The Bolsheviks in Russian Society

The Bolsheviks in Russian Society

THE REVOLUTION AND THE CIVIL WARS

EDITED BY Vladimir N. Brovkin

Yale University Press   New Haven and London

Published with assistance from the Charles A. Coffin Fund.

Designed by James J. Johnson and set in Aster Roman type by The Marathon Group, Inc.
Printed in the United States of America by Edwards Brothers, Inc., Ann Arbor, Michigan.

A catalogue record for this book is available from the British Library.

The paper in this book meets the guidelines for permanence and durability of the Committee on Production Guidelines for Book Longevity of the Council on Library Resources.

10 9 8 7 6 5 4 3 2 1

Library of Congress Cataloging-in-Publication Data

The Bolsheviks in Russian society : the revolution and the civil wars / edited by Vladimir N. Brovkin.
    p.   cm.
    Includes bibliographical references and index.
    ISBN 0-300-06706-2 (cloth : alk. paper)
    1. Soviet Union—History—Revolution, 1917–1921.   2. Rossiĭskaĭa kommunisticheskaĭa partiĭa (bol 'shevikov)—History.   I. Brovkin, Vladimir N.
DK265.B633133   1997
947.084—dc21   96-47127

Contents

Part Four
Representations and Actions

Part Five
Ideology, Mentality, and Culture

The Bolsheviks in Russian Society

VLADIMIR N. BROVKIN

Introduction:
New Tasks in the Study of the Russian
Revolution and the Civil War

The collapse of the Communist regime in 1989 revolutionized the terms of scholarly debate on Russian history. A movement to shed light on "blank" spots in Soviet history was begun. Even more important, new political forces appeared in Soviet society and identified themselves intellectually and politically with non-Bolshevik and anti-Bolshevik predecessors. The Social Democratic party appealed to those for whom the political experience of the Mensheviks and Socialist Revolutionaries was not of mere academic interest. The new Liberals identified themselves with the former Constitutional Democrats, and the new Monarchists strived to rediscover and reconsider the myth and reality of autocracy. The Soviet "republics" began to reexamine the terms of their incorporation into the union. Journalists, historians, and politicians all felt obliged to comment on the nature of War Communism and New Economic Policy. In other words, the Russian Revolution became not just a matter of the past but a matter of the present and future.

With the exception of the research done in the 1920s, most pre-1990 Soviet research on the Russian Revolution is worthless. Those books are illustrations of the party line and have little to do with history. They contain a requisite number of quotations from Lenin and the general secretary of the Communist Party of the Soviet Union and a few footnotes citing archives inaccessible to Western historians. The history profession in the Soviet Union responded slowly to the age of glasnost'. Only after the fall of Communism did the first truly innovative histories begin to appear. Today historians are examining formerly taboo topics: the Red Terror, the personality of Lenin, the plight of Russian peasants under the Communist dictatorship, anti-Bolshevik political parties, Mensheviks, SRs, and even the Whites. An interest in everything un-Soviet and anti-

Communist is sweeping the Russian intelligentsia and is reflected in new research on the Russian Revolution. And Russian historians are now beginning to use previously inaccessible archives, although these scholars sometimes are hampered by their ideological constraints and will unconsciously apply crude Marxist class analysis.

The best studies on the Russian Revolution until now have been written in the West. After the pioneering works of Merle Fainsod and Leonard Schapiro in the 1950s, the research agenda focused on the personalities of Lenin, Stalin, and Trotsky, and the actual course of events in 1917 and in the civil war. The main question for historians concerned the origins of Stalinism. The continuity thesis between the Lenin and Stalin dictatorship advocated by Fainsod and Schapiro was challenged by Robert Tucker, Moshe Lewin, Stephen Cohen, and others.

In 1968 an important collection edited by Richard Pipes appeared. *Revolutionary Russia*, the result of a conference that brought together leading historians of the Russian Revolution, set the research agenda for years to come. New studies broadened the scope of research and focused on soviets and other institutions and organizations, as well as on regions of the Russian empire. Marc Ferro's study of peasants in 1917, John Keep's study of the soviets, and Dietrich Geyer's research on revolutionary dynamics were among works that broadened our understanding of the Russian Revolution.

In the 1970s and 1980s the sociopolitical edifice designed by Lenin and Stalin was widely perceived in the United States as a stable and lasting system. Western research began to focus increasingly on social history, studying the classes and groups that were assumed to support the system. These historians strived to revise what they believed to be conservative, Cold War–biased, anti-Communist historiography. A spate of books showed workers' support for the Bolsheviks in 1917 and after. Some scholars went so far as to defend the official Soviet thesis of the workers' and peasants' alliance under the leadership of the Communist party during the civil war. Although it is methodologically sound to study history from below, the research on the revolution focused almost exclusively on 1917 and, as a result, produced a distorted picture of that turbulent year. The masses appeared as the main actors, and the decisions of politicians, generals, and entire political parties were considered irrelevant to the inevitable outcome: the Bolshevik victory, was no longer referred to as a seizure of power or as a coup, but as the Bolsheviks' coming to power.

Revisionist studies of the post-October period of War Communism and civil war center on the Bolshevik government, its policies and institutions—The Party, The State and Society, in that order. Contrary to the revisionists' avowed goal to view history from below, few of those histories cover the period of the civil war from the nonruling class perspective. There still are no books on the SR party, on monarchist organizations, on the church, or on other organized anti-Bolshevik entities in Russian society. All of these groups were considered unworthy of scholarly attention. But it is impossible to understand the nature of the Russian civil war without seriously considering the values, views, policies, and actions of the Bolsheviks' opponents. The cumulative effect of revisionist scholarship was to provide a certain degree of legitimacy to the Bolshevik seizure of power, an event that was increasingly called the October Revolution.

Critics of the revisionists disputed the social support thesis in studies of non-Bolshevik political parties and forces and by extending the focus from October 1917 to a longer historical period. In his *Russian Revolution* and *Russia Under the Bolshevik Regime,* Richard Pipes compared the nature of popular upheaval and the mechanics of power-wielding by the Bolsheviks to explain how the Bolsheviks managed to conquer Russia. Politics was back in the picture, and alternatives were again visible. Critics of revisionists (myself included) have argued that social support for the Bolsheviks was not a mandate for the Communist dictatorship. The very notion of support needs a definition. Support for what? Surely a vote for the Bolsheviks in 1917 was not a vote for Red Terror or even a vote for a dictatorship of the proletariat.

It is possible for a revolutionary minority to seize and retain power against the will of the majority of the population. Events in Russia since the late 1980s provide a new perspective on 1917 and beyond. Today nobody would question the fact that had a few individuals made different decisions in October 1993, Russia's current history would be different. This reminds us that October 1917 was just as volatile. Bolshevik victory and the terms of that victory could have been quite different.

The time has come to move beyond the narrow focus on Red Guards, Red Petrograd, proletarian consciousness, and Bolsheviks' achievements on the educational front to examine the complex and heterogeneous nature of Russian society. Only then might the victory of one faction of one party be seen in context. It is time to move beyond the assumption that because the Bolsheviks won they had social support. We must abandon the assumption that during the civil war there was the Party, the State, and Society in Russia. In fact, there were many parties and movements; there was no state, only pieces of the old state warring with one another; and there certainly was no one society during the civil war, but at best a society torn to pieces. And finally, it is time for historians to develop their own conceptual frameworks rather than elaborate on official Soviet categories. Proletarian consciousness, Socialist construction, Marxism-Leninism, and many other concepts are used in Western literature as if they mean what the official propaganda stipulated. Simply because the Bolsheviks declared that they were building Socialism does not mean that that was what they were doing—even if they themselves believed it to be the case.

This book brings together the work of Western and Russian historians reassessing the history of the Russian Revolution and setting a new scholarly agenda. The theme of this volume is the interaction of state authority—be it Red or White—and social and political groups pursuing their own objectives during the Russian Revolution and the civil war. The authors of these essays examine the disintegration of the Russian government in 1917 and its reemergence under the Bolshevik dictatorship on the one hand, and, on the other hand they describe the response of various social groups and regions to this new order. They focus on the neglected subjects of history of the Russian Revolution: non-Bolshevik and anti-Bolshevik political parties and movements; local and provincial history; the nature of peasant bands, war lords, and workers' independent councils; women, the church, and scores of other manifestations of autonomous action during the civil war. This history from below in fact demonstrates the degree to which various social groups in Russia defended their autonomy and resisted the imposition of centralized dictatorship.

1917—Collapse of the State and Authority

It has become a kind of a revisionist orthodoxy, elaborated in a dozen books on 1917, that the revolutionary action of the masses pushed the Bolsheviks toward their "coming to power" in 1917. This "from February to October" approach, with its focus on the Bolsheviks or on the "proletarian masses," obscured the volatility of the situation. Two chapters in this collection, by Michael Melancon and O. V. Volobuev, shift the focus to other political parties, Bolsheviks' allies or opponents. As a result, one begins to see that political parties offered alternative policies. Nothing was predetermined.

Images of the revolution are often associated with official events, such as the storming of the Winter Palace, the convocation of the Second Congress of Soviets, and the passing of countless resolutions and decisions at mass gatherings. In fact, the essence of the revolution was in the almost complete dissolution of authority. The liberated masses engaged in drunkenness, debauchery, and pogroms. The first thing the revolutionary soldiers did after the Provisional Government was declared overthrown, was to get drunk. They found huge stores of wine in the Winter Palace and kept entire regiments drunk for days. They smashed fine furniture and works of art to demonstrate their anger at the ruling elite, the officers, and educated society in general. In November and December 1917, entire regiments abandoned the front and slaughtered their officers. In many cities it was dangerous for an officer—a representative of the ruling class, a symbol of authority, privilege, and culture—to wear his epaulets. The people who dressed and spoke differently were now at the mercy of the revolutionary masses.

The settling of accounts, the wanton destruction of buildings and art objects, and the collapse of labor discipline all were manifestations of the same cultural phenomenon: Everything is permissible. In the early months of their power the Bolsheviks tried to ride the crest of this spontaneous movement and promote redivision of wealth. They encouraged peasants to seize landlords' estates, workers to seize factories, and army deserters streaming from the front to seize weapons. The official slogan was "Loot the Looted."

In the winter of 1917–18 the overthrown property owners, like a defeated party in a war, were ordered to pay indemnities. All over Russia, Bolshevik revolutionary committees published decrees demanding ransoms from bourgeois families and threatening to shoot hostages if the money was not paid. Millions of rubles were raised in this fashion. In Petrograd and other cities, the bourgeoisie were evicted from their homes, which, in the name of social justice, were to be distributed to the workers. In fact, these apartments went to Bolshevik functionaries. The Bolsheviks encouraged this anarchic movement in order to weaken their political opponents, the army, and the business class. They needed to destroy the material means of the propertied classes to resist them. Only a year later the Bolsheviks themselves would deal with the revolutionary masses in repressive manner, but in 1917 Bolshevism was indistinguishable from anarchy.

Intelligentsia

The year 1917 marked a sharp break in the relationship between the intelligentsia and the people. Before the Revolution, the Russian intelligentsia worshipped the Russian people, endowing them with all kinds of virtues. This cult of the revolution as a realization of this supreme goal is masterfully analyzed here by Anna Geifman. The Russian intelligentsia flocked to the revolutionary parties, participating in underground cells, in bank robberies, and in assassinations, all in the name of liberation. Even the Constitutional Democrats—the Kadets, as they were known—saw their main enemy in the established order.

After observing the wrath, anarchy, and senseless destruction of 1917, fear of the masses set in among the intelligentsia. The revolution caused tremendous dislocation. Population in the cities dwindled. Petrograd, a city of over 2 million people, lost more than half of its residents in the first year of Soviet power. Shops were boarded up, trade was banned, buildings were neglected, trams did not run, the water supply did not function, and the only source of fuel for heating cold apartments was furniture. The most destitute part of the population was the intelligentsia. Many left for the countryside to stay with relatives and friends. Many others had nowhere to go, especially clerks, typists, and employees of numerous offices that were now closed. By the end of the civil war, hundreds of thousands had emigrated. Those who stayed had been middle-class employees with no income other than their jobs. Only a few wanted to be associated with the new regime. For most, what was going on in Russia was incomprehensible. There was no Russia—no government, no law and order, no personal safety. The very notion of "Bolshevik government" seemed to many by early 1918 a contradiction in terms, ridiculous and frightening at the same time. Government was supposed to promote order, but the Bolsheviks appeared to be unleashing disorder, violence. and vengeance. The government was expected to fall at any time, yet months dragged on and the Bolsheviks remained in power.

This frame of mind was captured in the popular satirical journal *Novyi Satirikon*, edited by Arkadii Averchenko. The journal made no secret of its view that the anarchy was not a spontaneous outburst but a policy encouraged by the Bolsheviks. In December 1917 it published a series of cartoons criticizing Bolshevik social policies. In bold print on the front page the journal stated, "We are thankful to the Bolsheviks for . . . " (This headline was surprising because no one expected *Novyi Satirikon* to be thankful to the Bolsheviks for anything.) The next page continued, "For undercutting the speculation with paper at the source by shutting down all the newspapers" and, in a takeoff on a pompous Bolshevik slogan, "for making art the property of the people." The accompanying cartoon made it clear that this policy was little more than the destruction of art treasures and theft and speculation with them by the proletarians. "We are thankful to the Bolsheviks for leading the kind Russian people into the big highway." This big highway is a place for robberies, not for progress. At *Novyi Satirikon*, "socialist revolution" was viewed as nothing but destruction of culture, accumulated wealth, and resources. It was unbridled pursuit of personal gain in the guise of Socialist redivision of property.

In the summer of 1918 a frequent topic of conversation among the non-Bolshevik intelligentsia was the British landing in Arkhangelsk and the German capture of Rostov-on-Don. Should one adopt a pro-German or a pro-Allied orientation? Helplessness and doubt about their own strength generated an eagerness for the arrival of the Germans or Allies. It all sounded unreal. Russia had ceased to exist. How many governments were there? There was a Bolshevik "government" in hungry and empty Moscow and Petrograd. Was it a Russian government or the headquarters of the world revolution? The SRs had formed the government of the Constituent Assembly on the Volga, and General Kornilov was building the Volunteer White Army in the South.

Despite political orientations among the non-Bolshevik intelligentsia that ranged from Socialist to Monarchist, they all seem to have experienced a cultural shock in 1918. What could one do amid this chaos? Who was to blame? The Bolsheviks? The Germans? The tsar and his court? The Russian people? The intelligentsia themselves? Almost everyone pondered these questions in the first year of the "proletarian" dictatorship.

The Workers

One of the most puzzling facts in the research of this period is the scarcity of writing on the very social groups that the revisionists proclaimed to be the center of their attention—workers and peasants. Most books on workers do not go beyond early 1918. What were workers' attitudes toward actual Bolshevik rule, rather than to the promises? What we usually hear about popular attitudes after the Bolshevik seizure of power is a discussion of proletarian consciousness. In this context, increased consciousness means increased devotion to the proletarian cause and to the leadership of the Communist party. This view, very much in accord with the Bolshevik myth, postulates that the workers developed a proletarian identity directed against property owners and that the Bolshevik party was their natural leader. However, if we go beyond the official resolutions passed at workers' meetings and rallies to the level of values, behavior patterns, and attitudes of the common people, we might be able to decipher how the workers understood the revolution.

At the time when Bolshevik propaganda presented the seizure of power as a proletarian revolution, as liberation of labor from the chains of capitalist exploitation, workers understood this message as liberation *from* labor. This is beautifully described by Sergei Pavliuchenkov in his chapter. Unemployed workers demanded the same wages as employed ones, and unskilled workers demanded equal wages with the skilled ones. Labor discipline collapsed and factory administrators were overthrown. As a result, hardly any work at all was performed in the winter of 1917–18. It turned out, as the press reported at the time, that most workers did not like to work. They held their jobs to make a living but did not like their proletarian identity, and as soon as they could abandon it, they did. Even the Bolshevik press was full of accounts of workers passing the time in endless rallies and on smoking breaks. Many said, "Why should we work now? Let the overthrown classes of the bourgeoisie work." The Bolsheviks tried to capitalize on this attitude by drafting the bourgeoisie to dig trenches on the approaches to Petrograd. Workers, the supposedly conscious proletarians, stood guard as entrepreneurs, lawyers, doctors, and society ladies worked. This was supposed to generate a feeling of social justice in the minds of workers: now they were the masters. At the same time, this cultural practice confirmed the fact that if a worker had an opportunity to rise out of the ranks of workers, to supervise somebody else's work, he would. The last thing a worker who had achieved authority wanted was to return to the factory floor. He cherished the new difference between himself and those who remained simple workers. He would jealously guard his superiority over others and flaunt it in his relations with them. Yet he knew that he was indebted to the Bolvsheviks and that they could take away his privilege at any time. He thus was compelled to show his loyalty to the Bolshevik party not to demonstrate his proletarian consciousness but to protect his new authority.

In years that followed, the main antagonism was between workers who remained on the factory floor and those who had risen to the rank of boss. During the spring of 1918 workers complained bitterly about the privileges for the commissars, the refusal to hold elections, and the brutal suppression of strikes. As Michael Melancon and Scott Smith demonstrate in their chapters, the Left SRs, the Mensheviks, and the SRs, who had established a reputation of being sharp critics of the Bolsheviks, gained new popularity among the workers and were beginning to win elections in the urban and rural soviets of Bolshevik-controlled Russia. Faced with the new popularity of these opposition parties, the Bolsheviks in almost all cases disbanded the newly elected soviets and suppressed the opposition parties.

While the official propaganda continued to describe the working class as the ruling class in Russia, workers were complaining that they were deprived of even the simplest rights. Any attempts to criticize factory administration or to go on strike were suppressed as counterrevolutionary provocation. Most strikes during War Communism resulted in closing of the plant, screening of the workers, interrogations and searches of the troublemakers, infiltration of factories with informers, and exile of the most vocal workers to remote provinces or into the Red Army. On several occasions, hundreds of workers were deported and shot. Frightened workers responded by fleeing to the countryside, and by 1921 fewer than

100,000 workers remained in Petrograd out of the more than half million there had been in 1917.

The pattern of relations set up in 1918 between the Bolsheviks and the workers survived in some respects for many decades. Workers were told that since they were now liberated, they had to work harder. But their pay was worse than under the old regime. So they pretended to work, and the government pretended that it paid them. From this stemmed the corruption in the factory so eloquently described by Sergei Pavliuchenkov in his chapter. It was a system of fake accounting and kickbacks. It is naive to regard workers' culture and values during this upheaval either as Bolshevik (representing proletarian consciousness and obedience to the vanguard) or as resistant specifically to the new Communist tyranny. Workers' cultural practices were a response to the collapse of authority and to Bolshevik propaganda, and they represented workers' own interpretation of what they could get away with.

Women

Revisionist study of women during the civil war has remained focused on Bolshevik women leaders and on legislation concerning abortion and family matters. In fact, the collapse of labor ethics in Russia went hand in hand with the collapse of morality. The Bolsheviks denounced existing moral norms as bourgeois superstition, and family, order, decency, and private life as bourgeois norms of behavior. The immediate result of this attack on the code of public behavior was the collapse of mores. Stealing was no longer stealing but expropriation of bourgeois property. Faithfulness in married life could be easily disregarded, especially if a class motive was available. This shift in gender relations is discussed briefly in my chapter on women during the civil war. I suggest that there was a Bolshevik policy toward women as a social group. Variants of that policy applied to women workers, peasant women, or bourgeois women. The clash between the official representations of liberation and the dismal reality of policy is the main theme here.

Proletarian women were supposed to be a part of the ruling class. In reality, however, they were subjected to humiliating searches at the factories, and sexual harassment was rampant. Peasant women, whom the Bolsheviks viewed as backward and superstitious, were treated as easy to punish for the deeds of peasant men. Taking hostages from the families of peasant rebels, deporting large groups of the civilian population, incarcerating the Cossacks' wives in concentration camps—these were some of the shocking practices of the Bolsheviks.

Rape during the civil war has remained largely a taboo subject. Yet it was common. Worse, it was a matter of policy. Bourgeois women, and especially officers' wives, were systematically raped with the direct complicity of Bolshevik administration. On the other hand, Jewish women were mercilessly raped by the White troops in Ukraine.

The revisionist scholars have left the problem of terror, and of Red Terror particularly, outside the sphere of investigation. (Indeed, there are a dozen books on proletarian consciousness but only one study on Red Terror, done by an émigré historian in 1924.) It is impossible to understand the nature of civil war without the study of terror. The structure and processes of Red Terror against all political parties and entire social groups says much about the formation of institutions, habits, and cultural practices of the new regime. Several chapters in this book examine various forms of terror during the civil war. Peasant terror against state officials described by Taisia Osipova and Delano DuGarm and the White terror and lawlessness discussed by N. G. O. Pereira reveal the intensity of hatred that divided Russian society.

Peasants

Except for Oliver Radkey's and Orlando Figes's books on the peasant war in the Tambov and Volga regions, respectively, there are no studies of the peasants, the largest class in Russia, or of the Green movement, the most powerful movement during the civil war. What happened to history from below after October? Osipova and DuGarm discuss peasants' perceptions and reactions to Bolshevik policy during the civil war. What emerges in their accounts is a picture of popular resistance to dictatorship, resistance much more powerful and lasting than anyone realized.

The social, political, and cultural history of peasants during the years of War Communism and civil war went through three distinct but overlapping stages. The first stage was a carnival of the revolution. During 1917 and the first half of 1918, peasants celebrated the collapse of the Russian state. Finally the long-awaited freedom from the oppressive state [volia] had arrived, and the peasants appropriated what they believed was rightfully theirs in accordance with their own notions of justice.

By the summer of 1918 the peasants had redivided the land and settled down to their routine cycle of life. The Bolsheviks still had a good name, because they were perceived as the people who had made possible the seizure of the landlords' property. The Bolsheviks then started their notorious program of grain requisitioning, of establishing up Committees of the Poor, and, in 1919, of collective farms and agricultural communes.

The peasants resisted, avoiding the draft by bribing local officials, forming bands of Green rebels who hid in the forests, attacking requisition detachments.

They generated a rich folklore that reveals their incomprehension of Bolshevik rhetoric. The word *Bolshevik* was understood because in Russian it stemmed from the word *bol'she* (more). Bolsheviks were the people who gave more land to the people, the peasants reasoned. But Communists were the bad guys because they wanted to requisition grain. The Cheka reports to Lenin on peasant attitudes repeatedly mention that the peasants spoke well of the Bolsheviks but condemned the Communists. In some areas the peasants spelled "Communist" as *kamenist* (mason), because the closest-sounding word they knew was *kamen'* (stone). They reasoned that Communists were the people who worked with stone—that is, masons. In some areas rumor had it that Bolsheviks and Communists were at war. The leader of the Bolsheviks was said to be Lenin, and the leader of the Communists, Trotsky. Sometimes there was a distinction between Communism and the Soviet power. Soviet power was good, according to the peasants, but Communism was bad. It was no different than serfdom in the old times. Now peasants owed all kinds of obligations to the new regime, just as they had owed obligations to the old master. They were drafted to deliver grain to the provincial center; they were drafted into the army. They were mobilized for all kinds of projects, and in their minds, this was like serfdom.

The second stage in peasants' history started in mid-1918 and lasted roughly until the end of 1920. It coincided with the Bolsheviks' war first with the SR-led government of the Constituent Assembly, which had overthrown Bolshevik rule in the Volga River basin in 1918, and then with a number of White governments led by Admiral Kolchak in Siberia and General Denikin in the South of Russia. As Taisia Osipova masterfully demonstrates, peasants did not want to be drawn into a war among Russian elites. Their first concern was their own household and their own province. Peasants greeted the Whites as liberators, but shortly thereafter they had had enough and greeted the Reds with enthusiasm. A few months later they would form partisan detachments in the forests and attack the Reds. One of the most popular songs in the countryside during the civil war was this: "Ne khodil by ty Vanek vo soldaty [Vania, don't go to the army] / v Krasnoi armii shtyki [Red Army has enough bayonets] / chai naidutsia bez tebia bolshaviaki oboidutsia [The Bolsheviks can get along without you]."

Let the Bolsheviks fight their war without you. That was the essence of the peasants' view. Even those who could not avoid the draft showed a lack of enthusiasm for fighting in the civil war. From mid-1919 to the end of 1920 hundreds of thousands of deserters roamed the Russian country-

side. Some of them were simply hiding in the forests. Others formed regiments of Greens that attacked requisition detachments, burned draft lists,
and killed off local Communists.

The third stage in peasant history started sometime in 1919 and lasted
well into 1922. It was a period of all-out peasant war on the Bolsheviks
waged in virtually every province of grain-producing Russia, Ukraine, and
Siberia. It peaked in the winter of 1920–21 in Tambov province, the center of peasant rebellion so well described by Delano DuGarm. Hundreds
of peasant guerrilla bands engaged in a bloody war with the Communist
state. After the defeat of the White armies the Communist government
intensified pressure on the countryside, trying to envelop it with "socialist institutions." The peasants perceived this attack on market relations as
intolerable interference—no sowing committee was going to tell them
what and when to sow and at what price to sell their harvest. They saw
the Communist party cells in the countryside as outposts of urban intervention that had to be destroyed.

The Green movement was led by dozens of peasant leaders who tried
to articulate the peasants' grievances. In their proclamations echo the programs of the political parties, yet they were remarkably self-directed. The
uniqueness of this culture lay in its freedom from the intellectual guidance
of the Russian state. The appeals of the Committee to Exterminate the
Communists in Siberia spoke with profound hatred of all Communists and
cities. The anti-semitic pronouncements of numerous *bat'kos* in Ukraine
also sound virulently anti-urban. But there is an array of orders and
appeals from peasant leaders in the Tambov-Voronezh and lower Volga
areas echoing programs of the Right and Left SRs. They refer to revolution
as a positive event and appeal to the people as the highest authority.

Despite this diversity there is something in common to all the peasant
voices: it is a sense of local identity and readiness to defend homeland
from outsiders. Peasants craved tranquility and isolation. Their folklore
betrayed hostility to all city dwellers, even those, like the SRs, who had a
good reputation among them. Peasant popular culture during the civil
war was rooted in the traditional way of life that was so abruptly and violently destroyed.

Organized Opposition

Only a small part of anti-Communist political society took part in the
politics of resistance. The ideas and actions of the Mensheviks, SRs,
Kadets, and Whites is an enormous topic. Scott Smith, Leonid Heretz,
and N. G. O. Pereira focus on these issues in their chapters and paint a

picture of the regional diversity, warlordism, and ideological incompatibility of the Whites and the SRs, the factional infighting among the SRs, and the morbid geist of the White movement. A deeply traumatized anti-Bolshevik Russia was divided into groups with nothing in common.

People in all of these political currents defined the Bolshevik experience within an intellectual framework from the past. The Mensheviks tried to find a Marxist explanation for the Bolshevik experiment and act accordingly. The Socialist Revolutionaries saw reality through the lens of what they believed were peasant interests. The Kadets, their own identity based in European culture, perceived Bolshevism through this prism. By contrast, the main ingredients in the ideology of the Whites were professed patriotism and commitment to a Russia that was lost.

Faithful to their Marxist ideology, the Mensheviks did come to accept the notion that a proletarian revolution had taken place in Russia. They were horrified by the violence, atrocities, and brutality of the revolution but did not blame the Bolsheviks exclusively. They attributed excesses to the heritage of capitalist exploitation. For most Mensheviks the Bolsheviks were mistaken comrades on the left. Their policies were wrong-headed, hasty, and ill-conceived, failing to consider the well-being of Russian workers. From here stemmed the Menshevik policy of loyal legal opposition. They saw their historical role in culturalizing the Bolsheviks, as they put it—in making tough Bolshevik revolutionaries into kinder and gentler Socialists. To achieve this goal one had to strive for fair elections, freedom of speech, and independent social and political organizations.

As Marxists, the Mensheviks had to believe in progress. To admit that a catastrophe had occurred was tantamount to repudiating their very belief system. The Mensheviks constantly struggled with their understanding of what was supposed to be happening and with the gloomy reality. Only a few managed to resolve this contradiction. In 1920 an underground right Menshevik platform concluded that the system of political and economic relations in Russia under Communism was "unforeseen" by Marxism. It was a qualitatively new system. The proletariat was just as oppressed under the new masters as it had been under capitalism, if not worse, because it had no rights, no press, and no free unions. The new elite did not own the means of production but it controlled the means of production as a collective entity. The Communist party had turned into a new privileged self-recruiting estate aimed at perpetuating its dictatorship over the entire population. This was a non-Marxist and perceptive analysis, yet it left no way out.

Like other groups of Russian intelligentsia, the Mensheviks came out of the turmoil of the revolution with a profound fear of the masses. They had numerous chances to lead the people they claimed to represent, the workers. They were winning elections in a landslide in 1918, they were propelled to lead the strikes in 1919, they were again scoring well in elections in early 1920. Yet each time they chose to put on the brake, to calm down the workers and to defuse the workers' protests. The Mensheviks feared revolutionary upheavals, and they were embarrassed to admit that the only way forward was backward, to the capitalism and democracy of the February Revolution. In this sense the Mensheviks lost intellectual ground to the Communists, who convinced themselves that time was working for them and that they were going to inherit the capitalist world.

The Socialist Revolutionaries, by contrast, were on much firmer ideological ground vis-à-vis the Bolsheviks. Their entire ideology held that Russia was a peasant country and therefore even if the Bolsheviks did represent the workers, they could not claim to rule Russia. Unlike the Mensheviks, the SRs were not Marxists, although they considered themselves Socialists. They denounced the Bolshevik usurpation of power and fought the Communists on the battlefield in 1918, defending the government of the Committee of the Constituent Assembly. Scott Smith presents a detailed and perceptive discussion of the internal contradictions in the SR party. Both Right and Left SRs denounced Communists as usurpers and liars who had promised fair elections and never held them, who had promised land to peasants only to rob them of the products of their labor, who had promised peace but launched a war against Russian peasants to stay in power.

A cultural gulf divided the SRs from the peasants. There were some peasants who were in the party, but the main body was a rural intelligentsia.

Of all the educated groups in Russian society, the SRs were closest to the people, but they were not the people. Like the Mensheviks, they both idealized and feared the masses. They could not articulate and explain why violence and destruction had taken place in areas where there were no Bolsheviks. As part of intelligentsia the SRs were shocked by the experience of 1917, but as admirers of the people, they could not explain this phenomenon.

The SRs were unable to bridge the gap between what the peasants were doing and what the SRs thought they ought to have been doing. They thought that the peasants ought to have waited for peaceful agrarian reform, which the Provisional Government and the Ministry of Agriculture were preparing under party leader Victor Chernov. Instead, the peasants had started seizing land by force. In 1918 the peasants ought to have supported the Government of the Committee of the Constituent Assembly on the Volga because that was the only chance to provide a democratic alternative to the Communist dictatorship. Instead, the peasants had withdrawn from national politics and showed no inclination to support any government at all. To the SRs' credit, they never blamed the peasants for failing to live up to their duty as defined by the SRs. They just kept trying harder.

In 1919 and 1920 the peasants came closest to doing what the SRs thought was in their best interest. They started setting up peasant unions all over Russia led by local people, many of whom considered themselves SRs. It appeared for a moment in the winter of 1920–21 that a peasant war—led, coordinated, and supplied by an informal network of peasant unions—would break the back of Soviet power. Dozens of provinces were engulfed by peasant war. Most of rural Russia was ungovernable and the crops uncollectible. Some SR observers expected the Communist regime to collapse in the spring of 1921.

The SRs were unable to see that Russian peasants did not necessarily aspire to a legal order and representative democracy; their horizon was limited to the economic concerns of their province. Government was to be feared and resisted, not taken over. So economic concessions of the Bolsheviks defused the peasant war of 1920–21, ruined the SR party, and saved the Bolshevik regime.

The Whites

Two chapters in this book are devoted to the history of the White movement. Leonid Heretz provides an insightful analysis of the psychology of the Whites, and N. G. O. Pereira develops the theme further by discussing the culture of government under the Whites in Siberia. Pereira demolishes the image of the White regime as a coherent and well-entrenched military dictatorship. In fact, it was riddled with intrigue, rivalry, and infighting among various atamans. One begins to wonder whether the term *White government* is accurate at all. There was hardly any government in the territory the Whites claimed to control. There was instead naked assertion of a claim to rule the unfortunate population vis-à-vis other warlords. It was a social movement of officers, with few links to other parts of educated society.

The Whites dreamed about the Russia that was lost. Unlike the Socialists and the Liberals, the Whites turned to the past, unable to comprehend the calamity that befell Russia. They hated the comrades, those who had stolen and violated beautiful Russia. Love and hatred combined in the White culture—love for Russia, with its fields, endless space, and beauty, and hatred of the comrades, of foreign spies, and of Jews, with their imported ideology.

The Whites regarded themselves as valiant knights whose mission was to clear the Russian soil of miserable and wretched agitators and troublemakers. This imagery is well presented in a well-known poster that was quite effective during the civil war. In the background is the valiant White cavalry galloping, unstoppable, toward the spectator. These are the saviors and deliverers of Russia. In front of them are miserable creatures in black suits and ties: Lenin, Trotsky, Zinoviev, and others. They are running fast, but there is no way out. They are approaching an abyss, and in another moment they are going to fall to hell and pay for their crimes.

What is remarkable in this self-representation is the absence of the people. They are not involved in the struggle between the White and the Red, the good and evil. They are to be liberated without their own involvement. This failure to include the people, even in a propaganda appeal, reveals the White mentality. It is the agitators who mobilize the masses. The Whites believed that they were going to do the job alone. The power of the White movement was indeed in this self-reliance, which gave them courage and determination. A few thousand dedicated officers under General Kornilov in 1918 accomplished remarkable military feats. Always outnumbered and outgunned many times over, they won battle after battle from spring 1918 until September 1919.

In spite of their self-reliance, the letters, orders, conversations, and songs of that time reflect the Whites' doubts about the possibility of victory. They realized full well that they were cut off from the people, and even from the rest of educated society, which they despised. They believed that they were fighting in a hopeless cause to which only their honor bound them.

The Whites tended to regard Russians as naive and childlike, led astray by agitators, revolutionaries, and foreigners. In areas they controlled they dealt with the people as though they were disobedient children who had to be punished for their misdeeds. They expected gratitude and obedience.

Leonid Heretz notes an interesting cult of death in White folklore. Some regiments decorated their uniforms with black crosses, skulls, lightning bolts, and similar emblems. The Reds, stunned by the combat behavior of Whites, coined a term to describe it—psychological attack. The Whites would march into battle—with all their insignia, banners, and drums—straight toward the Red lines without trying to take cover even when machine-gun fire began to cut down row after row of officers. The message was that dying on the battlefield with honor was a blessing.

By late summer 1919 it began to appear as if victory over the Reds was around the corner. The Whites controlled huge areas of Russia and Ukraine, and the army kept advancing toward Moscow. At that point the psychology of the White movement changed. Many leaders of the White movement began to act as if victory was inevitable because theirs was the just cause. The aura of martyrdom was cast aside. The time had come to punish those guilty of treason. The White regime became more arbitrary and more cruel in punishing the comrades. Their patronizing and disdainful attitude gave way to dictatorial actions. Workers, soldier deserters from 1917, and peasants who had stolen other people's property had to pay for their crimes. Socialists must answer for their collaboration with the Communists, Liberals were going to pay for their alliance with the Socialist agitators in 1917. With each new victory the Whites were cutting themselves off further from the rest of the Russian society.

Defeats at the front in November 1919 opened the third and final stage in the history of the White movement. With each week it became more certain that the war was lost. The White armies rolled backward. The valiant ethos of the past could no longer be revived. Defeat meant death from a Cheka bullet if one was caught by the Bolsheviks or an uncertain future away from Russia. It was the end of the world—a carnival of death, a drunken orgy before the denouement. Whites vented their frustration on workers, peasants, Cossacks, and intellectuals. They believed that their defeat could only be the result of treason.

The fragmentation of anti-Communist Russia and its inability to act in cohesion discussed in this book bring a new dimension to the explanation of the causes of the Bolshevik victory in the civil war. This must be seen as the result of the self-destructive tendencies of various social groups in Russia rather than as a monument to Trotsky's talents or presumed social support for the Bolsheviks.

The Bolsheviks and Their Culture

Although the revisionists were the first to recognize the importance of studying the history of mentalities, identities, and attitudes, most of their studies in this area focus on proletarian identity, proletarian culture, and socialist values. The key theme of this book is that Russian Communism stemmed from Russian imperial culture. Jonathan W. Daly describes the Bolshevik policy toward the church; Richard Pipes discusses the words and deeds of Lenin, the leader; Christopher Read analyzes Bolshevik culture and values; and Dmitry Shlapentokh discusses the nationalist ideology re-created by the Bolsheviks.

These contributors analyze how intellectual currents developed. They discuss the intellectual affinities of Bolshevism at various stages of its development with other seemingly un-Bolshevik or anti-Bolshevik currents of the time, and they examine the cultural context of the time, the mental models and patterns of thinking the Bolsheviks re-created without even realizing that they had done so. They suggest that regardless of what the Bolsheviks called their system, it was in fact a centralized nationalist dictatorship that borrowed heavily from Russia's past. What reemerged after the revolution was an old Russian patrimonial autocratic culture in a new guise.

Orthodoxy and the New Religion

Orthodoxy, autocracy, and nationality were the pillars of official imperial ideology under the old regime. The Bolsheviks believed that religion was simply a trick invented by the ruling classes to dupe the masses and keep them in subservience. Their propaganda ridiculed the church and religious belief without addressing moral or philosophical questions. Among the intellectual Bolsheviks, science had replaced God. The church was presented as a tool of oppression of the laboring masses.

The attack on the church was not merely an assault on one of the pillars of the old regime. The Bolsheviks felt threatened by the permanence and stability of the church. To persuade the Russian people to adopt a new creed was not easy, since Orthodoxy was a peculiar mix of custom, belief, and blind faith.

The Bolsheviks treated the church as just another institution to be destroyed. Their main method of accomplishing this was to generate and exploit divisiveness in the opponents' camp. The Bolsheviks arrested thousands of priests on charges of counterrevolution, and they attempted to replace religious holidays and rituals with the new ones.

One campaign in this saga is described in great detail here by Jonathan W. Daly. Under the guise of raising funds for the victims of famine, the Bolsheviks desecrated the churches and confiscated valuables and icons. The party ordered cadres in all provinces to requisition gold and other church valuables by force if necessary. Much of this stolen booty was sold in bulk in the West. Recently released documents make it clear that these acts were done on Lenin's orders. This destruction of national heritage was supposed to sharpen division within the church between those who felt obliged to cooperate with the government in the cause of alleviating famine, and those who resisted confiscation. The campaign generated revenue for the Bolshevik party as it robbed the church of its wealth.

The idea of Communism replaced Orthodoxy as the new truth. It promised salvation not after death but on Earth. Communism could be achieved only by studying the objective laws of human development and acting on that knowledge under the leadership of the vanguard of the people, the Communist party and comrade Lenin.

Like the church, the Communist party was structured as a hierarchy. Like the church, it was intolerant of heresy. There could be no debate over the meaning of the truth. The party was the embodiment of the truth, and the party line was always correct. Like the church, the Bolsheviks had saints and martyrs, and they actually used such terms as "a martyr of the revolutionary struggle" and or "the saintly cause of the proletarian struggle." The Cheka was compared to the Inquisition, and the Chekists defined themselves as the holy knights of the revolution. Both Russian Communism and Russian Orthodoxy were based in ritual and dogma, whereas Western Christian philosophy and Marxism had developed as a quest for interpretation and understanding of the truth.

New Autocracy

In the old triad of Orthodoxy, autocracy, and nationality, autocracy was the anchor. The autocrat of all Russias was the embodiment of the permanence and endurance of Russia and of the holy Orthodoxy. In the minds of Russians, the tsar—the autocrat—had a mystique and an aura of love. He was a distant figure, almost a deity, a protector and father sanctified by God. The idea of the tsar was removed from the person of the tsar. The Bolshevik propaganda spent much effort on discrediting this idea. The tsar was represented as the chief exploiter, the head of the landlords.

In terms of real cultural practices, however, the old Russian idea of autocracy simply was adapted by the new regime. The Bolsheviks recreated, subconsciously perhaps, the idea of an autocrat in the concept of the *vozhd'*, the leader who became a representation of the supreme authority, protector and guarantor of the present and the future. Lenin created an autocratic government without division of powers, elected parliament, or independent judiciary. Instead, a group of handpicked commissars were put in charge of various branches of government and were accountable to Lenin personally. After his death, rituals were invented for adoration of his body, as if it were a deity. Examining newly declassified documents, Richard Pipes shows us a picture of Lenin with which many were familiar but some had refused to believe. It is of a dictator running his government as a personal chancellery, taking interest in minute detail and scheming and plotting throughout his life. It is a picture of a cruel man, personally responsible for numerous atrocities.

In 1917 the idea of a party in Russian political culture was similar to this concept as it existed in the West. There were several major parties, and one could change membership. Debate among political parties in public forums and in the press was a part of normal discourse. All this changed rapidly when the Bolsheviks seized power. Other political parties were suppressed, their members arrested and driven underground. The word *party* acquired a new meaning. The Communist party, Bolshevik propaganda tells us, is the vanguard of the proletariat, the best and most conscious detachment of the working class. The party was now understood not as a voluntary association of people but as a detachment of fighters. To belong to the party meant to belong to a unique category of people. It meant that one had acquired understanding of the meaning of history. This definition of party membership was similar to initiation into an order of monks. The party had a collective wisdom inaccessible to others. It was the repository of the truth, and only in the name of the party could changes in doctrine be inaugurated. Laws did not apply to party members. In terms of morality, code of behavior, self-definition, and legal status, party members had become a separate part of society by 1921.

Few have asked why the official projections of the image of the party in Russia took these forms and not others. References to Marxism are not helpful here because the Mensheviks were doctrinaire Marxists who never thought of a Marxist workers' party in Bolshevik terms. In his chapter Christopher Read tackles this complex question. Lacking voluntary popular support, the Bolsheviks relied increasingly on shortcuts to attain legitimacy. They substituted popular support with the enforced display of support. They were not aware themselves that they were acting on deeply internalized cultural practices, values, and understandings of what authority and power meant. Despite their Marxist Western veneer, they were reproducing Russian political culture in their "proletarian" party. Their ethical norms of obedience, order, fear of the master, and elitism; their condescending attitude to people, claim to superior wisdom, and hierarchical structure of authority and privilege—what are these traits other than the cultural heritage of the Russian service bureaucracy created by Peter and perfected through the eighteenth and nineteenth centuries?

Russia as a Beacon of Salvation

In the old triad of Orthodoxy, autocracy, and nationality, Russia was represented as a holy land, the third Rome, the defender of the true Christianity. The idea of Russia had always been defined in opposition to the West. Both for the Slavophiles and Westernizers, Russia was a land with a unique destiny and mission. Now the Bolsheviks adapted this vision by substituting the idea of Russia with proletarian internationalism. Russia was the motherland of the proletarian revolution. It was a homeland of all oppressed people suffering capitalist exploitation. As under the old regime, Russia still had a special destiny and mission. Only now it was not to defend the true Christianity but the laboring masses. The poster and verse of the revolutionary years depicted Russia as the first land in the world to be freed from capitalist exploitation. Russia is depicted as a chosen land, the first one to be freed, and at the same time it was a beacon of liberation for others. Here we have a subtle combination of a nationalist idea of Russia as the first and best and an internationalist idea of Russia as a workers' state to be joined by all the oppressed. Thus the Bolshevik propaganda fused the Slavophile exclusivity of Russia and the Westernizers' link to the West.

Lenin, Trotsky, Zinoviev, and other Bolshevik leaders believed that they were internationalists. Propaganda spoke of the federative republic of soviets the world over or of the United Soviet Republics of Europe. In practice, however, the way the Bolsheviks established the Communist International left no doubt that the Russian Communist party was to be the leader of all Communist parties. Every Communist party adhering to the Communist International had to accept twenty-one conditions. If these parties staged a successful proletarian revolution in their respective countries, they would join the federative Soviet republic led by Russian Communist party. In real terms, Internationalism meant Russian domination. From the beginning a substitution occurred in which words projected proletarian internationalism and deeds projected Communist expansion of the Russian state.

With the twentieth century in its last decade and the Communist era in Russia now history, the Communist revolution and its aftermath can be viewed as a prelude to catastrophe for Russia. The country lost millions of people in wars, civil wars, purges, terror, and repression. All these tragedies are increasingly perceived as having been suffered for nothing. Russia never has caught up with the industrialized Western world. And in some respects the gap today is wider than in 1917. The country's industrial base is still outdated. Its parliamentary institutions are just as fragile as they were in 1917. Nor has Russia resolved the crisis of its national identity—whether it should be an empire, a multi-national federation, or a unitary state. Russian society is left with the legacies of the Communist revolution. Democrats, Liberals, Communists, Nationalists, and even Monarchists are back in Russia's political arena. Their programs, values, and ideals are remarkably similar to those of their predecessors in 1917–22. An understanding of Russian society during this prelude to catastrophe is a starting point for an understanding of Russia as it enters the twenty-first century.

One

Paralysis of Politics and Bolshevik Seizure of Power 1917

ANNA GEIFMAN

The Russian Intelligentsia, Terrorism, and Revolution

The key difference between popular revolt or uprising and revolution is that the latter rationalizes primitive and instinctive popular grievances, verbalizes them into general programs, and carves out intuitively suitable and appealing slogans for the masses. The people responsible for formulating the theoretical principles that give a revolution its spirit are necessarily the educated members of a society in turmoil.[1] In the case of revolutionary Russia, they were members of the "intelligentsia," which—in the broadest meaning of this collective noun—included all individuals pursuing knowledge and the practical realization of abstract intellectual and ethical values.

Given the many past scholarly difficulties in defining the Russian intelligentsia, it would be presumptuous to present this delineation of the nearly amorphous social group as the all-encompassing one. It is essential, however, to keep in mind that it was this group—the literati, among the much larger group of individuals who called themselves revolutionaries and helped to shake apart the traditional establishment—that took on the role of turning the revolt into a revolution.

Interpreting the attitude of educated society in general and the intelligentsia in particular toward the overthrow of the old order, including its political forms and its socioeconomic structure and spiritual foundation, is central to understanding the Russian revolution. And yet—perhaps because of the current emphasis on social history, and the significant influence of Marxist class analysis in scholarship—scholars of the revolutionary process are primarily concerned with such mass movements (and the major social groups contributing to them) as peasant uprisings, workers' strikes, military and naval mutinies, student disorders, and armed demonstrations. While they also examine the lives and work of prominent members of the revolutionary intelligentsia, they usually place inadequate emphasis on the intelligentsia as a social entity whose members may be identified not by their predetermined inclusion in a particular economic class but by acquired intellectual characteristics. These characteristics, along with the deeper causes shaping the intelligentsia's attitude toward the Russian revolution—causes that frequently differed from the explanations offered by the intellectual participants in the antigovernment movement themselves—are the focus of this chapter.

The last two decades of Russian prerevolutionary history were the most explosive years of left-wing Russian terrorism, which was the most extreme form of antigovernment activity in Russia and claimed an estimated seventeen thousand casualties between the turn of the century and 1917.[2] The position of educated society vis-à-vis this most radical manifestation of political protest may therefore be regarded as a key issue in determining how far along the revolutionary path its more politically active members were prepared to go to achieve their objectives.

From the beginning of the organized revolutionary movement in the 1860s and 1870s, radical intellectuals usurped the term *intelligentsia* (introduced into the Russian language at that time as *intelligenty*) to represent themselves as defenders and servants of the oppressed and exploited, waging a relentless war against the autocratic regime. Even though the word *intelligentsia* in its original meaning implied a concept much broader than the revolutionary opposition, designating a more complicated phenomenon—"a 'class' held together only by the bond of 'consciousness,' 'critical thought,' or moral passion"[3]—the revolutionaries preferred to simplify things. Anyone who did not agree that the autocracy was responsible for all the misfortunes that had ever befallen Russia, giving rise to an urgent necessity to do away with the "brigand gang" in power, was not accepted as a member of this "self-designated class, with its explicit political and philosophical commitments." Members of the intelligentsia represented the "defensive self-consciousness of people who believed in their collectivity and defined this collectivity by their beliefs."[4] This mode of thinking was almost mandatory, given the gulf between politically conscious educated Russians and the conservative tsarist state, a breach that historians trace to at least the abortive Decembrist uprising and its brutal suppression in 1825.

Yet within intellectual circles the radical opponents of the autocratic regime allowed a significant divergence of opinion concerning the methods appropriate for the antigovernment struggle. They were even prepared to tolerate naive individuals who doubted the expediency of reorganizing the country's life in accordance with socialist principles, the most fashionable socioeconomic outlook in the educated milieu by the late nineteenth century. So long as these stubborn skeptics supported the political overthrow of the tsarist regime—which was the primary goal of all revolutionaries—they qualified as members of the intelligentsia.

The radical intellectuals usurped not only the term *intelligentsia* but also what they considered the key principle in its definition. To their minds, members of the intelligentsia could come from any social stratum and possess the most superficial education and intellectual training— barely enough to familiarize themselves with simplified theoretical justi- fications for antigovernment activity. Each person aspiring to the title *intelligent,* however, was required to dedicate himself wholeheartedly and selflessly to the people and the public good. And it was this trait of the intelligentsia that the revolutionaries attributed exclusively to themselves: a doctor, zemstvo agronomist, or public schoolteacher who did not sup- port the radicals but who rendered daily services to the people did not qualify as a true *intelligent* because ultimately the public good—so held the radical wisdom—could be attained only through revolution.

In fact, many radical intellectuals regarded all activities on the part of nonrevolutionary benefactors of the people as harmful in the long run precisely because their peaceful humanitarian aid indirectly strengthened the regime destined to be destroyed. This attitude was especially evident during a devastating famine that ravaged a number of central Russian provinces in 1891–92. When numerous volunteer doctors, doctors' aides, nurses, agronomists, and students rushed to join official relief operations in the countryside, where raged typhus and cholera, many revolutionaries argued against these humanitarian efforts as simplistic and inadequate. They openly agitated for violence, blaming state officials, the police, and the wealthy for the misfortunes of the poor in the hope of turning the starving masses against the authorities and sparking a new wave of peasant distur- bances.[5] This attitude on the part of the radical intellectuals translated into a slogan—"The Worse, the Better" (*chem khuzhe, tem luchshe*)—which quickly evolved into a general policy that became apparent when certain revolutionaries seemed to applaud the famine and express hopes for another bad harvest, which they assumed would instigate a peasant revolt. The policy became even more evident when many self-proclaimed liber- ators of the people openly rejoiced at the news that hundreds of workers and their families had been killed and many others wounded by govern- ment troops during the events of Bloody Sunday in St. Petersburg on 9 January 1905—events that surely heralded the anxiously awaited signal for the beginning of the revolution.[6]

The nonrevolutionary intellectuals apparently over time accepted the radical judgment of who qualified as a genuine *intelligent* and who did not. The radicals seemed to have proved the sincerity of their con- victions not only by renouncing personal and material comforts but also by accepting the grave consequences of their war against autocracy—imprisonment, exile, hard labor, and execution. This was especially true of the terrorists, many of whom justified their determination to spill their enemies' blood by their own willingness to die in the revolutionary struggle. Indeed, some of them even welcomed death, which they believed would exonerate them for their use of violence.

Other extremists, however, evaluated their situation in more practical terms. Many realized that the harsh government measures against the revolutionaries—persecutions characterized by frequent overreactions reflecting the administration's insecurity—failed to eliminate subversive underground activities and undermined the position of the authorities by turning society against the all-powerful regime and eliciting popular sympathy for the extremists. In this sense, the revolutionaries apparently sought through their terrorist attacks to provoke the authorities to further repressions, which would increase public dissatisfaction and protest.

To a large degree, the revolutionary intellectuals did achieve their objectives, for by the late nineteenth century they had become true martyrs in the eyes of educated society. No matter how strongly the liberals disagreed with radical doctrines and practices, they had to acknowledge the courage and determination of the freedom fighters. The fact that the revolutionaries supplemented lofty political demagoguery with a readiness to die for their principles validated those principles for the intelligentsia as a whole, largely because the nonradicals could not boast the same dedication to the people's cause.[7] And it is for this reason that so many educated Russians could barely conceal the sense of guilt that arose over the cautious behavior that guaranteed their personal security. Nor could they hide a certain inferiority complex before the daring and uncompromising extremists, not only allowing them to dictate the definition of what the revolutionaries never tired of praising as the freedom-loving, altruistic, and populist Russian intelligentsia, but also to formulate the rules for "politically correct" behavior for every *intelligent* in any confrontation between the reactionary and the revolutionary camps. In other words, to qualify as a member of the intelligentsia, it was no longer sufficient for an independent-minded person to exercise critical thinking with regard to state policies; he was also required to support, at least in spirit, the revolutionary cause. By the late nineteenth century even the conservatives found themselves dependent on the opinions prevailing in the educated milieu, which had been conditioned by the revolutionary outlook and values, including ethical values. The most revealing example of this dependence on public opinion dominated by revolutionary conscience is a familiar conversation between Dostoevsky and publicist Aleksei Suvorin in which the great novelist confessed that in a hypothetical situation in which he overheard terrorists plotting regicide, he would not have informed the police for fear of ruining his public image: "The liberals would never have forgiven me. They would have tormented me, driven me to despair."[8]

Liberal society thus remained unequivocally apologetic vis-à-vis the extremists, and by the outbreak of the 1905 revolution this stance had become a tradition; the pressure it exerted even in official circles helped to account for the initial hesitation of the government in the face of the crisis. Following the escalation of violence, many government functionaries, unable to withstand the influence of the prevailing liberal mentality, also viewed the radicals as selfless if misguided martyrs persecuted by the ruthless state. As a result, numerous civil, police, and military officials, including some in the highest rank, not only resisted implementing severe measures against the radicals and specifically the terrorists, but also could not conceal their personal admiration and sympathy for the "unfortunate politicals." Many government officials felt the pangs of guilty consciences as a result of their participation in suppression of the revolution; some began to drink heavily and even suffered mental breakdowns or committed suicide, unable to overcome their shame. Moreover, individual members of the tsarist administration occasionally risked their own careers to extend favors to extremists fighting the very establishment that these state servants represented.[9]

Contributing to society's tendencies to sympathize with the revolutionaries (which, incidentally, undermined the radical aplomb in singling out the intelligenty as necessarily enemies of the regime) was a marked transformation of the broader intelligentsia's attitude toward individual involvement in public life. This transformation, which originated in the late nineteenth century, is perceptively depicted in the reminiscences of Vladimir Korolenko, a prerevolutionary writer and liberal publicist. Korolenko describes his father, a provincial town judge whom he remembers as a cultured and remarkably honest man, proud of his strict adherence to the law. While the father never failed to help people to the best of his abilities, he always stayed within the legal norms and, with his "inner convictions not rocked by analysis," never questioned the legitimacy of any of the fundamentals of Russian life: "God, the tsar, and law for him were at a height inaccessible for criticism." In this way, Korolenko's father, representative of a generation of cultured Russians that included many members of the official superstructure, was different from his son: the young Korolenko and numerous other intellectuals of his day no longer considered it sufficient to admit responsibility only for their personal behavior or to serve their country by fulfilling honestly and competently the requirements of their positions and occupations. Indeed, they now deemed it unethical not to participate actively in public life on the side of the "forces of progress." Korolenko's father, whose "conscience was always invariably clear," and the other "honest people of his time did not know the profound spiritual distress flowing from awareness of personal responsibility for the 'whole order of things.'" They were free of the "bitter sense of guilt regarding social injustice" expressed by members of the later generation of intellectuals, who considered themselves accountable for all the evils in Russian society. This sense of personal responsibility required these intellectuals, entrapped by their quixotic urge to render their idealism rational and pragmatic, to become concerned and involved in any sociopolitical issues that had been the undisputed domain of the autocratic government.[10]

The tsarist administration refused to recognize that an entire generation of Russian intellectuals now considered it their moral duty to intervene in every aspect of the country's public life. To a significant degree, therefore, the authorities were responsible for a situation in which the radicalized intelligentsia, far from seeking to overcome its traditional estrangement from the ruling spheres, had assumed a generally antigovernment stand by the early years of the twentieth century. Failing to perceive the mutual hostility and distrust between the country's ruling spheres and its educated citizens as a symptom of the unhealthy state of Russia's internal life, the government of Nicholas II, at least in the initial decade of his reign, did nothing to overcome the alienation of cultured circles. Instead, it stubbornly preferred to regard every independent voice as a revolutionary manifestation and treat it accordingly, thus forcing all politically conscious people closer to the uncompromising radicals.

Indeed, the beginning of Nicholas II's reign was marked by a tragic lack of communication between the court and liberal society. When a delegation from various zemstvo assemblies came to St. Petersburg in January 1895 to address the tsar on the occasion of his coronation, Nicholas responded by proclaiming the dream of popular representation to be "senseless." This insensitive treatment of the zemstvo deputies naturally provoked a new wave of antagonism toward the establishment, with a prominent publicist, Petr Struve, summarizing the general mood in an open letter to the tsar in which he asserted that in hurling a challenge to society, the autocracy was digging its own grave, for inevitably, "it will fall under the pressure of living social forces."[11] It was no wonder, then, that almost from the beginning of his reign Nicholas II was nicknamed Nicholas the Last.

Precisely because the highest authorities in the Russian empire were so desperate, anxious, and insecure about their efforts to preserve the status quo, seeking to eliminate every sign of social discontent in their struggle against the extremists rather than striving to find its deeper causes, their policies were those of "hesitant ruthlessness—either too harsh or not harsh enough."[12] Although fearful that overtly repressive actions would portray the country's rulers as semi-Asiatic barbarians and also damage its credibility in Western political and financial circles, the government of Nicholas II nevertheless occasionally resorted to unusually cruel antirevolutionary measures that outraged even the moderates, who were far from revolutionary in their outlook yet held the autocracy responsible for the never-ending conflict with the radicals. The most renowned victim of this dilemma was Count Leo Tolstoy, who in his later years ardently opposed the rationalized use of violence. In his famous essay "I Cannot Keep Silent!" (*"Ne mogu molchat'!"*) he condemned the omnipotent state for its use of execution against the revolutionaries. In a private conversation with Korolenko, Tolstoy seemed to betray his own preaching of nonviolence by empathizing with the terrorists, whose tactics should have made them Tolstoy's adversaries: "I . . . understand that the terrorists should perhaps be condemned for certain things. Well, you know my views, but still . . . I cannot help saying: these things are necessary."[13] Tolstoy, obsessed with moral dilemmas, undoubtedly approached extremism from an ethical viewpoint and simply could not reconcile himself with the state's use of its seemingly abundant resources against individual daredevils, confused unfortunates, and selfless zealots.

Although a similar mood was widespread in educated and cultural circles, it would be incorrect to accept the idealistic assumption that the entire Russian intelligentsia took part in or supported revolution only as a result of the pangs of a collective guilty conscience and the desire to fulfill a moral obligation to help Russia. Nor is it accurate to assert that all members of the intelligentsia sympathized with the revolutionaries because they appeared to be the weaker side, persecuted by the merciless machinery of the state. Many who liked to think of themselves as genuine intelligenty cooperated with the radicals for a number of reasons that had little to do with ethics.

In contrast with the situation that developed in the late nineteenth century, on a personal level most members of the Russian intelligentsia in 1905 had little in common with the extremists. First of all, by the outbreak of the first Russian revolution, the social composition of the revolutionary movement had changed significantly, and the overwhelming majority of the radicals, especially the terrorists, no longer came from society's educated circles. Whereas nearly all members of the People's Will organization were descendants of the upper and middle classes, and by virtue of their education and general interest in abstract ideas and social issues belonged to the intellectual milieu, the new political groups and parties that multiplied rapidly after the beginning of the century included an increasing number of first-generation workers and artisans. Many of these new radicals were impoverished peasants who had left their homes in the countryside in search of suitable employment in developing industries in the cities and towns. They found life in the city strenuous and psychological adaptation to it difficult, making them easy prey for revolutionary agitators looking for recruits. Semiliterate young workers and artisans soon began to dominate the membership of the revolutionary movement, transforming it by the very fact that only a small fraction of these semi-literate radical upstarts considered it important to acquaint themselves with even the most fundamental theoretical principles and ideological creeds professed by the revolutionary leaders.

In fact, these newly enlisted freedom fighters frequently expressed contempt not only for the intelligentsia at large, which they considered too scrupulous to be effective, but even for their fellow radicals among the intellectuals. With a certain barbaric arrogance many revolutionaries discarded the intellectuals' devotion to ideas, asserting that reading, studying, and debating theoretical questions were simply excuses for not fighting.[14] And since few of the party intellectuals and theoreticians were prepared to become personally involved in hazardous underground operations, particularly terrorist enterprises, the combatants often departed from the ideological principles advocated by theorists abroad for the sake of immediate practical results, ignoring the decisions of the "generals," whom they saw as little better than idlers and cowards.

The relationship between intellectuals and nonintellectuals was hampered further by another phenomenon that transformed the antigovernment movement even more drastically by the time of the 1905–1907 revolution: the active participation of non-Russian nationalities in the radical struggle, especially in revolutionary terrorism, to an unprecedented degree. Although mass uprisings in the Kingdom of Poland were not news to the imperial government, never before had the people of the Baltic and Caucasian regions taken up arms against the tsarist regime in such large numbers. Even the relatively passive Finns embraced the revolution by turning the Duchy of Finland into a safe haven for the manufacture and transportation of weapons and explosives. Moreover, by 1900 almost 30 percent of the individuals arrested for political crimes in Russia were Jews, and while in 1903 only 7 million of the total 136 million inhabitants of the empire were Jewish, about half of the members of revolutionary parties were Jewish.[15] Although the leaders of non-Russian political organizations promoted the sociopolitical objectives outlined in their parties' programs, most rank-and-file members of the antigovernment groups operating in the border areas considered national independence their primary goal. The borderland movements were thus first and foremost nationalist, and only secondarily socialist or anarchist in character; their immediate regional demands often had little in common with the goals of the Russian radical intellectuals, and occasionally members of the ethnic intelligentsia neglected to conceal that they were merely using the empirewide revolution to attain their national objectives.

As was the case in the Russian revolutionary movement after 1905, the ranks of the national independence fighters in the borderlands consisted predominantly of lower-class individuals, most of whom possessed only a rudimentary education at best. They included, for example, the Latvian "forest brothers," inveterate rebels of peasant origin who terrorized the Baltic German nobility and Russian authorities in the countryside; many Georgian and Armenian revolutionaries; Polish terrorists; and the majority of the young Jewish extremists from the areas of the Pale. They were uneducated, had difficulty expressing themselves even in their native languages, and demonstrated little sympathy for or interest in the intellectual controversies of the day, including those within the socialist camp.

Perhaps the most important factor contributing to the lack of understanding between the intelligentsia and the burgeoning and increasingly egalitarian antigovernment movement was the appearance of what Petr Struve termed a "new type of revolutionary that developed unnoticed by society . . . in the prerevolutionary years and finally emerged during 1905–1906." This new type of radical was a "blending of revolutionary and bandit, whose extremist psychology was marked by liberation from all moral restraints."[16] Early signs of this tendency, already present in the second half of the nineteenth century, were perceptively noted by Dostoevsky and depicted in *The Devils*. The process reached its apogee, however, in the post-1905 period, when the indiscriminate combat practices of growing numbers of radicals qualified them as the "new type of extremists." By then, the phenomenon was evident not only to attentive observers but also to the general public, even if inside opposition circles only a few sincere souls, appalled by the corruption and irreversible disintegration of the revolutionary consciousness, were prepared to acknowledge it.

Radicals of the new type came to differ significantly from most of their revolutionary predecessors active between the 1860s and the 1880s, with the exception, of course, of a few pathological individuals in the antigovernment camp, including the infamous Sergei Nechaev, a forefather of this new type of extremism. The new radicals, most of whom were involved in terrorist activities, exhibited a considerably lower level of intellectual and ideological awareness, as well as less inclination toward altruistic idealism and dedication to the cause. They also demonstrated comparably limited discrimination in their methods, especially in the selection of targets for their attacks. For these radicals, terrorism became "so addictive that it was often carried out without even weighing the moral questions posed by earlier generations."[17] In fact, such renowned revolutionary figures as Grigorii Gershuni, the head of the Socialist Revolutionary Combat Organization, and anarchist leader Petr Kropotkin conceded that terrorism and other extremist activity now "extended beyond the boundaries of a narrow circle of people totally devoted to the cause of liberation," and also that the revolutionary organism was infected with Nechaevism (*nechaevshchina*), a "terrible disease . . . the degeneration of the revolutionary spirit."[18] It was not unusual for a variety of shady individuals, adventurers, and opportunists, including common criminals, hooligans, and the riffraff of Russian society (frequently referred to as "petty rabble," or *shpanka*), to join the ranks of the freedom fighters and use lofty slogans to justify their unrestrained banditry. This criminal activity was particularly evident in the practice of "expropriations," as revolutionary robberies were termed by the political parties that engaged in them. These widespread "ex's" assumed various forms, including armed assault, extortion, and blackmail.

Differentiating between revolutionaries and criminals in that period was not an easy matter, especially in cases involving an individual with a lengthy police record. Such a person might have been arrested initially as a common criminal, then returned to the court system several years later to be sentenced to a long term of imprisonment for participation in an attempted assassination, and finally sent back to court on rape charges. Contemporaries of the 1905 revolution often found it impossible to separate common criminality from politically motivated acts. It was not unusual, for example, for a revolutionary contemplating an expropriation to plan on using half of the loot to aid the downtrodden proletarians and the other half to buy himself a small estate abroad.[19] Many robberies (Gershuni went so far as to say nine-tenths of them[20]) traditionally considered revolutionary expropriations were in reality ordinary criminal undertakings. In the post-1905 period, when, as Struve observed, a "flood of fast-living and pleasure-seeking burst into the revolution,"[21] the proceeds of these robberies were often used by the new type of radicals strictly for personal gratification. In the nineteenth century, revolutionary robberies were extremely rare and a dissolute lifestyle was not an option for extremists, but in the 1905 era revolutionary banditry became so widespread as to be labeled by a popular cliché of the period the "seamy side of the revolution." The label also referred to the unusually large number of psychologically disturbed people attracted to the revolutionary camp, as was evident not only from the stream of mental breakdowns and suicides among the Russian extremists but also from the pervasiveness of unquestionably sadistic behavior, committing acts of striking, meaning-less, and pathological cruelty.[22]

As revolutionary circles assumed an increasingly democratized and mass character, accompanied by the inevitable dissipation of the lofty and idealistic atmosphere of the tightly knit clandestine society of the late nineteenth century, the Russian intelligenty became more and more alienated from the revolutionary practitioners, until most members of the intelligentsia no longer shared either intellectual or ethical values with the rank-and-file revolutionaries. Despite this tendency, however, by 1905 a number of factors had spurred the intellectuals to join the radical ranks.

The first of these factors was the intellectuals' evident desire to play a leading role in politics—an ambition warranted, in their opinion, by their possession of one tool essential for achievement of the *bien publique:* an educated and rational approach to statesmanship. This goal, however, was incompatible with the fundamental premises of the autocracy that Nicholas II was sworn to uphold "as firmly and as steadfastly as . . . [his] unforgettable late father."[23] As a result of this unyielding stance on the part of the monarch, intellectuals of every political shade were left with the sole option of pursuing their objectives by forming organizations that, under the circumstances prevailing before 1905, could operate only illegally.

In spite of its considerable success in preventing the revolutionaries from unifying into formidable organizations similar to the People's Will throughout the era of counterreforms in the 1880s and early 1890s, the administration of Alexander III could not eradicate the radicals' funda-mental desire to band together. This drive seems to be part of a general tendency of the Russian intelligentsia to overcome its frustrating loneli-ness, its separation and alienation from both the official bureaucratic realm and the backward world of the apolitical peasantry by joining soci-eties of likeminded individuals. After the dissolution of the People's Will in the early 1880s, the opponents of the tsarist regime, operating in numer-ous underground groups empirewide, never stopped trying to organize a unified antigovernment movement. Finally, in 1893, they celebrated a fleeting success in the formation of the Party of People's Rights (Partiia Narodnogo Prava), a short-lived and heterogeneous entity that encom-passed revolutionaries as well as liberals. Although the police destroyed the organization in April 1894, it established a precedent for modern political parties in Russia. The experience encouraged the revolutionaries to intensify their efforts to unify the antigovernment forces, and for many intellectuals it also revived the hope of realizing their political ambitions in the future.

After several other attempts to create revolutionary parties inside

Russia, a number of these extralegal politicians emigrated abroad and there assumed positions of prominence in several new organizations headquartered in Western Europe, including the Socialist Revolutionary and the Social Democratic Workers' parties, as well as the more moderate Union of Liberation. Significantly, the incessant rivalry among the party leaders, who were all devoted to the struggle against autocracy, began with their debut in the political arena. They apparently preferred to be generals of smaller armies rather than share authority over their cadres and—equally important—control over their parties' treasuries. Thus, whereas rank-and-file members of various political organizations throughout the Russian empire actively cooperated in the practical tasks of the revolution, exhibiting a comradely spirit and unequivocal disregard for their parties' theoretical differences,[24] their leaders in emigration devoted countless hours to interparty wrangling. This stubborn squabbling over the nuances of ideology and tactics, marked by obsessive attention to detail, elaborate intrigue, and personality conflicts, betrayed in many of these individuals an underlying drive to participate in the antigovernment movement that had much to do with personal political ambition and the desire for otherwise unattainable public prestige.

At the same time, realizing that in the face of an official policy of "hold and suppress" (*derzhat' i ne pushchat'*) it was virtually impossible for independent activists to participate in public life, many nonradical intellectuals, including zemstvo workers, also came to realize that Browning pistols and dynamite were the only practical methods of forcing the government to make concessions. Although for the most part unprepared to engage in extremism personally, they sought to participate in the revolution by providing the radicals with both pragmatic aid and ethical justification for political violence.

Specifically, this was the position of the Constitutional Democratic party, whose members, known simply as the Kadets, were generally held to be the stronghold and embodiment of Russian liberalism. The Kadet party, proud to have among its membership the "flower of the Russian intelligentsia,"[25] indeed included an exceptional number of talented writers, publicists, and prominent public figures among the country's zemstvo intellectuals, lawyers, journalists, and other educated professionals. None of them could be considered bloodthirsty villains who welcomed violence for its own sake, nor did they sympathize personally with the new type of radical, practicing indiscriminate violence. Nevertheless, the radicalization of Russian politics was undoubtedly to the Kadets' advantage, for the threat of expanding revolution and rampant terrorism forced the authorities to consider major conciliatory steps, the most essential of which, from the Kadets' standpoint, would be the formation of a new responsible cabinet (*otvetstvennoe ministerstvo*) composed of leaders from their party. Their desire to obtain the tsar's approval of this Kadet-dominated cabinet required them to be extremely cautious in maneuvering between the authorities and the extremists in their attempt to convince the former that the Constitutional Democratic party was the only group of respectable moderates opposed to violent tactics and capable of stopping the raging anarchy while hoping to use and control the latter, with whom they no doubt wished to break as soon as political victory was secured. Until that time, however, the Kadet leaders, always afraid to be compromised in the eyes of society by any rapprochement with the autocracy, were unwilling, despite individual voices of protest in their own party, to renounce their temporary solidarity with the revolutionaries, who were to do the dirty work necessary to undermine the regime. On the contrary, the Kadet leadership welcomed and often even indirectly encouraged the extremists in the party press and their Duma speeches, and also secretly provided the radicals with practical and material assistance, perceiving that their activities benefited the entire Russian opposition movement, liberals as well as radicals. In contributing in this way to the radicalization of the political process, the Constitutional Democrats must themselves be considered revolutionaries rather than liberals in the traditional sense of the word, for the political ambitions of their leaders prevented the Kadets from stepping into the gap between the radicalized intelligentsia and the conservative state. Consequently, the Kadets failed to contribute to the development of a more moderate political culture in the empire by declining an opportunity to correct one of tsarist Russia's fundamental flaws— the absence of a strong liberal tradition.[26]

"Revolution was becoming the fashion," recalled Victor Chernov, leader of the Socialist Revolutionary party,[27] providing another reason why individual intellectuals subscribed to the struggle against tsarism. At about the turn of the century, when moderate principles were regarded as the sad mistakes of an older generation, revolutionary activity became a favorite and fashionable pastime in educated (and not so educated) circles, whose members had already accepted the radicals' definition of intelligenty and went out of their way to prove themselves as such. Numerous professionals, representatives of the artistic community, and students—all aspiring members of the exclusive self-declared intelligentsia—volunteered to promote the revolution if not by personal participation in risky exploits then at least by less heroic enterprises, such as providing the activists with money, "clean" passports, shelter, and places to hide illegal literature, weapons, and explosives. Some of these individuals began to fear the consequences of this dangerous game almost as soon as they began playing it, and while a few pulled out with as much relief as self-loathing and contempt for their own cowardice, most continued to associate with the radicals, sometimes seduced by the excitement of the clandestine world and sometimes solely to avoid the shameful label of deserter.

Others, however, particularly the younger Russian intellectuals, felt the urge to proceed beyond voluntary or half-extorted favors to the revolutionaries, and plunged into the whirlpool of extremism. Increasing numbers of educated Russians had rejected not only the official Orthodox church but also the fundamentals of faith and Christian spirituality. Yet they still craved an all-encompassing set of guidelines; for these people, seeking a replacement value system became a way of life. Many pursued escape from their mundane existences and stifling routines by experimenting with the superficial and flashy features of the complex social and aesthetic process known as the Silver Age in Russia, a period of intense cultural and intellectual turmoil, artistic sublimity, and decadence. Always in search of exalted spirituality, which often entailed new and sometimes elaborate forms of unconventional behavior intended to shock, these restless and frustrated young people usually became bored with their hobbies almost as soon as they discovered them. And after every disappointment they resumed their frantic vacillation from one possibility for instant salvation to another. Sooner or later many of them stumbled onto the idea of revolution as yet another sufficiently progressive variant of self-liberation worthy of pursuit. At a time when highly turbulent minds sought, in their artistic ecstasy, "poetry in death,"[28] radicalism and political violence provided intriguing new avenues of self-expression and were transformed for some individuals into dramatic performance. For these people the pursuit of revolution thus differed little in its underlying motivation from the widespread use of alcohol and drugs, fascination with occultism and other forms of the supernatural, obsessive contemplation of suicide, indulgence in the prevalent pornographic literary bedlam and preoccupation with eroticism and sexual perversion, or dabbling in futurist poetry.

In this world, where grotesque vulgarity and sweet naivete tangled, shifted, and replaced each other in kaleidoscopic fashion, women came to play an increasingly active role among the Bohemians-turned-revolutionaries. A great deal of responsibility for this change lay with the Russian government, for during this time of rapidly changing family relations and the spread of education, it denied young, assertive females, who could no longer be confined to the home, access to higher learning and to opportunities to pursue intellectual and professional ambitions, not to mention a role in political or public life. The only place where women were accepted as social equals was the revolutionary milieu, and it is hardly surprising that so many emancipated females, acutely resentful of being treated as the "weaker sex" at home and in society, severed their ties not only with their restrictive parents and husbands but also with the traditional establishment as a whole. Almost by default they found themselves among the political outcasts.

By the beginning of the century, about one-fourth of all Russia terrorists were women.[29] Remarkably, many of their male comrades were eager to use female revolutionaries in the most risky and violent extremist operations. Many of these women were eager to prove their courage and assert themselves among their new radical friends by dedicating (or even sacrificing) their lives to the cause. Perhaps another factor accounting for this devotion and fanaticism was a projection of the Russian Orthodox concept of the woman-martyr into the strictly secular realm of radical politics. Correspondingly, a number of female Russian terrorists were perceived by their comrades as "monastic" types.[30]

This mode of behavior was equally common among Jewish women, who were even more restricted in their homes and within their traditional social environment than were their Russian counterparts, and who devoted themselves wholeheartedly to extremism, as demonstrated by their disproportionate presence in terrorist organizations. Their readiness to embrace terrorism had much to do with the fact that "in becoming revolutionaries, they severed links with their families and past traditions at a deeper level than men did. By joining the movement, a Jewish girl was not only opposing her parents' political beliefs, but was also flouting one of the very foundations of Jewish society—her role as a woman in the family."[31] In this way, Jewish females estranged themselves from their Orthodox community and, experiencing prejudice and discrimination in Russian society at large to an even greater extent than did Russian Orthodox women, they sought refuge among other outcasts in revolutionary circles, where, for the most part, religious and cultural tolerance prevailed to a degree truly remarkable for early-twentieth-century Russia.

In their attempts to realize their inner motivations and drives, individual members of the Russian intelligentsia thus plunged headlong into the revolution. Whether driven by a moral obligation not to remain passive in the face of the numerous problems evident in Russia's public life and frustrated by the inability to do so legally, by personal political ambitions, by a desire to be involved in fashionable radical activities, by an urge to experiment with extremism as part of the Silver Age pathos, by a need for self-assertion (particularly evident in many revolutionary females), or by any combination of these—the Russian intelligenty invested all their hopes in the revolution. It is thus not enough to speculate that "had the intelligentsia in Russia been given an opportunity to take part in political activities and political decisions, it would have learned to understand better the distance between the possible and the desirable, and therefore it would not have been so inclined to doctrinairism and extremism." Nor is it sufficient to offer a sweeping assertion that the "Russian autocracy, by its obstinate resistance to peaceful change and by its lack of sincerity when compelled to make concessions, provoked extremism."[32] Around 1905, when the most perceptive members of Russian society, especially among the literary elite, began to predict the imminent collapse of the entire traditional order, their pessimism reflected not only a sense of approaching political crisis, but also, more broadly, an awareness of the spiritual catastrophe befalling the country. To a few, most notably the greatest contemporary poet, Aleksandr Blok, it was evident that behind all the politics, revolutionary sentiments had become commonplace because "some different higher principle is needed. Since there is none, rebellion and violence of all sorts take its place."[33] A strictly political solution could thus do little to settle the profound inner conflicts of educated Russian society.

In their desperate search for new higher principles, the intellectuals gradually became accustomed to treating the revolution not merely as a panacea for all evil but even as a kind of deity to which traditional sociopolitical forms and fundamental ethical norms had to be sacrificed. This led them to accept the radicals' definition of the very word *intelligentsia*, to exonerate the extremists as martyrs to the people's cause, to validate the radical policy of "The Worse, the Better," to support violence out of political necessity, and, in general, to go along with the maxim that the means are justified by the evident glorious revolutionary end—a notion that prepared the intelligentsia for the crudest and most sanguinary version of revolutionary consciousness: the Bolshevik perception of reality.

And yet, the long-awaited revolution, from its outbreak in 1917, proceeded to undermine and eventually eliminate an essential characteristic of the Russian intelligentsia, its separation and alienation from both the official establishment and the masses, thus endangering its very existence as a group. Because "the new state made no place for the intelligentsia of the past, with its function of political criticism and articulation of alternative ideals,"[34] soon after 1917 the intellectuals faced a choice: either become conformists and thus violate their own basic requirement for membership in the intelligentsia, or suffer persecution at the hands of the new authorities.

Those who chose the first alternative eliminated the gap between themselves and the rest of the Soviet elite, and ceased to qualify as intelligenty, illustrating one scholar's observations: "One of the difficulties in the relation of intellect to power is that certain primary functions of intellect are widely felt to be threatened almost as much by being associated with power as by being relegated to a position of impotence. An acute and paradoxical problem of intellect as a force in modern society stems from the fact that it cannot lightly reconcile itself either to its association with power or to its exclusion from an important political role."[35]

Tragically, those intelligenty who dared to prefer the second option, retaining their independence in thought and criticism, suffered and died along with numerous other victims of a state far more ruthless than the tsarist regime had ever been. Nearly all of them were exterminated during Communist rule in Russia, a tragic loss that helps to explain a generally accurate observation about Russian society in the 1990s: while individual intelligenty may still be encountered as isolated members of a nearly extinct species, they have largely been replaced by a surrogate type of Soviet and post-Soviet intellectual. As a group, the intelligentsia—at least in the traditional sense of the word—no longer exists in Russia.

Notes

1. Richard Pipes, *The Russian Revolution* (New York: Random House, 1993).

2. Anna Geifman, *Thou Shalt Kill: Revolutionary Terrorism in Russia, 1894–1917* (Princeton, N.J.: Princeton University Press, 1993), 21.

3. For a discussion of the original use of the term "intelligentsia" see Martin Malia, "What Is the Intelligentsia?" in Richard Pipes, ed., *The Russian Intelligentsia* (New York, 1961), 2–4, 7.

4. Paul Miliukov, cited in Thomas Riha, *A Russian European: Paul Miliukov in Russian Politics* (Notre Dame: University of Notre Dame Press, 1969), 78; Jane Burbank, *Intelligentsia and Revolution* (New York: Oxford University Press, 1986), 6–7.

5. G. Ul'ianov, "Vospominaniia o M. A. Natansone," *Katorga i ssylka* 4(89) (1932): 73; Viktor Chernov, *Zapiski Sotsialista-Revoliutsionera* (Berlin: Grzhebin 1922), 95.

6. "Iz otcheta o perliustratsii dep. politsii za 1908 g.," *Krasnyi arkhiv* 2(27) (1928): 156; O. Piatnitskii, *Zapiski bol'shevika* (Moscow, 1956), 65.

7. James Frank McDaniel, "Political Assassination and Mass Execution: Terrorism in Revolutionary Russia, 1878–1938" (Ph.D. diss., University of Michigan, 1976), 97–98; Walter Laqueur, *Terrorism* (Boston: Little, Brown, 1977), 111.

8. A. Suvorin, *Dnevnik* (Moscow: Novosti, 1992), 15–16.

9. Geifman, *Thou Shalt Kill*, 223.

10. V. G. Korolenko, *Istoriia moego sovremennika*, vols. 1–2 (Moscow, 1985), 19–20.

11. Cited in Richard Pipes, *Struve: Liberal on the Left, 1870–1905* (Cambridge: Harvard University Press, 1970), 154–155.

12. Astrid von Borcke, "Violence and Terror in Russian Revolutionary Populism: The *Narodnaya Volya*, 1879–83," in Wolfgang J. Mommsen and Gerhard Hirschfeld, eds., *Social Protest, Violence and Terror in Nineteenth- and Twentieth-Century Europe* (New York: St. Martin's, 1982), 60.

13. V. G. Korolenko, *Zemli! Zemli!* (Moscow, 1991), 77.

14. See, for example, A. Lokerman, "Po tsarskim tiur'mam," *Katorga i ssylka* 25 (1926): 186, 189.

15. Norman M. Naimark, "Terrorism and the Fall of Imperial Russia," *Terrorism and Political Violence* 2(2) (Summer 1990): 174; Leonard Schapiro, *Russian Studies* (New York: Penguin, 1988), 266.

16. Cited in A. Serebrennikov, ed., *Ubiistvo Stolypina. Svidetel'stva i dokumenty* (New York: Teleks, 1986), 319.

17. Naimark, "Terrorism and the Fall of Imperial Russia," 189.

18. Petr Kropotkin, *Russkaia revoliutsiia i anarkhizm* (London, 1907), 40; Grigorii Gershuni, "Ob ekspropriatsiiakh," undated letter to comrades, 2, 1, Nicolaevsky Collection, box 12, folder 1, Hoover Institution Archives, Stanford, Calif.

19. Geifman, *Thou Shalt Kill*, 7.

20. Letter from Grigorii Gershuni, 23 February 1906, 4, Nicolaevsky Collection, box 12, folder 1, Hoover Institution Archives, Stanford, Calif.

21. Cited in Serebrennikov, *Ubiistvo Stolypina*, 319.

22. For a discussion of the "seamy side of the revolution" see Geifman, *Thou Shalt Kill*, 154–172.

23. Cited in Pipes, *Struve*, 154.

24. For a discussion of mutual assistance and cooperation among antigovernment activists of diverse political persuasions, a phenomenon underemphasized in current historiography on the Russia revolution, see Geifman, *Thou Shalt Kill*, ch. 6.

25. P. Miliukov, *God bor'by* (St. Petersburg, 1907), 118.

26. For a detailed discussion of Kadet policy with regard to extremism see Geifman, *Thou Shalt Kill*, 207–222.

27. V. M. Chernov, *Pered burei* (Moscow: Mezhdunarodnye otnosheniia, 1993), 165.

28. Cited in Viacheslav Venozhinskii, *Smertnaia kazn' i terror* (St. Petersburg, 1908), 28.

29. Laqueur, *Terrorism*, 121.

30. Boris Savinkov, *Vospominaniia terrorista* (Khar'kov, 1926), 117.

31. Amy Knight, "Female Terrorists in the Russian Socialist Revolutionary Party," *The Russian Review* 38(2) (April 1979): 145–46.

32. Boris Elkin, "The Russian Intelligentsia on the Eve of the Revolution," in Pipes, *Russian Intelligentsia*, 32–33.

33. Alexander Blok, "The People and the Intelligentsia," in Marc Raeff, ed., *Russian Intellectual History: An Anthology* (New Jersey: Humanities Press, 1978), 362.

34. Burbank, *Intelligentsia and Revolution*, 7.

35. Richard Hofstadter, *Anti-Intellectualism in American Life* (New York: Knopf, 1963), 229.

O.V. VOLOBUEV

The Mensheviks in the Fall of 1917: Decisions and Consequences

2

I feel with pain some kind of discord which is tearing Russia apart. There is no love for the motherland any more. Just about everybody is talking about love for the motherland but everyone thinks that he has the recipe for salvation. But to deny to oneself something that is his own for the sake of a possibility of common work and for the sake of joint efforts to save the country is not considered acceptable. In every history textbook we read about one country or another which perished from internecine strife. Now, consciously or unconsciously we are coming to it. This is called the "class struggle."
—From the diary of War Minister A. I. Verkhovsky, 16 October 1917

C ould the Mensheviks and Socialist Revolutionaries have presented realistic alternatives to the Bolshevik seizure of power? Which mistakes by the Socialist parties contributed to the success of the October coup? Could the Revolutionary Democracy, as these parties were called, have prevented the establishment of the Bolshevik dictatorship? Such questions remain at the center of political and scholarly debates on 1917 in Russia. Contrary to the established interpretation of Soviet historiography, the outcome of the revolutionary process in 1917 was not predetermined. Alternative modes of political development did not prevail, but this does not mean that they did not exist. The causes for a particular outcome lay in the disunity of various organized social forces. Among the most important of these social forces were the Mensheviks, the recognized leaders of the Petrograd Soviet up to September 1917 and of the Central Executive Committee (CEC) of soviets up to the October overturn. As the historian Ziva Galili pointed out, they were responsible for establishing the all-Russian network of soviets, with all its successes and failures.[1] After scrutinizing the Mensheviks' activity from February to July 1917, Galili concluded that the fate of the moderate Socialists was largely sealed by July.[2] She devoted only one chapter of her 1993 book on the overturn to the crucial July to October period, during which a search for a third political alternative was under way, she wrote. According to this point of view, nothing could have changed the outcome of the power struggle.

In this chapter I favor a different point of view. The field of possible political alternatives was widening and then narrowing during the late summer of 1917, depending on circumstances of the moment. Some alternatives were being realized, and others remained unrealized. Russia's contemporary history, which has much in common with its revolutionary past, shows that political victories and defeats are largely determined by the skill of leaders and parties and their ability to mobilize social forces in support of their ideas, as well as by their will and determination to achieve their objectives.

The leaders of the Mensheviks and SRs offered their own explanations for the defeat of democracy in 1917. Iraklii Tsereteli believed that the leaders of Russian democracy "found themselves ill-prepared to face an exceptional situation created by the Russian revolution, when for the first time in the history of all revolutions, the Socialists were propelled to a leading role and the main danger for the free order lay on the left."[3] Their main failure was not that they accepted the coalition with the liberals but that they did not maintain control of the initiative. The leader of the Socialist Revolutionaries, N. D. Avksent'ev, held similar views. He saw the tragedy of democracy in the failure of the Socialists to rally to the side of the Provisional Government at the critical moment.[4]

The left-of-center Socialists—Iulii Martov, Fedor Dan, Noi Zhordaniia, and Victor Chernov—saw the causes for the defeat of democracy differently. In 1940, the journal published by Fedor Dan, *Novyi Mir,* printed an editorial titled "The Two Paths." The author of the article, who contrasted views of left- and right-leaning Mensheviks and cited Martov, argued that the victory of Bolshevism was the result of the failures of Social Democracy, which "could not, did not know how to, and did not want to" lead the revolutionary process, having surrendered to Bolshevism the solution of the burning problems of war and peace, and land and organization of industry.[5] The leader of the Georgian Mensheviks, Zhordaniia, recalled that he had demanded that Nikolay Chkheidze, the Petrograd Soviet chairman, and Tsereteli undertake decisive measures to end the war and adopt reforms, because only then could the revolutionary intelligentsia convince the people who "lived and thought by facts alone."[6] Victor Chernov likewise believed that the Socialists' coalition with the Constitutional Democrats (Kadets) was disastrous, because attempts to safeguard the coalition neutralized the partners and left the government paralyzed.[7]

The Menshevik and SR leaders argued to their last hour about the defeat of democracy. Who was right and who was wrong? But we need not assume that one of the alternatives was necessarily doomed to failure and that the other had to succeed. Under certain circumstances, either of the alternatives, or those that have not been considered, may have had chances for realization, depending on the actions of specific entities, including leaders, parties, organized social groups, and army units. The history of contemporary Russia, with its ever-changing political and social circumstances, has taken many unforeseeable twists that occurred not so much because of attitudes concerning certain ideas but rather as a result of clashes among leaders and political forces and the institutions in their hands.

Let us follow the Mensheviks' policy from the end of August to the end of October 1917, reviewing the alternatives it offered and the initiatives the Mensheviks launched in order to find the way out of the government crisis. I focus here on the Mensheviks' policy in regard to the coalition government with the Kadets and the proposed all-Socialist government; their activity in the Democratic Conference, the Preparliament and the soviets; and their stance on the problem of civil war and civil peace.

In the Wake of the Kornilov Affair

General Lavr Kornilov's order to his troops to march on Petrograd, perceived by Prime Minister Alexander Kerensky as an act of rebellion, caused yet one more government crisis. The discord between the moderate and radical Socialists was obvious at the CEC session on 27–28 August. The Mensheviks put forward several proposals: to create a Committee to Struggle with Counterrevolution and to convene a conference of democratic organizations, an assembly of political forces which would form a new cabinet until the convocation of the Constituent Assembly. In debates on the composition of the new government, the moderate Socialists— Tsereteli, Mark Lieber, Avksent'ev, and others—defended the Kadets' participation. They believed that such participation was the most reasonable way to solve the government crisis and preserve civil peace. The Bolsheviks opposed coalition with the Kadets. They favored creating a new government accountable to the soviets—one that excluded the "bourgeois" parties.

In addition to the "coalition solution" and the "soviet solution" to the government crisis, another alternative was offered by the prominent Menshevik B. O. Bogdanov, who served on the Central Military Industrial Committee. Bogdanov sought the establishment of what he called a "dictatorship of democracy"—a government composed of representatives of the newly and freely elected city dumas, zemstvos, cooperatives, and other representative institutions. Martov, the leader of the center-left Mensheviks, also favored what he called "democratic dictatorship," but it differed somewhat from Bogdanov's vision. Martov advocated creating a democratic Preparliament, predominantly made up of the representatives of soviets, to which the government would be accountable.[8] Essentially, both Bogdanov's and Martov's proposals were attempts to find a middle ground between the coalition solution and the soviet solution.

On 31 August, the Menshevik CC resolved that no one with any connection to the Kornilov affair could participate in government. The Mensheviks' statement unequivocally pointed the finger at the Kadets as being sympathethic with Kornilov.[9] On the same day the SR Central Committee issued a similar statement. If the Kadets entered a new cabinet, the PSR ministers vowed to resign.[10] On the evening of 31 August the delegation of the CEC (Tsereteli, A. R. Gots, Vladimir Zenzinov, Dan, and others) arrived at the Winter Palace and informed Kerensky of the decision of the two Socialist parties. Kerensky reacted to this *demarche,* as he described it, "barely containing indignation." He called the Kadets' participation in the new cabinet essential and said that he could not accept "orders coming from political parties."[11] The CEC delegation, looking for a compromise, agreed that a five-person directorate would perform the functions of government until the new cabinet was formed. The Socialist leaders sought to prevent the sharpening of the government crisis in the wake of the Kornilov affair. Although their tractability is understandable, it nourished Kerensky's illusions that the cabinet was infallible and that he was irreplaceable.

The CEC resolved on 31 August to convene a Democratic Conference and form a Provisional Government "free from any compromises with the counterrevolutionary elements" and capable of "fulfilling the program of Revolutionary Democracy."[12] In his memoirs Kerensky referred to this resolution with irritation. He was particularly upset by the notion that the composition of the government was to be determined by the Democratic Conference and that the government's decisions were to be approved by the CEC of soviets.[13] It is important to note that the CEC resolution did not contain the latter provision: the text spoke only of close contact between the CEC and the government to safeguard order. Nevertheless, it conveyed the idea that the government would be held accountable to a representative body until the Constituent Assembly convened. Moreover, the resolution amounted to an attempt by the Socialist parties to determine the fate, composition, and policies of the Provisional Government. N. N. Sukhanov, a talented observer of the political scene in 1917, noted that the CEC had in fact adopted the principles of a dictatorship of democracy in the sense that "bourgeois" parties were removed from deliberations on the composition of the cabinet.[14] A breach appeared between the soviets, led by the Socialist parties, and the executive branch, personified by Kerensky. This breach had disastrous consequences for the fate of democracy in Russia.

General Kornilov's failure to establish a military dictatorship fundamentally changed the political situation in Russia. The realization that
there was a real danger on the right united the left-wing forces for a short
time. The soviets set up Committees to Struggle with Counterrevolution
made up of representatives of Socialist parties and trade unions. This
united Socialist front saved the Provisional Government of Kerensky even
as it acted independently of the government. Moreover, one of the main
forces in this alliance were the Bolsheviks, who were openly inimical to
the Provisional Government. In the wake of popular radicalization, new
revolutionary organizations were springing up, and the Bolsheviks were
gaining majorities in the soviets, which in turn gained importance as
powerbrokers. The soviets of Petrograd, Moscow, and other cities were
setting up all kinds of revolutionary committees and detachments of
armed workers, including the Red Guards. The CEC had to go along with
this process, and on 5 September it declared the Red Guards—the militarized workers' units—unaccountable to city authorities. The Bolsheviks
used these committees and detachments for their own purposes later in
their bid for power. Although Lieber and a few other leaders warned the
Menshevik and SR leaders of the danger, most did not anticipate the possible consequences of the fact that the soviets and Factory Committees
were setting up militarized detachments.

Perhaps the most dangerous developments for the Provisional Government and the moderate Socialists were changes in the armed forces.
The government was losing control over the generals, on the one hand,
and over the rear garrisons of the army and the Baltic sea fleet, on the
other. On 9 September the third regional congress of the Russian army
and fleet soviets in Finland voted for a Bolshevik resolution on the composition of government. That meant that the Bolshevik leaders of the
Baltic sea fleet could rely on the military units and ship crews in the three
main bases on the Baltic: Kronstadt, Helsinfors, and Revel (Tallin).

The moderate Socialists suffered a serious blow in the soviets of the
two capitals as well. On 5 September, the Moscow Soviet voted for the
Bolshevik resolution on the current political situation. On 9 September
the Menshevik-SR leaders of the Petrograd Soviet resigned because they
could no longer conduct policy based on the 31 August CEC resolution.
This meant that the Bolsheviks were in charge of the Moscow and Petrograd Soviets, which were growing increasingly opposed to the Provisional
Government. The interdistrict conference of soviets openly defied the
government right in Petrograd by refusing to carry out Kerensky's order
to dissolve the Committees to Struggle with Counterrevolution. In such
a situation the Socialist parties generally would either resolutely support
the government or oppose it. This time they did neither. Even the resolu-

tions of soviets on which the Mensheviks retained the majorities reflected the general leftward drift. On 9 September the Moscow province Bureau of Soviets resolved to support "creating a government which would include representatives of the soviets, trade unions, local self-government (Dumas) and cooperatives."[15]

The Democratic Conference appeared to the leaders of Socialist parties to be offering a way out of the crisis, allowing the country to hang on until the convocation of the Constituent Assembly. Fedor Dan, one of the CEC leaders, hoped that the Democratic Conference would form an all-Socialist government that excluded the Kadets. He was aware, however, that not all CEC leaders shared his views.[16] Even though the break with the Kadets was gaining adherents in the central committees of the Mensheviks and SRs, the official position of the CEC, thanks to Tsereteli's lobbying, was to preserve the coalition. Avksent'ev, a key SR leader, hoped that the Democratic Conference would broaden the social base of support for the Provisional Government and contain the spread of Bolshevik influence.[17] Despite their differences, all of the Socialist leaders hoped that this was the way to resolve the crisis and create a stable government.

Formally, the effort to seek cooperation with the Kadets prevailed in the Menshevik and SR Central Committees. But the compromise resolution on this question adopted by the Menshevik CC on 8 September stipulated that an all-Socialist cabinet be formed in case the Kadets refused to join the government. The vote was nine votes for the resolution, seven against, and two abstentions, a sign that serious disagreements divided the Mensheviks.[18] The struggle over this issue continued at the CEC session on 12 September, with Tsereteli arguing against Martov: "I am convinced that at the very moment when the banner of the revolution is in the hands of [Bolshevik leader Lev] Kamenev and Martov for a week or two, it will be trampled upon and torn into pieces." Tsereteli saw no difference between Bolsheviks and left-wing Mensheviks. In the end, five project resolutions were proposed, two along the lines favored by Tsereteli, two along the lines favored by Martov, and one favored by the Bolsheviks.[19]

The Mensheviks and SRs—faced with choosing between a coalition government with the Kadets and the all-Socialist government—found themselves in a difficult situation. These were antibourgeois parties, but they had agreed to share power with the Kadets. They had assumed governmental responsibility, but the Socialist parties still could not overcome doctrinal principles, the pressure of radicalized masses, as well as opposition in their own ranks to the "semi-bourgeois" government. The Socialist ideals and the antibourgeois propaganda on the one hand, and the practical necessity to cooperate with the Kadets on the other, inevitably led to political polarization. This made the moderate Socialists vulnerable, whatever course they might have adopted.

Antibourgeois attitudes in Russian society spread as quasi-religious consciousness rose. The key component of this quasi religion was adoration of the very notion of The Revolution—its symbols and institutions. The Revolution was associated with the miracle of liberation, purification, and resurrection.[20] This mood of the masses helped the Socialist parties to score a quick and bloodless victory over General Kornilov at the end of August and helped the Bolsheviks to overthrow the Provisional Government in October.

The Factions

Complex questions of war and peace, the nature of political power, land reform, food supply, and industrial relations were a source of intense infighting within the Socialist parties. It is possible to argue, in fact, that there was no united Social Democratic party but rather a number of autonomous groups. The Socialists could be divided into two main groups: the Defensists, proponents of war with external foes only and of peace within society, and the Internationalists, who demanded immediate peace with Germany and class struggle or even civil war "with the exploiting classes" in Russia. A. N. Potresov considered the bourgeoisie the natural ally of the Socialists in the revolution of 1917, and he defended this position in *Den'* (The Day), the newspaper that he edited. A slogan of this newspaper was "There Is No Salvation Other Than in Coalition." The so-called firm Defensists, grouped around Potresov, fought for unequivocal support of the Provisional Government and cooperation with the Kadets. The center-right Menshevik leaders, the so-called Revolutionary Defensists, such as Tsereteli, Chkheidze, M. I. Skobelev, and Lieber, also supported coalition with the Kadets, but their support was qualified. Dan, the editor of the CEC publication *Izvestiia*, shared their views until the end of August, when he began to criticize Kerensky sharply in his articles.

On the left wing of Menshevism were the Internationalists, led by Martov. They dominated the Petrograd city party committee, whereas the Revolutionary Defensists still held majority in the Central Committee. The Internationalists opposed coalition, and as of early September they favored an all-Socialist government accountable to a provisional representative institution like the Democratic Conference.

Outside of the official Social Democratic party were two political groupings that considered themselves Social Democrats. On the extreme right was G. V. Plekhanov's group *Edinstvo* (Unity), and on the extreme left were the so-called United Social Democrats–Internationalists, who were grouped around the newspaper *Novaia Zhizn'* (New Life), edited by N. N. Sukhanov and Maxim Gorky. Despite the appearance of variety among political groups, there actually were few political differences between Martov's Internationalists and United SD–Internationalists, or between Plekhanov's and Potresov's followers. Yet within the official SD party the rift between the left and the right was widening. As Plekhanov poignantly put it, the "Internationalist" Martov and the "Defensist Potresov" had nothing in common but a label—Menshevik.[21] The same kind of polarization was taking place in the party of Socialist Revolutionaries.

This rift clearly did not portend success for the Democratic Conference. In his opening remarks to the conference, entitled "Russia in Danger," Chkheidze said, "The Conference must show the way out of the current situation. The country desperately needs a revolutionary government, a government capable of pursuing a necessary policy without hesitation."[22] Intense struggle broke out between the Socialist factions over the question of coalition. The Menshevik caucus rejected the coalition, but the SRs and People's Socialists voted in favor. Tsereteli, Skobelev, and Avksent'ev tried to persuade their party colleagues to accept the coalition.

An informal bloc of opponents was formed out of the representatives of the Menshevik Internationalists, left-leaning SRs, and some Revolutionary Defensists. Their speaker, the left-leaning SR leader V. A. Karelin, argued that a new coalition cabinet would try to keep the balance between right and left on razor's edge and would have a policy devoid of meaningful content and lacking popular support. Therefore, the priority was to create an all-Socialist democratic government.[23] Martov spoke in a similar vein, calling the soviets the "embodiment of People's Power, institutions which exercised political authority in the country." Agreement with the Kadets was no longer possible. A truly revolutionary government had to be formed.[24] Fedor Dan's speech reflected the views of the Menshevik centrists. On the one hand, Dan rejected any implication that the soviets could be involved in government building. The Soviet leadership (the CEC) opposed any attempts by the extreme elements in the soviets to seize power. On the other hand, Dan proposed that the Democratic Conference form a representative assembly to which the new cabinet should be accountable and invite the Kadets to join that government.[25]

The crucial vote took place on 19 September. At first, the majority voted for the coalition with the Kadets. But then two amendments were tabled: one limiting the Kadets' participation in the cabinet and the other excluding it altogether. With the amendments the political meaning of the resolution was reversed. The second vote produced a majority against coalition. In the end it was decided that the Praesidium and the repre-

sentatives of the factions work out a compromise. The vote at the Praesidium was equally divided: sixty against the coalition and fifty for it. The
Democratic Conference, failing to reach a consensus on the composition of
the new government, was at a dead end. So yet another compromise decision was made: to keep on trying. The Democratic Conference formed the
Council of the Republic (the Preparliament), which was charged with iron-
ing out the differences between party factions and creating a cabinet. The
delegation of the Democratic Conference met from 22 to 24 September
with Prime Minister Kerensky and leading Kadet politicians. One of them,
S. N. Tret'yakov, summed up the political impasse very well: "The Democratic Conference says 'no' to the coalition, but Kerensky says the opposite: there can be no government without the coalition. The Democratic
Conference demands that the government be accountable to the Preparliament, but Kerensky says the opposite: the government is not accountable to the Preparliament and would shape the Preparliament itself as a
consultative institution. How is it possible to reconcile these diametrically
opposed views? I see no unification but only a gulf between the two.
Build a bridge over this gulf and then we could discuss unity."[26]

Clearly Kerensky was acting as an independent player, guarding his
cabinet against the encroachment of any institution to which it might have
to be accountable. The Kadets were siding with Kerensky because they felt
that the left-wing Socialists were trying to squeeze them out of government. While the Kadets and Kerensky stood firm, Tsereteli and other delegates of the Democratic Conference conceded point after point. They
were convinced that the coalition with the Kadets was indispensable.

After the Bolsheviks seized power, Martov reflected on the political
situation in a letter to Pavel Axelrod, the founder of the SD party. He was
convinced that had the Menshevik leaders displayed firmness, the SRs
and even Kerensky would have agreed to form an all-Socialist government that could have pursued immediate peace negotiations, land
reform, and speedy convocation of the Constituent Assembly.[27] There are
several reasons to believe that Martov's conviction was valid. In September the differences between the Socialist parties were easier to resolve
than they were a month later. At that time there was still a chance to
defuse the crisis by insisting on the right of the Preparliament to form a
government accountable to it, with the majority of the cabinet composed
of the Socialist ministers. Had the Provisional Government been led by
the leaders of the All-Russian Executive Committee of Soviets, the Bolsheviks could no longer have referred to the Provisional Government as
bourgeois and counterrevolutionary. It is no accident that Lenin rushed
his colleagues into a decision, fearing that he would lose the time needed
to undermine and overthrow the Provisional Government.

Kerensky scored a Pyrrhic victory over the Democratic Conference. He lost his chance to rely on a broader social base and to legitimate his government by accepting its accountability to the Preparliament. He believed that by insisting on the government's independence from any institution he was strengthening the government, but in fact he was weakening it. The failure of the Democratic Conference had disastrous consequences for the cohesion of the Menshevik and SR parties. The rift between factions widened, and by October the parties were on the verge of splitting. The Menshevik Internationalists formed a separate caucus in the Preparliament and began publishing their own newspaper, *Iskra* (The Spark). In Tula, Kharkov, Minsk, and other cities, the Menshevik Internationalists gained the majority. In Petrograd, the party split was so radical that the Internationalists put forward their own election slate for the forthcoming elections to the Constituent Assembly.

The Defensist Mensheviks, followers of Potresov, likewise drafted a separate election slate in early October. On the eve of the revolt the Defensists made one more step toward severing ties with the official Menshevik party. They opened their own headquarters and campaigned against the official party candidates and against the Internationalists.[28] The split among the Mensheviks weakened their positions not only in the soviets but also in the trade unions. They had a one-vote majority in the EC of the All-Russian Trade Union council. When the Trade Unions' delegation voted at the Democratic Conference against the coalition and for workers' control in industry, the Trade Unions' EC chairman V. Grinevich resigned and a coalition opponent, the Internationalist V. Chirkin, replaced him.[29] The deepening rift among the Mensheviks and SRs divided them into the proponents and opponents of the Provisional Government.

One political party, however, could not be both ruling party and opposition party. Some regional Menshevik leaders realized this, as is clear from the resolution adopted by the Menshevik conference in the Urals:

> The state structure created by the Revolutionary Democracy looks as if it is ready to collapse. . . . The government itself has become an arena for an irreconcilable internal struggle. Some provinces, even some cities are striving to separate or even to secede from the Russian republic, breaking it into pieces. Under these conditions of struggle of all against all, when cold and hunger are approaching in the midst of political and economic disintegration, general anarchy is on the way. The disintegration of economy and of the state itself, propelled by the war, nourishes polarization within the Democratic camp.[30]

The Army and the War

The disintegration that the Mensheviks so accurately described was most serious in the armed forces. Again the question arises over whether the Menshevik and SR leaders were prepared to stem that disintegration and the radicalization of soldiers and sailors. On 8 September, War Minister A. I. Verkhovsky reported on the conditions in the army to the CEC. He called the situation catastrophic and proposed declaring partial demobilization. The army had to be decreased at least by a third. The first priority was disbanding the garrisons in the rear; they were useless for the war effort and rebellious in internal affairs. The rights and duties of the army committees were to be clearly defined, so that normal relations could be established between them and the officer corps. The Allies would have to be informed that Russia could no longer continue the war and that peace negotiations were necessary. A number of steps were to be undertaken to ease the war burden on the population. On 4 September, Verkhovsky wrote in his diary:

> The more difficult the situation is, the clearer should be our policy. In the task of army organization one needs real authority. And the authority now is in the hands of democratic organizations. . . . My thoughts did not find approval in the government. Kerensky believes that my objectives are good but we had to rely on the authority of the Provisional Government, rather than on democratic organizations. I would have nothing against [that], except that now in September the authority of the Provisional Government, particularly among the soldiers, is negligible, and relying on it one cannot accomplish anything. . . . But here useless bias impedes contacts with the soviets.[31]

Verkhovsky's proposals were formally supported by the CEC, but in fact the war minister could not realize even a part of his plans. The right-of-center CEC leaders were apparently guarding the government against pressure from the leftists.

A partial demobilization of the army and a public announcement that agrarian reform had begun would have brought about temporary relief, possibly allowing the Provisional Government to survive until the convocation of the Constituent Assembly. If the moderate Socialists had accepted the break with the Kadets and formed an all-Socialist government, forcing Kerensky either to go along or to resign, they could have found ministers like Verkhovsky who would have been ready to work with the CEC of soviets. The right-leaning Mensheviks called the negative attitude concerning the coalition with the Kadets a case of "utopian tactics." "Utopian," as it turned out, was the policy of continued coalition.

The Preparliament

On 23 September the government crisis was formally resolved. The new coalition cabinet and the Council of the Republic (the Preparliament) were formed. Kadets took seats in both, a move that symbolized class peace in the country. *Izvestiia* expressed hope that the Preparliament would make it possible for Russia to overcome divisions between classes, parties, and factions, in the interest of avoiding civil war. These hopes were to be frustrated. The opening of the Preparliament coincided with a significant breakthrough by the Bolsheviks. On 25 September the Petrograd Soviet elected a new Praesidium with a Bolshevik majority. Trotsky became its chairman. On 23 September the CEC made a fateful decision to convene the Second Congress of Soviets on 20 October. What was even more ominous was that the Russian Committee of Soldiers, Sailors, and Workers' Soviets in Finland refused to comply with directives of the Provisional Government. This amounted to a bloodless revolt against the Provisional Government, which had no means by which to enforce compliance.

The revolt in Finland showed that the more the governmental authority was personified by Kerensky, the less actual authority he had. Tsereteli and his supporters made a great error in staking their reputation on Kerensky in late September. The political climate was changing quickly, and the prestige of the Provisional Government was falling. Under such conditions, concessions to Kerensky's demands undermined the local prestige of the CEC of soviets and deepened divisions among the Socialist factions. At the end of September, more political power could be found in the city and regional soviets than in the capital. Many of those soviets were still in Menshevik hands, and these regional leaders demanded the creation of a government accountable to the Preparliament.[32] The Menshevik leaders of the CEC—the makers of government coalitions—simply ignored the views of their regional party colleagues, misjudging the climate in the country.

The Preparliament suffered its first serious setback virtually at the outset. The Bolsheviks walked out, saying that they wanted to have nothing to do with the symbol of compromise and consensus. The center-right Mensheviks denounced the Bolshevik walkout as a declaration of war not only on the Kadets but also on all Socialists.[33] The Menshevik Internationalists criticized the Bolsheviks, but the main target of their attack was the coalition. Factional infighting simply moved from the Democratic Conference to the Preparliament. Its three major political groupings—the revolutionary leftists, the moderates, and the liberals—found no agreement on any important issue of the day. To make things worse, Kerensky's government ignored the Preparliament, depriving it of any significant political role. The Preparliament quickly became the target of derision and disdain on the part of various political groupings. *Novaia Zhizn'* described it as an "ephemeral and arbitrarily composed institution, a strange and ugly monstrosity borne by our young republic."[34]

The third coalition government tried to distance itself not only from the Preparliament but also from the leaders of the CEC and the soviets as such. According to Dan, in October all personal and unofficial contacts between the leaders of the Socialist parties and the government ceased. The government clearly sought to rise above the bickering. The moderate Socialists wrote in early October in their editorials that the compromise between the Revolutionary Democracy and Kadets was temporary, because the latter hardly would cooperate with the Socialists for long. This rhetoric clearly did not promote understanding between the nominal coalition partners. Nor was the Constituent Assembly election campaign of the right Mensheviks very wise. The right-leaning Mensheviks did not consider the soldiers' rural origin and the workers' impatience. Their appeals for an alliance with the "progressive bourgeoisie" could hardly have caused anything but irritation in the workers' milieu.

The Congress of Soviets

One of the most serious political mistakes the Mensheviks made concerned their policy regarding the Second Congress of Soviets. The Menshevik leaders feared its convocation and tried to delay it. The *Izvestiia* editorial "The Crisis of Soviets" on 13 October argued that the soviets were losing their democratic potential. By their very composition they represented only the workers, soldiers, and peasants. They began to act as centers of political authority, and were divisive and counterproductive. The Mensheviks preferred to support institutions of local self-government, the dumas and zemstvos, which were elected on the basis of universal franchise and represented the entire society. It is difficult to reproach the Mensheviks for this reasoning, for their goal was establishing a parliamentary republic in Russia. Moreover, the Mensheviks' and SRs' share of elected representatives in the dumas and zemstvos was substantial. Among the eighty-four city dumas elected in the fall of 1917, the SRs held 44 percent of the seats and the Mensheviks 8 percent. A united Menshevik-SR bloc held a solid majority in many city dumas, and the SRs' share in the zemstvos was even larger.[35] Nevertheless, the moderate Socialists' drift away from the soviets was counterproductive, allowing the Bolsheviks to seize political initiative and portray themselves as champions of direct People's Power represented in the soviets.

In the middle of October, regional Menshevik party conferences debated the election campaign to the Constituent Assembly and the convocation of the Second Congress of Soviets. Further polarization among the Mensheviks and the leftward shift of some key organizations is noticeable. The Tula Mensheviks' conference stated on 14 October, "The coalition government has proved to be unable to resolve the tasks posed by the revolution. The further development and the victory of the revolution can only be achieved if Revolutionary Democracy takes state power into its own hands." Lest it be misunderstood that the words *Revolutionary Democracy* referred to the power of soviets, the resolution explained, "The takeover of political power by the soviets exclusively would inevitably lead to the isolation of the proletariat, the break-up of the revolutionary front, and defeat of the revolution."

In other words, the Tula Mensheviks wanted an all-Socialist government, including the Bolsheviks, to be formed within the confines of the all-class state structure and without transfer of political power to the soviets. The Internationalists' caucus was even more radically inclined: "In order to avoid the break-up of the Democratic camp, we must support the Bolsheviks in the decisive hour and overthrow the present government."[36] The right-leaning Mensheviks argued that the Second Congress of Soviets should not debate the composition of government at all. This privilege was in the domain of the Constituent Assembly. The takeover of power by the soviets, they said, would lead to anarchy and civil war.

The Menshevik party leaders tried to convince others—and perhaps themselves as well—that most soviets were against convening the congress. When it became apparent that they were wrong, it was too late. The congress was going to take place, and the Bolsheviks were likely to have a majority. The Menshevik and SR leaders were unable to act decisively, perhaps because that would have led to a formal party split. Torn by factional infighting, the parties could not effectively oppose the Bolsheviks, as Potresov and Tsereteli urged, or support the all-Socialist government project, as Martov demanded. This paralysis played into the hands of the Bolsheviks, who could then attract workers and soldiers, as well as the prominent politicians who opposed Kerensky's administration. The crisis could have been overcome by the formal break-up of the party into two Social Democratic parties. In late September and early October, the calls for a formal split were heard in both camps. The Menshevik Internationalists in Petrograd argued at their meeting on 29 September that they could no longer remain in the same political party with Potresov. Yet they decided against secession because Martov had convinced his supporters that the Internationalists were winning over more and more adherents. Martov hoped to win the majority in the party and then the leadership of the organization.[37] He was successful in this endeavor at the December 1917 party congress, but his success came more than a month after the Bolsheviks had seized political power.

The search for an alternative to October overturn ended dramatically in the Preparliament on 24 October. Just as the Bolsheviks were sending detachments of Red Guards into action, making preparations for a coup d'état, Kerensky asked the Preparliament to support government efforts to suppress the Bolshevik attempt to "raise the mobs against the existing order." The Socialists were, as always, disunited and unable to act. In his response to Kerensky, Martov condemned government use of force against revolutionary crowds and denounced the rumored coup preparations of the Bolsheviks. He demanded that the government adopt a policy of radical reforms, transferring authority over land to the provincial land committees and beginning peace negotiations immediately. The Constituent Assembly should be convened as soon as possible, he said. Martov's draft resolution was voted on and won a slight majority. Dan recalled years later how he, Avksent'ev, and Gots delivered the Preparliament resolution to Kerensky in the Winter Palace on 24 October. According to Dan, the resolution amounted to a vote of no confidence in Kerensky government.[38]

In the meantime, the Bolshevik attempt to seize power antagonized the moderate Mensheviks and SRs who had just voted no-confidence in Kerensky. The Second Congress of Soviets opened on 25 October amid a new government crisis. The Menshevik party caucus at the Soviet Congress denounced the Bolshevik coup and walked out in protest. Martov's Internationalists, who remained, proposed that the congress call on all parties to help resolve the crisis peacefully. Supported by the Left SRs, the army delegates from the war front, and even some moderate Bolsheviks, Martov's resolution was accepted by the congress. An all-Socialist government was to be formed. Trotsky changed the direction of the congress, however, when he condemned the "bankrupt Socialists" who had left the congress, and he denounced any compromises with them. Martov's Internationalists then walked out in protest as well. The Bolsheviks now could form their own government in the name of the Second Congress of Soviets. Having concluded a temporary coalition with the Left SRs, the Bolsheviks began to move steadily toward establishing one-party dictatorship.

Notes

1. Ziva Galili, *Lidery Menshevikov v russkoi revoliutsii. Sotsial'nye realii i politicheskaia strategiia* (Moscow: Respublika, 1993), 7.

2. Ibid., 12

3. Iraklii Tsereteli, *Vospominaniia o Fevral'skoi revoliutsii*, 2 vols. (Paris: Mouton, 1963), 2: 408.

4. N. Avksent'ev, "Bol'shevistskii perevorot," *Istoriia SSSR*, no. 5 (1992): 152.

5. Fedor Dan, "Dva puti," *Novyi Mir*, no. 1 (Paris, 20 March 1940), 3–8.

6. Noi Zhordaniia, *My Life* (Stanford, Calif.: Hoover Institution Press, 1968), 77.

7. Viktor Chernov, *Pered burei. Vospominaniia* (New York: Chekhov, 1953), 338.

8. "Plenarnoe zasedanie TsIK s Ispolkomom krestianskikh deputatov," *Rabochaia Gazeta* (Petrograd), 3 September 1917.

9. "Plenarnoe zasedanie TsIK s Ispolkomom krestianskikh deputatov," *Rabochaia Gazeta* (Petrograd), 1 September 1917.

10. Ibid.

11. Aleksandr Kerensky, *Rossiia na istoricheskom povorote. Memuary* (Moscow: Respublika, 1993), 288.

12. V. Vladimirova, *Revoliutsiia 1917 goda. Khronika sobytii*, 4 vols. (Leningrad: Gosizdat, 1924), 4: 351, app. 37.

13. Kerensky, *Rossiia na istoricheskom povorote. Memuary*, 290.

14. N. N. Sukhanov, *Zapiski o revoliutsii* (Moscow: Respublika, 1992), 3: 158–159.

15. V. Vladimirova, *Revoliutsiia 1917 goda. Khronika sobytii* (Leningrad: Gosizdat, 1924), 4: 191–192.

16. Fedor Dan, *K istorii poslednikh dnei Vremennogo Pravitel'stva. Oktiabr'skaia revoliutsiia. Memuary* (Moscow: Orbita, 1991), 115.

17. Avksent'ev, "Bol'shevistskii perevorot," 144–145.

18. "TsKa RSDRP o Demokraticheskom s'ezde," *Izvestiia TsIK* (Petrograd), and *Rabochaia Gazeta* (Petrograd), 9 September 1917.

19. "Zasedanie TsIK Soveta Rabochikh i Soldatskikh Deputatov," *Izvestiia TsIK* (Petrograd), 13 September 1917, and *Rabochaia Gazeta*, (Petrograd), 14 September 1917.

20. B. I. Kolonitskii, "Antiburzhuaznaia propaganda i antiburzhuaznoe soznanie," *Otechestvennaia Istoriia*, no. 1 (Moscow, 1994), 24.

21. G. V. Plekhanov, *God na rodine* (Paris, 1922), 2: 68.

22. "Vserossiiskoe Demokraticheskoe Soveshchanie. Otchet o zasedanii. Pervyi Den'," in Gosudarstvennyi Arkhiv Rossiiskoi Federatsii, GARF, f. 1798, op. 1, d. 3, p. 3.

23. Ibid., "Otchet o zasedanii. Tretii den'," d. 5, p. 1.

24. V. Vladimirova, *Revoliutsiia 1917 goda. Khronika sobytii*, 4: 386, app. 66.

25. Ibid., 387–389, app. 67.

26. Ibid., 258.

27. Iulii Martov, *Pis'ma, 1916–1922* (New York: Chalidze, 1990), 14–15.

28. "Protokoly zasedanii PK i biuro men'shevikov oborontsev (2 September 1917–20 March 1918), in RTsKhIDNI, f. 275, TsKa RSDRP, op. 1, d. 150, p. 4, and d. 152, pp. 1–2.

29. Petr Garvi, *Profsoiuzy i kooperatsiia posle revoliutsii (1917–1921)* (New York: Chalidze, 1989), 23.

30. RTsKhIDNI, f. 275, TsKa RSDRP, op. 1, d. 87, p. 34.

31. A. I. Verkhovsky, *Rossiia na Golgofe (Iz pokhodnogo dnevnika, 1914–1918)* (Petrograd: Delo Naroda, 1918), 116–118.

32. "Korrespondentsii mestnykh men'shevistskikh organizatsii," RTsKhIDNI, f. 275, TsKa RSDRP, op. 1, d. 87, p. 6, 17, 19.

33. "Sotsial Demokratiia v Sovete Respubliki," *Rabochaia Gazeta* (Petrograd), 10 October 1917.

34. "Predparlament," *Novaia Zhizn'* (Petrograd), 30 September 1917.

35. "Partiia Sotsialistov Revoliutsionerov na vyborakh v gorodskie Dumy," *Partiinye Izvestiia* (Petrograd), no. 3, TsKa PSR, 19 October 1917, col. 8.

36. Editorial, *Golos Truda* (Tula), 18 October 1917, 3.

37. "K raskolu v RSDRP," *Novaia Zhizn'* (Petrograd), 30 September 1917.

38. Dan, *K istorii poslednikh dnei Vremennogo Pravitel'stva*.

MICHAEL MELANCON

The Left Socialist Revolutionaries and the Bolshevik Uprising

3

B y the fall of 1917 there existed two distinct Left Socialist plans of action concerning the Provisional Government. The government's supporters of course hoped that the government would remain in power until the Constituent Assembly convened. In this chapter I focus on the groups—Bolsheviks of various tendencies, Left Mensheviks, and Left Socialist Revolutionaries—who wished to supplant the existing moderate socialist-liberal government with a purely Socialist one; more pointedly, I examine the disagreements among these groups about the timing and auspices of the government's proposed quietus. Historians have largely overlooked the role of the leftist coalition and the debates within it in favor of describing internal Bolshevik arguments and sharply delineating a Bolshevik versus SR-Menshevik dichotomy, a misleading if hallowed set of priorities.

Most scholars have portrayed the Left SRs as gradually splitting off (under Bolshevik tutelage) from the PSR during the summer and fall of 1917. Oliver Radkey, however, notes that most SR activists were more radical than the party's leadership, a situation that gave birth to the leftist movement early in the year.[1] Even before World War I the issue of illegal activities had divided the party. Senior party leaders, such as E. Breshko-Breshkovskaia, A. Argunov, N. Avksent'ev, and M. Vishniak, suggested replacing underground operations with legal activities within the semiconstitutional tsarist state; other prominent figures, including V. Chernov, M. Natanson, N. Rakitnikov, and most activists rejected this heresy, with the result that the moderates, rich in leaders but poor in following, largely abstained from party organizational work.[2]

At war's outbreak, the moderates, who found at least some merit in the existing state, supported its military efforts ("defensism"), whereas the redoubtable Chernov, Rakitnikov, and Natanson, plus B. Kamkov, led the PSR in opposing the war ("internationalism"). Chernov and Natanson even espoused the Russian government's defeat ("defeatism"), because a victorious tsarism would be a resurgent one.[3] The SRs' antiwar stance reflected the party's doctrine of Russia's uniqueness: peasant revolutionism coupled with a weak bourgeoisie forecast Socialism rather than liberal capitalism. The SRs had first expounded the theory of (and coined the unfelicitous term) *permanent revolution*, boycotted three out of four state dumas, and, pari passu, maintained their radical course. By 1917 both leftists and moderates had orientations of earlier provenance, while the PSR as a whole was inclined leftward.

The February revolution wrought sharp permutations in the party, with fateful results for the SRs and for Russia. If leftism—identified as staunch opposition to the war, to the tsarist regime, and to capitalism—characterized most SR activists and organizations before February 1917, a shift to the center commenced immediately afterward. The Revolutionary Defensism that swept the Socialist parties during the early euphoric days played a role. Rejecting the tsarist government's war was easier than opposing the (same) one that now beset revolutionary Russia: Socialists had something worth defending. Furthermore, the Right SRs (illustrious personages with ample prior party service), at the forefront of endless intellectual cadres, helped organize and lead the new legal party structures, whose policies were therefore not based on the stern stances of the pre-February underground groups.[4]

Chernov's new, unwonted moderation was also a factor. Across the country, leaders and activists of untempered socioeconomic radicalism looked to Chernov for signals on how to proceed. On his return to Russia, however, Chernov aligned himself with the new rightist majority in the Central Committee and entered the Provisional Government, thus associating himself and the party with the fate of the government and its future head, A. Kerensky. Chernov never explained this deviation from his accustomed path; but by late summer he reemphasized leftist positions on war and land. After the October Revolution he led the PSR to adopt a range of resolutions reminiscent of those adopted earlier by the Left SRs.[5] In any case, the post-February PSR had a right-leaning central and (often) local leadership grafted on to a left-leaning rank and file, which stamped it with an unclear physiognomy that pertained not so much to the program as to the lack of agreement about how vigorously to pursue it. The rightist leadership then concluded an alliance with liberals that brought the PSR to the pinnacle of power even as it threatened to alienate much of its peasant, worker, and soldier following.

These circumstances tempered the leftists' joy at the overthrow of tsarism. They were implicated in an exquisitely unhappy marriage of convenience with the reigning rightists, and from February on they acted with waxing independence of the SR Central Committee. A mere two days after tsarism fell the first crisis occurred: P. Aleksandrovich, with the aid of worker SRs and the cooperation of the *Mezhraionka* (non-Bolshevik leftist Social Democrats), attempted to induce the Petrograd Soviet to seize power. However, Kerensky and others argued passionately in the Soviet and at SR gatherings that caution must prevail in order to prevent counterrevolution and to consolidate revolutionary gains: Revolutionary Defensism on the battlefield and at home became the watchword. Even so, the Petrograd SR organization, the largest in the country, soon adopted left-centrist positions and, during April, almost approved leftist resolutions; during late summer the leftists assumed full control.[6]

Early clashes within other large party organizations led to outright leftist predominance only in Kronstadt, Kharkov, and Kazan. The moderate or centrist leadership of most organizations did not, however, prevent a steady leftward drift; when the Third SR Congress met in May 1917, roughly 40 percent of the delegates voted for some leftist planks. The majority, led by Chernov and others to the right of him, elected a new Central Committee, with Natanson as the single leftist, thus ignoring the left's burgeoning nationwide presence. Although they failed to mold the determinations of the congress, left wingers created an "organizational bureau" with the goal of coordinating policies and activities; this outraged the moderates but allowed the left to begin an orderly growth.[7]

From the outset, Left SR leaders distanced themselves from their own Central Committee by openly allying with other leftists, most notably the Bolsheviks (but also the Menshevik Internationalists, the Mezhraiontsy, and the Anarchists). At the All-Russian Conference of Soviets of late March 1917, the "minority" SR faction with Kamkov at its head joined with the Bolsheviks to sponsor an antiwar resolution officially registered as "Bolshevik–Left SR." Kamkov told the delegates that "because of the new government's class composition, it can't be with the revolution." In view of its dilatoriness on the eight-hour day, he asked the delegates, "Do you imagine that the Provisional Government will solve the land question in the manner that the revolution will demand?" Only the "new revolutionary organ" (that is, the Soviet) could resolve the problems of the day, he concluded. On 2 May, the Left SRs in the Petrograd Soviet voted with the Bolsheviks and Menshevik Internationalists against allowing the Socialists into the Provisional Government; the very next day they told a citywide meeting of still-wary SR members that "only possible solution of the [current] crisis . . . is the creation of revolutionary power in the name of the soviet."[8] At the First Congress of Soviets in June, a coalition of Left SRs, Mezhraiontsy, and Bolsheviks condemned the planned offensive at the front, and N. Mazurin, an arch-leftist from Krasnoiarsk, orated for the Left SRs against war and government.[9]

When the failed offensive spurred the famous July crisis, the Left SRs, centered in the PSR's Northern Regional Committee, gave the green light to the descent of Kronstadt sailors on the capital and aligned themselves with the mass movement in the streets. On 4 July Kamkov told the All-Russian Central Executive Committee that it was impossible to ignore the demands of the Petrograd proletariat and armed forces: "I suggest trans-ferring power to the soviets." Furthermore, on 12 July the Left SR orga-nizational bureau issued a statement absolving itself of responsibility for the Central Committee's policies and "reserving for itself full freedom of expression."[10] Thus with escutcheons emblazoned with the post-February mottos of Soviet power, of an end to the war, and of timely redress of peasant and worker injustices, the Left SRs had undertaken open battle against the SR Central Committee. Reality intervened in the form of the Central Committee's expulsion orders, which drew hasty letters of apol-ogy from Left SR leaders. This unheroic denouement reflected the Left SRs' too-sanguine estimate that they were poised to take over the party from within (they later regretted not splitting).

Regardless, the gauntlet was thrown, the battle engaged. The Left SRs accused the "ruling circles in the party" of deliberately alienating the "most conscious elements of the laboring masses," which hindered party work among soldiers, workers, and peasants and threatened to "throw the center of party support to layers of the population which, because of their class composition, cannot advocate real policies of revolutionary socialism." In their view, the leadership was abandoning the revolution-ary cause in favor of policies suitable for the middle levels of society. As the Penza SRs later queried Kerensky, "Are there no limits to your . . . retreat from revolutionary positions? Who is dearer to you: the laboring people or the bourgeoisie? Are you with us or against us?"[11]

The result was that the Provisional Government's repression after the July Days disorders was aimed at the Left SRs and other leftists as much as at the Bolsheviks. By mid-July the government was blocking the sup-ply of paper to the Petrograd Left SR newspaper *Zemlia i Volia*, whose editorial board was soon cleansed of leftists by the Central Committee. This flagship of the leftist SR movement had become a thorn in the side of the moderates through its regular reports on the increasing manifestations of leftism in the party and its open suggestion that "Soviet power" was the solution to the country's crisis.[12] The authorities also shut down the Left SR newspapers *Narodnaia niva* and *Sotsialist-revoliutsioner* in the Baltic Fleet area and other Left SR–oriented garrison papers throughout the country. The radical SR agitators P. Proshian, A. Ustinov, and P. Shishko in the Baltic Fleet, F. Khaustov at the northern front, Gol'man (chair of the Mogilev Province Peasant Soviet) at the Western front, and many others in the south suffered arrest; in Petrograd numerous Left SRs and Menshevik Internationalists were also jailed. The demotion of V. Algasov, V. Chaikin, and Kamkov from the Bureau of the All-Russian Executive Committee of the Soviets capped the campaign.[13]

In moderate Socialist circles close to the Provisional Government and the All-Russian Executive Committee, the embarrassing topic of leftism within their own (SR and Menshevik) parties received little open attention. True, the extreme Right SRs referred coyly to the leftists in the party as "our party Bolsheviks" or "our Bolsheviks."[14] However, it was easier for SR and Menshevik leaders to level contumely against the Bolsheviks as the villains of mass Russia's radicalization (or, as they put it, anarchy) than against their own parties' fractious ranks. That many non-Bolsheviks were suffering arrest was hardly unknown to informed observers, but top-level government, Soviet, and Menshevik-SR circles forebore public reference to it.[15] The restriction of animadversions to the Bolsheviks (now connoting "promoters of anarchy") had unexpected results. Although the Left SR movement also suffered material damage, the obloquy that fell entirely on the Bolsheviks turned to the latter's advantage. Bolsheviks first became identified as the group that had suffered (unfairly, many thought), and then, in a stunning dialectical turn, reemerged into mass consciousness as the party of the people's tribunes and whose title now signified "staunch revolutionaries."[16] Largely excluded from public discourse and further burdened by the twin albatrosses of Kerensky and their own Central Committee, the Left SRs, as continuing members of the PSR, watched as their considerable activities were credited to another party. For example, the agitators—misleadingly known, even today, as "Kronstadt Bolsheviks"—who stirred up such a firestorm during mid-1917 all had graduated from the naval base's LSR school of agitation.[17]

Despite these problems, the Left SR movement was on the ascent, though at a slower rate than the Bolsheviks, whose exemplary activism received a big boost from other leftist groups. By mid-spring the PSR's Northern Regional Committee, under the guidance of Kamkov, Natanson, and P. Proshian, had become a leftist citadel that, among other things, issued *Zemlia i Volia;* the Kharkov and Kazan organizations functioned as outposts to the south and east. By early summer many garrison and army committees in the interior had fallen under the control of leftist Socialists, mostly Left SRs, who edited newspapers carrying their anti-war and anti–Provisional Government calls. At the fronts, a block of Left SRs, Bolsheviks, and Left Mensheviks propagated the same message. Furthermore, by late spring the SRs in some peasant Soviet executive committees (Mogilev, Penza, and Kazan) had begun ignoring the Provisional Government and the SR Central Committee in transferring land to the peasants and otherwise quietly manifesting "Soviet power."[18]

The radical ideas expressed by worker, soldier, and peasant SRs were further reflections of this process. For example, at the late March Soviet conference, the worker-SR Mikhailov attempted to strengthen the resolution against the war, and Kotliarov, an SR from the front, warned that "if [the Provisional Government] takes one step off the [correct] path, we will . . . recognize the soviet as the government"; another SR *frontovshchik* (front soldier) rejected a coalition with the bourgeoisie and insisted that only a congress of Soviets could solve the problems facing the country. At the June Soviet congress an SR sailor dismissed the importance of the Provisional Government since in the localities the soviets "already have power"; he advocated a revolutionary peasant, worker, and soldiers' government "that will actively legislate."[19] In a similar vein, an SR in the Ekaterinoslav Soviet defended Bolshevik criticisms as "healthy": "their cause will prosper as long as the [existing] conditions continue." During the fall, in a letter to *Znamia truda*, a non-leftist Petrograd worker insisted that "worker-SRs in no way agree with the Central Committee's policies about power. . . . The coalition with the wealthy must come to an end."[20]

On this basis the Left SRs concluded that the Central Committee did not accurately represent the party's active cadres and mass following, a problem also reflected in a certain number of SR-to-Bolshevik crossovers, loudly touted by the Bolshevik press.[21] As Radkey long ago noted, the Central Committee blithely ignored the opinions of the rank and file, a phenomenon that enhanced the status of Left SRs in local organizations.[22] The early leftist organizations (Kronstadt, Kharkov, and Kazan) were joined during the spring by those in Tomsk, Odessa, Ufa, Helsinki, and Ekaterinburg, and, by midsummer, Kherson, Kaluga, and Pskov. The entirely worker-oriented SR organizations of some industrial towns (Taganrog, Lugansk, and Nikolaev) also developed along leftist lines, as did the Siberian organizations of Kansk, Atkarsk, and Novo-Nikolaevsk. In addition, an array of organizations (Penza, Kursk, Mogilev, Riga, and Omsk) issued leftist resolutions on war, power, and land, as did the Western Siberian SR conference and the SR faction at the Urals Soviet congress.

By early fall, huge organizations in Petrograd, Voronezh, Finland, and Tashkent had gone to the left, which eventually drew the Central Committee's draconian (and utterly ineffective) measure of "dissolving" them. Important SR organizations in Tambov, Saratov, and Revel (Tallin) suddenly voted leftist planks, as did smaller ones in Fort Ino, Buguruslan, and Vyborg; so did three-quarters of the SR-dominated executive committees of provincial peasant soviets, formerly moderate bastions. In addition, many organizations—Astrakhan, Ivanovo, Krasnoiarsk, Baku, Tula, and Tver—split, with worker, peasant, and soldier cadres usually going to the leftists, whereas the voluminous intelligentsia stayed with the PSR. In Samara, where the rightist Brushvit held tight rein over the huge SR organization, the SR Maximalists (allies of the Left SRs) grew from a splinter group to a major party.[23]

Their large delegations at various assemblies suggest the growth of Left SR influence. On 23 August, the congress of the All-Russian Railroad Union elected its executive committee (the famous Vikzhel), giving the Left SRs the largest contingent and the chairmanship of the union.[24] At provincial, frontal, regional, and national congresses held between August and November 1917, resolutions often could not pass without Left SR support. For example, at the North Caucasus Soviet congress, the Left SRs and the Bolsheviks had ten delegates each for just over 50 percent of the total (Mensheviks and SRs had the balance); at the Volga Soviet congress, the Bolsheviks had twenty, the Left SRs eight, for slightly over 50 percent of the deputies; and at the Siberian Soviet congress, the Bolsheviks had sixty-four, the Left SRs thirty-five (the Right SRs had the largest single delegation), giving the Bolshevik-LSR block just over 50 percent. The front congresses before and after October had a similar make-up, in which only the split of the SRs into right and left allowed the passage of left block resolutions. At several important gatherings the Left SRs exceeded other groups, as at the railroad congress, the Black Sea Fleet congress, the Turkestan regional soviet congress, and the all-Russian peasant congress.[25] The Left SRs had become an independent force even prior to their late November formation of a separate party.

Given their waxing influence, what were the SRs saying? On the pages of their publications—*Zemlia i volia*, their new Petrograd workers' paper *Znamia truda*, and their journal *Nash put'*—the Left SRs insisted that they alone maintained the party's ideology unblemished.[26] With a touch of irony, M. Kogan-Bernshtein wrote that they set themselves the "modest task" of struggling against the "reformist mood" and "preserving the revolutionary-Socialist and consistently internationalist character of the entire party." They insisted that the party's ruling circles were "turning off from the path laid down by the SR program and traditions" and "had completely abandoned . . . revolutionary socialism."[27]

The leftists insisted that for SRs (as populists), the Russian revolution was Socialist in character, as confirmed by the year's events. A necessary corollary was that the SRs had nothing in common with capitalism or the bourgeoisie. According to Spiridonova, in light of the SRs' task of creating Socialism and fighting for it as "the highest moral value," the greatest enemy was the bourgeoisie. She also emphasized the SR program's land socialization plank, whose function was to spark societal changes in a Socialist direction. Thus the leftists demanded the immediate organized transfer of land to the land committees and, in short order, to the peasantry. Kamkov and others insisted that the revolution in Russia had not changed the nature of the war: it was still imperialist and must be ended. Some Left SRs demanded real rather than pallid half-measures toward peace, whereas others, such as V. Mstislavskii, advocated an immediate armistice and a separate peace. Thus the June offensive and the reimposition of the death penalty at the front especially outraged all Left and many regular SRs.[28]

The Left SRs affirmed the workers' right to unionize, to a fair wage, and to an eight-hour day, even during wartime. They also noted that the concept of workers' control was part of the SR minimum program, in light of which they played a considerable (as yet undocumented) role in the Factory Committee movement. The committees, they thought, should exercise control in keeping plants operating, but with a strong element of organization under the auspices of a national coordinating body.[29]

Internationalism constituted a final noteworthy aspect of Left SR thought (the term "Internationalists" became part of their party title). V. Ivanov-Razumnik asserted that the ultimate victory for Socialism in Russia depended on the "victory of democracy not in Russia alone, but in other European countries." N. Trutovskii noted the positive role of Russia, the former "gendarme of Europe," in international Socialism and even found merit in "backwardness" in that Socialism in agrarian countries such as Russia (and possibly India and China) would remove them from the list of exploited nations and thus hasten the collapse of imperialism.[30]

This complex of ideas led the Left SRs to the conviction that a Socialist government based upon the soviets, the natural offspring of revolutionary society, was the best matrix for accomplishing the desired programs. They did not fetishize the soviets, nor did they use the slogan "all power to the soviets" in their published propaganda. At public meetings and in the pages of their newspapers and journals, however, they argued the case for Soviet power in terms of revolutionary society's aspirations and the crises the nation was experiencing. Since the Provisional Government based on the liberal coalition carried out inadequate reforms and continued its war policy, an authoritative Socialist government should replace it, they maintained. After the July Days, they described the All-Russian Executive Committee of the Soviets as the appropriate (and de facto) locus of power; Kamkov, A. Kalegaev, and others decried the lack of a people's government.[31] During August and September the Left SRs hammered at the inability of the existing government to handle various crises: only a Socialist government based on the soviets would have the authority to end the growing economic collapse, fight the counterrevolution, and achieve other revolutionary goals, including the Constituent Assembly. The Left SRs popularized the famous term *odnorodnaia sotsialisticheskaia vlast'* (roughly "all-Socialist government").

The issue that perhaps best captures the Left SR character was the group's refusal to oppose the aspirations of democracy (workers, peasants, and soldiers), which has prompted commentary about an alleged cultism of the masses. Indeed, Spiridonova and others could sometimes wax grandiloquent, as when just before October she wrote, "Our revolution, our revolution . . . Its tone was high and clean, its songs . . . inscribed in silver letters. The abolition of the death penalty, the call for peace to all laborers, the creativity of the revolutionary *narod* ever grew and ascended." Such rhetorical flights should not obscure the seriousness of most Left SR analyses. For example, a regular theme in *Zemlia i volia* editorials and articles during May and June was the failure of the moderate Socialists to comprehend mass society's revolutionary mood. Would the leaders of the PSR and the Soviet executive committee hear soldier and worker voices in time, they wondered?

Again, just after the July Days, Kamkov adjured the All-Russian Executive Committee not to "ignore the demands of the soldiers and workers." When members of the executive committee saw the sea of banners calling for "power to the soviets" they were bound by revolutionary discipline to take heed: theirs was not to impede the revolution. Thus, democratic aspirations for the Left SRs constituted a prime value. Each failure to carry out revolutionary programs and each abuse of revolutionary power only swelled the numbers of Bolshevik followers, cautioned *Znamia truda*. Spiridonova noted with consternation that the Seventh SR Council of August, with only a slight majority of moderates over the leftists, could formulate no better program than further support for the Provisional Government, coalition with the bourgeoisie, and the death penalty. Mstislavskii intoned about the widening chasm between government and people.[32]

The Left SRs proposed the painfully obvious solution of counterposing the power of democracy (democratic social elements) with the power of the bourgeoisie. Mstislavskii reminded his moderate comrades that where the revolution ended for the bourgeoisie it began for Socialists; the bourgeoisie was not the future enemy, but the current one. The liberal and moderate Socialist slogans about "saving the Motherland to save the revolution" actually meant saving the bourgeois state and destroying the revolution. Socialists must therefore unify around democratic organs, namely, the soviets. If the soviets experienced tiredness and absenteeism, active programs must revive the democratic cause. The Kornilov affair's obvious reenergizing of the soviets ensured the success of democracy.

The axis on which Left SR advocacy of Socialist (Soviet) power

turned during the fall was that the Kornilov episode had shown the counterrevolution's helplessness—a helplessness that would endure as long as
democracy remained united, as it had been when the revolution was
under direct threat. "Democracy was strong" whereas the "counterrevolution [or the bourgeoisie] was weak," they reiterated, but with the
caveat—only when democracy is united. The true "living forces" were not
the capitalist classes, as maintained by the moderates, but democracy.
Because the democratic elements and Socialist parties were united in the
soviets, labor unions, and factory committees throughout the country,
these democratic organizations showed the correct path. The crisis of
power would end with the casting aside of the coalition with the liberals
and the creation of all-Socialist power based on the soviets. Finally, the
Left SRs' constant refrain was that only a government of all the Socialist
parties would have the authority to unite democracy, end the economic
crisis, and, above all, prevent civil war.[33]

The Left SRs dismissed accusations that they were riding on Bolshevik coattails: How could the SRs be accused of Bolshevism for advocating
the transfer of land to the land committees, when immediate transfer of
land to the peasantry had always been the party's programmatic center-
piece? One Left SR quoted N. Bykhovskii's comment earlier in the year
that if the SRs fell through on the land question, they fell through completely: yet the SRs had done little, even with Chernov as minister of agriculture. The Left SRs often framed their pleas to the Central Committee
in terms of heading off the Bolshevik surge. A regular theme of Left SR
commentary during September and October regarded the "rumors" of a
Bolshevik putsch. Although they felt that the rumors came from sources
hostile to the revolution, they used them as pretexts for a series of warnings to the Bolsheviks that any demonstrations in the streets would split
democracy, stimulate counterrevolution, and, in any case, be superfluous
since the upcoming congress of soviets would assume the task of overthrowing the Provisional Government. In the Petrograd Soviet they
accused the Bolsheviks of "Hottentot tactics," sparking a heated exchange
with Trotsky. Thus, as Algasov and Kamkov pointed out at the party's first
congress, in many concrete activities the Left SRs acted in concert with
the Bolsheviks but with their own agenda, which excluded measures not
issuing from democratic organizations.[34]

From their perspective, the Left SRs offered a solution both to the
threat of counterrevolution and to the precipitous leaching of support to
the Bolsheviks. Given the depth of the crisis, they argued, one had to
choose between the laboring masses and the bourgeoisie, between Socialism and counterrevolution; no middle ground existed on which to maintain
broad popular support, and, in any case, SR theory and programs provided

no such safe haven. "Workers and soldiers began the revolution in the first place, without help from the bourgeoisie, and . . . [their organizations] will be the center of the government now."[35] Whatever one makes of the Left SR attitude toward the democratic elements, one can hardly doubt that had the SR leaders even partially heeded the leftists (likewise for the Mensheviks) the groundswell of support for the Bolsheviks would have ebbed sooner or never taken place at all, perhaps changing history. The irony herein is that, immediately after October, both the Mensheviks and SRs adopted positions not dissimilar to those they had so recently and vehemently rejected.

During the early fall, the Left SRs participated with propaganda goals in the Democratic Conference and the Council of the Republic (or Preparliament), both of which they held to be undemocratically constituted. Spiridonova told the Democratic Conference that "not even the hottest supporter of the bourgeois coalition has told us . . . what [it] has brought for rank and file workers, soldiers and peasants." I. Shteinberg lectured the Preparliament that only Socialist power could bring peace and create an army capable of fighting for peoples' liberty; and the Left SR officer Iu. Sablin painted a sad picture of an undisciplined, disenchanted army: only a revolutionary army would protect Russia.[36]

An all-Socialist government was a Left SR *idée fixe*. After the failure of various tactics to lure the moderates into agreeing to end the liberal coalition, the Left SRs focused on a congress of soviets that they first urged and then supported when the All-Russian Executive Committee issued a call for it.[37] They also began applying pressure for a new party congress and a congress of peasant soviets, all of which the Left SRs believed would now adopt leftist positions. During early September the workers of the giant Izhorsk plant passed a resolution based upon Spiridonova's speech to them. They sought an immediate armistice, the transfer of land, an end to the death penalty, an eight-hour day, and the immediate gathering of the congress of soviets. Toward the end of the month the Petrograd Provincial SR Conference passed a similar resolution, plus planks espousing the confiscation of excess wealth and workers' control exercised through the Factory Committees.[38]

Meanwhile, the right-leaning Socialists wished to avoid congresses at all costs. For example, after first summoning the Soviet congress, the All-Russian Executive Committee tried to cancel it because of alleged lack of interest, a claim contradicted by the numerous resolutions from all over the country that had prompted its call in the first place. After finally approving the Soviet congress for 25 October, the All-Russian Executive Committee later denied its legitimacy. Similarly, the Right SRs maneuvered to induce peasant soviet delegates to vote against a congress by offering a resolution that forced delegates to choose between a congress and a Constituent Assembly. A majority thus rejected the congress, even though a larger majority had just voted for a Socialist government.[39]

In this tense atmosphere, the Left SRs assigned themselves the task of supporting the development of the revolution and restraining the Bolsheviks. Thus they entered the Petrograd Soviet's Military-Revolutionary Committee (MRC) when it formed in October. The newly elected head of the Petrograd Soviet's soldiers' section, a Left SR named P. Lazimir, who had played a major role in the organization of Petrograd's defenses during the Kornilov affair, headed the MRC. At this time MRCs were forming in many soviets throughout the country in order to coordinate defenses against counterrevolution. In most places they included Bolsheviks, SRs, and Mensheviks. (The Petrograd MRC was unlikely to have been conceived as a hidden staff for a Bolshevik coup, since the Bolshevik Central Committee had still not agreed on a plan of action, and a majority usually opposed any separate steps at all.) Kamkov later explained that when the Left SRs became aware of Bolshevik plans to use the MRC for a unilateral move against the government, they withdrew from it. After the October Revolution they reentered, only to withdraw again when it began to take measures against the freedom of the press; finally, in mid-November, they rejoined the MRC for the duration of its existence. The Left SRs' tactic involved pressuring the Bolsheviks, who clearly wanted their presence, by withholding it at crucial moments. Overall, the records of the Petrograd MRC show that considerable numbers of Left SRs served there, as did a great number of nonparty activists.[40]

Algasov, an MRC activist, judged the withdrawal tactic a failure, because in their absence the Left SRs were unable to exercise any restraint on the Bolsheviks. When they were present they had often tempered improper activities. The Left SRs faced a dilemma: how to remain faithful to the revolution, which associated them with the Bolsheviks, and maintain a level of integrity as regards their opposition to unilateral actions and violations of basic rights. As the Left SR labor activist V. M. Levin had said in August about the Red Guards and the workers' militias, the Left SRs could either join them or allow them to be dominated by the Bolsheviks.[41] Although the Left SRs warned their followers not to take part in any activities against the Provisional Government prior to the congress of soviets, many Left SRs in fact joined in the overthrow when the Bolsheviks launched it. As a group of Left SR sailors told Mstislavskii when he reminded them that they had just voted against participation, "a resolution is one thing, the revolution is another."[42] On their own, the Left SRs would have waited for the Second Congress's autonomous decision to end the Provisional Government; however, if a revolutionary act were otherwise launched against the unpopular existing government, whose days were numbered, many Left SRs felt obliged to participate.

The soviet congress that opened on 25 October 1917 hardly fulfilled the vast expectations that the Left SRs and many others had had for it. The Left SRs had warned that the congress would not be entirely representative, since some soviets and front organizations of moderate orientation were boycotting it in line with their theory that the soviets had "outlived themselves." They felt that this tactic threatened not so much to deprive the congress of authority as to "artificially exaggerate the left wing over the center." Still, the Left SRs hoped that the congress would be "creative," for its failure would be a fatal blow to the revolution. They warned the gathering delegates against the "destructive tactics enunciated by Lenin" and hoped that, despite possibly faulty representation (actually the congress was quite well attended), it would carry out the revolutionary task of replacing the government, since the Soviet gatherings of March and June had also had less-than-perfect representation.[43]

By the next day, things had turned out as the Left SRs feared: the Bolsheviks had launched their attack (with some Left SR involvement) and thereby presented the congress with an unsavory choice of approving an objectionable activity or ratifying the Provisional Government, which in reality most delegates wished to abolish. As Lenin and Trotsky had foreseen, the Second Congress accepted the fait accompli, though many Boshelviks and other Socialists had reservations about the methods. The Left SRs remained at the congress after the PSR and the Mensheviks had abandoned it in protest (many SRs joined the leftist faction, whose positions many of them shared, doubling its size). Kalegaev, Kamkov, and V. Karelin expressed support for the congress's land and peace programs. As Karelin said about Lenin's declaration on peace, "We will vote for it [because] it is close to our ideas"; and Kalegaev greeted "Lenin's draft [on the land] as a celebration of our program." On the question of power, however, the Left SRs drew the line. They demanded a government that would "unify all democracy around it" (Karelin) and create a "unified revolutionary front" (Kamkov). In the first harbinger of the post-October Vikzhel negotiations, Karelin, as Left SR spokesperson, threatened to oppose Soviet power and boycott the government "until the two sides of democracy had met one another face to face" and Kamkov importuned the Bolsheviks not to "isolate the moderate portion of democracy. . . . Find an agreement with them!"

Later, in a key speech Karelin offered an olive branch to the Bolsheviks by noting that it was not their fault that the moderates had walked out but, still, he repeated, "life demands all-Socialist democratic power." Karelin then explained Left SR motivations for not walking out themselves (despite the Bolsheviks' "crude steps"). "We did not want to isolate the Bolsheviks since their . . . . downfall will be the downfall of the revolution." He then outlined the Left SR program: "Our group wants a ministry of provisional commissars, subject to the central organ of the congress of soviets [the new All-Russian Executive Committee]. . . . We protest the exclusion of representatives from the peasant soviets in the government list [offered by the Bolsheviks]. . . . We will not enter [the government] since this would create a gap between ourselves and those who left the congress. . . . A reconciliation of the Bolsheviks and those who left is the principal task of the Left SRs." Karelin finished by protesting steps that the Bolsheviks had already taken against the freedom of speech of other parties.

Left Mensheviks and some Bolsheviks also spoke in this vein, thus commencing, at the inception of Soviet power, a struggle over the nature of Soviet power.[44] The Left SRs acted consistently with a line they had developed step by step since February: Socialist Soviet power that would immediately carry out revolutionary programs and that would include all of democracy (all the Socialists unifying all workers, soldiers, and peasants) because only such a government would have the authority to prevent or lessen the impact of civil war. The struggle, however, had just begun.

The main outlines of the post-October struggle for an "all-Socialist" government, rather than a Bolshevik-oriented one, are as follows. Just prior to 25 October, Kamenev and Zinoviev, who opposed separate Bolshevik action as likely to precipitate a civil war, published a warning about their Central Committee's plans. Thus the Left SRs had highly placed allies among the Bolsheviks in favor of the "all-Socialist" variant (the Left SRs claimed that they played a key role in splitting the Bolsheviks). Regardless, they made good their vow to refuse a Bolshevik offer to enter the Council of Commissars (Sovnarkom) with agriculture and other portfolios. Instead, with the agreement of the Martov wing of the Mensheviks and, quietly, the Kamenev-Zinoviev Bolsheviks, they set about persuading—or, in lieu of that, forcing—the Bolsheviks to carry on negotiations with the SR-Menshevik bloc. They were uniquely situated to do this because of their position in the railroad union committee (Vikzhel), where Left SRs A. Malitskii (chair), I. Krushinskii, and N. Stamo wielded great influence. As B. Malkin told the Left SR Congress in November, "we sabotaged the Bolsheviks by pulling out of the MRC and refusing to enter the government. . . . We isolated . . . Smol'nyi's [the Bolsheviks'] tactics" and, in effect, forced the Vikzhel negotiations.[45]

The story unfolded in dramatic fashion. On 26 October, the Moscow-based Vikzhel, after voting overwhelmingly to take measures to create an "all-Socialist government," embarked en masse for Petrograd.[46] On arrival, Vikzhel delegates contacted the congress of soviets, the Ministry of Transport, and moderate Bolsheviks, including Riazanov, Rykov, and Nogin, after which they blockaded troop movements in or out of the city and threatened a railroad strike if the Bolsheviks did not agree to negotiations with the various Socialist parties. Meanwhile, news arrived that Kerensky was returning to the capital with Cossack units under Krasnov and that a tense situation had arisen in Moscow (by 29 October armed conflict flared there between those supporting the Provisional Government, including many Right SRs, and those opposing it, with quite unfavorable initial results for the Bolsheviks). At the same time, the idea of all-Socialist negotiations engendered sweeping support in Petrograd and throughout the country.

The 27th passed desultorily, and both the Bolsheviks and the Committee for the Salvation of the Revolution (a right Socialist coordinating body) tried to enlist the railroad delegates to their respective sides (Riazanov even threatened Vikzhel with arrest by the MRC). The first signs that the Left SR-Vikzhel strategy was working came on 28 October when the Committee for Salvation agreed to the principle of an all-Socialist government (albeit without Bolsheviks) and when Riazanov sent word that Vikzhel delegates should come to the Smol'nyi for initial negotiations. Meanwhile, a desperate struggle between the MRC (which led the defense of Petrograd) and Vikzhel had broken out and would continue throughout the crisis over Vikzhel's blocking of transports of pro-Bolshevik and pro-Kerensky forces. The MRC arrested personnel from Vikzhel, whose armed detachments sprung them; threats and counterthreats flew as the negotiations peaked. (One of many ironies is that at this point the Left SRs Ustinov, Algasov, and M. Levin were on the MRC.)

By the 29th fighting had started in Moscow, with an initial advantage to the pro-Kerensky forces, and firm news arrived about Kerensky-Krasnov's approach to Gatchina and Tsarskoe Selo. Vikzhel sent delegates to both Kerensky and the MRC to try to bring about an armistice. Finally, toward evening the first meeting of the Vikzhel negotiations took place at the transport ministry's offices. Reports differ about exactly who attended, but stenograms of the meetings show that at this and other sessions through early November, an array of Socialist leaders participated, including Riazanov, Nogin, Rykov, Kamenev, Zinoviev, Sokol'nikov, and Stalin from the Bolsheviks; Malitskii, Krushinskii, and Stamo (all Left SRs) from Vikzhel; Kamkov, Kalegaev, Karelin, and Malkin from the Left SRs; Znamenskii and Planson from the People's Socialists; Gendel'man, Rakitnikov, and others from the SRs; Filipovskii, a Right SR from the Committee for the Salvation; and the Mensheviks Martov, Dan, Gutman, and Skobelev. The first round of talks continued into midmorning of the 30th, with the Bolsheviks agreeing in principle to the Vikzhel plan that called for an all-Socialist government from the Bolsheviks to the People's Socialists and immediate negotiations toward an armistice; the right Socialists, meanwhile, held out for an all-Socialist government without Bolsheviks. Each side insisted that the opposing alternative would be unacceptable to the "rest of democracy." The meeting finally broke up for further consultations and votes in the various party committees.

Meanwhile, plans for an armistice foundered on the dilatory tactics of Kerensky and the Petrograd right Socialists (the latter wanted to wait "two or three days" because of their soon-to-fade military prospects). This was an important, indeed crucial, development, because had an armistice been reached, negotiations could have proceeded without a known military outcome in either Petrograd or Moscow, placing heavy pressure on the Bolsheviks, who as yet were on the defensive.

While fighting continued in or near both capitals, the next round of negotiations took place on 31 October with the broadest representation of all the sessions. Both sides edged closer to the Vikzhel–Left SR planks. The Bolsheviks, who had insisted that the "all-Socialist government" would have to stand firmly on the decisions of the Second Congress and comprise at least 51 percent Bolsheviks, now seemed more conciliatory. Strikingly, the Right Mensheviks offered support for (but not entry into) a government with Bolsheviks; and the Right SRs agreed to enter a government with Bolsheviks, but under a plan that would have excluded Lenin and Trotsky. Overall, this session had a character of give and take, but right Socialists' exclusion of Lenin and Trotsky from government posts seems to have precluded agreement.

By the next day, news came of a full Bolshevik victory in Moscow and the retreat of Kerensky-Krasnov from the capital. In a dramatic recorded telephone call on 1 November between Trotsky and Riazanov in the Smol'nyi and Malitskii on the other end, the Bolsheviks reiterated their willingness to negotiate but now ruled out an armistice, thus ending any opportunity of an agreement under military pressure on the Bolsheviks. Further sessions on 2 and 3 November witnessed a gradual withdrawal by Bolsheviks and right Socialists from the common ground of the 31st. By the 5th, Malitskii wired to Moscow that the negotiations had failed and Vikzhel was returning to Moscow.

Nevertheless, the stand-off continued. With hefty backing from social organizations, the Left SRs continued to press for an all-Socialist government, while numerous Bolsheviks resigned from their Central Committee and from Sovnarkom, largely with the goal of reestablishing the all-Socialist negotiations. On 4 and 5 November, all Left SRs resigned from the MRC in protest of Sovnarkom's propensity to act without the All-Russian Executive Committee's prior approval, in this case by ordering the MRC to make arrests and close oppositional newspapers.[47] Regardless, all subsequent attempts to pressure Lenin and Trotsky to share power with moderate Socialists (or subordinate themselves to the soviets) failed, and the Left SRs eventually entered the government with the Bolsheviks.

I have noted the irony of Left SR participation in anti–Provisional Government actions that the Left SR leadership abhorred; likewise, while the MRC was arresting Vikzhel activists, who were pursuing a Left SR plan, Left SRs served on the MRC. This does not exhaust the list. As Left SRs maneuvered desperately to force agreements during the Vikzhel talks (they had a sober estimate of the prospects for success), Left SR military commanders achieved the victories that lifted the pressure from the Bolshevik hardliners: N. Muraviev organized and led the troops that repelled the Krasnov forces; Sablin's unit captured a large contingent of the anti-Bolshevik forces in Moscow, ending the conflict there; and even the cruiser *Aurora* operated under a Left SR captain as it fired its blanks at the Winter Palace.[48]

This lack of consistency reflected their exquisitely difficult position: for Left SRs, the revolution's fate directly concerned them. They noted the Bolsheviks' heavy popular support in the cities and at the fronts. The overthrow of the government and formation of a new one under Bolshevik auspices were unfortunate political realities; a defeat of the Bolsheviks would be a defeat of the revolution. For the duration of civil conflict, all the Socialists walked the razor's edge between the Bolsheviks and the Whites. During October and November, all the parties, including the Bolsheviks, split badly and worked at cross purposes; furthermore, as a group still formally operating within the PSR, the Left SRs hardly disposed of the wherewithal to impose discipline.

Legitimate questions arise about the viability of the Left SR plan for an all-inclusive Socialist government: Could Lenin, Trotsky, Kamenev, Kamkov, Chernov, Martov, Dan, Avksent'ev, Skobelev, and Peshekhonov have worked together? Regardless, a broad Socialist government would have commanded enormous support in Russia. The national railroad and postal-telegraph unions, the national labor union movement and numerous factories, soviets, and soldiers' committees communicated their wish for a government of all the Socialists. During the negotiations themselves, delegates from factories, garrison units, and the fronts arrived to demand an agreement.[49] Advocates saw it as their one chance to keep democracy unified to prevent the horrors of civil war, certainly the leitmotif of Left SR analysis. Lenin and Trotsky held that civil war was inevitable, and Lenin lectured the party not to fear the conflict. For him civil war demarcated old from new, a sine qua non of revolution.

The Left SRs adhered doggedly to SR theory and programs, which seemed adequate to revolutionary tasks in Russia. They felt that they, as much as anyone, had developed the revolution. As Spiridonova later indignantly exhorted her cohorts, "We made this revolution, not the Bolsheviks." (Future research will determine her accuracy.) Steps to deepen the revolution struck the Left SRs as naturally reflective of the needs and aspirations of mass society. They opposed one-party rule and unilateral actions as violations of democracy. Democracy was not only an ethical goal for Left SRs but also a vital guarantor of noncoercive governmental authority. The Left SR approach to democratic rule included demands for the government to subordinate itself to democratically elected bodies and an insistence on full representation for the peasantry. A split within democracy (defined as workers, soldiers, peasants, radical intelligentsia, and the institutions that represented these groups) would strengthen the counterrevolution, spurring in turn harsh measures from the revolutionary government. As early as November Kamkov warned that steps the Bolsheviks were taking could lead to "mass arrests and . . . mass shootings."[50]

The Left SRs' outlook on the Bolsheviks was realistic. Their measures to restrain them ultimately failed, but then so did everyone else's. In their view, SR and Menshevik policies contributed directly to Bolshevik popularity, which the SRs and Mensheviks then refused to accept as a reality. For the Left SRs, it was a reality so significant that, for the time being, the downfall of the Bolsheviks would signify the victory of counterrevolution, a dilemma that, as noted, plagued even the moderate Socialists throughout the civil war.

During the fall of 1917, Left SRs, numerous other Socialists, and, more important, much of laboring and thinking Russia strove for the achievement of Soviet power rather than the power of one party. This was to have been the victory of democracy rather than of a group (the Leninist leadership) within one party that saw fit to set priorities for the country without regard for the desires of vast social groups, all other Socialists, and even its own serried ranks. For deliberately subverting a democratic (albeit imperfectly so) revolution in favor of a far less democratic one, the Lenin-Trotsky leadership and ultimately the Bolshevik Party bear direct responsibility for the travails that promptly ensued.

Several potentially useful historiographical suggestions arise out of this account. The lightly sketched picture of pre-October Left SR activities adumbrates the actual case in which a broad coalition of leftists worked to deepen the revolution. The concepts involved—replacing the Provisional Government with a Socialist one, locating power in the soviets, ending the war and ameliorating laboring Russia's plight—constituted a shared revolutionary heritage rather than the ideas of one party. Workers and soldiers threw considerable support to the Bolsheviks out of the political calculation that the party seemed to offer what they wanted.

One may argue that in the chaos of post-October Russia the authoritarian variant of the Leninist leadership had the best chance of surviving; one may just as plausibly argue that specific Bolshevik policies sharply intensified the chaos. The Left SR variant involving a broad Socialist coalition, whatever its shortcomings, alone promised sufficient social support to preserve aspects of the new hard-won democracy. Instead, a faction of one party prevailed because, for specific agendas, it located allies outside its own confines within other parties and, temporarily, across broad societal lines; but its narrow vision soon necessitated coercion even against its social and political allies. In the eyes of the post-October Bolsheviks, the revolution (Soviet power) and Communist power assumed an essential identity, a stance not to be conflated with the fleeting instrumental identity recognized by Left SRs and others. The very social elements that brought about Soviet Socialist power failed to view one-party rule as even tolerable, let alone permanent. No October epiphany had occurred, except in Soviet propaganda and febrile historiographical formulations.

The Left SRs' admirable idealism remained untested by lengthy contact with political power; thus we recall them—if we recall them at all—as eternal naifs or Bolshevik handmaidens. Regardless, in this study I aim at using their experiences to re-create certain forgotten realities. The revolutionary strivings of October 1917 were far less "Bolshevik" than has been imagined. Communist rule was not the only revolutionary alternative to the Provisional Government. Coalitional Socialist power, sanctioned by longtime Socialist practice, was the variant with the broadest popular backing; it alone held out the prospect of avoiding the prolonged civil war, out of whose cauldron untrammeled dictatorship was forged. The chances for an all-Socialist government were slim, the benefits incalculable.

Notes

1. K. V. Gusev, *Krakh partii levykh eserov* (Moscow: Izd. sots.-ekon. lit., 1963) is perhaps the most important of numerous Soviet articles and books about the Left SRs. Oliver Radkey's two studies are *The Agrarian Foes of Bolshevism* (New York: Columbia University Press, 1958), and *Sickle Under the Hammer* (New York: Columbia University Press, 1962).

2. Interesting discussions of SR activities, programs, and theory can be found in Manfred Hildermeier, *Die Sozialrevolutionaere Partei Russlands* (Cologne: Boehlau Verlag, 1978); Maureen Perrie, *The Agrarian Policy of the Russian Socialist-Revolutionary Party from Its Origins Through the Revolution of 1905–1907* (Cambridge: Cambridge University Press, 1976); Christopher Rice, *Russian Workers and the Socialist Revolutionary Party Through the Revolution of 1905–1907* (New York: St. Martin's, 1988); and Radkey, *Agrarian Foes*.

3. Information about the wartime SRs can be found in M. Melancon, *The Socialist Revolutionaries and the Russian Anti-War Movement, 1914–1917* (Columbus: Ohio State University Press, 1990).

4. For information about this period of SR history see Radkey, *Agrarian Foes*, chap. 1.

5. V. M. Chernov, "Ideinye pozitsii P.S.R. posle Oktiabr'skogo perevorota v 'Tezisakh' 1918 g.," Hoover Institution, Nicolaevsky Collection, no. 7, p. 53.

6. A. G. Shliapnikov, "Fevral'skie dni v Peterburge," *Proletarskaia revoliutsiia*, no. 1 (1923): 133–134; V. Zenzinov, "Fevral'skie dni," 67–68, manuscript in Hoover Institution, Nicolaevsky Collection, box 393, file 3; *Znamia truda*, no. 18 (13 September 1917).

7. *Zemlia i volia* issues from spring and summer 1917 provide much information about the growth of leftism within the party. On the complicated affairs of the Third Congress see Radkey, *Agrarian Foes*, 185–237.

8. *Vserossiiskoe soveshchanie sovetov rabochikh i soldatskikh deputatov. Stenograficheskii otchet* (Moscow: Gosizdat, 1927), 103–104, 139; N. Avdeev, ed., *Revoliutsiia 1917 goda: khronika sobytii*, 6 vols. (Moscow, 1923–1930), 2: 99, 103; *Delo naroda*, no. 4 (4 May 1917). At early gatherings the leftist SR minority factions were about the same size as the Bolshevik groups.

9. *Pervyi Vserossiiskii s"ezd sovetov r. i s. d.* (Moscow: Gos. izd-vo, 1930), 42–43, 126–129, 290.

10. *Izvestiia kronshtatskogo soveta*, nos. 88–94 (6–13 July 1917); Gosudarstvennyi arkhiv rossiiskoi federatsii (henceforth GARF, formerly TsGAOR), f. 6978, op. 1, d. 93 (Protokoly ob"ed. zasedaniia VTsIK i IK VSKrD, 4 July 1917), ll. 4–5.

11. V. Vladimirova, ed., *Revoliutsiia 1917 goda. Khronika sobytii*, 3: 177; M. Ol'minskii, *1917 god* (Moscow: Izd. Kom. un-ta im. Ia.M. Sverdlova, 1926), 186–187.

12. *Izvestiia kronshtatskogo soveta*, no. 53 (24 May 1917), no. 98 (18 July 1918); *Zemlia i volia*, no. 78 (27 June 1917), no. 85 (9 July 1917); *Volia naroda*, no. 43 (18 June 1917).

13. GARF, f. 6978 (VTsIK pervyi soz., 1 iiunia–25 okt. 1917), op. 1, d. 228, l. 12; d. 584, l. 98; d. 695, ll. 42–43, 46; f. 3875 (IK Vser. sov. kr. dep.), op. 1, d. 4. *Izvestiia kronshtadtskogo soveta*, no. 93 (12 July 1917); *Volia naroda*, no. 69 (19 July 1917); D. E. Grazkin, "Revoliutsionnaia rabota v XII armii nak. okt. (1916–1917). Vosp. i mat.," *Voprosy istorii*, no. 9 (1957): 3–16; A. S. Smirnov, "Ob otnoshenii bol'shevikov k levym eseram v period podgotovki oktiabr'skoi revoliutsii," *Voprosy istorii KPSS*, no. 2 (1966), 18; Tseitlin, "Soldatskie organizatsii," 43, 183, 187.

14. *Volia naroda*, no. 30 (3 June 1917), no. 32 (6 June 1917), no. 41 (16 June 1917), no. 45 (21 June 1917), no. 62 (11 July 1917), no. 90 (12 August 1917), no. 92 (15 August 1917), no. 102 (26 August 1917), no. 106 (31 August 1917).

15. Messages from the Kazan Soviet and the Urals Regional Soviet Conference are in GARF, f. 6978, op. 1, d. 421, l. 2; d. 458, l. 7.

16. For one of numerous examples see the declaration of Bolshevik support from a Petrograd garrison unit in GARF, f. 6978, op. 1, d. 581, l. 115.

17. The Left SR–oriented Kronstadt peasant soviet founded and ran the course for agitators. When the Left SRs turned to the main Kronstadt soviet (workers, soldiers, and sailors) for help with funding, the Bolsheviks opposed the measure on the grounds that the course was entirely "Left SR." See *Izvestiia Kronshtatskogo soveta*, no. 57 (28 May 1917) and no. 67 (9 June 1917).

18. GARF, f. 1797, Ministerstvo zemledeliia, op. 1, d. 20, Postanovleniia biuro Penzenskoi gubernii IK ot 15 maia i 15 iiunia 1917; Tsentral'nyi Gosudarstvennyi Arkhiv Narodnogo Khoziaistva (TsGANKh), f. 478 (Narkomzem RSFSR), op. 1, d. 147 (Materialy o mestnykh sov. organakh Penzenskoi gubernii); d. 215 (Perepiski s vol. i uezd. gub. sem. otd.). *Izvestiia Kazanskogo soveta*, all issues from May, June, and July 1917, especially no. 1 (12 July 1917) and no. 4 (20 July 1917); R.S. Tseitlin, "Soldatskie organizatsii v period podgotovki vel. okt. sots.-rev. (na materialakh Kazanskogo voennogo okruga)," Cand. diss., Kazan University, 1972, 36–43, 129–130, 150, 165, 171–172.

19. *Vserossiiskoe soveshchanie*, 33, 65, 92, 166–167; *Pervyi vserossiiskii s"ezd*, 210–212.

20. GARF, f. 6978, op. 1, 16–18; *Znamia truda*, no. 48 (19 October 1917).

21. *Rabochii put'*, no. 20 (21 September 1917), no. 27 (4 October 1917), no. 32 (10 October 1917), no. 36 (14 October 1917).

22. For considerable evidence about the central committee's neglect of its own mass organizations see Rossiiskii tsentr khraneniia i izucheniia gokumentov noveishei istorii (hereafter RTsKhIDNI—formerly TsPA IML), f. 274 (Materialy TsK PSR), op. 1, dd. 13, 14.

23. *Zemlia i volia*, no. 5 (28 March 1917), no. 15 (12 April 1917), no. 27 (26 April 1917), no. 29 (28 April 1917), no. 31 (30 April 1917), no. 36 (6 May 1917), no. 60 (6 June 1917); *Znamia truda*, no. 11 (3 September 1917), no. 12 (5 September 1917), no. 20 (16 September 1917), no. 23 (20 September 1917), no. 24 (21 October 1917), no. 25 (22 September 1917), no. 26 (23 September 1917), no. 38 (7 October 1917), no. 39 (7 October 1917), no. 48 (19 October 1917). GARF, f. 6978, op. 1, d. 423, ll. 12–42; d. 458, ll. 5–7; d. 460, ll. 49–52. Radkey, *Agrarian Foes*, 384; Gusev, *Krakh levykh eserov*, 84; *Protokoly pervogo s"ezda*, 5–12.

24. GARF, f. 5498 (Vikzhel, 25 August 1917—ianv. 1918), op. 1, d. 4, l. 79; P.N. Khmylov, "K voprosu o bor'be bol'shevikov protiv soglashatel'stva 'levykh' eserov v dni oktiabria," *Uchenye zapiski Moskovskogo gos. bibl. inst.*, no. 3 (1957), 30.

25. P. A. Golub, "O bloke bol'shevikov s levymi eserami v period podgotovki i pobedy Oktiabria," *Voprosy istorii KPSS*, no. 9 (1971), 65; *Bor'ba za vel. Okt. na Niko-laevshchine* (Nikolaev, 1927), 190. At the congress of the 3rd Army on 9 November, there were 155 Bolsheviks, 110 SRs (Left and Right), 20 SR-Maximalists, and about 50 Mensheviks (*Pravda*, no. 184 [9 November 1917]).

26. *Nash put'* appeared under the editorship of Mariya Spiridonova and with a stellar staff of future Left SR party leaders that included A. Bitsenko, V. Algasov, I. Shteinberg, A. Kalegaev, M. Kogan-Bernshtein, V. Trutovskii, A. Ustinov, B. Kamkov, and A. Kachinskii.

27. *Zemlia i volia*, no. 68 (15 June 1917), no. 85 (9 July 1917).

28. *Nash put'*, no. 1 (August 1917), 4–7, 9, 14–19, 31–32, no. 2 (October 1917), 31–32; *Zemlia i volia*, no. 29 (28 April 1917), no. 50 (25 May 1917). At a session of the Petrograd Soviet at which the death penalty was debated, the SR Iakovlev pre-dicted that the "reintroduction of the death penalty will force simple soldiers to think—why isn't the death penalty applied to Sukhomlinov and the Romanovs . . . and it's being introduced [for us] by our comrade SRs—Kerensky and Savinkov," at which point the Bolsheviks broke out in laughter. "Don't laugh," yelled the SR. "It is tragic that old revolutionaries are doing this!" The SR resolution against the death penalty passed overwhelmingly, with only Tsereteli voting against (*Volia naroda*, no. 96 [19 August 1917]).

29. GARF, f. 472 (Ts. sov. fab.-zav. kom., Mai 1917-Ian. 1918), op. 1, dd. 1, 2, 62; *Nash put'*, no. 1 (August 1917), 56–57; *Znamia truda*, no. 16 (10 September 1917).

30. *Nash put'*, no. 1 (August 1917), 28–28, 43, 53–55; *Znamia truda*, no. 29 (27 September 1917).

31. *Izvestiia kazanskogo soveta* (2nd series), no. 8 (26 July 1917).

32. *Zemlia i volia*, nos. 73, 76, 77 (21, 24, 25 June 1917); *Nash put'*, no. 1 (August 1917), 9–10, no. 2 (October 1917), 31–32.

33. This summary of Left SR analyses is a composite from speeches and writings, sources for which are *Protokoly pervogo s"ezda partii levykh sotsialistov-revoliutsionerov (internatsionalistov)* (Moscow: Izd. "Rev. Sots., 1918), 38–41; *Nash put'*, no. 1 (August 1917), 9–11, 13–14, 19–20, no. 2 (October 1917), 31–34, 46–47; *Zemlia i volia* (Pet-rograd), nos. 73, 76, 77 (21, 24, 25 June 1917), no. 147 (18 September 1917); *Znamia truda*, no. 1 (23 August 1917), no. 3 (25 August 1917), no. 5 (27 August 1917), no. 10 (2 September 1917), no. 14 (7 September 1917), no. 15 (8 September 1917), no. 17 (12 September 1917), no. 22 (19 September 1917), no. 28 (26 September 1917), no. 45 (15

October 1917), no. 48 (19 October 1917); and *Zemlia i volia* (Kharkov), no. 166 (13 October 1917).

34. *Protokoly pervogo s"ezda,* 47–49; *Znamia truda,* no. 4 (26 August 1917), no. 17 (12 September 1917), no. 43 (13 October 1917), no. 49 (20 October 1917).

35. *Znamia truda,* no. 46 (17 October 1917).

36. *Zemlia i volia,* no. 147 (20 September 1917); *Znamia truda,* no. 23 (20 September 1917), no. 24 (21 September 1917), no. 45 (15 October 1917), no. 46 (17 October 1917), no. 48 (19 October 1917).

37. GARF, f. 6978 (VTsIK), op. 1, d. 138; *Volia naroda,* no. 107 (1 September 1917), no. 108 (2 September 1917).

38. *Znamia truda,* no. 16 (10 September 1917), no. 38 (7 October 1917).

39. GARF, f. 1235 (VTsIK, I–IV sozyva), op. 1, d. 1, ll. 2–4; d. 2, ll. 12–13; d. 15, 3–6; f. 6978, op. 1, d. 197, l. 2; d. 510, ll. 1–3. *Znamia truda,* no. 24 (21 October 1917), no. 34 (3 October 1917); *Izvestiia VTsIK,* no. 185 (October 1917).

40. *Protokoly pervogo s"ezda,* 47–48; GARF, f. 1236, op. 1, d. 9, ll. 84–86.

41. *Protokoly pervogo s"ezda,* 47–49; *Znamia truda,* no. 5 (27 August 1917).

42. S. Mstislavskii, *Five Days Which Transformed Russia* (Bloomington: Indiana University Press, 1988), 112.

43. *Znamia truda,* no. 52 (24 October 1917).

44. *Vtoroi Vserossiiskii s"ezd Sovetov rarochikh i soldatskikh deputatov. Stenograficheskii otchet* (Moscow: Gosizdat, 1928), xxxv, 8–9, 14, 25–26, 54, 82–84; GARF, f. 1235, op. 1, d. 8, l. 1.

45. *Protokoly pervogo s"ezda,* 96–97.

46. This account of the Vikzhel negotiations (roughly 28 October through 4 November) is from GARF, f. 5498, op. 1, dd. 22, 24, 55, 56, 57, 58, 61, 62 (*Materialy Vikzhelia v Oktiabr'skie dni*) (d. 58 consists of the stenograms of the Vikzhel negotiations); d. 13 (*Stenogrammy chrezv. s"ezda Vikzhel,* zasedaniia 29 Dekabria 1917, doklady ob oktiabr'skikh dniakh); f. 1236 (*Materialy Petrogradskogo VRK*), op. 1, dd. 1, 2, 4, 6, 12, 14, 18, 19, 27, 56, 95, 96.

47. GARF, f. 1236, op. 1, d. 1, l.47.

48. One telegram from Muraviev states, "Gatchina has been taken by the Finland Regiment. Cossacks are retreating and marauding. Taking steps to restore order" (GARF, f. 1236, op. 1, d. 12, l. 107). See also P. Krasnov, "Na vnutrennem fronte," *Arkhiv Russkoi Revoliutsii,* no. 1 (1922), 171–177; K. Eremeev, *Plamia—Episody oktiabr'skikh dnei* (Moscow, 1928), 127–191 passim; A. Arosev, *Kak eto proizoshlo (oktiab'skie dni v Moskve). Vospominaniia, materialy* (Moscow, 1923), 8–12.

49. Support for an all-Socialist government was virtually universal. For resolutions and proclamations to this effect see GARF, f. 1236, op. 1, d. 1, ll. 42, 47; d. 12, ll.100, 129, 160; d. 18, ll. 14, 21, 23, 29–30; d. 19, 12–14, 24–26.

50. *Protokoly pervogo s"ezda,* 45–46, 73.

TWO

Anti-Bolshevik Forces: Fragmentation
and Alienation, 1918–1920

The Socialists-Revolutionaries and the Dilemma of Civil War

T he dissolution of the Constituent Assembly shattered the fragile
vessel of peace in Russia: civil war, now inescapable, soon engulfed
the Russian empire.[1] Accustomed to the political language of the
French Revolution, the SRs felt certain that this civil war would end in
the triumph of "Bonapartist counterrevolution" and had therefore predi-
cated their whole strategy in the revolution on averting its outbreak. They
argued that only the reconvocation of the Constituent Assembly could put
an end to civil war and avert counterrevolution. This reasoning framed
the SRs' central dilemma after January 1918: in order to reconvene the
Constituent Assembly, the SRs—the assembly's principal advocates—
would have to fight for it, which meant participating in the civil war; yet
by their logic civil war doomed the revolution, the advancement of which
was the principal purpose of convening the assembly. This contradiction
bedeviled the SRs throughout the civil war and accounts for much of
their vacillation and many of their shifts.[2]

The SRs at first abandoned active efforts to reconvene the Constituent
Assembly. Although reconvocation remained their primary strategic goal,
the SRs were not prepared to fight for it. Instead, the SR Central Committee in January 1918 drew up a set of theses that outlined a policy of
peaceful opposition to the Bolsheviks within the framework of the Soviet
regime.[3] The Central Committee's rejection of armed struggle against the
Bolsheviks was underpinned by its analysis of the social basis of the new
regime. Objectively, the Central Committee contended, Bolshevism was a
counterrevolutionary movement because of its attack on the fragile institutions of Russian democracy and because it had, by launching the civil
war, opened the way to counterrevolution. But the methods of struggle
that the SRs would normally use against counterrevolution—in the party
tradition, chiefly terrorism—were inappropriate, because "Bolshevism,
unlike the Tsarist autocracy, is based on workers and soldiers who are

still blinded, have not lost faith in it, and do not see that it is fatal to the cause of the working class."[4] The Russian masses' political inexperience and the embryonic form of their class organizations had left them susceptible to the Bolsheviks' maximalist program, in which they grasped only the "naked demands for the chaotic plundering of national and private property."[5]

To use the favorite metaphor of the SRs and other Socialists after October, the salvation of the revolution, and therefore of the country, depended on the masses "sobering up"—overcoming the intoxicating effects of Bolshevism and returning to the realm of the possible. The SRs, like the Mensheviks, sought to persuade the workers and soldiers that the Bolsheviks' utopian attempt to leap directly into Socialism had sparked the spectacular collapse of Russian industry, the ballooning unemployment, and the crisis in the food supply. The SRs hoped to rally the workers and soldiers around a "healthy Socialist policy" that recognized the social and economic constraints on the immediate building of Socialism in Russia, but at the same time did not preach a return to unvarnished capitalism. Such a policy could include the socialization of the land, selective nationalization, and state regulation of industry if such moves were carried out in a systematic, organized fashion.[6] The SRs sought to convince workers that the revitalization of the industrial economy hinged on the overthrow of Bolshevik rule and the reconvocation of the Constituent Assembly, because only the Constituent Assembly could put an end to civil war and reunify the country as a single economic entity.[7]

A prominent party presence in Soviet politics, the SRs believed, would bring these arguments to the masses and, by strengthening the soviets, erect a barrier both to Bolshevik dictatorship and to the expected onslaught of counterrevolution. The party therefore returned to the All-Russian Central Executive Committee (CEC), to the Petrograd Soviet, and to other Soviet institutions that it had abandoned after October. In the CEC, in the soviets, in the press, and in propaganda and agitation in the factories, the SRs concentrated on a war of words with the Bolsheviks. With no opportunity to shape policy or block Bolshevik proposals, the Socialists were relegated to criticizing the regime's policies and to agitation for new soviet elections in an attempt to win back the "blinded" workers and soldiers. Strikingly, the SRs aimed their propaganda almost entirely at workers and soldiers. The urban thrust of the party's propaganda runs counter to the SRs' image as the party of the Russian peasants and illustrates one of the party's most important weaknesses as it faced the Soviet regime and the unfolding civil war: it had no rural party apparatus and no practical ability to bring the peasants out in defense of the party's goals. As a result, the party's profile differed little from that of the

Mensheviks, and the two parties worked together closely in an effort to build a mass urban opposition in the first months of 1918.

In retrospect, the SRs' hopes to work as a Soviet opposition—hopes that were even stronger among the Mensheviks—seem naive. The willingness of the Bolsheviks to use force against their opponents was no longer open to doubt after the dissolution of the Constituent Assembly; the removal of the Bolsheviks, to which the Socialists aspired, would require force as well. The Socialists' reluctance to accept the necessity of force grew out of their obsessive fear of counterrevolution, which led them to organize opposition to the Bolsheviks only within the framework of the regime, in retrospect a quixotic effort. But if the efforts of the SRs and Mensheviks to organize a mass opposition movement were beset by a variety of problems—arrests and harassment, the intermittent persecution of the non-Bolshevik press, and the resolve of the Bolsheviks to retain state power—the Socialists had one important strength: the trajectory of popular political attitudes, which swung around once again in their direction in early 1918.

Serious opposition to the Bolsheviks sprouted immediately after the dissolution of the Constituent Assembly. In the countryside, the peasants paid no mind to the assembly's fate, but in many cities where the Bolsheviks had enjoyed the support of most workers, the months after the dissolution of the assembly witnessed a rapid reversal of fortunes. The dissolution was not itself the most important cause of this shift, though it played a role. Worker discontent was grounded instead in the intensifying economic crisis and in the arbitrary, violent nature of Bolshevik rule. As anti-Bolshevik sentiment developed throughout the country, the SRs and Mensheviks sought to use it to win new elections to the soviets and to build a mass opposition movement.

Petrograd offers one of the earliest examples of the evolution of such worker dissatisfaction and its interaction with party politics. The demonstration in favor of the Constituent Assembly in the city on 5 (18) January included a significant number of workers; workers figured among the casualties as well. As proved to be the case in many other cities, Bolshevik violence, in particular the killing of workers, triggered immediate condemnations of the regime. Those condemnations mushroomed into calls at many factories for new elections to the soviet, the resignation of the Council of Peoples' Commissars, and the reconvocation of the Constituent Assembly.[8] The Socialists made the call for new elections to the Petrograd Soviet the focus of their propaganda and were able to achieve at least a partial success. Despite the efforts of the Bolsheviks and the Factory Committees they controlled, the movement for new elections to the soviet spread to more than twenty factories by early February and resulted in the election of fifty new delegates: thirty-six SRs, seven Mensheviks, and seven nonparty delegates.[9]

The Bolsheviks' unwillingness to recognize the elections and to seat the new delegates pushed a group of Socialists who had been active in the Workers' Conference of the Committee for the Defense of the Constituent Assembly to lay plans for an alternative workers' forum. In mid-January they formed an initiative group that began to organize elections in the factories for what later became the Assembly of Workers' Plenipotentiaries; the leaders of the initiative group were mainly right Mensheviks but included one SR, E. S. Berg.[10] The first session of the Assembly of Workers' Plenipotentiaries took place on 13 March, with eighty-three delegates in attendance, representing twenty-five factories. The delegates issued a declaration condemning the Bolsheviks' betrayal of their promises of a democratic peace, land, and freedom, and denounced the Bolsheviks' refusal to sanction new elections to the soviet. By April, there were 110 plenipotentiaries: 42 nonparty delegates, 35 Mensheviks, 33 SRs, and 1 People's Socialist.[11] The background for the formation of the assembly was the growing sense of despair over unemployment and the collapse of industry in Petrograd, but according to one of the Menshevik organizers, the catalyst in turning these Petrograd workers against the Bolsheviks was the shooting of the workers at the demonstration in defense of the Constituent Assembly.[12]

As in Petrograd, the first serious discontent with the regime in the provinces derived from the proclivities for violence and arbitrariness displayed by many local Bolsheviks in the context of an economic crisis that stoked opposition to Bolshevik policies. Under the circumstances, there were no effective restraints on local Bolsheviks' exercise of power: even the central Bolshevik leadership would have been unable to rein them in. In Astrakhan', for example, a group of local Bolsheviks broke from the party organization to set up a rival Bolshevik organization in spring 1918. In explaining their decision to the Bolshevik Central Committee, the representatives of this new organization cited their disgust with the behavior of the official party organization in the city: it had, they thought, been taken over by newcomers who considered that to be a Communist "one must do one thing only: beat, shoot, cut up, and squeeze all who do not want to think the way they think and act the way they act."[13] The central party leadership signaled its priorities by denouncing as schismatics those who had split from the original Astrakhan' Bolshevik organization.[14]

Such uncontrolled terror in the provinces had a devastating effect on the Bolsheviks' popularity with workers. One of the first and most dramatic such cases was in Tula, where the local Bolshevik N. V. Kopylov's report to the Bolshevik Central Committee presents a succinct summary of the situation: "After the transfer of power to the soviet, a rapid about-face began in the mood of the workers. The Bolshevik deputies began to be recalled one after another, and soon the general situation took on a rather unhappy appearance. Despite the fact that there was a schism among the SRs, and the Left SRs were with us, our situation became shakier with each passing day. We were forced to block new elections to the soviet and even not to recognize them where they had taken place not in our favor."[15] As the same source confirms, the collapse of worker support for the Bolsheviks in Tula antedated mass unemployment in the city.

The decisive factor seems to have been a murder carried out by a local official, which formed part of a broader pattern of disorder, lawlessness, and violence. A certain Kozharinov, a Maximalist member of the Tula Military Revolutionary Committee, shot and killed the commander of the railroad workers' militia and seriously wounded another member of the militia at a session of the Tula railroad workers' soviet. Kozharinov fled, but the railroad workers remained assembled to discuss the situation. Kozharinov then returned with a squadron of Red Guards armed with machine guns to disperse the railroad workers' meeting, which it did by opening fire, wounding seven. Appeals for Kozharinov's trial and the recall of Bolshevik and Left SR delegates from the soviet immediately rolled through the workshops of the Tula Arms Factory, the main industrial enterprise of the city. This escalated into a call for new elections to the soviet, the resignation of the Council of Peoples' Commissars, and the transfer of all power to the Constituent Assembly.[16] Layoffs of Tula workers, the result of the demobilization of war industries, aggravated the crisis in the city. Shortly, as the same Tula Bolshevik reported, the "remnants of sympathy for the party among the working masses began to melt away not by the day, but by the hour." The unsystematic guerrilla campaign of the Bolsheviks against new elections to the soviet proved insufficient: the local party leader G. N. Kaminskii was effectively forced to abolish the city soviet and to vest power in the Provincial Executive Committee. The Provincial Executive Committee refused to convene a plenum of the city soviet for more than two months, knowing that if it contained newly elected delegates it would be dominated by the opposition.[17] In the interim, a Workers' Conference materialized and became one of the strongest provincial movements of plenipotentiaries.

From these sparks, discontent with the Bolsheviks spread throughout Russia in the winter and spring of 1918. Although workers constituted a small minority of the population, their dissatisfaction with the regime held special significance for the SRs and Mensheviks, because the Socialist parties focused on workers their effort to build an organized opposition to the regime. One of the Socialists' chief priorities in this effort was winning control of the soviets. In April and May elections to the city soviets were held in provincial capitals around the country: in almost all cases they returned SR and Menshevik majorities. Moreover, as the often-despairing private analysis of local Bolsheviks reveals, the collapse of the Bolsheviks' fortunes was more acute than the numbers in many of these elections would suggest, because the ruling party had a variety of methods at its disposal to pack the soviets with its own supporters. The Bolsheviks' response to these defeats—annulment of the results, dissolutions of the soviets, and maneuvers to stack new elections—only reinforced the workers' image of Bolshevik rule, fueled discontent, and fanned the movement of plenipotentiaries.[18]

A survey of these elections and provincial soviet politics in the main regions of European Russia—the Central Industrial and Agricultural regions, the Volga, and the Urals—reveals the scope and intensity of worker dissatisfaction with the new regime in the spring of 1918. Broadly speaking, the intersection of the Bolsheviks' arbitrary, violent political behavior with the economic crisis, unemployment, and food shortages in particular, drove worker opposition around the country in much the way it did in Petrograd and Tula. This was certainly true in the Central Industrial region, where in the fall of 1917 the workers were among the most radical of Russian workers; by the spring of 1918 those workers had become some of the strongest supporters of the opposition Socialist parties. Tula, one of the most important industrial centers in this area of the country, is a case in point. In the other provincial capitals of the Central Industrial region for which reliable information is available, only Tver' gave the Bolsheviks a majority in city soviet elections. Even there, on the eve of the election the local Bolsheviks complained nervously to the Central Committee of the "very real danger" of a Menshevik victory and demanded that the best party orators be sent.[19]

In Yaroslavl', calls arose in some factories for new elections to the soviet in January; judging from the sketchy reports, the major issue seems to have been the behavior of the Red Guards.[20] Political tensions mounted through the winter as the Menshevik-led opposition tried to organize elections. In partial elections held at the beginning of April, the opposition secured a solid victory: when the soviet convened on 9 April it contained forty-seven Mensheviks, thirty-eight Bolsheviks, and thirteen SRs. After the new soviet elected a Menshevik chairman, the Bolshevik delegation walked out and declared the soviet dissolved.[21] In response, workers in the city went out on strike, which the Bolsheviks answered by arresting the strike committee and threatening to dismiss the strikers and replace them with unemployed workers.[22] These tactics only prompted more workers to strike: virtually the entire industrial work force in the city stopped work. In the end, the Bolsheviks were forced to agree to hold new elections for the soviet at the end of the month.[23] The opposition won these elections handily—the Mensheviks far outdistanced the Bolsheviks, with the SRs in third place—but the Bolsheviks dissolved this soviet as well and placed the city under martial law.[24]

Industrial strikes also figured prominently in the politics of Kaluga. In January the Mensheviks and SRs won the city soviet elections.[25] A Kaluga Left SR conceded in the spring that anti-Bolshevik sentiment in the province was "extraordinarily strong."[26] On the night of 19–20 March the Bolshevik and Left SR authorities carried out mass searches of the population to confiscate weapons. Undoubtedly they were accompanied by violence, because the Kaluga railroad workers went out on strike in response. Summing up the situation in a meeting of the Kaluga Provincial Executive Committee on 25 March, the local Bolshevik leader P. Ia. Vitolin explained that the strike was a "counter-revolutionary action against Soviet power. One cannot call [the strike] economic, because the railroad workers are sufficiently well provided for in this regard. In view of this our attitude to the strikers must be completely merciless: we should spare their families, but immediately throw them into the open snow fields to live with the wolves. Simultaneously, we should inform all the Soviet republics that they should not be hired anywhere. In their place we should hire worker-cadres from Moscow."[27] The Bolsheviks broke the strike in Kaluga but were understandably reluctant to hold new elections to the soviet in this atmosphere. When elections were finally held later in the spring, the opposition emerged victorious.[28]

In Riazan', the last of the provincial capitals in this region, the opposition won elections to the city soviet in April. The Bolsheviks promptly dissolved the soviet and declared a dictatorship under a Military-Revolutionary Committee.[29] When the soviet was allowed to reconvene, roughly half of its membership was sympathetic to the opposition, and it entered into immediate conflict with the Military-Revolutionary Committee. A Bolshevik concluded at the end of April that "political life in Riazan' is not especially trustworthy. Many elements, even among the Red Army soldiers, are obvious counter-revolutionaries."[30]

Soviet politics in the provincial capitals of the Central Black Earth region followed a rather different pattern. In most of these cities worker support for the Bolsheviks in 1917 was much less significant than in the Central Industrial region. If the weakness of the Bolsheviks' position in these cities in 1917 tended to work against them in 1918, they had in their favor the absence of the acute crisis in food supply that helped to drive opposition sentiment in the cities to the north. Even so, the political situation was tense. In Kursk, scanty information suggests that the soviet was dissolved several times in April.[31] In Penza, six people were killed in a religious procession on 15 February, and the chairman of the Penza Soviet reported to Moscow that the mood in the city was "uneasy."[32] Politics in Voronezh was fairly calm for much of the spring. This quickly changed under the impact of the Bolsheviks' preparations for the evacuation of the city in the face of the German advance in mid-May, which brought a quick collapse of Bolshevik support and the formation of a Workers' Conference led by the socialists.[33]

In Orel, the Socialists retained their support among the workers through the upsurge of extremism in the fall of 1917. In January, the workers' section of the city soviet, led by the Socialists, passed a resolution opposing the transfer of power to the soviet. The Mensheviks and SRs agreed to stay in the soviet on the condition that the organs of local self-government would be left intact, that the Executive Committee would carry out only those measures of the Council of Peoples' Commissars that were "possible and expedient," and that new elections for the soldiers' section would be held.[34] In April the soviet consisted of forty-five Mensheviks and SRs, thirty-five Bolsheviks, and twenty Left SRs. The Bolshevik who reported these figures to the CEC added, "In general, the right socialist parties enjoy a large influence. The mood of the workers is against the Bolsheviks and Soviet power, which they understand as a purely Bolshevik party power. At meetings of the railroad workers the Bolsheviks were not allowed to speak. There were shouts of 'Down with them,' etc."[35] When new elections were held in May, the opposition won a majority, and the Bolsheviks disbanded the soviet.[36]

Elsewhere in Orel province, the industrial region of Briansk and Bezhitsa was an important center of opposition to the Bolsheviks, with a strong local movement of plenipotentiaries. An SR-Menshevik victory in soviet elections in mid-January pointed up the Bolsheviks' weakness there.[37] In Briansk, opposition intensified when the local military command, engaged on the front with the Ukrainians, carried out mass searches with attendant thefts and violence that resulted in the death of one worker. The angry workers gathered at a mass meeting and threatened to lynch the local Bolsheviks. An instructor from the Commissariat of Labor who traveled to the region reported that the searches had aroused the whole population against the Bolsheviks and that the hostility of the workers to the Bolsheviks was "very clearly expressed. It was the first time I have participated in a meeting of workers' organizations that viewed the present political situation with such bitterness."[38] In new elections to the soviet in Briansk, the SRs received twenty-three seats, the Bolsheviks nineteen, and the Mensheviks four.[39] These figures, however, understate the hostility the local workers felt toward the Bolsheviks: a Bolshevik informed the

CEC in May that the "Briansk workers are hostile to the Bolsheviks and Soviet power," while in Bezhitsa the "mood of the workers is anti-Bolshevik—there are sharp attacks on Soviet power."[40]

Tambov produced the most complicated political drama of all the towns in the Central Black Earth region. On 13 February a protracted political crisis began there when the city soviet passed a resolution in favor of all power to the Constituent Assembly: apparently under the impact of the rupture of the peace talks with the Germans at Brest, some of the Tambov Bolsheviks panicked and defected to the SRs and Mensheviks to form a new soviet majority. In response, the Tambov Bolshevik leadership formed a provincial soviet of workers', peasants', and soldiers' deputies that declared itself the organ of government in the province and city until a Provincial Congress of Soviets could be held. This Congress opened on 1 March and was packed with Bolsheviks and Left SRs, who controlled all but 60 of the 487 seats. It dissolved the city soviet, set new elections to it for the end of the month, and vested power in a Provincial Executive Committee.[41] At the end of March the elections to the new city soviet gave the SRs and Mensheviks a majority of the seats. Although the Bolsheviks and Left SRs formed a minority in the soviet, they demanded a majority of the seats in the Executive Committee and walked out when they were refused.[42] In the Provincial Executive Committee, the Bolsheviks and Left SRs disagreed on how to solve the political deadlock in the city. The Left SRs argued for the dissolution of the soviet and its replacement by a "Revolutionary Committee." The Bolsheviks agreed on the need to dissolve the soviet but were more reluctant to break so openly with the appearance of Soviet power. Instead, they reestablished the Executive Committee of the old city soviet, which had a Bolshevik majority. The Bolsheviks did, however, inform Moscow that they considered it necessary to raise the possibility of the "replacement of Soviet power by the power of the Communist and Left SR parties" as perhaps the only way out of the impasse.[43] Such a naked dictatorship proved unnecessary. The Provincial Executive Committee remained the real authority in the city. This organ, a Tambov Bolshevik conceded, was an "alien organization" for the city's workers, who had not elected it and considered it hostile to their interests.[44]

Along the Volga, the political situation in the towns in the winter and spring of 1918 closely resembled that of the Central Black Earth towns. In these smaller cities, workers' political passions were generally not as fierce as in Petrograd and in the more industrialized cities in the Central Industrial region. Unrest typically issued instead from the garrisons and from a motley array of armed bands controlled by Maximalists, Anarchists, and others, who staged uprisings in many of these towns over the course of the spring.[45] Nizhnii Novgorod and the factories of Sormovo, however, had long irritated the Bolsheviks with their provincial opposition to Bolshevik rule. Elsewhere, prospects were slightly better for the Bolsheviks, but the opposition probably had the support of most workers in the Volga towns.[46]

In Saratov, elections to the city soviet were held in April. Definitive evidence is lacking, but they apparently resulted in a victory for the SR-Menshevik opposition. On the eve of the elections, the chairman of the Saratov Bolshevik committee urged the Central Committee to send prominent party workers to aid in the Bolshevik campaign "in view of the mood that has formed among the workers."[47] At the Second Congress of the Left SRs in April, the delegate from Saratov reported that "new elections of the city soviet are now being held in Saratov. There is a definite anti-Bolshevik mood. . . . The complete ruin of the Bolsheviks is expected, and probably the huge majority in the soviet will belong to the Mensheviks and Right SRs."[48] In view of this evidence, as well as the hints in the Bolsheviks' newspaper in Saratov, a Menshevik-SR victory in the election seems likely.[49]

In Samara, there were no elections to the soviet in the spring of 1918. P. D. Klimushkin, a leading local SR and later one of the principal figures in the Committee of Members of the Constituent Assembly in Samara, estimated that the Bolsheviks might have retained the support of the majority of the workers, though he was uncertain. At the Tube Factory, the biggest industrial enterprise in the city, the Bolsheviks and SRs had roughly equal levels of support; the printers, as elsewhere, were Menshevik, and the railroad workers wavered in their loyalties.[50] According to an officer and a Kadet journalist who were in the city at the time, the Samara Bolsheviks were relatively moderate, which might explain the weakness of the SR-Menshevik opposition there.[51] Still, Bolshevik sources conceded that the "political mood among the masses was far from favorable for Soviet power" in the spring of 1918 and that many workers defected to the Mensheviks, SRs, and Maximalists or lapsed into apoliticism.[52] The Bolsheviks meanwhile ensured that they maintained a majority in the Samara Soviet by continuing to seat the Bolshevik delegates to the soviet from the Samara garrison even after the dissolution of the garrison in February.[53]

Sormovo witnessed the strongest opposition to the Bolsheviks among workers in the Volga towns. Here some workers passed resolutions in defense of the Constituent Assembly at the beginning of January, but the SRs' call for new elections suffered defeat in the soviet.[54] Over the course of the month worker dissatisfaction with the Bolsheviks mounted in reaction to the Bolsheviks' arrest of the Sormovo Menshevik leader and the high-handedness of the Red Guards.[55] In February, a local SR named

Chernov was murdered with his wife. Amid suspicion of Bolshevik complicity in the murder, a new majority coalition of SRs, Mensheviks, Left SRs, and nonparty delegates coalesced in the Sormovo Soviet. The new majority set up a commission to investigate the circumstances of the murder, and it agreed to finance Chernov's funeral and to compensate his family monetarily. And, over the objections of the Bolsheviks, the majority decided to hold elections to the soviet on 2 March.[56]

The elections were delayed until April, but the Bolsheviks knew that defeat awaited them. M. S. Sergushev, the secretary of the provincial Bolshevik organization, informed Moscow that "in the workers' district of Sormovo a grandiose collapse of spirit may be observed" and pleaded for help from the center: "Our situation as a provincial committee is not very pleasant! Rescue us!"[57] The elections returned a soviet in which the SRs and Mensheviks held twenty-one seats, of which thirteen were held by the SRs, while the Bolsheviks and Left SRs had seventeen delegates.[58] The situation was considerably worse for the Bolsheviks than the numbers would suggest. The Bolshevik committee in Nizhnii Novgorod, responsible for work in Sormovo, conceded the "complete break with the soviet by even the previously revolutionary workers."[59] Sergushev also reported this to Moscow and warned, "The position of Soviet power in the province is now threatened."[60] When the soviet convened, the Bolsheviks and Left SRs walked out and declared their own parallel soviet. In May, however, the two sections of the soviet were reunited after negotiations led by the prominent Bolshevik F. F. Raskol'nikov: the SR-Menshevik majority acquiesced in the exercise of political power by the Bolshevik minority, in return for a promise that it would be granted control of economic and cultural affairs.[61] This peculiar arrangement, however, did little to solidify the Bolsheviks' position in Sormovo.

Not far from Sormovo, in the Urals, worker opposition to the Bolsheviks also manifested itself, though information is sparse for some cities. The Left SRs claimed a Bolshevik–Left SR victory in Ekaterinburg, and Menshevik sources reported an opposition victory in Perm', but there are no details about either place.[62] In Zlatoust, the SRs controlled the soviet until March, when new elections were held: as a Zlatoust Left SR put it, "We were able to disperse and arrest all the initiators of the city soviet" and organize new elections.[63] These elections, however, ended in a Bolshevik defeat and the election of an SR as chairman of the soviet Executive Committee. The new Executive Committee consisted of nine nonparty delegates, seven SRs, three Bolsheviks, and two Mensheviks. On 17 March, Red Guards who were brought in from Cheliabinsk and elsewhere dissolved the soviet over the protest of the Zlatoust workers, who went out on strike.[64]

The armaments factory at Izhevsk was the most important center of worker unrest in the Urals: in the summer of 1918 the workers joined with the SRs to overthrow the Bolsheviks there. In February the SRs and Mensheviks secured a majority in elections to the local soviet and elected a Menshevik, A. I. Sosulin, chairman of the Executive Committee. On the first day of the new soviet, Red Guards conducted searches of the SR organization, confiscated weapons they found there, and arrested some SRs. The next day two bombs thrown by unknown persons exploded in the building of the SR organization, where the SRs and Mensheviks were meeting to discuss strategy. Two days later Sosulin was killed in an ambush on his way home; the SR S. Naslegin was wounded with him. The SR V. I. Buzanov, later a prominent figure in the overthrow of the Bolsheviks in Izhevsk, was wounded in a separate attack.[65] The Bolsheviks were able to maintain control of the situation until elections to the soviet were held again in May, but these elections ended in a massive Bolshevik defeat. Economic difficulties were not the root of the opposition victory: the Izhevsk Bolshevik party committee informed Moscow that it possessed grain, raw materials, and fuel "in abundance" but that the composition of the soviet was nevertheless "absolutely rightist."[66] The Bolsheviks walked out of the soviet and dissolved it.[67]

The sum of this evidence from around the country makes clear that the majority of Russian workers were hostile to the Bolsheviks by the spring of 1918. As the SRs and Mensheviks discovered, however, this antagonism was not easily translated into an open mass opposition movement. In part, this was because the Bolsheviks simply dissolved opposition-controlled soviets, disregarded workers' opinions, and cracked down brutally on such manifestations of discontent as strikes. But the problem posed by Bolshevik repression was compounded by the collapse of SR party organizations and by mounting political apathy among workers. In 1917 the SRs had a membership of about 700,000, but only a fraction of it remained active in the party in the spring of 1918.[68] A delegate to the Eighth Party Council of the PSR in May reported that the party organizations in the northwest were in disarray. In the Central Industrial region, another speaker observed, the organizations had been nearly destroyed, though they were later partially rebuilt. And in the Urals, of ninety SR party organizations in January 1918 only forty remained four months later.[69] A contraction in party membership in the first half of 1918 was not unique to the SRs. It afflicted the Bolsheviks and Mensheviks as well, and it testifies to the withdrawal of many people from politics in the wake of the establishment of the new regime.[70] This decline in the SRs' membership greatly complicated the task of mobilizing discontent to construct an opposition movement.

The second problem for the Socialists in their effort to build an opposition movement was the accelerating loss of interest in politics among the mass of workers who were not members of political parties. Observers of all political stripes bear witness to the apathy and disillusionment among workers generally, even in the cities where worker anti-Bolshevik sentiment was most vehement. In Petrograd, for example, newspapers at each end of the non-Bolshevik spectrum, the Social Democratic–Internationalist *Novaia zhizn'* and the Kadet *Nash vek*, took note of worker apathy, which was conceded privately by the SRs as well.[71] In Izhevsk, an SR admitted that the workers were reluctant to take any action against the Bolsheviks more decisive than protest resolutions, were increasingly apathetic, and were sick of all the political "windbags."[72] Surveying the situation around the country in May, the SR Central Committee member E. M. Timofeev concluded that apoliticism, passivity, and a desperate desire for order were overcoming all strata of the population.[73] Disgust with political violence, partisan squabbles, and civil war, and the increasing difficulty of satisfying basic needs for food, fuel, and housing—that is, the same forces that fostered worker discontent with the regime—were undoubtedly also at work in the growing disinterest in politics.

This combination of popular apathy and hostility to the Bolsheviks forms the backdrop against which the SR leadership revised the party's political strategy at the Eighth Party Council of the PSR in May. Although the main cause of this change in strategy was the SRs' understanding of the implications of the Treaty of Brest-Litovsk, the SRs would have been loath to move to a more aggressive policy had they not believed that the masses had outlived their Bolshevik "illusions." And as several delegates to the council pointed out, mass enthusiasm for Bolsheviks had cooled, but the SR effort to build a legal opposition movement seemed to be foundering on Bolshevik repression and mass inertia.[74] The new strategy approved at the Eighth Party Council abandoned the idea of a legal mass opposition that had been the keystone of the Central Committee theses of January. Unlike the Mensheviks, who stuck doggedly to their effort to build a mass opposition within the framework of the regime, the SRs shifted their focus to organizing an uprising to establish a government under the Constituent Assembly and to resume the war with the Germans.

The rethinking that culminated in the resolutions of the Eighth Party Council began shortly after the conclusion of the Treaty of Brest-Litovsk. For the SRs the treaty marked not only a capitulation to Germany but also the transformation of the Germans into the masters of the Bolsheviks, and hence into the true rulers of Russia. When Count Mirbach arrived in Moscow to open the German Embassy, the SRs, like many Russians, assumed that the Bolsheviks would be taking their orders from him. The SRs believed that the logic of German policy would compel the establishment of a reactionary Russian government to complete the country's subordination to German imperialism. This assumption found seeming corroboration in the German overthrow of the Ukrainian Rada and the establishment of a new Ukrainian government under Hetman Skoropadski at the end of April, which pushed the SRs to consider the possibility of fighting the Germans and their Bolshevik henchmen.[75]

At the end of March, representatives of the SR Central Committee participated in negotiations organized by the Party of People's Socialists aimed at forming a united political front against the Bolsheviks and Germans. This front, the People's Socialists hoped, would also include the SRs, the Kadets, the tiny Marxist group Unity, and perhaps the Mensheviks. These negotiations quickly broke down over the impossibility of bridging the gap between the SRs and the Kadets, who disagreed about the role of the Constituent Assembly as constituted on 5 (18) January. The Kadets insisted that the old Constituent Assembly could not be resurrected and that any discussion of the role of the Constituent Assembly had to center on an Assembly that would be created by new elections. This view was unacceptable to the SRs, and a *Delo naroda* editorial lashed out at the "bourgeoisie" for abandoning the Constituent Assembly.[76] Still, the willingness of the Central Committee even to participate in such negotiations, which clearly violated the spirit of the resolutions of the Fourth Party Congress of December 1917 against coalition with "bourgeois" parties, testifies to the shifting attitudes within the party leadership.

Although the Central Committee blocked the formation of a united political front with other parties, the leaders of the right wing of the party, notably N. D. Avksent'ev and A. A. Argunov, forged ahead and played a central role in the formation of the Union for the Regeneration of Russia. This became one of the most important underground anti-Bolshevik organizations in Soviet Russia in 1918. It united on a personal basis leading political figures from the center and left of the Russian political spectrum who accepted a straightforward political program: the resumption of the war with Germany in cooperation with the Allies; struggle with the Soviet government; the formation of a strong collegial directory to serve as the Russian government for the duration of the war; and the convocation of the Constituent Assembly at the end of the war to reestablish a united, democratic Russia. By structuring the organization as a personal union instead of a formal political bloc, the initiators of the Union circumvented the SR and Kadet Central Committees. The relative simplicity of the program reflected an effort to sketch a minimum platform on which right SRs and left Kadets could agree. The initial core of the Union of Regeneration consisted of the People's Socialists N. V. Chaikovskii,

V. A. Miakotin, A. A. Titov, and A. V. Peshekhonov, the Kadets N. N. Shchepkin and N. I. Astrov, and the SRs Avksent'ev, Argunov, and B. N. Moiseenko. They were joined by a number of other Socialists, Kadets, and persons not affiliated with any political party.[77]

The Union of Regeneration's goal was the formation, with Allied aid, of an eastern front against the Germans and Bolsheviks. In April, representatives of the Union began discussions of such a plan with Allied representatives in Moscow, chiefly the French Consul General Fernand Grenard. Simultaneously they began to recruit officers for eventual transfer to the eastern front, which they hoped to create.[78] Aware of the Union's plans, the SR Central Committee also began to assess the possibility of establishing an eastern front. It put out its own feelers to the Allies and, like the Union of Regeneration, began to gather officers.[79] Discussions with the Allies and recruitment of officers were not, of course, the monopoly of the Union of Regeneration and the SRs in this period: Moscow in April and May was a beehive of such activity on the part of Boris Savinkov, the Right Center, and a number of underground officers' organizations.

By the time of the Eighth Party Council of the PSR, which opened in Moscow on 7 May, the party as a whole, not just the right wing active in the Union of Regeneration, had come around to the necessity of adopting armed struggle against the Germans and Bolsheviks. The main political report to the council, written by Timofeev, declared that the Council of Peoples' Commissars, "hoping to acquire as a result of the Brest treaty breathing space to carry out its domestic political aims, in reality has transformed itself into the unconditional executor of all the demands of the conquerors. It maintains its existence only on condition of its complete subordination to the orders of Berlin and Vienna, and only for as long as this is convenient to the latter."[80] Faced with the German conquest and the Bolsheviks' destruction of the country by quasi-socialist experiments and civil war, the SRs felt obligated to make a last heroic effort to defend the achievements of the revolution. To fulfill this task, however, the SRs had to liberate Russia from the Germans and Bolsheviks, which the council made the order of the day for the party. Impressed by the scale of peasant rebellions on the Volga described by A. I. Al'tovskii, the chairman of the Volga regional SR organization, the council followed the lead of the Union of Regeneration and made the Volga the staging ground of the planned rebellion. There the SRs intended to overthrow the Bolsheviks, reconvene the Constituent Assembly, and reestablish the organs of local self-government; with Allied support they would reopen the eastern front against Germany.

The thorniest problem for the SRs as they contemplated the uprising was whether to cooperate with nonsocialist forces in the organization and leadership of the planned campaign. Avksent'ev and other leaders of the right wing of the party were eager for such cooperation, without which an effective movement seemed exceedingly unlikely. This view was anathema to the left wing of the party, which saw in it a revival of the failed policy of coalition that had been buried at the Fourth Party Congress. The resolutions of the council, which referred to the need for the cooperation of all the "creative forces" of the country, seemed to hold out the possibility of joint work with the nonsocialists. That impression is belied, however, by the SRs' conception of the organization of power in the territory to be liberated from the Bolsheviks and Germans. Power was to be entrusted not to the coalition directory envisioned by the Union of Regeneration but to the Constituent Assembly as it was constituted on 5 (18) January—minus the Bolsheviks and Left SRs. In other words, the SRs were to be in full control. In essence, these divergent plans are the germ of the disagreements that were to plague the politics of the eastern front later in 1918.

The SR leadership drew up plans for underground work to prepare the uprising, which was to center on Saratov. This work was in full swing at the end of May when, fortuitously, the rebellion of the Czechoslovak Legion overthrew the Bolsheviks in Samara. The SRs shifted their focus there and organized the Committee of Members of the Constituent Assembly, which assumed power behind the newly organized eastern front and opened a new period in the civil war for the SRs. It cannot be overstressed, however, that despite their anti-Bolshevik rhetoric, the SRs conceived both the uprising in its planning stages and the subsequent campaign on the eastern front as aimed principally at the Germans, not the Bolsheviks. The prominent SR V. Ia. Gurevich recalled in emigration that the overthrow of the Bolsheviks was not the SRs' central consideration, "since we mistakenly believed the Soviet government was doomed to a quick and inescapable death, independent of the planned uprising. The latter very many of us saw as primarily a struggle against the Brest peace, which it seemed then would lead to the economic and political enslavement of Russia to triumphant German imperialism for many years and also to a lengthy period of domestic reaction."[81]

The decision to launch armed struggle with the Bolsheviks thus represents much less of a revolution in the SRs' position than it might at first seem. The complex of attitudes underlying the decision to plan the rebellion remained fundamentally the same when the SRs refused to engage in armed struggle: both decisions were dictated chiefly by consideration of the best means of resisting counterrevolution. The dilemma posed in January 1918—how to secure the reconvocation of the Constituent Assembly without intensifying a civil war that was likely to end in the victory of reaction—continued to haunt the SRs and set limits on the possibilities of struggle with the Bolsheviks. In light of this, it should come as no surprise that when the German revolution of November 1918 removed the threat of counterrevolution implicit in the Treaty of Brest-Litovsk, the SRs promptly abandoned armed struggle with the Bolsheviks.

At the end of 1918, however, in the wake of the Red Terror and amid full-scale civil war, the SRs' effort to resume peaceful opposition work within the Soviet framework was far more problematic than it had been in the first half of the year. Indeed, in retrospect early 1918 presented a unique opportunity for the Socialists, and the successes and failures of the SRs and Mensheviks in building a mass opposition to the Bolsheviks reveal much about the shifting political and social terrain in Russia after October. The prevalence of opposition sentiment among workers virtually nationwide makes it difficult any longer to sustain the thesis that the narrowness of the opposition's social base was the cause of its failure in 1918 or, more broadly, that worker support for the Bolsheviks was a major factor in the Bolshevik victory in the civil war.[82] Moreover, the often virulent hostility displayed by many workers toward the Bolsheviks cannot be explained, as has been customary, in purely economic or social terms: that hostility also sprang from the arbitrary and violent nature of Bolshevik rule—which is to say that worker opposition had political sources as well. Although it is true, as William Rosenberg has argued, that the negligible commitment of Russian workers to Western concepts of law and political liberty posed a serious obstacle for an opposition movement in defense of the Constituent Assembly, workers nonetheless had political values of their own that pushed them into the camp of the opposition.[83] Prominent among them was a desire to escape the arbitrariness and occasional violence that had traditionally characterized worker relations with the state authorities. Even before the well-known massacre at Kolpino in May 1918, the Bolsheviks had dashed such worker hopes, and the role of violence in galvanizing worker opposition had added a new chapter to an old regime tradition whose most famous episode was Bloody Sunday in 1905.

At the same time, one should not be too sanguine about the chances of the SR-Menshevik opposition in 1918.[84] Severe institutional and organizational weaknesses hobbled the SR and Menshevik parties, even as their popularity among workers rebounded; the Socialists, like the Bolsheviks, felt acutely the sense that they sat atop a volcano they were powerless to control. This institutional weakness was largely a legacy of the old regime political tradition, which bequeathed to revolutionary Russia a weak civil society and inchoate political parties that had shallow roots in the population and were easily eradicated by the Bolsheviks in the summer of 1918. As Iulii Martov observed of the Mensheviks, the success of Bolshevik repression simply laid bare the weaknesses of the Mensheviks' own party structure.[85] Likewise, the SR organization collapsed as quickly as it had grown up in 1917, and by the fall of 1918 the party reverted to what it had been under the old regime: a congeries of urban radical groups dominated by intellectuals whose basic assumptions differed very little from those of the Bolsheviks and who therefore feared a White victory far more than the preservation of the Soviet regime. As such, of course, the party was doomed to paralysis and agonizing death in Soviet Russia.

Notes

1. Research for this chapter was supported by a grant from the International Research and Exchanges Board (IREX), with funds provided by the National Endowment for the Humanities, the U.S. Information Agency, and the U.S. Department of State, which administers the Russian, Eurasian, and East European research program (Title 8).

2. Soviet historians, by contrast, depict the PSR as committed to counterrevolution and armed struggle against the Bolsheviks; they also stress (and exaggerate) SR involvement in peasant rebellions, to the neglect of the urban SR activities on which I focus in this chapter. For an early Soviet account see Vera Vladimirova, *God sluzhby 'sotsialistov' kapitalistam* (Moscow: Gosizdat, 1927). K. S. Gusev, *Partiia eserov. Ot melkoburzhuaznogo revoliutsionarizma k kontrrevoliutsii* (Moscow: Mysl', 1975) is the most complete work of later Soviet scholarship. The standard Western accounts are Oliver Radkey, *The Sickle Under the Hammer: The Russian Socialist Revolutionaries in the Early Months of Soviet Rule* (New York: Columbia University Press, 1963), which stresses the muddle-headedness of SR leaders and the collapse of the party's peasant support, and Manfred Hildermeier, *Die Sozialrevolutionäre Partei Russlands. Agrarsozialismus und Modernisierung im Zarenreich* (Cologne: Böhlau Verlag, 1978), which argues that the SRs' neopopulist program was incompatible with the obective tasks of Russia's modernization. Several more recent Western studies have revised the traditional image of the party: Christopher Rice, *Russian Workers and the Socialist-Revolutionary Party Through the Revolution of 1905–1907* (Basingstoke: Macmillan, 1988); Anna Geifman, *Thou Shalt Kill: Revolutionary Terrorism in Russia, 1894–1917* (Princeton, N.J.: Princeton University Press, 1993); and Michael Melancon, *The Socialist-Revolutionaries and the Russian Anti-War Movement, 1914–1917* (Columbus: Ohio State University Press, 1990).

3. See V. M. Chernov, "Ideinye pozitsii P.S.-R. posle oktiabr'skogo perevorota v 'Tezisakh' 1918 g." in Marc Jansen, ed., *Partiia sotsialistov-revoliutsionerov posle oktiabr'skogo perevorota 1917 goda. Dokumenty iz arkhiva P.S.-R.* (Amsterdam: Stichting Beheer IISG, 1989), 45–53; the theses are published in the same work, 53–119.

4. "Tsentral'nyi komitet P.S.-R. Tezisy dlia partiinykh agitatorov i propagandistov. No. 1," *PSR posle oktiabr'skogo perevorota*, 55.

5. Ibid., 54.

6. Chernov, "Ideinyie pozitsii," *PSR posle oktiabr'skogo perevorota*, 50.

7. "Tsentral'nyi komitet P.S.-R. Tezisy dokladov dlia partiinykh agitatorov i propagandistov. No. 11," *PSR posle oktiabr'skogo perevorota*, 101.

8. "Na zavodakh i fabrikakh," *Novaia zhizn'* (Petrograd), 9 January 1918, 2; "Probuzhdenie proletariata," *Delo naroda* (Petrograd), 12 January 1918, 3; "Perevybory v Petrogradskii Sovet," and "Obukhovtsy protiv Smol'nogo," *Delo narodnoe* (Petrograd), 17 January 1918, 2.

9. "Perevybory v Petrogradskii sovet," *Novaia zhizn'* (Petrograd), 7 February 1918, 3.

10. "Interview with George Denike," in Leopold Haimson, ed., *The Making of Three Russian Revolutionaries: Voices from the Menshevik Past* (Cambridge: Cambridge University Press, 1987), 446–448; G. Ia. Aronson, *Dvizhenie upolnomochennykh ot rabochikh, fabrik i zavodov v 1918 godu* (New York: Inter-University Project on the History of the Menshevik Movement, 1960), 5–6.

11. "Bespartiinaia rabochaia konferentsiia," *Novaia zhizn'* (Petrograd), 20 March 1918, 3; G. Baturskii, "Sredi rabochikh," *Delo* 3–9 (1918): 14–15.

12. "Interview with George Denike," in Haimson, *Making of Three Russian Revolutionaries*, 445, 448.

13. RTsKhIDNI, f. 17, op. 4, d. 26, l. 6.

14. Ibid., l. 8.

15. Ibid., d. 82, l. 1.

16. *Golos naroda* (Tula), 16 January 1918, 2–3; in subsequent issues appear many calls by local workers for new soviet elections, the resignation of the Council of Peoples' Commissars, and the transfer of all power to the Constituent Assembly.

17. RTsKhIDNI, f. 17, op. 4, d. 82, l. 1; *Novyi narodnyi golos* (Tula), 10 March 1918, 2.

18. On this see the groundbreaking work of Vladimir Brovkin, *The Mensheviks After October: Socialist Opposition and the Rise of the Bolshevik Dictatorship* (Ithaca: Cornell University Press, 1987), to which my analysis is much indebted; see also William Rosenberg, "Russian Labor and Bolshevik Power After October," *Slavic Review* 44 (1985): 213–238.

19. RTsKhIDNI, f. 17, op. 4, d. 48, l. 1; RTsKhIDNI, f. 17, op. 4, d. 73, l. 14b; "Perevybory v Sovet. Tver'," *Vpered* (Moscow), 25 April 1918, 4; "Tver'," *Znamia truda* (Moscow), 23 April 1918, 4. No reliable information is available for Vladimir and Smolensk. In Kostroma, elections held in April returned thirty-one Bolsheviks, thirty-one nonparty delegates, twenty-one Mensheviks, eight Left SRs, and five SRs (GARF, f. 393, op. 3, d. 1, l. 241). These figures are impossible to interpret, because the views of the nonparty delegates cannot be established; in other cities, however, nonparty delegates generally sided with the opposition.

20. "V provintsii," *Dela naroda* (Petrograd), 31 January 1918, 3.

21. "Yaroslavskii proletariat na skam'e podsudimykh," *Vpered* (Moscow), 24 April 1918, 2. For more detail on the political background to the elections see Brovkin, *Mensheviks*, 138–141.

22. GARF, f. 393, op. 3, d. 473, l. 65.

23. "Tsentral'naia oblast'. Yaroslavskii proletariat na skam'e podsudimykh," *Vpered* (Moscow), 23 April 1918, 4; "Yaroslavskii proletariat na skam'e podsudimykh," *Vpered* (Moscow), 24 April 1918, 2; "Poslednie razgromy, razgony, rasstrely," *Novaia zaria* 1 (1918): 38–40.

24. Brovkin, *Mensheviks*, 141.

25. *Delo* (Petrograd), 23 January 1918, 2.

26. RTsKhIDNI, f. 564, op. 1, d. 1, l. 108.

27. GARF, f. 393, op. 3, d. 160, l. 36.

28. Brovkin, *Mensheviks*, p. 131.

29. GARF, f. 130, op. 2, d. 625, l. 5; Brovkin, *Mensheviks*, 134.

30. Ibid., f. 393, op. 3, d. 217, l. 119; "Po Rossii. V Riazani," *Novaia zhizn'* (Petrograd), 26 April 1918, 4.

31. "Poslednie razgromy, razgony, rasstrely," *Novaia zaria* 1 (1918): 40; Brovkin, *Mensheviks*, 143–144.

32. GARF, f. 130, op. 2, d. 622, l. 2.

33. "G. Voronezh. Sovetskaia vlast'," *Novaia zaria* 5–6 (1918): 63–65.

34. "Rabochaia sektsiia Orlovskogo soveta r. i s. d.," *Delo sotsial-demokrata* (Orel), 16 January 1918, 4.

35. GARF, f. 1235, op. 93, d. 242, l. 1.

36. Brovkin, *Mensheviks*, 142–143.

37. RTsKhIDNI, f. 71, op. 33, d. 463, ll. 20–21; "Otkhod ot bol'shevizma," *Delo sotsial-demokrata* (Orel), 14 January 1918, 1; *Golos naroda* (Tula), 14 January 1918, 4; "Rabochie protiv Smol'nogo," *Delo narodov* (Petrograd), 18 January 1918, 1.

38. RTsKhIDNI, f. 71, op. 33, d. 463, l. 21.

39. "G. Briansk, Orlovskaia gub.," *Novaia zaria* 3–4 (1918): 44.

40. GARF, f. 1235, op. 93, d. 242, l. 2.

41. Ibid., f. 393, op. 3, d. 378, l. 40; *Bor'ba rabochikh i krest'ian pod rukovodstvom bol'shevistskoi partii za ustanovlenie i uprochenie sovetskoi vlasti v Tambovskoi gubernii (1917–1918 gg.). Sbornik dokumentov* (Tambov: Partiinyi arkhiv Obkoma KPSS, 1957), 99; "Tambovskaia gub. Sovetskaia epopeia," *Novaia zaria* 1 (1918): 51.

42. GARF, f. 130, op. 2, d. 581, l. 8; "Tambovskaia gub. Sovetskaia epopeia," *Novaia zaria* 1 (1918): 54.

43. Ibid., f. 393, op. 3, d. 377, l. 151.

44. Ibid., f. 393, op. 3, d. 378, l. 134.

45. See A. P. Nenarokov, *Vostochnyi front 1918* (Moscow: Nauka, 1969), 38–44.

46. For more on this region see Brovkin, *Mensheviks*, 147–155.

47. RTsKhIDNI, f. 17, op. 4, d. 64, l. 1.

48. Ibid., f. 564, op. 1, d. 1, l. 128.

49. Brovkin, *Mensheviks*, 150.

50. GARF, f. 5881, op. 2, d. 403, ll. 9–10.

51. V. I. Vyrypaev, "V. O. Kappel'. Vospominaniia uchastnika belogo dvizheniia," 2; S. A. Elachich, "Obryvki vospominanii," 11–12. Both manuscripts are in the Hoover Institution Archives, Stanford University.

52. S. Gruzdev, "Bol'shevistskoe podpol'e v Samare v dni uchredilovshchiny," *Proletarskaia revoliutsiia* 12/35 (1924): 178; Ia. Andreev, "Rabochie i Komitet chlenov U.S.," *Chetyre mesiatsa uchredilovshchiny. Istoriko-literaturnyi sbornik* (Samara, 1919), 42–43.

53. On the conflict between the Samara Bolsheviks and the local garrison see the sketchy reports in F. G. Popov, ed., *1918 v Samarskoi gubernii. Khronika sobytii* (Kuibyshev: Kuibyshevskoe Knizhnoe Izdatel'stvo, 1972), 44–45, 54–55, 61.

54. *Zhizn'* (Nizhnii Novgorod), 9 January 1918, 3; *Narod* (Nizhnii Novgorod), 13 January 1918, 3; "V zashchitu U.S.," *Novyi luch* (Petrograd), 20 January 1918, 3.

55. RTsKhIDNI, f. 275, op. 1, d. 120, l. 1; *Zhizn'* (Nizhnii Novgorod), 21 January 1918, 1.

56. *Svobodnaia zhizn'* (Nizhnii Novgorod), 19 February 1918, 4, and 20 February 1918, 3.

57. RTsKhIDNI, f. 60, op. 1, d. 53, l. 65.

58. "Provintsial'naia khronika," *Delo naroda* (Petrograd), 16 April 1918, 4; "Perevybory Soveta R. D. Sormovo. Nizh. gub.," *Vpered* (Moscow), 16 April 1918, 4.

59. RTsKhIDNI, f. 17, op. 4, d. 50, l. 21.

60. Ibid., d. 51, l. 12.

61. GARF, f. 130, op. 2, d. 642, l. 1; "Doklad o rabochikh volneniiakh v Sormove," *Novaia zhizn'* (Petrograd), 24 May 1918, 3.

62. "Po Rossii. Ekaterinburg," *Znamia truda* (Moscow), 16 April 1918, 4; Brovkin, *Mensheviks*, 154.

63. RTsKhIDNI, f. 564, op. 1, d. 1, l. 81.

64. "Po Rossii. Sobytiia v Zlatouste," *Nash vek* (Petrograd), 7 April 1918, 4; "K razgonu Sovetov," *Zaria* (Tomsk), 24 April 1918, 1.

65. RTsKhIDNI, f. 274, op. 1, d. 5, l. 41; M. S. Bernshtam, ed., *Ural i Prikam'e. Noiabr' 1917-ianvar' 1919. Dokumenty i materialy* (Paris: YMCA Press, 1982), 280; "Iz-za ugla," *Delo naroda* (Petrograd), 28 March 1918, 1.

66. RTsKhIDNI, f. 17, op. 4, d. 35, l. 35; GARF, f. 130, op. 2, d. 606, l. 1.

67. RTsKhIDNI, f. 17, op. 4, d. 35, l. 36; Brovkin, *Mensheviks*, 154; Bernshtam, *Ural i Prikam'e*, 280.

68. For SR membership in 1917 see Kh. M. Astrakhan, *Bol'sheviki i ikh politicheskie protivniki v 1917 godu. Iz istorii politicheskikh partii mezhdu dvumia revoliutsiiami* (Leningrad: Lenizdat, 1973), 233.

69. RTsKhIDNI, f. 274, op. 1, d. 5, ll. 36, 64, 66.

70. On the Bolsheviks' membership see L. M. Spirin, *Klassy i partii v grazhdanskoi voine v Rossii (1917–1920 gg.)* (Moscow: Mysl', 1968), 124–125; on the Mensheviks see Brovkin, *Mensheviks*, 201.

71. "Rabochaia zhizn'," *Novaia zhizn'* (Petrograd), 16 February 1918, 3; "Sredi rabochikh," *Nash vek* (Petrograd), 16 April 1918, 3; RTsKhIDNI, f. 274, op. 1, d. 5., l. 66. Rosenberg, in "Russian Labor," also stresses worker disillusionment with party politics.

72. RTsKhIDNI, f. 274, op. 1, d. 5, l. 44.

73. Ibid., l. 6.

74. Ibid., ll. 41, 66.

75. A. R. Gots, "Mezhdunarodnaia politika," *Delo naroda* (Petrograd), 23 April 1918, 1; V. V. Sukhomlin, "Politicheskie zametki," *Volia Rossii* 10–11 (1928): 163.

76. *Delo naroda* (Petrograd), 5 April 1918, 1; *Krasnaia kniga VeCheK*, 2nd ed. (Moscow: Politizdat, 1989), 2: 79–80; V. A. Miakotin, "Iz nedalekogo proshlogo," *Na chuzhoi storone* 2 (1923): 180; A. A. Argunov, *Mezhdu dvumia bol'shevizmami* (Paris: Union, 1919), 3–4.

77. Miakotin, "Iz nedalekogo proshlogo," 180–181; Argunov, *Mezhdu dvumia bol'shevizmami*, 4–6.

78. Miakotin, "Iz nedalekogo proshlogo," 188–192; Argunov, *Mezhdu dvumia bol'shevizmami*, 5–7.

79. GARF, f. 1005, op. 1A, d. 1341, ll. 74–75; GARF, f. 1005, op. 1A, d. 1342, ll. 26–29; V. M. Zenzinov, "Bor'ba Rossiiskoi demokratii s bol'shevikami v 1918 godu. Moskva—Samara—Ufa—Omsk," Hoover Institution Archives, Nicolaevsky Collection, box 8, folder, 24, 26–29.

80. RTsKhIDNI, f. 274, op. 1, d. 1, l. 6.

81. GARF, f. 5910, op. 1, d. 441, l. 13.

82. Rosenberg stresses the narrowness of the opposition's social base in "Russian Labor"; for a broader claim for the importance of worker support in the Bolshevik victory, see Leopold Haimson, "Civil War and the Problem of Social Identities in Early Twentieth-Century Russia," in Diane Koenker, William Rosenberg, and Ronald Suny, eds., *Party, State, and Society in the Russian Civil War: Explorations in Social History* (Bloomington: Indiana University Press, 1989), 36. Sheila Fitzpatrick also attaches importance to worker support for the Bolsheviks, though she argues that it was peasant support that tipped the balance in favor of the Bolsheviks during the civil war: see Fitzpatrick, *The Russian Revolution, 1917–1932* (Oxford: Oxford University Press, 1982), 70. Western local studies have generally argued that most workers continued to support the new regime and that the sources of opposition were economic, not political: for Petrograd see David Mandel, *The Petrograd Workers and the Soviet Seizure of Power: From the July Days 1917 to July 1918* (London: Macmillan, 1984), 390–413; S. A. Smith, *Red Petrograd: Revolution in the Factories, 1917–1918* (Cambridge: Cambridge University Press, 1983), 246; Alexander Rabinowitch, "The Evolution of Local Soviets in Petrograd, November 1917–June 1918: The Case of the First City District," *Slavic Review* 46 (1987): 35–37; and Mary McAuley, *Bread and Justice: State and Soci-*

ety in Petrograd, 1917–1922 (Oxford: Oxford University Press, 1991), 107. For the Volga Towns see Orlando Figes, *Peasant Russia, Civil War: The Volga Countryside in Revolution (1917–1921)* (Oxford: Oxford University Press, 1989), 159–162.

83. See William Rosenberg, "Reply," *Slavic Review* 44 (1985): 254–256.

84. Brovkin's assessment of the state of the Menshevik party structure, and hence his view of the organizational strength of the opposition, contrasts with my sense of the moribund state of SR organizations in the summer of 1918. In view of the SRs' accounts of provincial politics and the Mensheviks' own membership figures, I doubt whether the Menshevik organizations were more than marginally better off than the SR organizations. See Brovkin, *Mensheviks*, 201.

85. Cited by Frederick Corney in *Russian Review* 52 (1993): 115.

LEONID HERETZ

The Psychology of the White Movement 5

T he fall of the Romanov dynasty and the failure of the Provisional Government cleared the way for two grand utopian experiments: Bolshevism and the peasant revolution. The Bolsheviks made a vehement effort at destroying the old world of inequality and imperfection and building a new, perfect order according to the precepts of Marx and Lenin. At the same time, the Russian peasantry set about the long-relished task of purging the land of the alien and parasitical ruling class and culture that had stifled and oppressed it since the time of Peter. The prime target and chief victim of these concurrent and interrelated experiments was Russian educated society as a whole and its culture in the broadest sense.[1] In the months following the Bolshevik seizure of power the defining categories of the civilization of the Petrine Empire were dissolved by the force of anarchy and violence. The vortex of revolutionary events reduced Russian educated society to a state of confusion and desperation. Against this backdrop of helplessness and hopelessness the White movement emerged as an active minority within the old Russian elite.

The contrast between the activism of the Whites and the passivity of the educated society of which they were a product poses a fundamental analytical problem—namely, the identification of those factors that set the Whites apart from their broader cultural milieu. In this study I attempt to determine the psychological processes that gave rise to the White movement by analyzing the formative experience of the premier White force, the Volunteer Army.[2] I hope that this work will help to fill a major gap in the historiography, which has devoted insufficient attention to the White struggle in general and to its psychological and cultural aspects in particular. I present not a discussion of military operations or politics, which have been the focus of most scholarly work on the Whites,[3] but rather an examination of the perceptions and ways of thinking that characterized the White mentality.

105

Within the broad and rather elusive topic of portraying and analyzing the mentality of the Volunteer Army I give special attention to the following basic issues: the White understanding of the Russian and world situation at the outset of the struggle; the identification of the enemy; the impulses that motivated the Volunteers; the formation of Volunteer identity and the development of group cohesion; and the ways that the first campaign served to intensify the psychological processes at work in the initial phase of the organization of the Volunteer Army. It will be argued that the Volunteers viewed their struggle in religious—absolute—terms. For them the condition of Russia in the aftermath of the Bolshevik seizure of power was one of chaos and triumph of evil in the ultimate, apocalyptic sense, involving the complete degradation and defilement of everything of value. The Whites were spurred to action by an intense sense of duty and devotion to Russia; given the apparent hopelessness of the situation, acting on this impulse required a willingness and desire for martyrdom or self-sacrifice. Their first campaign was not a practical military operation but a statement of principle, and in the course of this formative experience the Volunteers developed an exalted conception of their own group identity and mission that would continue to motivate through the rest the civil war.[4]

The Call to Arms and the Initial Response

The White movement eventually grew into a large and disjointed agglomeration of forces operating on several fronts in diverse local circumstances. The core of the movement, however, the White army par excellence, remained the Volunteer Army, the anti-Bolshevik formation called into being by Generals Lavr Kornilov and Mikhail Alekseev in the chaotic months following the Bolshevik coup. The Volunteer Army initiated the White struggle and served as both the engine and cutting edge of the movement until the end. It is specifically the first phase of the Volunteer Army—from the call-to-arms through the crucible of the Ice March on the Kuban'—that offers us the greatest insights into the process of selection which produced the core of the White movement.[5] Moreover, this initial experience had a decisive formative impact on the nature and mentality of the Volunteer Army. The attitudes, personal ties, and style forged at that time would continue to play the crucial role even as the movement grew in size and diversity during the civil war.

In the immediate aftermath of the Bolshevik seizure of power, and in the midst of the chaotic disintegration of the old Russian order, a small group of the most implacably anti-German and anti-Bolshevik members of the Russian army command sent out the call to arms that would result in the formation of the Volunteer Army. This declaration, made public at the end of 1917, appealed for a spontaneous, general levy in the style of Minin and Pozharskii to counter the advance of anarchy and the German/ Bolshevik onslaught. In the heterogeneous style that would be character- istic of all subsequent White propaganda, it contained evocations of the mythic Russian past as well as the democratic agenda of the present, call- ing for the defense of defiled sanctuaries and the Constituent Assembly. Essentially, the appeal was an emotional one, ending with a call to "all those who love the long-suffering Motherland, and whose soul aches with filial compassion for her, to join the Russian host."[6] Although the decla- ration was ostensibly addressed to the whole nation, it was obviously directed at Russian educated society. It is striking testimony to the demoralization of this class that the appeal, as well as subsequent orga- nizational efforts, found resonance among a tiny minority. As Denikin wrote, "Officers, cadets, academic youth and very, very few others re- sponded. The levy of the whole people did not work."[7] Even within these limited subgroups a negligible proportion volunteered. Most shared in the general mood of the Russian cultured class, which Slashchev, an early Volunteer who later gained notoriety as White dictator of the Crimea and then as a defector to the soviets, noted that "the intelligentsia as a whole was completely befuddled. It could not comprehend what was occurring and belonged to the party of 'I. I.' (*ispugannyi* [frightened] intelligent)."[8]

The initial Volunteer Army was, therefore, extremely selective—even though this policy went against the stated hopes of its organizers. Joining required an act of will that set one apart from the overwhelming majority of one's social class, not to mention the peasant mass of the Russian pop- ulation. The following account of recruitment efforts in Rostov gives a good sense of the resistance that the Volunteers faced:

> Although in its mass the academic youth in the middle schools yearned to fight against Bolshevism, it was still under the strong influence of family, society and school. . . . Officers came to the commercial middle school . . . and explained their mission to the director—to call on the youth to defend the Motherland, the Don, Rostov, the family and the Church. . . .The direc- tor hesitated and summoned the inspector and the priest. The priest, with- out giving the matter much thought, firmly declared, "You would call on the youth to commit murder?" and demanded that the officers give up on their idea. The director supported the priest with another argument: "If the older students leave, who will the school be left with?" The inspector remained silent.

Although the organizers were eventually allowed to speak to the students and engage in other recruitment activities, their efforts yielded only a few more than two hundred volunteers out of the thousands of students then in Rostov.[9] The reluctance of the students' guardians typifies the attitude of educated society as a whole. In the face of the open and freely declared hostility and promises of annihilation directed at it by the Bolsheviks, the old elite hesitated to take the risk of active resistance to the new regime. Moreover, this passivity was characteristic not only of civilians, of whom it might be expected, but also of military men, who had endured the dangers of the Great War. Here is a description of Rostov in early 1918, when several hundred Volunteers made up the entire defense of that city: "Thousands of officers from regiments which had deserted from the front wandered about the city. They looked on with equanimity as some eccentric types in officers' uniforms and rifles on their shoulders carried out garrison duty and remained in a constant state of complete combat readiness. At this time, the situation was very precarious on the outskirts of the city, and Red detachments were approaching the city itself."[10] Passivity and the hope that the threat will somehow pass by itself might well be a natural response to extreme danger. This raises the question of identifying the factors that set the Volunteers apart from their cohorts and led them to make the choice of armed resistance.

The Life Experience and Motivations of the Volunteers

The first Volunteers shared the common experience of Russian educated society—the malaise born of the intense and unresolvable prerevolutionary conflict between the autocracy and the opposition in its variants; the exultation at the outbreak of the Great War, followed by the demoralization caused by the strains of the protracted war effort and the resultant morbid turn of the internal Russian political struggle; the sudden collapse of the centuries-old governmental order and the fleeting period of euphoria that followed; the unraveling of the social and political fabric during 1917 and the ultimate trauma of the Bolshevik seizure of power, with all the attendant catastrophes of class and cultural warfare, social revolution and the shameful end of Russia's participation in the war. In the case of the majority of Whites who were military men, this experience was greatly intensified by direct involvement in the war effort, which had been the crux of all of these developments and aggravated by the much more violent form that social conflict took in the army and navy. The academic youth contingent of the Whites was wholly a product of the war years in terms of formative experience. In sum, this was a pool of people who had expended the most extreme effort in a cause that ended in disaster. This disaster brought with it the collapse of the foundations and basic categories of their lives and subjected them to degradation and brutalization as individuals and as members of a social-cultural class. Although this series of developments is well known to anyone familiar with Russian history, it must be reviewed in stark form in order to provide the context for the emergence of the Volunteer Army.

The force that prevented the Volunteers from succumbing to the passivity and resignation which characterized educated society during the Revolution was an exalted sense of duty, whether in the military variant of loyalty to Russia and the brotherhood of arms or, in the case of the academic youth, devotion to Russia as a cultural ideal. Given the dire circumstances of the time, acting on this sense of duty and obligation required that one be willing to give one's life for the cause, and, as shall be discussed at greater length below, it was specifically the Russian officer and student subcultures that had the most developed cults of self-sacrifice. The urge to action was stimulated by feelings of shame, both collective and personal. L. V. Polovtsov, an organizer of the Army, described the military men among the first volunteers as "the best of the officers . . ., whose dignity had been so deeply offended . . . , who had suffered the trampling of Russian military honor, and who with all their heart yearned to wash away the badge of disgrace from the motherland with their blood."[11] Of the civilians, primarily students, Polovtsov wrote: "The same feeling of love for the motherland drew them to the army. . . . They were ruined, torn away from their families. Many had passed through the hands of the terrible Bolshevik Cheka. Some had been completely ruined and seen their beloved family estates burned down, others had seen their fathers or brothers tortured to death, and all had been robbed down to their last possession. They had seen Orthodox sanctuaries turned into movie houses. They knew, from Bolshevik newspapers, that their mothers, wives, and sisters had been socialized—that is, given over to Chinese and Latvians [Red Guards] for complete defilement."[12] These passages, written in the dramatic style typical of most White literary production, convey the fusion of patriotism, duty, grievance, shame, and the urge for self-sacrifice that motivated the Volunteers.

Perceptions of the Condition of Russia and the World

The Whites' understanding of the context of their struggle was marked by a similar complexity. At root, the Whites saw themselves as fighting the *stikhiia*, the elemental destructive force of nature that had been unleashed by the war and the Revolution and was now eradicating civilization and order. The determining component in the psychological atmosphere on the eve of the formation of the Volunteer Army was chaos in the strongest, metaphysical sense of the word, what one White officer writing in 1918 referred to as the "unprecedented, almost inconceivable, frankly 'supernatural' collapse in which the former 'Russian state' now finds itself."[13]

The Whites believed that, at a minimum, Russia had entered into a new time of trouble, a period of anarchy in which the evil and base instincts of mankind were given free reign. However, conditions were such that even the Russian historical archetype for national disaster could not convey the extent of the breakdown. The events of the day evoked in some the notion that the world was coming to an end. Among the Russian intelligentsia, the apocalyptic forebodings that had permeated conservative high culture in the past took on a greatly expanded relevance and currency. The months following the Bolshevik seizure of power saw a flourishing of the whole gamut of Russian apocalyptic thinking, from the belief that Russia was finished and the deity of European culture was a sham, to the explicit application of eschatological prophecy to the current state of Russia and the world. The Whites also manifested this tendency, and their accounts of the period are replete with apocalyptic imagery.

The following passages illustrate how the early Volunteers felt the apocalyptic spirit of the times. In *The Red Horse*, one of his series of memoirs and autobiographical novels on the civil war, Roman Gul', a participant in the Ice March, tells of what he, as a student who had volunteered for service in the Great War, felt when the Russian war effort collapsed: "And now everything, having turned upside down, will sink to the bottom. But the most terrifying thing is that not even the bottom can be seen, that everything will drown in a murky, bloody abyss."[14]

In his novel *Evening Sacrifices*, a mythic, explicitly apocalyptic depiction of the Kornilov campaign, Ivan Rodionov describes the emotional state of his youthful White martyr in the aftermath of the Bolshevik coup: "The soul-sickness became unbearable. . . . Iurochka felt that something formless, bloody, nightmarish and horrible was moving in on him from all sides and beginning to crush him like a heavy press. . . . And there was nowhere to escape from that formless and terrible force, nowhere to hide, no salvation."[15] This sense of disaster and utter hopelessness is of crucial importance for understanding the dynamic of the White struggle, for it shows that the first Volunteers were not motivated by rational calculations for success. Rather, their actions took place on a moral and emotional plane and represented a protest against the forces that had destroyed their world.

It was in this context that the personality of Kornilov came to play the crucial role. Although a number of well-known and capable officers and political figures were involved in the organization of the Volunteer Army, it was Kornilov, with his reputation for decisiveness and legendary courage, who served as the magnet and inspiration for the people who were drawn to its ranks. In the eyes of the Volunteers, it was he alone who knew what had to be done; others were confused and disoriented. Given the disruption of social structures and familial ties, as well as the youth of the majority of the Volunteers, Kornilov filled the place of the father, the affirmation of the principles of authority and order in the midst of chaos.

Identification of the Enemy

Although the Whites were unanimous in their perception that Russia had been reduced to chaos, their identification of the culprits was marked by deep and fateful contradictions and ambiguities. At the outset, and in a continuation of the Great War mode of thinking, the Whites focused on the Germans as the cause of all the trouble. In January 1918, Kornilov stated his conception of the struggle: "Germany is the sworn [mortal] enemy of Russia and all Slavdom. Either complete victory over Germany, or the doom of Russia. There is no other choice."[16] Thus, the chief organizer of the Volunteers viewed his work as a continuation of the war with Germany, assigning the Bolsheviks the lesser dignity of being merely agents or pawns. As Kornilov's political program put it: "Russia has fallen into the hands of political adventurers who, under the flag of social revolution, are doing the Great-German work of destroying the military might of the country. Playing . . . on the base instincts of the ignorant popular masses . . . and on the moral and physical weariness of the broad layers of Russian society caused by the difficult four-year war, the so-called Council of People's Commissars has set up a despotic dictatorship of the rabble [chern'] which is bringing ruin to all the cultural-historical achievements of the country."[17] Kornilov's summation of the developments of the recent past reflects the thinking of his followers at the time. Primacy is given to the German factor, and in that sense the Volunteers, products of the Great War, were continuing the struggle which had defined their lives.

With its fundamental idea of an epochal conflict between Germandom and the Russians/Slavs, Kornilov's thinking is an example of the (racialist) nationalism coming to the fore in Russia and throughout Europe as a result of the Great War. Among many of his followers, this tendency was much more pronounced. One participant in the Ice March prefaced his account of the campaign with an exegesis on Revelation, identifying Wilhelm as the Beast of the Apocalypse and placing the Volunteers' fight against him and "the demons of Bolshevism" in the context of eschatology.[18] Moreover, the slogan of this work—"May Russia rise from the dead and may her enemies be scattered"[19]—is an striking expression of how nationalism had assumed the functions of religion for many Whites.

Thus, the initial focus was on the Germans as the archenemy. However, as the full elemental force of the Revolution became apparent, and as the early Volunteers came into conflict not with the distant Germans but with the Red Guards and other hostile forces close at hand, attention shifted to the Bolsheviks themselves, and especially to their relationship with the people. The two poles of the White view of the Bolsheviks can be stated as follows: 1) the Bolsheviks were a chance assortment of scoundrels and psychopaths brought to the fore by the elemental power of the Revolution, like scum and debris at the crest of a wave; 2) the Bolsheviks were the embodiment or at the very least plenipotentiary agents of the cosmic force of evil, who had called forth and mastered the stikhiia. Thus, "Soviet power" could be seen as either contemptible charlatanry, laughable but for its monstrous criminality, or as the vanguard of a universal, metaphysical assault on Good.

This polarity did not reflect a factional divergence of opinion—rather, it was the core internal conflict within the psychology of the White movement as a whole and within the minds of individual Whites. The well-known conservative journalist V. V. Shul'gin, who took part in the Kornilov campaign, conveys the essence of this polarity and the coexistence and the interaction of its elements in the following extract of the White view of the Bolsheviks: "They have destroyed and devastated the country. . . . People perish by the millions because they continue their cursed, demonic socialist experiments, their Satanic Vivisection of the unfortunate Russian body."[20]

The Whites' perception of the Russian people was marked by a similar and related polarity. Although there was unanimity in the White camp that the people as a whole were behaving in a beastly fashion, the explanations for this beastliness varied along two lines: 1) exhausted by the exertion of the Great War and disoriented by the fall of the tsardom, the essentially decent, God-fearing, patriarchal Russian peasantry accepted the elixir offered by the revolutionaries and now found itself in a temporary state of psychosis or intoxication; 2) the breakdown of authority and the absence of the knout allowed the base and savage Russian people to show their true nature and act on the instinct to smash anything and anyone noble, refined, and good. Although the Volunteers would attempt to differentiate between the "good" peasants, who could be brought back to their senses, and the depraved types, who constituted the vicious and destructive "rabble," they would always view the people as a potentially dangerous group requiring strict control that they, as the embodiment of the principles of Russian patriotism and statehood, were obliged to provide.

The Ice March as a Symbolic Act

It was in this complex and contradictory psychological state that the first Volunteers set out through the Kuban' steppe on the bloody peregrination that came to be called the Ice March, the decisive formative experience of the movement. The Ice March shows most starkly the essence of the White cause—implacable struggle in the face of overwhelming odds for the sake of principle. Indeed, the campaign was forced on the army. The Don Cossack region, which the organizers of the Volunteer Army had, in their first appeal, described as the "last bastion of Russian independence and the last hope for restoring a Free and Great Russia"[21] and on which they made whatever minimal plans they could, was overtaken by the Bolshevik revolution in early 1918. The Volunteers left Rostov without concrete strategy or hope. Denikin described the situation as follows: "We left. Madness followed in our footsteps. It forced its way into the cities we left behind with shameless abandon, hatred, robbery and murder. . . . We began the campaign in extraordinary circumstances: a handful of people, lost in the wide steppe of the Don, amidst the raging sea which had engulfed our native land. . . . We walked out of the dark night and spiritual bondage and wandered into the unknown—Searching for the blue bird."[22]

The extremity of the situation provided the impetus for the movement: the Volunteers refused to accept what they understood to be the death of their country and submit to what they saw as the force of evil. General Alekseev expressed the symbolic nature of the undertaking in a statement he made as the army prepared to leave Rostov: "We are leaving for the steppes. Perhaps we shall return, if God in His mercy allows. But we must light a beacon, so that there be at least one point of light in the midst of the darkness which has engulfed Russia."[23]

These passages convey the Volunteers' sense of the exalted nature of their own mission. The Ice March was not a tactical maneuver toward a tangible goal of success. Rather, it was conceived as a statement of the principles of honor and duty in a world in which baseness and criminality triumphed.

Self-Sacrifice for the Sake of an Idealized Russia

The main components of the Volunteer Army (the military men and the students) brought two highly developed and intense cults of self-sacrifice to the movement. In the case of the professional officers, this was a continuation, albeit in extreme form, of the glorification of death in battle that had animated the old officer corps. The students represent a more complicated phenomenon. The impulse toward self-sacrifice prevalent among the academic youth had, in previous generations, expressed itself in such revolutionary movements as the People's Will and Socialist Revolutionary terrorism, which represented a refusal to accept the injustice and imperfection of the world as it existed, specifically in the concrete circumstances of Imperial Russia. With the multiple traumas of the World War and the Revolution, and with the Bolshevik trampling of the ideals of the Liberation Movement, the way was cleared for academic youth to shift to a nationalist ideal. There was in fact a degree of direct personal continuity between the Volunteer Army and previous manifestations of youthful idealism: most of the junior officers who joined Kornilov's shock troop in 1917 and then regrouped with their leader in Rostov were republicans or sympathizers of the Socialist Revolutionary party,[24] and one participant had spent twelve years in Siberian exile for his activities as a student revolutionary in 1905.[25]

The students and junior officers gave the White movement an unmistakable cast of youthful rapture. The idealized Russia of White youth (and of the movement as a whole) shimmered like a mirage beyond time or place. Ivan Shmelev, who wrote a series of psychologically insightful stories and novels on the early Volunteers, stated this in the tone customary for White discussions of the Ice Campaign and its participants: "The Russian Volunteers, like the 'poor knight,' had 'one vision, incomprehensible to the mind'—Her, Russia, and everything fused with Her, embodied in Her, personified by Her, and 'faithful to the sweet dream, filled with pure love,' they traced her sacred name on their shield with their blood."[26] Prerevolutionary Russia did not serve as this ideal, although it was infinitely preferable to the Bolshevik order. As the anthem of the Kornilov regiment put it, "We have no regret for the past. The Tsar is not our idol."[27] Instead, the Russia for which the White youth fought existed as a sort of city of Kitezh, a lost and hidden ideal of purity that could be reached only by passage through the crucible of combat and by victory over the mighty Bolsheviks.

Success was not seen as an immediate and realistic possibility; rather, the exalted beauty of the ideal and the utter monstrosity of Bolshevism made self-sacrifice a moral imperative, and the greater the hopelessness, the greater the significance of the act. Here is a characteristic expression of how White youth understood the matter: at Easter, the words of the Paschal canon "Christ is risen from the dead, having trampled death by death" reached two mortally wounded Volunteers in their hospital beds. One said to the other, "'It won't be anything terrible if the two of us don't survive. . . . We also trampled death. . . . Because the Bolsheviks are death itself, and even more terrible than death. . . . Death destroys the body, but they are killing not only Russia's body, but also her soul.'"[28] The suffering of the Volunteers was associated with the archetype for sacrifice, and the salvation of Russia was declared the ultimate purpose.

The Cycle of Atrocity

The Whites' sense of the magnitude of their own self-denial as well as their perception of the evil nature of Bolshevism were enhanced by the cruel form that the conflict took from the outset. The Ice March set the pattern of atrocity that would characterize the Russian civil war. The innumerable acts of cruelty and inhumanity committed in the course of that conflict are usually explained within the context of civil war in general, the argument being that struggles within a country or people naturally arouse more intense hatreds than do international wars, and that this qualitatively greater vehemence expresses itself in atrocity. The psychological mechanisms by which internal conflicts inevitably become vicious are never really explained in the literature (and this despite contradictory evidence, the American Civil War immediately coming to mind). This phenomenon makes more sense if viewed within the framework of the apocalyptic currents that permeated the psychological atmosphere of Russia during the Revolution. Both sides viewed the conflict in terms of cosmic significance. For the Bolsheviks this was the beginning of the "final and decisive battle" for the eternal happiness of mankind, while the Whites saw themselves as engaged in a desperate defense of what little good remained in a world overwhelmed by chaos and evil.

It would seem reasonable to assign the Bolsheviks the role of initiators of the cycle of atrocity. Although systematic, state-sponsored violence did not begin until somewhat later—with the institution of the so-called Red Terror—peasant and soldier rebellion, with its hoary tradition of crude, unsanitized brutality, provided the actual physical force for the initial phase of Bolshevization. More important, the chief agents of anarchy and violence in this period were largely deserters from the front, men who had been loosed from traditional moral constraints and had developed an intense hatred for the officer class in the course of the world war. Attacks on the early Volunteers can be seen as direct outgrowths of the mutinies that accompanied the collapse of the Russian army in 1917. In fact, the specific forms of torture that the Red Guards inflicted on captured Whites were usually the same as those which officers had suffered at the hands of their rebellious men. These acts of cruelty centered on the insignia that identified the officer and set him apart from the soldiers. Here is a typical listing: "They [the Reds] carved epaulets out of [captured

White officers'] shoulders, instead of stars they pounded in nails, they branded the cocarde on the forehead, they tore strips of skin off the legs in the form of sidestripes. There were instances when even gravely wounded officers were slowly roasted over bonfires."[29] Knowledge of Bolshevik atrocities intensified the Whites' sense of purpose. The heightened savagery of the conflict made the defining act of courage required to join the movement seem all the more heroic; at the same time, it fostered an intense feeling of group cohesion and mutual responsibility as the Volunteers strove to keep their members from falling into the hands of the Reds. The Volunteers, for their part, gave no quarter to the Bolsheviks. Here is how one participant described the underlying principle:

> Using the threat of extermination, the Bolsheviks forced everything and everyone in Russia to submit to them, and in fact they did mercilessly and basely exterminate everything which was alive and refused to bow down before them immediately and without resistance. Kornilov answered them with the exact same kind of extermination! . . . We knew that any Kornilovets—whether healthy or wounded, soldier or doctor, man or woman, or even a child—who fell into the hands of the Bolsheviks would be shot. And all armed Bolsheviks captured by us were shot on the spot, in ones, tens, hundreds. . . . The Bolsheviks' challenge was accepted by their stern opponent, and we saw how this war of extermination, which had been declared without forethought by people with weak nerves on people with nerves of steel, ate away at the morale of the Bolshevik forces.[30]

Thus, retribution was seen as necessary for the defense of freedom and honor against a vicious and cowardly enemy, and as a manifestation of the qualities of determination and hardness which the conflict required. In this way, the White urge for vengeance was given a logical justification.

Once the Whites responded in kind, a cycle of atrocity and vengeance began which intensified the mutual demonization. One observer offers a picture of this process and its psychological effects on the Volunteers:

> The unimaginably cruel tortures to which the Bolsheviks subjected wounded and captured "Cadets" evoked a response in kind from the latter. . . . The Volunteers subjected captured Bolsheviks to cruel beatings and executions. A typical sight were the garlands of hanged commissars on the crossroads of those villages and Cossack settlements through which the Volunteer Army passed. . . . And no one was shocked or upset by such a sight.
>
> On the contrary, such decisive measures satisfied the feelings of vengefulness, grievance, and malice against the looters, torturers and killers which had built up in the hearts of the Volunteers. Everyone

believed that this was the only way to deal with such merciless, possessed animals. . . .

[The campaign as a whole] was unimaginably hard for the Volunteers, hard both physically and morally.

This was not life . . . but a bloody nightmare, gnashing of teeth, uttermost hell.[31]

The vicious struggle with the Reds was a continuation and deepening of the cultural process initiated by the Great War, as the logic and psychological mechanisms of interminable and relentless combat stripped away the ethical conventions of the previous age and elevated killing to the status of a moral imperative. The experience of life and death in the course of this moral apocalypse gave the White movement a ruthlessness that stood in sharp contrast to its ideals.

The Cult of Death

From the outset, death had occupied a central place in the consciousness of the Volunteers. These men, products of the Great War, had witnessed the demise of their civilization. This experience was represented in the emblems of the movement. The insignia of the Kornilov regiment was a skull-and-crossbones over crossed swords and a lit bomb. When Kornilov formed his shock troop in 1917, he explained that this symbol meant "Victory or Death" and that "it is not death which is terrible, but disgrace and the loss of honor."[32] In 1918, "Victory or Death" had been replaced by "Better Death Than Slavery."[33] There was also symbolism in the regimental banners: the black and white of the Alekseevtsy was understood to represent mourning for order, and the black and red of the Kornilovtsy was taken to mean mourning for freedom.[34] Thus, death and loss dominated the thinking of the Volunteers, a tendency intensified by the experience of the Ice March. During the months of bloody skirmishing, the drive for self-sacrifice and the number of casualties produced the cult of death that would characterize the White movement.

Given the youth of many of the Whites, especially the combat forces, and the religious element of their mindset, it is natural that White literature's treatment of the movement's fallen heroes would reveal elements of the uniquely Russian cult of the Passion-Bearers (*strastoterptsy*), in the tradition of Boris and Gleb, the Tsarevich Dimitrii, and others: the tearful consideration of youthful, noble innocence and purity cut down by the conspiratorial forces of evil. In this context, death in battle was seen as both a redemptive act and a release. Here is one picture of the idealized White view of death: "Fortunate and pure, a hero without blemish, Vitia left this world which had been defiled by scoundrels and enveloped in falsehood and deceit. . . . He laid down his life for his unfortunate and mocked motherland."[35]

It was not only the rank and file who died in battle. Many of the most prominent leaders took the same risks as the men, and this, too, was seen as an expression of how the army was qualitatively different from all others. General Kornilov himself was killed by a stray Bolshevik shell in one unsuccessful operation, and in death, as in life, he was seen by the Whites as the model to be emulated. In subsequent months more of the Volunteers' commanders would die. Given the improvisatory nature of the army, its commanders were able to put a strong stamp on their units, which developed an intense sense of group identity. The death of several of these leaders resulted in the rather macabre situation in which the best regiments of the Volunteer Army—the Kornilovtsy, Alekseevtsy, Markovtsy, Drozdovtsy,[36] and so forth—proudly bore the names of dead men. This means of identification was not only an expression of loyalty to the fallen leaders, but also an affirmation of the principle of self-sacrifice.

The White Mentality in the Context of Religion

The density of religious imagery in the expressions of White thinking cited thus far offers the key to understanding the nature of the White movement. The Whites perceived the world and their struggle in religious categories, and it is in the context of religion that their mentality can best be explained. However, their religiosity was not that of traditional Orthodox piety. The Whites, as products of the secularized educated society, were not notably devout. Rather, their cult, developed under the pressures of the Great War and the Revolution, involved the transfer of religious impulses to a new object—Russia. The Whites did not fight for a restoration of the prerevolutionary order, nor indeed for any mundane political goal, but rather for the mythical "Holy Russia."

As we have seen, the Whites often depicted the state of Russia in terms of "defilement," "impurity," and "blasphemy." Their choice of words reflects religious categories that were imbedded in Russian culture. Although it has taken various superficially secularized forms in the course of historical development, the Russian ideal of perfection—derived from Christian and specifically Byzantine asceticism—has always been one of purity and of the triumph of the spirit over matter. The Revolution involved an attack on the values of the culture as a whole as well as on countless individual people. In the aftermath of October, educated society witnessed the trampling of its ideals as its members suffered brutalization and violation. The

Whites perceived the revolutionary assault on their Russia as a combination of sacrilege and rape, and their reaction fused the psychological responses to these experiences.

The Whites' struggle was an attempt to cleanse and purify Russia by means of self-sacrifice. They conceived of this in terms of Christian civilization's archetype for redemptive suffering—the crucifixion of Christ. During the Ice March the Volunteers demonstrated their willingness "to walk the Way of the Cross"[37] and die for their mythic vision of Russia. This self-perception was given symbolic representation—each participant in the Kornilov campaign was awarded a St. George's cross bearing a crown of thorns. Thus, the first Volunteers associated their act with the central event of the Christian conception of history.

The Whites' essentially religious understanding of the world condition was marked by a fundamental polarity. The Volunteers viewed their struggle in terms of opposing principles—nobility and baseness, freedom and slavery, purity and defilement, light and darkness, life and death, and, ultimately, God and Satan. Moreover, they believed that the epochal conflict between Good and Evil was coming to its summation and that Russia was its battleground. This mindset is an expression of the dualist tendency which is so deeply ingrained in Russian culture and which helps to explain the vehemence of political and ideological clashes in Russia.

The Ice March was the decisive event in the psychological formation of the Volunteer Army, and the exalted sense of group identity, and mission that it engendered would continue to drive that premier anti-Bolshevik force. The purpose of my study has been to improve the historical understanding of the Russian civil war by providing an analysis of the perceptions and beliefs of the first Whites and an identification of the factors that motivated them to undertake armed resistance against the Bolsheviks. I hope that this outline will enhance the historical picture of the complex psychological and cultural dynamic at work in Russia during the Revolution.

Notes

1. "Educated society" (derived from the Russian usage) is used here to denote the Westernized segment of the Russian population. This term, which stresses the decisive importance of the cultural factor yet avoids the narrower and more specific connotations of *intelligentsia*, is the best way to convey the essential distinction between the modernizing Russian elite and the great mass of the people who continued to live in the traditional culture.

2. I base my study almost entirely on a diverse body of primary sources found in the collections of Harvard University, the archives of the Hoover Institution, and the library of the Holy Trinity Monastery in Jordanville, New York. Foremost among these

is the large corpus of memoirs—whether published or preserved in manuscript form—produced by participants in the struggle. I have concentrated on those written during or shortly after the conflict, before the passage of years and the accumulation of new experiences had dissipated the psychological atmosphere of the civil war. Pamphlets, posters, and other minor publications also offer numerous insights into White thinking. In addition, the most strongly subjective genres (novels and stories, poetry and song) have been most useful. Here I examined not only the works of the most gifted of the artists who have written on the Whites, but also that substantial body of obscure and forgotten émigré literature that expresses the ideas of the rank-and-file participants in the movement. Finally, I have had the opportunity to get to know and interview several veterans of the Volunteer Army.

3. Studies of the White movement have tended to focus on military matters, which present little of interest to anyone besides professional military historians and hobbyists with somewhat exotic interests. There are, however, a number of works that deal with the question in a broader social and political context. The best of these is Peter Kenez's *Civil War in South Russia, 1918: The First Year of the Volunteer Army* (Berkeley: University of California Press, 1971). Although Kenez provides a thorough and useful examination of military, organizational, and political problems, he does not delve very deeply into the psychology or culture of the Whites, beyond stating the fact that the rank-and-file Volunteers were radically anti-Bolshevik and militarist in attitude. In terms of conveying the psychological atmosphere of the civil war, one of the earliest works—William Henry Chamberlin's *Russian Revolution 1917–1921* (New York: Macmillan, 1935)—remains the most successful.

4. The language used by the Whites in their own writings reflects this exalted conception of the movement and its participants. Many of the excerpts of White literary production cited in this work are overdramatic and turgid in style, but they are an accurate and characteristic manifestation of the Volunteer mindset.

5. Strictly speaking, the Ice March [*Ledianoi pokhod*] refers to one particularly dramatic episode in the course of the Volunteer Army's first campaign in the Kuban' Cossack region. I am using it in a broader sense to denote the entire winter and spring of 1918, when the Volunteers were essentially alone and fighting against what seemed to be insurmountable odds.

6. A. Denikin, *Ocherki russkoi smuty* (Paris: J. Povlozku, 1921–1925), 2: 198–199.

7. Ibid., 199.

8. Ia. Slashchov [*sic*], *Krym v 1920 g.: Otryvki iz vospominanii* (Moskva: Gosizdat, 1926), 16. Here Slashchev is referring to the situation in Russia as a whole in early 1918.

9. V. E. Pavlov, ed., *Markovtsy v boiakh i pokhodakh za Rossiiu v osvoboditel'noi voine 1917–1920* (Paris: Union des combattants de la Division du Général Markoff, 1962), 66–67.

10. M. A. Kritskii, ed., *Kornilovskii udarnyi polk* (Paris: Val, 1936), 56–57.

11. L. V. Polovtsov, *Rytsari Ternovogo Ventsa* (Prague, n. d.), 91.

12. Ibid., 92. The "socialization" of women, actually decreed by some local Soviets (Denikin reproduces one of these orders in his *Ocherki*, 2: 273), made a great impression on popular consciousness, and this, with the widespread incidence of rape (especially of women from the educated classes) added even greater intensity and psychological complexity to the social conflict of the period. The aspect of sexual violence in the revolution has been almost completely ignored in the historiography, even though it stands out as a major issue in the sources.

13. S. Arefin, "Razval armii," *Belyi Arkhiv* 2–3 (1928): 55. First published in *Ob"edinenie*, 1918.

14. R. Gul', *Kon' ryzhii* (New York: Izdatel'stvo imeni Chekhova, 1952), 88. The title and epigraph for this work are drawn from Revelation.

15. I. A. Rodionov, *Zhertvy vechernie: Ne vymysel, a deistvitel'nost'* (Berlin, 1922), 16. Rodionov's biography offers an interesting illustration of movement between the extremes of the Russian political spectrum. Initially a revolutionary populist, Rodionov gained fame with his book *Nashe prestuplenie*, a novel on the demoralization of peasants in the city. Even before the revolution he converted to right-radicalism, and it was from this perspective that he wrote on the civil war.

16. M. Lembich, "Politicheskaia programma generala Kornilova," *Belyi Arkhiv* 2–3: (1928): 178.

17. Ibid., 180.

18. A. Suvorin, *Pokhod Kornilova* (Rostov na Donu: "Novyi chelovek" [1918]), 2nd ed., reverse of title page. This work was widely read and caused quite a stir in White-controlled areas of South Russia because of its virulent militarism and intense hostility to civilians in general and politicians in particular.

19. *"Da voskresnet Rus' i rastochatsia vragi eia!"* Ibid. In this paraphrase of one of the cardinal moments in the Orthodox Paschal service, "God" is replaced by "Russia."

20. V. V. Shul'gin, *1920 g.* (Sofia, 1921), 276.

21. Denikin, *Ocherki*, 2: 198.

22. Ibid., 2: 224.

23. Cited in Pavlov, *Markovtsy*, 116. These lines, written in a letter that Alekseev left in Rostov as a sort of testament of the movement at what was possibly a fatal moment, were widely known within the army and are cited prominently in many contemporary accounts and memoirs as an encapsulation of the Volunteers' motivations.

24. Kritskii, *Kornilovskii udarnyi polk*, 11.

25. Pavlov, *Markovtsy*, 76–77. According to Pavlov, this man, Aleksandr Vasil'e-vich Kalashnikov, had been a military commissar of the Provisional Government.

26. Cited in *Ledianoi pokhod* (New York: Soiuz uchastnikov pervogo Kubanskogo pokhoda, 1953), 49.

27. *My bylogo ne zhaleem, Tsar' nam ne kumir.* Cited in Kritskii, *Kornilovskii udarnyi polk*, 12. The author notes that the regiment dropped these lines later in the course of the civil war. This shift in tone is a minor manifestation of an important phenomenon, namely, the way that the dynamic of the conflict drove many opponents of the Bolsheviks toward the right.

28. Kritskii, *Kornilovskii udarnyi polk*, 97.

29. Ibid., 57.

30. Suvorin, *Pokhod Kornilova*, 37.

31. Rodionov, *Zhertvy*, 122.

32. Kritskii, *Kornilovskii udarnyi polk*, 18.

33. Suvorin, *Pokhod Kornilova*, 128–129.

34. Ibid., 90.

35. Rodionov, *Zhertvy*, 117.

36. The Drozdovskii regiment did not take part in the Ice March but linked with the Volunteers shortly afterward. Its composition and formative experience (a campaign across the chaotic southern Ukraine) was similar to that of the Volunteer Army, and the two forces fused naturally.

37. This is a standard poetic image for the Ice March. See, for example, a November 1919 speech by Denikin cited in A. Loukomsky, *Memoirs of the Russian Revolution*, trans. M. Vitali (London: T. F. Unwin, 1922), 206.

Siberian *Atamanshchina:*
Warlordism in the Russian Civil War

T he Cossacks were a warrior caste of free Russian and Ukrainian rural residents who traded military service for privileges and land along the frontier of the expanding Russian empire in the eighteenth and nineteenth centuries. Unlike most Russian peasants, they never experienced serfdom, and even to the limited extent that they were part of the communal land tenure system they were not subject to quitrent (*obrok*), corvée (*barshchina*), or land redemption payments. Most important, Cossacks were exempt from the soul tax or capitation (*podushnaia podat'*).[1]

Because of these privileges, the Cossacks were widely seen as set apart from the peasantry.[2] The gulf was increased by the militarism of the Cossacks, who often expropriated their neighbors' belongings. Strong corporate identity, loyalty to the chosen leader (ataman), and a distinct form of regionalism were features of the Cossack worldview. (The term *ataman*, which roughly translates as headman or chieftain, was the title used initially among the Don Cossacks and subsequently by all the other *"voiska"*—administrative units created by and directly subject to the personal authority of the tsar.[3]) Cossacks defined themselves by their geographic region—thus *Dontsy, Uraltsy,* and *Kubantsy,* which reflected variations in local customs and autonomy.[4] It could hardly have been otherwise, considering the enormous distances between the groups. Thus, the Trans-Baikal Cossacks, inhabiting an area of eastern Siberia encompassing more than 42,000 square miles with a 1916 population of 265,000, were by far the most numerous—about three times the combined totals of their Amur and Ussuri cousins.[5] Several hundred miles to the west were the Orenburg and Siberian hosts, with three minor voiska in between. Bordering Siberia on the west were nearly 160,000 Ural Cossacks, who were known for their ferocity and fractiousness.[6]

Eastern Siberia was ethnically and topographically more diverse than the western region, with a larger proportion of Asiatic non-Russian peoples, but it was less populated and habitable. It was not developed agriculturally or industrially, and it was under constant threat of foreign intervention, particularly from Japan. Its extreme remoteness from the centers of commerce and government administration made the eastern part more vulnerable to Cossack warlordism, known as *atamanshchina*.

Service under the atamans in Siberia was a high-risk/quick-reward proposition that appealed to fringe elements of society (apart from Cossacks themselves). Petty criminals, bandits, deserters, and ethnic minorities—Chinese, Koreans, and Mongols—were prominent in the entourage of the Far Eastern atamans. Loyalty hinged to a great extent on the personal magnetism of the leader, his success in battle, and his ability to provide tangible rewards. Desertion and redeployment were not uncommon, and rank-and-file Russian Cossacks often transferred their service to another, more successful, ataman. But the Asian minorities, who were more vulnerable to the vagaries of official policy and to xenophobia, tended to stick to a leader with whom they had some ethnic or linguistic connection.[7] The Siberian Cossacks were landowners and officers whose political and social conservativism often put them at odds with the surrounding rural population. Indeed, the peasants identified the Cossacks with many of the worst coercive aspects of the old prerevolutionary order, and the Cossacks' quick association with the Whites worked to discredit the latter.[8]

Nevertheless, the Siberian peasantry's initial response to the October Revolution was also unenthusiastic. Soviet agrarian policies offered little to a region with virtually no history of bondage or land shortage.[9] Social tensions in Siberia existed not so much between wealthy landlords and poor field workers as between land-rich Cossacks and free peasants who suffered by contrast (even though they too were better off than their counterparts in European Russia). Cossacks controlled the most desirable and productive land even though they constituted a distinct minority of the total population; their per capita allotments were three to five times greater than those of neighboring peasants.[10]

Lenin's clear understanding of rural prejudices and mentality was evident in his decision to abolish the Cossacks' special privileges and obligations on 13 December 1917. In Siberia this did much more to win popular support for his cause than did his land decree a month earlier, especially in areas where many peasants and Cossacks lived side by side.[11]

The greatest power vacuum existed in Eastern Siberia, principally because of the atamanshchina. Whether the phenomenon was a spontaneous response to the existing situation or the proximate cause, the important thing was its physical location behind the White lines. Thus, despite its overtly anti-Soviet outlook, atamanshchina did much greater harm to the Whites than to the Reds. This was especially true in the Trans-Baikal, where Ataman G. M. Semenov held sway. In Western Siberia, such Cossack leaders as A. I. Dutov, B. V. Annenkov, and P. P. Ivanov-Rinov were more disposed to side early on with the main White government in Omsk, though perhaps not to fully subordinate to it.

Because of its geography and history, Eastern Siberia, from the Pacific Coast to Irkutsk, was much more affected by the militarism of imperial Japan and the centrifugal tendencies prevalent in warlord China (with its numerous petty feudal fiefdoms and regional autonomy).[12] By the summer of 1918 there were several conflicting claims to power in Eastern Siberia. These ranged from isolated municipal administrations to improbable "All-Russian" governments that aspired to be the legitimate successor to the Kerensky and old imperial regimes.

Over the next three and a half years the claims included those from the Provisional Government of Autonomous Siberia under the moderate Socialist Revolutionary P. Ia. Derber; the conservative nationalist "Business Cabinet" of General D. L. Khorvat (director of the Chinese-Eastern Railway in Harbin); Admiral A. V. Kolchak's military viceroys; civilian zemstvo boards in Vladivostok (A. S. Medvedev) and Verkhneudinsk; a pro-Soviet municipal government in Blagoveshchensk (M. A. Trilisser); the short-lived but far-flung Far Eastern Republic (led by the veteran Communists A. M. Krasnoshchekov and P. M. Nikiforov), which was recognized by Moscow as a temporary buffer state between Soviet Russia and Japan; the Japanese-backed Provisional Priamur Government (S. D. and N. D. Merkulov); and a revival of the ancient Russian Land Assembly (*Zemskii Sobor*) in Vladivostok, which nominated the eccentric Kolchakovite General M. K. Diterikhs as military dictator.[13] None of them, however, could assert effective control of more than small enclaves within the region, leaving much of the territory vulnerable to the atamanshchina, notably as practiced by G. M. Semenov and his sadistic associate Baron R. F. Ungern-Sternberg in the Trans-Baikal and Mongolia, respectively, along with their ally I. P. Kalmykov of the Ussuri voisko, and the mysterious I. M. Gamov in the Amur.

Semenov himself was of Buriat-Russian heritage. Cossacks considered him to be a Cossack, and Buriats naturally saw him as one of their own, as did the Mongols.[14] But he had admirers even among the Jews. He had seen service as a tsarist officer in Poland and the Carpathians during the First World War, and in the summer of 1917 he returned (with Ungern) to the Trans-Baikal at the behest of the Provisional Government to mobilize non-Russian recruits. When Soviet power was suddenly established in the fall of 1917, Semenov immediately organized a following of Cossack and indigenous forces to oppose the Bolsheviks and restore "legitimate Russian government" in Siberia.[15]

But following his installation during the summer of 1918 as ataman of the Trans-Baikal Cossacks, Semenov dismayed the local Russian military by raising the issue of an independent Buriat-Mongolian state rather than concentrating on fighting the Bolsheviks.[16] The opinions of the Russian military, however, mattered less to Semenov than the wishes of his Japanese benefactors, who wanted the Mongols under their "exclusive influence" and saw in him a congenial vehicle for their own expansionist designs on the Russian Far East.[17] Tokyo, moreover, was prepared to back Semenov with material support: to subsidize his activities and to pay his men's salaries when no Russian civilian or military authority was willing to do so.[18]

In spite of the connection to Japan, Semenov and his fellow Cossack leaders always maintained that their first allegiance was to the Great Russian state principle. They denied vigorously that their presence destabilized or weakened central government authority in Eastern Siberia. Gamov spoke on behalf of all the atamans when he stated that "only the Cossacks, representing the statist point of view, can save Russia."[19] It would be consistent with the Cossacks' traditional allegiance to the central Russian government (and to an autocratic head of state) for them to have welcomed Admiral A. V. Kolchak's ascension to power in Omsk on 18 November 1918. It was also the case in Western Siberia, where there was a surge of spontaneous declarations pledging that "all Cossacks, as in the past, . . . will [continue] to defend the motherland and the Orthodox faith under the high leadership of the Supreme Ruler."[20]

In the fall of 1918, Western Siberia and the Urals witnessed an end to the bewildering variety of regional governments, to the Socialist-Revolutionary committee of former members of the Constituent Assembly (KOMUCH) in Samara, and to their replacement by the statist militarism of the new All-Russian regime in Omsk. In addition, major White leaders, such as Generals Denikin and Iudenich, as well as most of the important political figures of the defunct Provisional Government (including many Socialist Revolutionaries and even some Mensheviks), put aside their differences and rallied to Kolchak. It was thus all the more significant that Semenov and his allies in Eastern Siberia—despite continuing insistence on their loyalty to traditional Cossack values and Russian nationalism—steadfastly refused to recognize Kolchak's authority.[21]

From the beginning of his administration the supreme ruler could not count on the security of his rear or on the vital communications link along the Trans-Siberian Railway eastward. That vast territory should have been a reservoir of critical support for his government. Instead, the presence of the atamans made it a no-man's land where the authority of Omsk remained merely nominal. Kolchak's armies received no recruits from Eastern Siberia, and supplies along the Trans-Siberian Railway, especially east of Irkutsk, were subject to constant raids by renegade bands practicing a vicious form of taxation cum plunder. In the Trans-Baikal, virtually no train passed through without paying the infamous "Chita tariff."[22]

The chief reasons given by Semenov himself for his differences with the White leadership and Kolchak in particular were their opposing attitudes and loyalties toward Japan and the West.[23] From the moment Semenov met Kolchak in the spring of 1918, just after Kolchak had joined General Khorvat's Chinese-Eastern Railway administration in Manchuria, an antagonistic tone was established. It continued almost until the end of their relationship.

Neither the admiral nor the ataman was disposed to like or trust the other. Kolchak regarded Semenov as little better than a brigand who encouraged his followers to engage in excesses against the civil order, such as the wanton seizure of private property, bringing disrepute to the authority of their common employer, the Chinese-Eastern Railway in Harbin. Their mutual antipathy quickly came to a head when, following a raid by Semenov's men on a store in the railway zone, Kolchak took forceful punitive actions that exposed the touchy ataman to public humiliation.[24]

In justifying his position, Semenov naturally chose to avoid the details of this particular episode as well as his mistreatment of civilians in general. He preferred to emphasize his differences with Kolchak over relations with Tokyo: "The Admiral considered my pro-Japanese orientation to be almost criminal and demanded that I renounce totally my independent political line on this matter and subordinate myself to [the railway authority in] Harbin."[25] But the ataman refused to sever his ties with the Japanese. Neither Kolchak nor Khorvat, he argued, had any legal mandate as a regional or national government, and they were in any case incapable of defeating the Bolsheviks. On the other hand, he said, "Imperial Nippon was . . . interested in seeing a nationalist Russia at its side rather than some hotbed of permanent revolution and source of Communist propaganda for the whole world."[26]

Semenov's resistance to Omsk cannot be explained by policy differences alone, however. In the first place, his disagreements with Kolchak were not that great, especially in light of the gulf which separated them from Bolshevism, and the far greater threat that the latter presented to both. The magnifying factor was personality, which, because of the peculiar combination of circumstances and forces in Siberia, assumed a disproportionate significance.[27] In Russia's "wild east" of the civil war period, idiosyncratic whims and prejudices became historical fissures.

In this regard, the personality of the supreme ruler was of particular importance. Semenov characterized him as a "highly nervous, hot-tempered individual who knew very little about the peculiarities of conditions in the Far East" and whose strong likes and dislikes blinded him to the virtues of Japan as well as to the unpromising realities of Western assistance to Russia.[28] But the ataman also believed that Kolchak, far from being too dictatorial or tough, was "very soft and subject to the influence of surrounding conditions and personalities."[29]

Semenov was not alone in noting the admiral's unsuitability for the role of supreme ruler.[30] Despite his high ethical standards and strict devotion to duty, Kolchak seemed incapable of inspiring similar qualities, or even obedience, among his subordinates in both the civil and military service at Omsk: "Unreservedly brave, direct and sincere, of crystalline honesty and nobility, Kolchak lacked the one quality essential for a dictator—a strong will. . . . It was not Kolchak who led the government, but a crowd of intriguers and politicos who controlled Kolchak."[31] This was hardly consistent with the forceful image of competent government that the admiral hoped to project at home and abroad.[32]

The immediate dilemma facing Kolchak's administration was how to respond to the terrorist activity of some of its more active agents, such as ataman B. V. Annenkov's men in Semipalatinsk, who, rather than take on the dangerous job of battling the Bolsheviks at the front, preferred to pass the time by beating up local villagers. This was not what Kolchak had in mind, but he was notoriously slow and tentative about disciplining the men lest they stop fighting for him altogether. Only when the Cossacks became so unmanageable that they threatened the property of respectable middle-class merchants did the Omsk government take some action.[33]

Even so, Kolchak did not dare do much, because he remained heavily dependent on the good will of Annenkov and the other Cossack chiefs to secure both recruits and supplies for his armies. The supreme ruler's passivity was less a sign of indifference to or of tacit approval of the transgressions than of fundamental weakness. The inadequacy of his response compounded the social malaise and added to the atmosphere of personal insecurity, lawlessness, and arbitrariness—precisely what the Omsk government could least afford under the circumstances. Public confidence continued to decline as Annenkov expanded his random confiscation of private property and violation of civil liberties; in the words of one eyewitness, his men behaved as though they were in a "conquered country."[34]

Kolchak was warned on several occasions by his most reliable intelligence agents that these activities were doing irreparable damage to his reputation and to the standing of his government.[35] Moreover, Annenkov's example was not the exception, even in those areas of Western Siberia and the Urals where the Omsk government ostensibly exercised the most direct control. In Orenburg and environs, ataman A. I. Dutov behaved similarly. This established a pattern in the public mind that could not be erased by any number of counterarguments—such as those of Dutov, who believed that the absence of "basic necessities" for his men forced him to requisition supplies and provisions from the civilians.[36] The violations became so numerous and egregious that many members of educated society and the upper classes concluded that "even the Bolsheviks did not behave in this way."[37]

In Eastern Siberia the chaos and the insecurity of person and property were even more severe. In addition to Semenov's multiethnic marauders, several smaller Cossack bands roamed at will, leaving a trail of havoc and devastation. Ataman Kalmykov in Khabarovsk district *uezd* was notorious for his violent measures, including the taking of children as hostages, ostensibly to force their parents to provide information on "Bolshevik agents" but in fact as a brazen means to extort ransom.[38]

The Khabarovsk zemstvo board pleaded with Kolchak for help, noting that the "coercive activity of the different military detachments totally terrorizes the population, disorganizes its economic life . . . , disrupts the schooling [of children], and in general creates the conditions of civil war—all of which, in the absence of the appropriate apparatus, [we are] utterly powerless to do anything about."[39] Kolchak lacked the resources to correct the situation, even if he had wished to. In fact, Kalmykov was by no means the worst transgressor in Eastern Siberia. That distinction belonged to the far-ranging and ferocious Baron Ungern-Sternberg, whose "infernal figure . . . elicited an almost superstitious horror."[40] Ungern was driven by a fantastic plan (which he shared with Semenov) to reconstitute much of the Trans-Baikal and bordering Chinese territories into a great independent Mongol state, and he saw much of the Russian peasantry in the region as hopelessly unworthy and corrupt.[41]

While Semenov was generally tolerant of religious and ethnic diversity and pragmatic in political questions, Ungern was a mystic and staunch monarchist. He detested the Jews, and he was a great admirer of Chinese civilization and Mongolian Buddhism. Ungern considered Jews and Mongols to be ethnic and spiritual antipodes with incompatible worldviews, though that did not prevent him from employing Jews in certain tasks.[42] Moreover, the baron (despite his own Baltic origins) personified the demotic anti-Westernism that was an underlying theme of Siberian atamanshchina. This quality appealed to many Cossacks as well as to other segments of the premodern indigenous local populations. It was particularly effective against Bolshevism, which represented the encroaching preponderance of the industrialized, atheistic West that was destroying the mores and values of the East.

Anti-Westernism was a major characteristic shared by Siberian ata-manshchina and Chinese warlordism. Soviet contemporaries who fought both movements remarked on the similarities between them. These included regional particularism as well as spontaneous skepticism toward all forms of national and central governments. The sentiments of Chinese recruits were echoed by many Siberians: "We were raised [and] . . . given a lot of kindness by our families, and we should love them. The country is another thing—what does it have to offer us? It can't be seen, it can't be heard, it doesn't respond to our calls. It is nothing but a few rogues who want to bully and oppress us, and to dupe us."[43] Other similarities between Siberian atamanshchina and Chinese warlordism were the loy-alty of followers to the ataman/warlord himself, not to his organization or cause, and the presence of an environment in which "decline in central power both stimulated the growth of regionalism (as an alternative to anarchy) and lessened the government's ability to restrain that growth."[44]

The anarchic militarism of spreading atamanshchina in Eastern Siberia was the subject of grave concern among moderately conservative Russians like Baron A. P. Budberg, who warned Kolchak that the ata-mans were the "most dangerous submerged rocks in our path . . . , and [that] it is essential to . . . insure that the[y] . . . are broken without mercy, not stopping at anything."[45]

Kolchak received similarly alarmist assessments from other private and official informants (including zemstvo boards). In addition, there were offers of material support from such loyal backers as the powerful cooperative unions to cover the costs of a campaign to curtail the ata-mans' reign of terror. A strong consensus existed in educated society that the establishment of lawful order was essential to the reconstruction of the Russian state.[46] The supreme ruler's continuing failure to act deci-sively was puzzling. He had to be aware that the more public outrages of the atamans—described in graphic detail in the leading Western news-papers—were seen as direct challenges to his authority that severely undermined his credibility and prestige.[47]

Unfortunately, Kolchak could not clean up his own backyard, much less keep order across the vast eastward span of Siberia. It was said that corruption and political intrigue were rampant in Omsk, where a camar-illa of youthful adventurers—led by the precocious (twenty-three years old in 1918) Minister of Finance I. A. Mikhailov and the equally inexpe-rienced Chief-of-Staff General D. A. Lebedev—was aggressively pursuing personal agendas that had little to do with the public interest.[48] Whatever the truth of these and other damaging allegations, the atmosphere around Kolchak was poisoned by intrigue and bad faith, which could not but hurt his relations with both his military field commanders and civil society. This in turn accelerated centrifugal tendencies, especially in Eastern Siberia. If Semenov and his comrades needed additional evidence that they were right to withhold their support from Kolchak, they had no difficulty finding it in the news coming from Western Siberia.

Kolchak's reaction to Semenov's continuing impertinence, however, had little effect. By Executive Directive No. 60, on 1 December 1918, he relieved Semenov of his official functions and remanded him to court-martial for "banditry and insubordination." Kolchak made a point of informing the Allies and Western public opinion that he had "suspended Semenov from his command and all his posts, and ordered [the] military to force him . . . to curtail [his] wild arbitrariness and anarchy."[49] But these brave words could not be enforced, and they served only to highlight the unreality of the supreme ruler's perspective.

In the meantime, the absence of Russian governmental authority in Eastern Siberia encouraged Tokyo's military—there ostensibly to provide neighborly assistance as well as protect Japanese nationals in Vladivostok—to wander far afield and behave like an army in "de facto occupation of Russian territory."[50] The Japanese commander in Eastern Siberia did not hesitate to issue a peremptory warning to the All-Russian Government in Omsk that any attempt to attack Semenov would be rebuffed by his 70,000 troops, and if Kolchak "should attempt to move troops into Transbaikalia, the Japanese forces would be compelled to act against them."[51]

Tokyo's aggressive support for Semenov and the other atamans in Siberia was a calculated slap at Russian national pride in general and at the Kolchak administration in particular. But for the Japanese military it also was natural to assume that the Cossack heads were the "closest counterpart to themselves, and . . . therefore that the [atamans] could be helped to power by methods familiar to Japan; and that, once in power, they could be depended upon as sound allies."[52]

Semenov and Khorvat predicted that Kolchak's adamant refusal to follow their example and adopt a conciliatory approach with Tokyo would prove fatal to his military and political fortunes in the Russian Far East. For his part, Kolchak found nothing improper in Khorvat's conduct: "With regard to the Japanese, Khorvath . . . adhered to a policy of avoiding the straining of relations, although on the whole he did not collaborate with them and had no connections with them."[53] But it is not certain that the Japanese were at any point genuinely interested in supporting a strong and an independent Russian government in the region. Thus, it may not have mattered how scrupulously Kolchak heeded their advice or a similar warning from the Russian ambassador to Tokyo: "You have assumed from the beginning too independent a position with regard to

Japan, and they have understood it. You allow yourself to speak to them in a too imperative and independent tone. . . . They have come to regard you as an enemy of theirs who is going to oppose anything they initiate. . . . Therefore, naturally, they not only will not help you but will oppose your work."[54] Anything short of major concessions that seriously compromised the economic and territorial integrity of Russia, however, would have been insufficient to satisfy Tokyo's war party. Kolchak testified that the head of the Japanese Expeditionary Mission in Siberia, General Nakashima, told him unequivocally that Japanese support was contingent upon "compensation" in these strategic areas.[55] No patriotic Russian officer could have agreed to such a quid pro quo, even in exchange for full military backing and support, regardless of how urgent and expedient the trade-off.[56]

Force of circumstances, especially the failure of the great White offensive in the spring of 1919 in Western Siberia and the Urals, finally obliged Kolchak to modify his position toward Semenov, if not the Japanese. On 9 April the supreme ruler rescinded his decree against the ataman and restored to him all his rights and functions as commander-in-chief of the Fifth Amur Corps, with a promotion to lieutenant-general.[57] Only then did Semenov recognize the Omsk regime, promising his "disinterested service" for the sake of the motherland.[58] The ataman's triumph over Kolchak was the clearest indication of the extent of the military and political debacle in White Siberia and an unmistakable sign that the cause was lost. It convinced the Western Allies that they could no longer afford to waste precious materiel on Kolchak and should concentrate their efforts elsewhere (as on Denikin in the south).[59]

Semenov's reconciliation with the supreme ruler came not as the result of any modification of behavior or attitude on his part but because of the deterioration in Omsk's military and political position. In fact, Semenov continued to terrorize and plunder the civilians under his control. Even after ostensibly accepting Kolchak's authority, he did not set aside his own self-serving agenda. A reliable informant reported that Semenov said that he recognized the Omsk Government but took no orders from it. The same source warned that Semenov was "undoubtedly preparing a coup, and . . . only waiting for a good moment to start a sharp conflict with the Omsk Government and declare himself Far Eastern dictator."[60] There was also tacit confirmation of this disposition in a message to Kalmykov: "I have 30 million [Japanese] yens. I am declaring a complete autonomy. Do not give one man to the front [to help the retreating Kolchak army]."[61]

Nevertheless, after the long and disastrous summer campaigns of 1919, when Kolchak was forced to move his capital from Omsk to Irkutsk,

Semenov and his four thousand or so men appeared to be the only alternative available to the beleaguered supreme ruler.[62] Kolchak was profoundly frustrated and humiliated by his treatment at the hands of the Czechoslovak Legionnaires and their French mentors, who refused to expedite his eastward retreat. He expressed his outrage in a perverse decision to appoint Semenov (in October 1919) to the posts of military governor of Trans-Baikal province and assistant to General S. N. Rozanov, who was commander of the Far Eastern and Irkutsk military theaters.

As the eastward Red advance gained momentum, a desperate and exhausted Kolchak took the final step in sealing his own unhappy fate by further antagonizing the departing Czechs—who still controlled the railway west of Irkutsk and alone could have provided him with safe passage into a dignified exile abroad. The admiral's already strained relations with the Legion became openly hostile when his official train passage eastward was constantly interrupted and literally sidetracked for days at a time by the Czechs—whose own echelons, packed with luxuries as well as family members and retainers, were given precedence in using what were, after all, Russian facilities on Russian soil.

Kolchak responded with the one threat he still had at his disposal: unless the Czechs immediately allowed his personal train to pass, he would order Semenov to blow up the tunnels east of Irkutsk, effectively blocking all rail passage to Vladivostok, the Czechs' main port of embarkation. To give additional substance to the threat, the ataman was put in command of all White forces in the Russian Far East—"with the fullness of both military and civil power"—who were squarely in the path of the departing Czechs.[63]

This threat was certain to remove any vestige of Czech goodwill or sense of responsibility for the admiral's fate, and to eliminate all possibility of Allied intercession on his behalf. When the supreme ruler arrived in Irkutsk he was immediately relinquished to the revolutionary authorities and summarily executed in the first week of February 1920.

Over the next several months the other anti-Bolshevik governments in Siberia collapsed. At the same time there was a surge from below in spontaneous resistance to Soviet authority. It became evident that the much of the rural population of Siberia had been opposed to both the Reds and the Whites but had hesitated to do anything that might contribute to the greater immediate danger, that of restoring the old regime (which was how the Bolsheviks effectively portrayed White victory) while Kolchak was alive. After the admiral's defeat and death, however, the peasant partisan movement that had been such a major factor in helping the Red Army against the common White foe turned against Soviet rule.[64]

In places where *partizanshchina* (a derogatory term for partisan warfare and its excesses) was strong, atamanshchina was relatively weak. Thus, in Western Siberia—the area most affected by Kolchak's rule—the partisan movement became most active after his death, particularly in the form of the anti–Soviet Siberian Peasant Union. Conversely, there were far fewer partisans in Eastern Siberia, where the atamans dominated. To the extent that Semenov's rough-and-ready brand of regionalism struck a chord among peasants—especially among Cossacks and the national minorities of Eastern Siberia—it preempted the partisan movement. And while it would be difficult to describe the ataman's politics as democratic, at least he knew enough to recruit an army of volunteers rather than resort to the tremendously unpopular coercive drafts employed by the governments of Omsk and Moscow.

In the end, Semenov was no match for the advancing Red Army, and he was fortunate to escape with severely diminished forces to Vladivostok. In early 1921 there was still talk of his regrouping with Ungern in the Maritime Province and (possibly with Japanese assistance) liberating the Trans-Baikal from the Soviets. But this was sheer fantasy. Moreover, the Kappelite remnants of Kolchak's armies in the Russian Far East opposed Semenov's involvement, and the struggle for political power in Vladivostok among competing anti-Bolshevik factions once again blocked any concerted White military effort.[65] By the end of the year, even the Japanese had concluded that they should withdraw from Siberia.[66]

With the Western Allies and especially Japan out of the picture, the elimination of the threat from Baron Wrangel in the Crimea, and Soviet borders with Poland stabilized, Lenin could afford to shift his focus back to Siberia. At the end of October 1922, as soon as the Red Army had secured Vladivostok and the railway line, steps were taken to suppress all remaining resistance to Soviet rule in the region. Still, sporadic antigovernment eruptions continued for several more years in both Eastern and Western Siberia.[67] Semenov himself, along with Kalmykov and the remnants of their forces, crossed the frontier into Manchuria in 1921 and entered the direct employ of the Japanese secret service. The final chapter of his extraordinary saga was written when Semenov was captured by the Red Army in 1945, taken to Moscow, tried in camera, and executed.[68]

In the years before his final reckoning with Soviet justice, Semenov made every effort to justify his own role and to explain the White defeat. In his analysis, the ataman emphasized the absence of a single, clear White ideology or slogan that could win over the broad sympathies of the peasant and working masses. He added that the Whites offered no plan or vision of the future, thus allowing their enemies to define them. By ignoring and putting off the peasants' chief demand for land, they played into the hands of Lenin's Bolsheviks, who could then claim that their real intentions were to restore the landlords' estates. While the Whites talked about the people's obligations and responsibilities toward the state, the Soviets quickly proclaimed popular rights to land and control of the factories.[69]

The final irony is that all these factors were at the same time greatly exacerbated by Semenov's role as the chief practioner of atamanshchina in Siberia. He was the ultimate expression of the "endemic spirit of anarchy within . . . the White ranks."[70] That anarchy—or, more precisely, political centrifugation—shattered an already fragile anti-Bolshevik coalition and opened the way to the new Red order.

Notes

This research was made possible through the continuing support of the Social Sciences and Humanities Research Council of Canada.

1. While indigenous peoples fished, hunted, and herded for a living, and peasants were almost exclusively engaged in farming, the Cossacks' chief peacetime occupation was raising cattle. See I. P. Poddubnyi, "Naselenie aziatskoi Rossii," in *Aziatskaia Rossiia* (Cambridge, Mass: Oriental Research Partners, 1974), 1: 93–178.

2. R. H. McNeal, *Tsar and Cossack, 1855–1914* (New York: St. Martin's, 1987), 7–11.

3. C. F. Smith, "Atamanshchina in the Russian Far East," *Russian History* 1 (1979): 65. Also *Entsiklopedicheskii slovar'*, 86 vols. (St. Petersburg: F. A. Brokgauz and I. A. Efron, 1890), 3: 411–412.

4. See M. P. Golovachev, "Rapport du Professeur Golovatchoff," Bakhmeteff Archive (Columbia University), box 2.

5. Smith, "Atamanshchina in the Russian Far East," 58.

6. McNeal, *Tsar and Cossack, 1855–1914*, 20–21.

7. Gosudarstvennyi Arkhiv Rossiiskoi Federatsii (GARF), f. 5873, op. 1, ed.khr. 8, l. 41ob. D. Lary offers this description of similar patterns in the Chinese context: "No stigma of a moral kind attached to deserting. They could either go home, find another unit to enlist in . . . or go into banditry" (*Warlord Soldiers* [Cambridge: Cambridge University Press, 1986], 95–96).

8. The term *White* is used here to describe the broad and unwieldy anti-Bolshevik political coalition that, after 1917, encompassed monarchists on the right and Socialist Revolutionaries and Mensheviks on the left. D. Dacy has suggested that "insofar as the Whites had any claim to be a people's movement, the Cossacks were that people. There was no one else. . . . The Cossack component of the White armies made up perhaps 50% of the total." Of course, Bolshevik propaganda did its best to reinforce this view, depicting both Cossacks and Whites in Siberia as an undifferentiated gang of reactionary predators whose purpose was to restore the "kulak-landlords-tsarist regime" ("The White Russian Movement" [Ph.D. diss., University of Texas, 1972], 198). For similarities with the situation in southern Russia see P. Kenez, *Civil War in South Russia, 1918* (Berkeley: University of California Press, 1971), 220–222.

9. *The Soviet Peasantry* (Moscow: Progress Publishers, n.d.), 54. See also V. K. Logvinov, *V bor'be s kolchakovshchinoi* (Krasnoiarsk: Krasnoiarskoe knizh. izdat., 1980), 89.

10. A. A. Gordeev, *Istoriia Kazakov* (Moscow: Strastnoi bul'var, 1992), part 3, 330–332.

11. The famous edict, enacted by the Second Soviet Congress in Petrograd during the night of 26 October (OS) [8 November NS] 1917, took over property from both public institutions and private landlords: that is, state, appanage, monastic, and church lands, as well as the estates of powerful landowners and even some holdings of more affluent peasants.

12. E. A. McCord, "The Emergence of Modern Chinese Warlordism: Military Power and Politics in Hunan and Hubei," 2 vols. (Ph.D. diss., University of Michigan, 1985), 1: 5, defines Chinese warlordism as a "political system in which individual military commanders exercise autonomous political power by virtue of their personal command of military force."

13. P. Balakshin, *Final v Kitae*, 2 vols. (San Francisco: Sirius, 1958), 1: 97–98.

14. The approximately 200,000 Buriat Mongols were the most organized and self-conscious of the "minority nationalities" in the region and were concentrated in the area south of Lake Baikal. See N. V. Turchaninov, "Naselenie aziatskoi Rossii," in *Aziatskaia Rossiia*, 2 vols. (Cambridge, Mass: Oriental Research Partners, 1974) 1: 64–92.

15. Semenov spoke several local dialects fluently. His philosemitism was ascribed to the influence of a Jewish chanteuse mistress. In any case, Semenov's Chita had a Jewish Society and a Yiddish theater. See L. Iuzefovich, "Samoderzhets pustyni," *Druzhba narodov* 9 (1992): 29. C. F. Smith, "The Ungernovscina—How and Why?" *Jahrbücher für Geschichte Osteuropas* 28 (1980): 592. Semenov had indicated his conservative political leanings when he urged the Trans-Baikal Cossacks to support General A. Kornilov's abortive coup d'état in September 1917 (G. M. Semenov, *O sebe. Vospominaniia, mysli i vyvody* [Harbin: Zaria, 1938], 57).

16. Semenov made his intentions public in February 1919 at a conference in Chita when he proposed the organization of a Mongol state that would include Mongolia, Tibet, and a large part of the Trans-Baikal bordering on Manchuria (GARF, f. 200, op. 1, ed.khr. 404, l. 49). Similar ideas existed on the Chinese side of the border. In the years that immediately followed, the Chinese warlord Chang Tso-Lin created a prosperous and autonomous regional state in Manchuria. See M. P. Pillsbury, "Environment and Power: Warlord Strategic Behavior in Szechwan, Manchuria, and the Yangtze Delta" (Ph.D. diss., Columbia University, 1980), 260.

17. Telegram from Klemm, 2 April 1919, GARF, f. 200, op. 1, ed.khr. 405, l. 119.

18. Not all Russian officers were critical of Semenov for his close ties with the Japanese. Captain N. F. Romanoff, in *Russia Posol'stvo* (United States), Hoover Institution Archives (HIA), 1914–1933, box 18, p. 5, came to his defense: "It is charged against Semeonoff that he is considered pro-Japanese, that he is receiving arms and money from the Japanese. . . . When it is necessary to pay officers and men and when you have no money you accept money from anyone who will give it to you."

19. Quoted in a telegram from Blagoveshchensk, 10 December 1918, GARF, f. 200, op. 1, ed.khr. 407, l. 14.

20. Telegram from Major-General Popov, 28 August 1919, GARF, f. 176, op. 4, ed.khr. 71, l. 146. Emphasis added.

21. Strong nationalistic sentiments were common among Cossacks in the region at this time: "We don't recognize any Siberian government, and will submit ourselves only to a Russian government" (quoted in a telegram from a security agent named Fet, 15 August 1918, *Russia [1918–1920], Vremennoe Sibirskoe Pravitel'stvo* [Derber Government], HIA).

22. The situation seems remarkably similar to that which existed in northern China at about the same time. J. E. Sheridan, *Chinese Warlords* (Stanford: Stanford University Press, 1966), 26: "Peking badly needed fuel and food, which was ordinarily shipped to the city in large quantities over the Peking-Hankow Railroad, [but] the warlord of Honan refused to permit railroad cars on this line to leave his own domain."

23. Semenov, *O sebe*, 112.

24. E. Varneck and H. H. Fisher, *The Testimony of Admiral Kolchak and Other Siberian Materials* (Stanford: Stanford University Press, 1935), 126–127: "[Semenov's] adventure made me [Kolchak] boil, as this constituted an invasion of the territory directly subordinate to me. I immediately gathered a detachment . . . to have that gang arrested and to restore the seized property."

25. Semenov, *O sebe*, 112. The Soviet view, however, has minimized both the differences between Semenov and Kolchak and between Russian atamans and Chinese warlords. All have been described as agents of the landlords, wealthy peasantry (*kulak*), and foreign interests. See the discussion in A. Waldron, "The Warlord: Twentieth-Century Chinese Understandings of Violence, Militarism, and Imperialism," *American Historical Review* 10 (1991): 1087–1088.

26. G. M. Semenov, "Istoria moei bor'by s bol'shevikami," HIA, box 1, p. 24.

27. In a candid moment, Semenov confessed that he could never forgive Kolchak for initially preventing his men from getting needed arms and supplies from Harbin (GARF, f. 193, op. 1, ed.khr. 3 [Lichnyi fond P. V. Vologodskogo], l. 8).

28. Semenov, *O sebe*, 112.

29. Ibid., 127.

30. V. G. Boldyrev, *Direktoriia, Kolchak, Interventy* (Novonikolaevsk: Sibkraiizdat, 1925), 143–144.

31. S. A. Elachich, "Obryvki vospominanii," HIA, 67–69.

32. G. K. Guins (Gins), *Sibir', soiuzniki, i Kolchak*, 2 vols. (Peking: Izd. Russian Mission, 1921), 1: 306–307.

33. L. H. Grondijs, *La guerre en Russie et en Siberie* (Paris: Editions Bossard, 1922), 383.

34. From Ia. Egoshkin's appeal to Kolchak, 12 December 1918, GARF, f. 176, op. 4, ed.khr. 9, l. 70.

35. See the report to Kolchak, 11 March 1919, GARF, f. 176, op. 7, ed.khr. 30, l. 2.

36. GARF, f. 5873, op. 1, ed.khr. 8, l. 142.

37. Ibid., f. 193, op. 1, ed.khr. 3 (Lichnyi fond P. V. Vologodskogo), l. 18.

38. S. P. Mel'gunov, *Tragediia Admirala Kolchaka*, 4 vols. (Belgrade: Russkaia tipografiia, 1930–31), part 3, 1: 237, refers to Kalmykov as "in many ways nothing more than a common criminal." During several of their most brutal raids Kalmykov's men were observed in the company of Japanese officers (GARF, f. 176, op. 1, ed.khr. 2, ll. 23–26). For more about his connection with the Japanese see Varneck and Fisher, *Testimony of Admiral Kolchak*, 231–233.

39. GARF, f. 176, op. 1, ed.khr. 2, ll. 26–26/ob.

40. Iuzefovich, "Samoderzhets pustyni," 31. Ibid., 26–27, provides contemporary descriptions of Ungern as having the "eyes of a maniac" and as being a man who "loved war the way others loved cards, wine, and women." A. P. Budberg, "Dnevnik," 21 February 1919, *Arkhiv Russkoi Revoliutsii* 13 (1924): 287, quotes one of Ungern's aides as saying that the ataman "regards the younger generation as cannon fodder, and believes that it must be sacrificed for the destruction of the Bolsheviks." See also A. S. Makeev, *Bog voiny—baron Ungern* (Shanghai: Zaria, 1934), 104–105, and F. Ossendowski, *Beasts, Men, and Gods* (New York: Blue Ribbon Books, 1931), 227–228.

41. Ossendowski, *Beasts, Men, and Gods*, 240–247.

42. See Iuzefovich, "Samoderzhets pustyni," 55.

43. Quoted from a letter written in August 1920, in Lary, *Warlord Soldiers*, 150.

44. Sheridan, *Chinese Warlord*, 1. Also see L. W. Pye, *Warlord Politics* (New York: Praeger, 1971), 5. Sheridan, *Chinese Warlord*, 8, elaborates this point: "The last century of the Ch'ing dynasty witnessed two related developments. On the one hand, the central government steadily weakened under the blows of domestic rebellion and foreign

wars; as the central power declined, regional economic and political autonomy increased. On the other hand, the influence of military men steadily grew . . . and military rather than civilian forms of administration characterized by terror and semi-institutionalized banditry." See also J. E. Sheridan, *China in Disintegration* (New York: Free Press, 1975), 78–79.

45. Budberg, "Dnevnik," 14: 226.

46. GARF, f. 176, op. 1, ed.khr. 2, l. 1.

47. S. C. Graves, "The Truth About Kolchak," *The New York Times Current History Magazine*, July 1921, 671. Foreign diplomatic missions, however, tended to be more sympathetic to Kolchak's dilemma in dealing with the unruly atamans; see telegram from Prince Kudashev, 26 July 1919, GARF, f. 200, op. 1, ed.khr. 407, l. 40.

48. Budberg, "Dnevnik," 14: 227. See also Mel'gunov, *Tragediia*, part 3, 5: 144–145.

49. GARF, f. 200, op. 1, ed.khr. 407, l. 13.

50. From Kolchak's note to the Russian ambassador in Washington, D.C., 8 December 1918, GARF, f. 200, op. 1, ed.khr. 407, l. 13.

51. Quoted in Varneck, *Testimony of Admiral Kolchak*, 195; also GARF, f. 200, op. 1, ed.khr. 407, l. 1.

52. J. W. Morley, *The Japanese Thrust into Siberia, 1918* (New York: Columbia University Press, 1957), 78. Also R. Jackson, *At War with the Bolsheviks: The Allied Intervention into Russia, 1917–1920* (London: Tom Stacy, 1972), 57; J. A. White, *The Siberian Intervention* (New York: Greenwood, 1969), 199–200; and Budberg, "Dnevnik," 13: 304.

53. Quoted in Varneck, *Testimony of Admiral Kolchak*, 139.

54. Ibid., 128.

55. Ibid., 120.

56. Semenov, *O sebe*, 112, denied that the Japanese had ever attempted to extract any such concessions from him.

57. GARF, f. 200, op. 1, ed.khr. 405, l. 124. See also Semenov, *O sebe*, 132–133.

58. GARF, f. 200, op. 1, ed.khr. 405, l. 153. See the telegram from Chita to Omsk,17 March 1919, in ibid., l. 100, which makes clear that as of that date Semenov still withheld his "recognition of the government of Admiral Kolchak."

59. For evidence of the British shift see the telegram from Klemm, 17 June 1919, GARF, f. 200, op. 1, ed.khr. 405, l. 165.

60. From Captain A. Spitsyn in Harbin (October 1919), citing Chang Tso-Lin as his source, in G. K. Guins (Gins) Collection, HIA, box 1, *Svodka* no. 14, 1–4.

61. Ibid., 25 October 1919, 9.

62. The most generous estimate of the number of men under Semenov's command at any moment was 10,000. But there were probably far fewer by this time. See *Russia Posol'stvo* (1914–1933) (United States), HIA, box 18, report of Captain N. F. Romanoff, 3; and GARF, f. 200, op. 1, ed.khr. 405, l. 102.

63. See Kolchak's decree of 4 January 1920 from Nizhne-Udinsk, GARF, f. 200, op. 1, ed.khr. 405, l. 229.

64. See my "Partisan Movement in Western Siberia, 1918–1920," *Jahrbücher für Geschichte Osteuropas* 1 (1990): 87–97; also "Lenin and the Siberian Peasant Insurrections," in G. Diment and Y. Slezkine, eds., *Between Heaven and Hell* (New York: St. Martin's, 1993), 133–150.

65. V. O. Kappel was the most talented of Kolchak's generals and the commander of the main White army that in retreating eastward tried to rescue the supreme ruler from execution in Irkutsk. After failing in this attempt, Kappel's men continued on their "Icy March" to Vladivostok, but their leader died in transit.

66. It was not until January 1925, however, that Japan finally removed its last troops from the northern half of Sakhalin Island. See V. Parfenov, *The Intervention in*

Siberia, 1918–1922 (New York: Workers Library, 1941), 51, and H. K. Norton, *The Far Eastern Republic of Siberia* (London: G. Allen & Unwin, 1923), 79.

67. GARF, f. 130, op. 3, d. 414, ll. 34–36; GARF, f. 393, op. 22, ed.khr. 219, l. 18. See also T. Shanin, *The Awkward Class: Political Sociology of Peasantry in a Developing Society: Russia, 1910–1925* (Oxford: Clarendon, 1972), 161.

68. Ungern-Sternberg was captured and executed at the end of the Civil War by Red partisans under P. E. Shchetinkin. See *Istoricheskii Arkhiv* 4 (1957): 71–81, and *Izvestiia*, 23 September 1921, 2.

69. Semenov, *O sebe*, 136–137, 153.

70. Dacy, "White Russian Movement," 393–394.

Three

Popular Resistance to Bolshevik Dictatorship

Workers' Protest Movement Against War Communism

7

> Between capitalist and socialist society lies the period of the revolutionary transformation of the one into the other. Corresponding to this is also a political transition period in which the state can be nothing but the dictatorship of the proletariat.
> —Karl Marx, "Critique of the Gotha Program"

The period of Russian history that started in October 1917 has long been referred to officially as the dictatorship of the proletariat. It was a difficult period that embodied numerous hardships and ordeals: revolution, civil war, intervention, economic devastation, epidemic, rebellion, and terror. Part of society was at war with the other, subjecting the enemy to merciless repression. Dictatorship was established in Russia.

But to what extent did the Russian proletariat take part in the dictatorship bearing its name? Did the workers practice dictatorship, or were they merely the human raw material used for the creation of the new system? The evidence is contradictory. Thanks to Soviet historiography, examples of workers' participation in the revolution and of their role in the construction and defense of the new society are well known. However, facts on workers' participation in the October events and in the civil war for the other side are far less known or studied. This participation has been brushed aside as an insignificant example of "petty bourgeois consciousness," which itself could be written off as a philosophical holdover from the past. It is now time for historians to devote attention to both sides of workers' actions during the first years of the Soviet regime in order to verify to what extent the term *dictatorship of the proletariat* describes the social reality of the period.

The course of events in the October seizure of power contains contradictory evidence. On the one hand, the Red Guards, made up of workers, occupied the post, the telegraph, and the rail stations, evidence frequently cited to prove workers' direct involvement with the Bolsheviks. On the other hand, the All-Russian Rail Workers' Union refused to endorse the

Bolsheviks' action and demanded that a coalition government of all Socialist parties be formed. In the following months railroad workers remained
a source of trouble for the Bolsheviks. On numerous occasions railroad
workers found themselves in the first ranks of opposition during strikes,
protests, and uprisings.

In elections to the Constituent Assembly held in November–December 1917, the Bolsheviks won convincingly in the main industrial cities of
central and northwestern Russia. Their victories were largely the result of
workers' dissatisfaction with the Provisional Government. These victories
in turn allowed Lenin to carry out his October overturn by relying on the
bolshevized workers' soviets. What is less well known is that workers'
political preferences changed after the Constituent Assembly elections.
With each passing week it was increasingly apparent that workers' hopes
that the Bolsheviks could improve the economic situation were going to
be frustrated.

The Bolsheviks launched an unprecedented social, economic, and
political transformation. Their avowed aim was to destroy the old state
apparatus, a goal that would sharpen social dislocation and cause hard-
ship in the cities. In December, as a result of the total collapse of the
transportation caused by the October overturn, the state-run food supply
system halted. The prospect of a cold and hungry winter cooled workers'
sympathies considerably to the victors of October. By the end of 1917,
political preferences among the workers had changed drastically. These
new attitudes were apparent in the sharp increase in the popularity of the
soon-to-be convened Constituent Assembly and in the political parties
that supported it.

The well-known workers' demonstration in support of the Constituent
Assembly on 5 January 1918, the assembly's opening day, revealed that a
large part of the working class had abandoned the Bolsheviks. The events
of that day revealed the depth of division among the workers. Red Guards
were shooting at other workers in Moscow and Petrograd who were taking part in the procession. The Menshevik delegates were indignant at the
session of the Moscow Soviet Executive Committee: "When the Bolsheviks felt that political popularity was on their side, the demonstrations in
early December went through without any obstacles. But the demonstration on 5 January was subjected to the most ferocious shooting even
though the victims were not some 'bourgeois' but workers, representatives of democracy and Socialists."[1]

The Mensheviks argued that the Bolsheviks feared the workers' participation in the demonstration because they knew that workers' attitudes
were reversing. The Bolsheviks were ready to use any means to keep
workers from marching in protest. On the eve of 5 January, all the oppo-

sition newspapers in Moscow were shut down. The Factory Committees of several plants threatened to fire anyone who took part in the demonstration. In some cases the Red Guards locked the workers inside the factories and took away their banners. Those who managed to take part in the demonstration were shot at without warning by the Red Guards, who showed more ardor than the regular soldiers did.[2] It is fair to conclude that during this period a part of the working class still supported the Bolsheviks. However, the processes of decomposition, which gained momentum during the first months of 1918, brought about changes in loyalties even in this privileged stratum of workers.

The problem was that the CEC decree of 14 (27) November on workers' control resulted in the spontaneous liquidation of private property rights. The financially struggling workers' collectives resorted to disposing of their assets in order to support themselves. Tempted by the opportunity to improve workers' living standards quickly, the Factory Committees worked with factory owners and administrators in withdrawing enterprise assets from the nationalized state bank. In other words, they were eating up the assets without thinking about the sustainability of production. A considerable part of these assets simply disappeared, and there was no improvement of workers' conditions or the production process. In a sense, the workers' control decree ushered in a "golden reign" for the Factory Committees and owners. By March 1918, when all the assets had been spent, the bankruptcies and closures of enterprises began. Unemployment rose. By spring, representatives of the ever-growing number of bankrupt enterprises lined up to plead for state subsidies. In this situation armed detachments of Red Guards reflected the frustration of their bankrupt enterprises. They turned into a source of trouble for the Bolsheviks, who in turn began to dissolve these armed detachments. The process of disbanding the Red Guards was still not complete by early summer. In the upper Volga provinces, for example, the Red Guards constituted the main force of anti-Soviet rebellions.

The growth of the workers' dissatisfaction with the Bolshevik regime is linked directly with the full-fledged civil war. For example, workers expressed their views and demands at a rally in Kostroma on 23 May 1918. At 2 P.M. that day, factories closed and five thousand workers rallied. Opposition speakers demanded reconvocation of the Constituent Assembly and freedom of trade, and the agitated workers would not let the Bolsheviks respond. After boisterous debate the workers adopted a resolution demanding that free trade be legalized under the supervision of a democratically elected non-Bolshevik government.[3] A local correspondent reported, "The mood in the city is agitated, especially in view of the news coming from Rybinsk and Yaroslavl' on workers' discontent there."[4]

This was a vague reference to events in these cities; street clashes had in fact erupted in Yaroslavl' between Red Army units and the still-active detachments of the Red Guards.[5] These clashes were merely a prelude to the events that were about to unfold.

After the rebellion of the Czechoslovak legion and the formation of the SR-led Committee to Reconvene the Constituent Assembly in June 1918, a full-scale front-line civil war cut through the Volga provinces. The diminishing food supply triggered an uprising in the Volga region in July. In a classified report to the Bolshevik CC, N. I. Podvoisky, the chairman of the High Military Inspection, admitted that the workers in the Volga provinces and the Urals supported the Czech-SR rebellion and that "masses of workers" joined the insurgent Peoples' Army fighting the Bolsheviks in an effort to reconvene the disbanded Constituent Assembly. They fought under the slogan "Long live the Constituent Assembly."

> This slogan enjoys tremendous popularity here. . . . During the entire period of the revolution no other slogan has attracted the masses so profoundly as this one does here in the areas engulfed by the Czechoslovak rebellion. Even those workers who had preserved their wages [jobs] had succumbed to this view, not to mention those unemployed. . . . With a few exceptions workers here are hostile toward Soviet Power. A considerable part no doubt is indifferent to the current political struggle. The unemployed workers at "demobilized" factories are mostly inimical to us, and some workers from the Tube and Cartridge plants in Samara joined the Cossacks.[6]

The report stressed that railroad workers were particularly irreconcilable and that their actions could be described only as undisguised sabotage of and resistance to Bolshevik orders.[7] It was largely because of the railroad workers' refusal to evacuate trains from the war zone that the fate of the gold reserve of the Russian empire was sealed. It was seized by the Czech-SR forces in Kazan'.

The official Soviet historiography maintains that the proletariat was the main force behind the Red Army's struggle against the counterrevolution of the bourgeois landlords. However, the Bolsheviks drew their strength, especially in the beginning, not from the workers but mostly from peasants, who had a vested interest in determining the results of the agrarian revolution and feared the return of the landlords and the tsar. The workers, on the other hand, displayed political indifference and in some cases animosity toward the Bolsheviks; this attitude was called counterrevolutionary disposition. Contrary to the expectation implicit in Communist doctrine, the working class of Russia displayed alienation from its historic mission of liberation. In the overwhelming number of

cases, workers' political dispositions were linked to the economic situation, particularly the food supply. It is no accident that at the CEC session
on 23 October 1919, M. I. Kalinin admitted that the most "counterrevolutionary mood" in the entire Soviet republic was present at the capital
and in those areas to which the masses of workers were fleeing in order
to escape famine.[8]

Many refugee workers flocked to the Smolensk province, far from the
civil war fronts, a shift that showed in the elections to the city soviet in
early 1920. Workers at factories and plants did not let the Bolsheviks
campaign. With a few exceptions, the Communists elected to the soviet
were voted in not by the workers but by the Red Army units. Workers of
almost all enterprises voted for the Mensheviks or for unaffiliated candidates.[9] In Petrograd it was common to hear the workers say: "We don't
care who has the political power, just give us bread."[10] A well-known dis-
sident in the Bolshevik party, G. I. Miasnikov, remembered the following:

> Petrograd was not so Red . . . as it appeared at the parades. Strikes and
> "go-slow" [actions] broke out under every possible pretext. Usually [the
> Bolsheviks] blamed the Mensheviks and SRs for the strikes and arrested
> them, but strikes went on and even intensified. Because of repression the
> Mensheviks and SRs acquired the aura of heroes, and entire plants rose
> up in their defense. And, in the eyes of the workers, the Communists
> turned into bloodhounds looking for hidden enemies. The Mensheviks
> and SRs criticized the established disorder and spoke out, calling the
> truth comprehensible to a common worker. The Communists, on the
> other hand, spoke about abstract matters and about the coming paradise
> on Earth. A Communist had to say that everything was fine.[11]

The political campaigning of the Mensheviks and SRs often channeled workers' indignation into political protests, especially in 1918 and
1919. A wave of strikes shook Petrograd in the spring of 1919 on the eve
of the Eighth Communist Party congress. Ten thousand Putilov plant
workers, led by the Left SRs, on 10 March almost unanimously passed a
resolution against the "dictatorship of the Bolshevik CC." The resolution
accused the Bolsheviks of betraying the October revolution and the interests of workers and peasants. It protested the regime of terror and repression against the Left SRs, and it condemned the "serfdom at the factories"
and the "disarming [of] revolutionary soldiers and sailors and their relo-
cation out of Petrograd." The resolution demanded the transfer of political
power to the freely elected soviets, abolishment of executions and torture,
liquidation of the Cheka (Extraordinary Commission, political police), and
guarantees of freedom of assembly and of the press.[12]

The week after the adoption of the Putilov plant resolution, other factories and plants came out in support of the demands. The authorities responded by launching unprecedented repressions against the workers in Petrograd. The Bolsheviks stationed armored cars outside the factories and plants of striking workers. Cheka agents and cadets from military schools, many of them Latvians and Chinese, occupied the plants. On several occasions these detachments opened fire at general meetings of workers, including meetings held at the Treugolnik factory and Rozhdestvensky street car depot. Police arrested hundreds of workers. At the Putilov plant, sixty-five workers were arrested, mostly Left SRs who disappeared without a trace in the cellars of the Cheka.[13]

The front-line civil war was at its height in 1919 when workers demanded ever more persistently that the Bolsheviks stop the slaughter. Railroad workers resolved to stop military operations immediately and establish peace with Admiral Kolchak, the leader of the Whites.[14] By June the main demand of the striking workers at the Tver' textile mills was no longer improvement of food supply or conduct of free elections to the soviets but immediate cessation of hostilities at the front.[15] In Moscow—during the successes of General Anton Denikin's offensive and on the very day that the Bolshevik CC published "Everyone Rise To Fight Denikin," an appeal signed by Lenin—workers in the Sokolniki district were marching, as we have learned from private letters, with white flags printed with the slogans "Down with the Bloody Slaughter," "Give Us Bread," and "Long Live the Constituent Assembly." The workers of Prokhorov textile mill refused to be drafted into the Red Army. They paraded with white flags instead, openly demonstrating their allegiance to the Whites.[16] Bolshevik campaigns to draft workers into the Red Army encountered difficulties just as serious as those they met in drafting peasants. Unlike peasants, however, workers were unionized and could act with more cohesion. Special CC and CEC plenipotentiaries dispatched to the provinces in May 1919 to conduct a Red Army draft campaign reported cases in which "entire trade unions refused to deliver a single person."[17]

Workers' oppositional attitudes were often apparent in the results of elections to the city soviets. In fact, the preponderance of the opposition was overwhelming in many industrial cities during the civil war, despite the difficulty of staging a fair campaign and the outright electoral fraud of the Bolsheviks. For example, the Communist party had no influence whatsoever at the two large military plants in Tula. From 1918 to 1920 the Mensheviks won solid majorities in the Tula city soviet, thanks to the workers. The Mensheviks in Tula consistently criticized Bolshevik dictatorial practices while defending the striking workers. Even though the military plants in Tula were crucial for the war effort, strikes at those plants broke out as frequently as in any other industrial city. In April 1919, for example, the

Tula workers went on a "go-slow" strike after putting forward the usual economic demands. The Bolshevik CC considering the matter concluded that the demands were political.[18] M. P. Tomsky, the chairman of the All-Russian Trade Unions Council, proposed settling the dispute "in the spirit of reconciliation and partial concessions," but his approach was rejected because it "gave no guarantees that the strike would end." It was decided to adopt "tough and decisive measures." Feliks Dzerzhinsky, the chairman of the Cheka, telegraphed to his subordinates in Tula: "Be decisive to the end. Do not enter into any agreements."[19] The Cheka threatened to dismiss everyone who would not resume work immediately. The threat worked, and on 10 April some employees at the armaments plant showed up for work. The strike was broken, and 290 strikers were arrested.

A year later, the Tula CP Committee reported to the CC that "at the cartridge and armaments plants strikes took place caused by food supply difficulties and agitation of the Mensheviks."[20] The strikers' main demand, here as almost everywhere else, was to remove the so-called anti-profiteer detachments that enforced the ban on private trade. Yet the ban was one of the main planks of the economic system known as War Communism, which is state monopoly on all forms of economic activity, including food supply. The so-called food supply dictatorship—that is, an attempt by the state to control production and distribution of food—was an essential ingredient of the Bolshevik political dictatorship. Therefore, the workers' struggle against food supply dictatorship can be seen as a manifestation of their opposition to the Bolshevik dictatorship as such.

Outbreaks of worker discontent were not limited to the railroad and armaments industries. Equally tense was the atmosphere in the textile industry region, east of Moscow. The lack of food was perhaps the main source of trouble in Ivanovo-Voznesensk, an important textile center. Even though warehouses were stocked with rotting cloth, weavers suffered continual food shortages beginning in 1918. In early January 1920 workers in Shuya, Bychuga, Rodniki, and other towns quit work, demanding that anti-profiteer detachments be dismantled.[21] The Province CP committee admitted on 17 February that the "food supply crisis sharpened in the extreme."[22] On 23 February the CP committee discussed the spreading rumors that workers in Ivanovo-Voznesensk itself were going to go on strike. On the same day the city party committee received information on workers' rallies and meetings held to protest Soviet power. Rumors spread at the factories that on 25 February workers were going to stage some kind of political action. The mood of the workers was described as heightened, excited, and angry. They were reported as saying: "If you took power, then give us bread, but if you can't, get the hell out and vacate the place for somebody else." At the Kuvaev factory in

Rykhlin district, soldiers' representatives assured the workers that the soldiers were not going to open fire.[23] On the 25 February agenda of the city party committee was the issue of the workers' rally at the central square; 1,500 people participated.[24] These kinds of outbreaks were taking place almost every other month. The Ivanovo-Voznesensk province party committee telegraphed the CC that difficulties with the food supply mean that "everywhere . . . an atmosphere is ripening for strikes, disturbances, and street processions, which so far have had an unorganized character but which could escalate into mass spontaneous protests."[25]

The food supply was most limited in the summer, on the eve of the new crop, and in the height of winter, with its snowstorms and unpassable railroads. On 6 December 1919 the Moscow chapter of the Metalists' Union described the situation in its address to the seventh All-Russian Congress of Soviets. "The food supply crisis has become sharper lately. The masses of workers find themselves in the tightening grip of famine. The stores of food made in the summer and early fall are used up. Food supply agencies give nothing to their consumers. Workers are undernourished, they are losing the physical capacity to work. . . . These conditions may provoke workers' action at a number of metal plants in Moscow."[26] A workers' delegation from a Gakhental factory declared that employees had quit work and were demanding that prohibitions on individual procurement of food in the countryside be abolished. Workers' delegates from factories in Dobrov and Nabholts warned the congress about the likelihood of their joining the strike. At the Ikshansk wire and nail factory, workers began a go-slow "Italian" strike.[27]

The forms of protest were not limited to petitions, resolutions, and strikes. Sometimes workers' demand that free exchange of goods be legalized meant, in practice, free exchange of manufactured goods for foodstuffs from the countryside. In January 1920 a scandal broke out in the All-Russian People's Economy Council over events at the soap factories Ralle and Brokar. Workers broke into the warehouses and distributed twelve pounds of soap to each worker as part of wages for January. It was an unauthorized removal of hundreds of pounds of soap, and neither the factory administration nor the Factory Committee did anything to prevent it.[28] In response, the soap industry directorate decided to close the plants, fire the employees, and ask the Cheka to investigate the actions of the administrative personnel and the factory committees.

In order to survive, everybody had to have something to sell. Practically every urban dweller sold goods on the black market, mostly old possessions but also new items, some of them stolen. The extent of theft reached a critical level. In a 29 June 1920 letter to Lenin, Kamenev wrote that the Moscow Cheka found it impossible to combat theft and speculation any longer. Arrests and executions no longer served as a deterrent, and the scope of undertakings was growing.[29]

Theft as a form of social protest was a serious problem. Warehouses typically were raided quietly and surreptitiously but on a scale that surpassed anything reasonable. The military censorship department's survey for April 1920 reveals that the workers in Gus Khrustal'nyi township of Vladimir province had decided to steal everything they could find at the textile factory. Hundreds of rolls of cloth were taken to the countryside to be exchanged for bread and potatoes. "The factory was literally turned into an open marketplace," the survey reported. The workers told the guards, "'Steal yourself and do not report on us.'" To the authorities the workers responded, "Give us bread and we won't steal." One day a crowd of workers besieged the building of the Food Supply Committee shouting, "Give us bread, or else we shall take away everything." Armed Communists dispersed the crowd and arrested some offenders. Remaining workers received twenty-five pounds of bread each if they promised not to steal any more.[30] They did not keep their promise for long. At the tenth CP congress in 1921, held after the New Economic Policy was adopted, someone pointed out that workers at the Gus Khrustal'nyi township had decided not to steal during the two weeks when their delegates were in Moscow negotiating. Later it was determined that during these two weeks the manufacture of cloth increased by 200 percent.[31]

Food supply dictatorship was one of the main components in the general system of Bolshevik dictatorship. The flight of hungry workers from enterprises—and the general flight from cities to the countryside—contributed to the mounting troubles of Russian industry. In part to counter this process, the CP ninth congress in early 1920 introduced new principles of industrial relations, known as *militarization of labor*. Under these principles workers lost their remaining rights, including free movement and free choice of work. They were bound to their employers, just as the serfs had been bound to the factories in the eighteenth century. This measure deprived workers of any opportunity to travel to the countryside in order to procure food independently. As a result, workers grew even more bitter, and they turned to malicious wrecking and sabotage.

In September 1920 the CC received a report from Perm' on the situation at the Motovilikha armaments plant, one of the most important in the Urals: "The authority of the plant administration does not exist. . . . The labor force is disintegrating. [Absenteeism] reached 50 percent. Arson, theft, and deliberate damage of locomotives, as well as hidden sabotage, are going on."[32] At the Kolchuginsky copper plant in Tver' province, the only plant in Russia casting cartridge brass, the ruling that added two hours to the workday produced an "incredible atmosphere."

Workers attempted to set fire to the warehouses of the plant; had they succeeded, production would have stopped.[33] Laconic but all-embracing information on workers' attitudes can be found in the regular surveys by the All-Russian Cheka. For example, in the survey covering the second half of August 1920, strikes were reported in the following provinces: Kaluga, Moscow, Vladimir, Nizhnii Novgorod, Smolensk, Orel, Kursk, Tambov, Voronezh, Kharkov, Poltava, Donetsk, Saratov, and Irkutsk.[34]

The end of the war with Poland and the defeat of General Wrangel's White army in the fall of 1920 pacified workers temporarily. The Food Supply Commissariat had managed to set up an effective system of transporting grain from the countryside to the industrial centers. But greater upheavals were to come. By the beginning of 1921 the general agricultural crisis and the growing peasant protest against grain requisitions led to unprecedented rebellion by the peasants. In fact, a new stage of civil war had begun.

In January the food supply system was largely paralyzed, partly by the actions of the rebels and partly by the snowdrifts. The political situation in Petrograd and Moscow was complicated by the lack of food, the closing of factories because of the lack of fuel, and the party debate on the role of trade unions. Communist leaders attacked each other verbally in front of workers and soldiers.

Early in 1921 the workers rejected the system of War Communism entirely and began to identify with the interests of peasants. A. Slepkov remembered this shift in the outlook of workers. As recently as 1919 the workers were saying: "We are swelling from hunger here in the cities and they are swelling from gluttony in the countryside." But by the beginning of 1921, workers were asking the Communists: "You demand that the countryside deliver grain, but what are you giving them in return?" About 60 percent of workers had some connection to the countryside—relatives, black market trade links, or land plots.[35]

Workers' disturbances broke out in Petrograd on 24 February, triggering a sailors' rebellion in Kronstadt. Petrograd was paralyzed by the general strike. The strikers were circulating openly anti-Bolshevik leaflets demanding a fundamental change of policy, release of arrested Socialists and workers, and free elections to the soviets. On 28 February leaflets calling for the overthrow of Soviet power and convocation of the Constituent Assembly were posted in the Nevsky district. The unrest spread: on 3 March the Communist caucus of the All-Russian Council of Trade Unions debated the "outbreak of the new wave of strikes in Moscow."[36] Factory Committees at numerous enterprises were expelling Communist members.

After the cruel suppression of the Kronstadt rebellion, conciliatory gestures were made toward workers in Petrograd. Authorities distributed four pounds of meat and other consumer items to each person, removed antiprofiteer detachments, and convened the meeting of workers' representatives with a guarantee of freedom of speech.[37] But the most important consequence of the social explosion of early 1921 was the abolition of War Communism and the transition to the New Economic Policy (NEP). This retreat by the Bolsheviks was a serious victory of workers and peasants over the Bolshevik dictatorship in Russia.

As we know from the Marxist-Leninist teachings of the recent past, utopian Socialism became the scientific teaching of Socialism after the discovery of Karl Marx had been made on the universal historical role of the proletariat as a social force for carrying out a Socialist revolution and improving society on through equality, justice, and scientific management. This discovery laid the foundation for the theory of the dictatorship of the proletariat, and the twentieth century was supposed to bear out this forecast. But history has provided no such confirmation. If we consider only the facts of this period, we learn that the "dictatorship of the proletariat," did not exist. The proletariat had only an indirect relation to the real dictatorship, which in fact was the dictatorship of the new state apparatus headed by Lenin's party leadership. Lev Sosnovsky, a well-known Bolshevik functionary, did discover in a remote uezd of Tver' province that three-fourths of the local Soviet Executive Committee members had been workers in Moscow and Petrograd. But this does not prove the existence of the dictatorship of the proletariat, only the existence of the dictatorship of Executive Committees. Representatives of the proletariat were merely used to fill the vacancies of the new state structure. The common workers felt the oppression delivered by the new bosses, their former brothers.

Bolshevik policy was being seriously criticized by other Socialist parties as early as 1918. These Socialists made it clear that the power of the commissar meant the defeat of the workers' and peasants' revolution. They claimed that state power as practiced by the Bolsheviks actually was a return to the principles of prerevolutionary times, freed from restraint and social compromises. The Bolsheviks set themselves toward achieving absolute domination over civil society. From the point of view of adherents of Socialism, this was nothing but treason. Was this the realization of the scientific laws of history or of utopian visions?

V. K. Volsky, the chairman of the Committee of the Constituent Assembly in Samara, in 1919 addressed the proletariat and its historical mission this way: "We have to cast aside illusions about the dictatorship of the proletariat. The proletariat has not reached either the maturity or the intellectual level to be able to 'introduce Socialism' not only in the countryside but at its own place."[38]

Notes

1. "Protokoly zasedaniia Mossoveta" (6 January 1918), TsGAMO, f. 66, op. 7, d. 8, p. 11.

2. Ibid., p. 12.

3. "Telegramma sobraniia rabochikh i grazhdan Kostromy Predsedateliu SNK V. I. Leninu" (23 May 1918), GARF, f. 130, op. 2, d. 705, p. 308.

4. *Izvestiia Narkomproda* (Moscow), nos. 6–7 (1918): 35.

5. *Znamia Truda* (Moscow), 22 May 1918.

6. N. Podvoisky, "Doklad o zadachakh Sovetskoi Vlasti v borbe s Chekhoslovatskim miatezhom," RTsKhIDNI, f. 17, RCP Central Committee, op. 84, Biuro Sekretariata, d. 4, p. 13.

7. Ibid., p. 14.

8. "Stenogramma zasedaniia VTsIK" (Fourth convocation, 23 October 1918), GARF, f. 1235 VTsIK, op. 21, d. 18, pp. 5–6.

9. N. Shutko, "Otchet o deiatel'nosti Smolenskogo Gubkoma" (10 March 1920), RTsKhIDNI, f. 17, op. 5, d. 209, p. 2.

10. "Svodka otdela voennoi tsenzury RVSR" (July 1919), RTsKhIDNI, f. 17, op. 65, d. 453, p. 126.

11. G. I. Miasnikov, "Voennyi Kommunizm v Petrograde" (2 May 1921), in documents on Miasnikov's group in the Motovilikha plant organization, Ekaterinburg Oblast Archive, f. 41, op. 2, d. 418, p. 83.

12. "Listovka Petrogradskogo Komiteta Partii Levykh SR" (9 March 1919), RTsKhIDNI, f. 17, op. 84, d. 43, p. 20.

13. Ibid., pp. 21–22.

14. "Stenogramma soveshchaniia upolnomochennykh VTsIK i TsKa RKP b po mobilizatsii" (June 1919), RTsKhIDNI, f. 17, op. 65, d. 7, p. 146.

15. "Svodka voennoi tsenzury RVSR" (June 1919), RTsKhIDNI, f. 17, op. 65, d. 141, p. 42.

16. Ibid., d. 453, p. 123.

17. "Stenogramma soveshchaniia upolnomochennykh VTsIK i TsKa RKP(b) po mobilizatsii" (June 1919), RTsKhIDNI, f. 17, op. 65, d. 7, p. 141.

18. "Protokol zasedaniia Orgburo TsKa RKP(b)" (11 April 1919), RTsKhIDNI, f. 17, op. 112, d. 3, p. 17.

19. "Razgovor po priamomu provodu s Tul'skoi Gubcheka" (5 April 1919), RTsKhIDNI, f. 17, op. 65, Documents of the Tula Gubkom, d. 86, p. 9.

20. "Svodka o partiinoi rabote Tul'skogo gubkoma RKP(b) (April 1920), RTsKhIDNI, f. 17, op. 12, d. 640, p. 36.

21. "Telegramma Ivanovo-Voznesenskogo gubernskogo s'ezda RKP(b)" (16 January 1920), RTsKhIDNI, f. 17, op. 65, d. 489, p. 2.

22. "Protokol zasedaniia Ivanovo-Voznesenskogo Gubkoma" (17 February 1920), RTsKhIDNI, f. 17, op. 12, d. 188, p. 12.

23. Ibid. (23 February 1920), d. 191, p. 12.

24. Ibid. (25 February 1920), d. 188, p. 15.

25. "Telegramma plenuma Ivanovo-Voznesenskogo Gubkoma v TsKa RKP(b) (23 May 1920), RTsKhIDNI, f. 17, op. 65, d. 327, p. 14.

26. From Komitet Moskovskogo otdeleniia Vserossiiskogo soiuza metalistov to VII Vserossiiskii s'ezd Sovetov, RTsKhIDNI, f. 2, Sovnarkom Secretariat, op. 1, d. 11957, p. 8.

27. Ibid., p. 5.

28. "Postanovlenie kollegii Tsentrozhira" (2 January 1920) in Protokol zasedaniia VTsNKh (5 January 1920), TsGANKh, f. 3429, VTsNKh, op. 1, d. 1302, p. 34.

29. From L. B. Kamenev to V. I. Lenin (29 June 1920), RTsKhIDNI, f. 2, Sovnarkom Secretariat, op. 1, d. 14521, p. 1.

30. "Svodka otdela voennoi tsenzury" (April 1920), RTsKhIDNI, f. 17, op. 65, d. 453, p. 70.

31. "Stenogramma plenarnogo zasedaniia X konferentsii RKP(b) (27 May 1921), RTsKhIDNI, f. 46, op. 1, d. 2, p. 186.

32. "Telegramma Permskogo Gubkoma v TsKa RKP(b)" (September 1920), TsGANKh, f. 3429, op. 1, d. 1431, p. 146.

33. From Tsentral'noe upravlenie gosudarstvennymi predpriiatiiami to Orgburo TsKa RKP(b) (22 May 1920), RTsKhIDNI, f. 17, op. 84, d. 68, p. 4.

34. "Informatsionnye svodki Sekretnogo Otdela VeCheKa" RTsKhIDNI, f. 2, op. 1, d. 68, p. 4.

35. A. Slepkov, *Kronshtadtskii miatezh* (Moscow-Leningrad, 1929), 8–9.

36. "Protokol zasedaniia biuro Kommunisticheskoi fraktsii VTsSPS" (3 May 1921), RTsKhIDNI, f. 95, op. 1, d. 22, p. 44.

37. G. I. Miasnikov, "Voennyi Kommunizm v Petrograde" Ekaterinburgskii oblastnoi arkhiv, f. 41, op. 2, d. 418, p. 84.

38. *Istoricheskii Arkhiv* (Moscow), no. 3 (1993): 146.

TAISIA OSIPOVA

Peasant Rebellions: Origin, Scope, Dynamics, and Consequences

The Reds and the Whites, the Bolsheviks and the Kadets, the Mensheviks and the Socialist Revolutionaries—all agreed that the political sympathies of the peasants, who constituted three-quarters of the country's population, determined the outcome of the civil war in Russia. Nevertheless, there are few studies on many aspects of civil war history, including peasants' attitudes to the war, behavior in the armies of the warring sides, desertion from the Red Army (evidence of opposition to the Soviet regime), resistance to War Communism, and peasant rebellions as integral to the civil war. As early as the 1930s, the study of the war's unsightly history gave way to a politicized effort to find a scapegoat for the peasant rebellions. For almost fifty years the rebellions were ignored in historiography as a legitimate subject of research. They could be mentioned only as confirmation of the correctness of the party's aim to split the peasantry along class lines and conduct uncompromising struggle with the so-called kulaks. The true history of the peasants' struggle against Communist dictatorship was replaced with a myth of an alliance between the working class and the peasants. Since the late 1930s, Soviet historiography has tended to treat the party line and reality as one. This approach has made it impossible to question the existence of the alliance and to scrutinize departures from the alleged party policy. It made it impossible to explain the rebellions, which had escalated into war by 1919.

From the late 1930s to the late 1980s Soviet historiography touted a standard interpretation of the character of peasant resistance. According to this interpretation, the revolutionary center of the country was counterpoised to the counterrevolutionary periphery, where the success of antisoviet forces was explained by the intervention of foreign powers. This thesis was defended with quotations from Lenin and Stalin, since no other proof was necessary. As a result, the entire period of peasant history during the civil war in central Russia was ignored by scholars for many decades. In this chapter I reconstruct the role of the peasants in central Russia during that period.

Grain—its ownership and the methods of procuring it—was the main problem in the peasants' relations with the Bolshevik authorities. According to Lenin, everyone in the countryside who retained grain for the market was a kulak—a speculator and an enemy of the revolution who had to either submit to the Communist dictatorship or be crushed by it. "Merciless war on the kulaks, that is our Socialist duty," declared Lenin on 5 July 1918 at the Fifth Congress of Soviets.[1]

In fact, this definition of *kulak* was nothing but a rhetorical abstraction. Despite their social differentiation, the wealthier peasants in central Russia had not broken with the traditional peasant commune. They still followed the same patriarchal laws as the rest of peasants. However, the 1917 ban on private ownership of land, on land lease, and on hired labor, and the equalization of land allotment aimed to undermine the position of these better-off peasants. The measures made the wealthier peasants hostile to the power of the soviets and turned them into supporters of the Constituent Assembly, led by the Socialist Revolutionaries.

In the spring of 1918 the Bolsheviks began to rely increasingly on coercive methods of grain procurement. Any peasants who had grain in their possession were defined as kulaks, regardless of their income. The peasants responded by refusing to sell their grain, thereby intensifying the food procurement crisis. They relied on the SRs to pressure the authorities to stop such coercion. Although there were too few of the better-off peasants to pose a danger to the government, their affinity with peasants at large and their leadership role in the countryside gave them strength. What united them with the middle-income peasants and some of the poor peasants was their resistance to the Bolsheviks' policy of coercion. For three years rebellions shook Russia, on the periphery and in the central provinces, as peasants fought against this state coercion.

The Initial Response to Arbitrariness—1918

Peasant resistance to the government first arose on a mass scale in the summer of 1918 in the eastern provinces. On 12 June a general mobilization was declared in fifty-one uezds of the Volga basin, the Urals, and Siberia. This was the first test of the peasants' attitudes toward Soviet power, and the results were much worse than the Communists had anticipated. Instead of the expected 275,000 draftees, the Red Army received only 54,000.[2] When the Soviets tried to enforce the mobilization order, the peasants responded with armed resistance and mass insurrections.

For example, in Kungursky uezd in Perm' province, one insurrection was registered in June and seventeen in July in connection with the Red Army draft campaign. Ten thousand peasants took part in these two insurrections.[3] Peasants of twelve cantons in Okhanky uezd and twenty-one cantons in Krasnoufimsky refused to obey the mobilization order, and insurrections foiled mobilization in Ufa, Samara, Saratov, Simbirsk, and Kazan' provinces.[4] The army draft in these provinces was officially canceled in view of "peasants' passive mood and unsympathetic attitude to mobilization."[5] The majority in these provinces, the middle-income peasants, sent a clear message that they had no interest in participating in the war between the Bolsheviks and the SRs backed by the Czechoslovak Legion. The peasants had achieved their main objectives in 1917: land and peace. Now they wanted to remain neutral in the war between rival governments. Peasants' unwillingness to participate in the civil war was evident in their reluctance to join the People's Army as well, which was being formed by the Committee of the Constituent Assembly (Komuch) government.

The Bolshevik strategy in the countryside was to split the peasant community along class lines. On 20 May 1918 the chairman of the CEC, Yakov Sverdlov, defined the task as "inciting the civil war in the countryside by creating two opposing forces. It was necessary to organize and arm the poor peasants in order to strangle the kulaks."[6] The decrees of May 1918 introduced the food supply dictatorship, centralized the procurement and distribution of grain, and set up the Food Supply Army. On 11 June the decree on the committees of the poor provided a legal basis for inciting civil strife in the countryside. And finally, the order of the Internal Affairs Commissariat of 2 July, "On the Struggle with Kulaks in the Soviets," demanded that wealthier peasants and other kulaks be deprived of their voting rights. This was confirmed by the Constitution, adopted a few days later at the Fifth Congress of Soviets.[7] At the CEC session on 4 July, Trotsky explained: "It is self-evident that the Soviet power conducts the civil war against the landlords, the bourgeoisie, and the kulaks. The Soviet power is not afraid to admit it openly. It is not afraid to appeal to the masses and organize the masses for this war."[8] He called for a merciless fight against the kulaks.

The political parties in the soviets were in opposition, but they all disagreed with the direction that internal policy and the methods of implementation were taking. The SRs proposed ending the food supply crisis by restoring market relations. The Menshevik leaders declared in the CEC that the Bolshevik policy was leading toward creating an "internal front" in the countryside. The idea of playing the poor peasants off the richer ones was unsound and utopian, Iu. Martov warned, because by "hitting the kulaks you will actually hurt the middle peasants."[9] Another Menshevik speaker, N. N. Sukhanov, proposed to dissolve the soviets and, instead of creating committees of the poor, restore institutions of local government elected on the basis of universal suffrage (such as the dumas and zemstvos). This is exactly what the Mensheviks and SRs started doing in the eastern provinces, where they overthrew the Bolsheviks.

The Left SRs believed that the food supply dictatorship reflected the Bolsheviks' lack of trust in the laboring peasantry. Bolshevik methods were inappropriate for solving food supply problems. The Left SRs rejected the Bolshevik interpretation of class struggle as war on an internal front. And they vigorously opposed dictatorial methods. They saw the solution in the state regulation of prices and in centralizing the distribution of consumer goods. They did not deny that the kulaks had to be induced to surrender grain, but only by economic incentives implemented by local soviets. The Left SRs opposed the idea of the Food Supply Army, and they banned party members from joining the requisition detachments. The Left SRs regarded the "committees of the poor" as undermining the very principle of Soviet power—that is, the local government of all peasants in the countryside. Their party policy was to energetically oppose requisition detachments and the committees of the poor.[10]

Tension between the partners of the ruling coalition, first noticeable in March 1918, developed into confrontation by May–June. Left SR leaders resolved to break with the Bolsheviks unequivocally. At the Third Congress of the Left SR party, on 28 June, party leader Mariya Spiridonova defined the tasks: "Our party must take upon itself the burden of leadership of the insurrection. We shall call upon the masses to rise, we shall incite, ignite, and organize. Only by means of the insurrection shall we be able to overcome that which is moving upon us."[11]

"We are entering a new stage of political development, a stage when we probably shall be the ruling party," she said.[12] The Left SRs hoped to become leaders of the peasant revolution and form a new government. Their immediate objective was to win majorities in the soviets and to cancel the Brest-Litovsk peace treaty with Germany. The sympathies of the peasants were the main rewards in the political struggle of opposition parties. Only with the peasants' support did a party have a realistic chance at overthrowing the Bolsheviks.

The Communists' idea to use the committees of the poor to ignite civil war in the countryside was not realized by the summer of 1918. The decree on the committees of the poor specified that the canton soviets were to oversee their organization. As a result of the spring elections, however, the representatives of the better-off peasants and the Left SRs predominated in the local soviets. In twenty-two provinces the Left SRs refused to act on the committees of the poor decree, forestalling the break-up of the peasant commune for three months. There were too few armed detachments of Communists in the countryside to be effective, and the poor peasants were not able to break the traditions of peasant communal life on their own. Moreover, they hardly strove to accomplish that. During the summer months the committees of the poor were formed in only 10 percent of the cantons.[13]

The most common expressions of peasant discontent in central Russia were protests against requisitions. During the summer of 1918 there were 130 incidents directed against local soviets, 73 insurrections, and 154 clashes with the requisition detachments.[14] In Orel, Kursk, and Voronezh provinces there were numerous cases of junior officers refusing to show up for the army draft.[15] For example, in Livensky uezd, Orel province, two thousand noncommissioned officers mutinied. They ransacked the uezd soviet, killed the Communists, and disbanded committees of the poor in the villages.[16] Serious peasant rebellions, triggered by requisition of cattle and grain, broke out in July and August in Porechsky and Belsky uezds of Smolensk province, Dmitrovsky uezd of Moscow province, and in several uezds of Voronezh, Penza, Novgorod, Pskov, and Petrograd provinces. In Varnavinsky uezd of Kostroma province the Red Army fought peasant rebels for more than a month.[17]

Lenin attentively followed the growth of peasant resistance. In his telegrams to Orel, Voronezh, Penza, and other provinces he insisted on merciless reprisals against the insurgents. He ordered local Bolsheviks to hang the inciters, seize hostages, "expose" the Left SRs, and requisition the entire stock of grain in areas of rebellion.[18] The only appropriate response to "kulak sabotage" was intensification of repression. Lenin's ideas were codified into the CEC decrees of August 1918. By the end of August the countryside was saturated with workers' requisition detachments, which established outright control over 70 percent of the grain-producing provinces of central Russia.[19] Their main objective was to seize the new crop, end the sabotage of the peasant commune, and transfer power to the committees of the poor. The policy of terrorizing the population into submission was legalized by the CEC Red Terror decree, announced on 2 September 1918. This decree summarized the experience accumulated in the provinces and outlined avenues of its intensification. The "enemies of the revolution" were to be interned in concentration camps, and those who were involved in the White Guards and in conspiracies and mutinies were to be shot on the spot.[20]

The terror, especially at the local level, was unprecedented in its arbitrariness and in its lawlessness in identifying the "enemies." All kinds of marginal individuals (drunkards, hooligans, criminals) surfaced during the civil war, and many found jobs in the soviets, especially at the local level. They easily appropriated the rhetoric of class struggle for their own needs and, defying the norms of morality and humanism, gave way to their baser instincts and to violence. They appropriated requisitioned goods for personal use. Their actions were outright criminal. Various theories justified the violence as a fundamental principle of Communist construction. N. I. Bukharin, the "favorite of the party," as Lenin called him, explained the role of revolutionary violence: "Proletarian coercion in all its forms, starting with executions and ending with the labor conscription, is, no matter how paradoxical this may sound, a method of creating Communist mankind out of the human raw material of the capitalist epoch."[21]

The committees of the poor and the requisition detachments forced people in the countryside to submit to Communist dictatorship. They broke the SR resistance and drove it underground, and arrested or executed SR leaders. At the party conferences and congresses of soviets or committees of the poor the Communists talked about the strengthening of proletarian forces, successes in the struggle against class enemies, and the loyalty of the majority of the population to Soviet power. The peasant protests and the ongoing rebellions were perceived by the authorities as normal manifestations of class struggle and as evidence of the growing role of poor peasants. Nevertheless, it soon became apparent that the committees of the poor were failing in their most important task: to collect and register the "surplus" grain. They managed to deliver no more than a third of the estimated "surplus." Moreover, the committees of the poor often hindered removal of grain from their provinces and engaged in what was officially called speculation—that is, private grain trade. The committees of the poor, even from the Bolsheviks' point of view, did more harm than good. They destroyed the network of peasant cooperatives and divided the assets but created nothing to replace it. They "nationalized" the windmills, consumer cooperatives shops, and inns but failed to keep them operating. On 14 October the interdepartmental commission discussed the performance of the committees of the poor. Instead of the power of the proletarian masses in the countryside the Bolsheviks faced the power of local cliques that used the "class struggle" approach to enrich themselves. Before long the Bolsheviks decided to abolish the committees of the poor.

Peasant Resistance to Army Draft, 1918

In September 1918 the Military Revolutionary Committee issued the order to mobilize former officers, noncommissioned officers, military doctors, and workers and peasants in five age groups. The draft was postponed until November so that the peasants could finish the harvest. This was the first mass draft of peasants into the Red Army in central Russia. From the beginning of the campaign the peasants rebelled. Between 1 November and 25 November rebellions broke out in 80 uezds of central Russia: in 11 uezds out of 12 in Ryazan' province, in 9 uezds of Smolensk province, 7 uezds of Tambov, in 6 uezds of Kaluga and Kostroma, and in 4 uezds of Vladimir, Moscow, Tula, and Cherepovetsk provinces.[22] The insurgents, led by former officers, set up regular headquarters and besieged uezd towns. In Ryazan' province they seized the township of Kasimov; in Tambov province, the town of Shatsk; in Smolensk, Dukhovshchina, Gzhatsk, and Porech'e; and in Kaluga province they seized several small towns and railroad stations.[23] Angered by the actions of the committees of the poor, middle-income and even poor peasants supported the mutinous draftees. The number of reported insurgents in a given uezd by far exceeded the number of those drafted. In Vareisky uezd, for example, the number of insurgents was estimated at 10,000 and in Medynsky uezd at 8,000.[24]

Insurgents destroyed local soviets, committees of the poor, and local Chekas. In Sapozhnikovsky uezd, for example, they killed forty Communists and soviet members.[25] Generally the rebels tried to restore their traditional peasant commune and, under the influence of the SRs, the all-estate institutions of local government, the zemstvos. In the summer of 1918 officers attempted to organize units of a regular insurgent army, the People's Army, following the example of the Komuch government. Peasants, however, were reluctant to join any army, and they often agreed only under pressure or threat that their village would be burned.

For the suppression of this movement the Bolsheviks deployed regular units of the Red Army and detachments of the Cheka and Food Supply Army. In Ryazan' province, for example, they formed a special detachment of 1,000 men. In addition, punitive detachments from the Moscow military district dispatched to Ryazan' numbered several hundred each to each insurgent uezd.[26] The military objective of these units was to provide relief to the besieged areas and to seize towns where insurgent headquarters were located. Heavy artillery was deployed against one village in Pronsk uezd, and in Tambov province armored cars were deployed in forty cantons.[27] Upon completion of the operation, the ring leaders and hostages routinely were executed. It is impossible to ascertain the total number of victims, but the data on some uezds suggest that it was high. In Pronsky, Rannenburgsky, and Kasimovsky uezds of Ryazan' province 750 persons were executed; in Velizhsky uezd of Smolensk province, 600; and in Tula, Voronezh, Orel, and Kostroma provinces, 1,200. Within just seven days, 200 peasants were executed in Tver' province. In their search for the ring leaders the Bolsheviks conducted mass arrests among suspect groups of the population: former imperial officers, schoolteachers, civil servants, and others who were known to be members of opposition parties (Kadets, Mensheviks, or SRs).

Spiridonova was the first to denounce Bolshevik reprisals against the peasants. At workers' rallies in Moscow in January 1919 she spoke of the reign of terror during the suppression of the peasant uprising in Varnavinsky uezd, Kostroma province. M. V. Frunze, the military commissar of Yaroslavl' military district, was in charge of this operation. Spiridonova likened the Soviet regime to the Tsarist one. In fact, it was much worse. "How many executions were there? . . . The Communists shoot, whip, suppress, and then impose an indemnity [upon the peasants]. There was a time when the Tsarist government also suppressed, but then they did not bring to ruin completely. . . . Peasants hate not only Soviet power and the Communists, they are set against the urban workers as well."[28]

Spiridonova called the Bolshevik policy counterrevolutionary, she likened the Cheka to the Okhrana (Tsarist secret police). The party cells were nothing but agents of the government, she said, and the committees of the poor were filled with hooligans, the scum of village community. She accused the committees of the poor of all kinds of abuse of authority—confiscating personal belongings and clothing, forcing peasants to deliver young girls to be abused sexually. Peasants rebelled, she said, and tortured the commissars.[29]

What Spiridonova was speaking about was commonplace in the Russian countryside. In the township of Skopin the uezd soviet chairman executed eleven hostages, and in Kasimov township the uezd soviet chairman arrested and executed the praesidium of the soviet congress because he was not elected as member.[30] The accuracy of Spiridonova's accusations is confirmed in a letter dated January 1919. It is from A. Ivenin, from Saransky uezd, Penza province, to the People's Commissar of Internal Affairs G. I. Petrovsky:

> The population is set against the soviets. . . . Local uezd authorities are entirely responsible for this. Their arbitrariness knows no limits, and very often it exceeds all that is most vicious from the times of the cursed Tsarism. When they collect the Extraordinary tax, they resort to torture of the Middle Ages. One can hear yells of "I'll shoot you" much more often than the threat of flogging was heard under serfdom. In some villages the so-called "Communist cells" impose their own "taxes" on some households, such as dinners, and then demand payment of an "indemnity" from these households for not serving them meals to their liking. They do not tolerate any objections and particularly they do not like reference to any. . . . They collect taxes, requisitions, and confiscations without any con-

nection to the considerations of expediency. . . . The people who are doing all this are known among the local population as persons with shady pasts, persons with criminal records. . . . Popular discontent is on the rise, and by spring it may acquire stormy character.[31]

Ivenin saw a way out in the strengthening of the "most severe dictatorship of the Socialist center over the clearly anti-Socialist authorities in the provinces." He recommended rapid and merciless reprisals for the slightest violation of instructions. Violence clearly was not only the main method of governing by the local authorities, it was the ideological pivot in the Bolshevik creation.

Bolshevik punitive actions in the countryside in December 1918 aimed not only to suppress peasant resistance to the army draft but also to extract the so-called Extraordinary Revolutionary Tax in the amount of ten billion rubles. This nationwide campaign generated uprisings in 58 uezds of central Russia. All in all, data show that in November– December 1918 peasant rebellions were under way in 138 of the 286 uezds of central Russia.[32] This was the first mass protest by peasants against the emerging system of War Communism—against coercion, violence, and destruction of a traditional way of life. After the suppression of these uprisings the Bolsheviks managed to enforce the draft of almost 600,000 peasants from central Russia into the Red Army.[33] It appeared that the authorities prevailed. Yet the peasants brought their discontent with them into the army ranks, hence the mass desertion, the garrison mutinies, and the defection of entire peasant regiments to the Whites in 1919.

Deserters, Cossacks, and the Greens—1919

The year 1919 has been depicted in Soviet historiography as the time when forces rallied countrywide for the implementation of the decisions of the Eighth Party Congress, which proclaimed an alliance with middle-income peasants. Historians analyzed the efforts of the CP and the soviets to defeat the White armies of Kolchak and Denikin, and 1919 is known as the year of brilliant victories by the Red Army. Since the 1930s, however, no one has written on the intensification of the internal war against the peasants. In fact, peasant war continued in the Russian countryside.

Even though the committees of the poor were abolished, the Food Supply Army remained to enforce collection of grain. The amounts levied on uezds and cantons exceeded what the peasants could reasonably deliver. But this was not the only burden the peasants had to bear. The state monopoly on grain procurement, which banned private trade, was broadened to include all agricultural products, even mushrooms and berries. Moreover, peasants were required to perform all kinds of work. They had a carting obligation, which required that they deliver to rail stations or towns without pay any goods ordered from their localities. Their labor obligation meant that they could be ordered to show up to clear railroad tracks of snow or to work on other projects deemed necessary by the authorities. These levies and labor obligations exceeded the costs extracted from peasants under serfdom. As the peasants struggled, the army draft campaigns continued.

One consequence of the mobilization campaigns was that the pro-Bolshevik elements in the countryside, considered the most loyal, were drafted into the army. As a result, the CP cells fell apart, and the soviets ceased to exist. The countryside was returning to its traditional form of government: the peasant assembly and its village elder. The central government was losing political control over the countryside. Hence it relied on appointed Military Revolutionary Committees (MRCs), which practically replaced the uezd Executive Committees (ECs) of soviets. Issuing of orders, taking of hostages, imposing of fines or indemnities on defeated enemy villages, confiscation of property and executions—these were the methods of government in the countryside in 1919. Peasants responded by sabotaging all instructions from authorities. The forms of passive resistance—avoiding the draft, hiding deserters, hoarding grain, bribing officials, and ignoring orders—varied a great deal. As repression intensified, the peasants went beyond passive resistance to the war: terror against Communist and Soviet functionaries, destruction of collective farms, and partisan warfare.

From January to June 1919 peasant uprisings took place in 124 uezds of European Russia. The insurgency peaked in March, when peasants were required to deliver 30 percent of the target amount of the levy. The local authorities were in fact trying to raise the entire yearly target at once. Food Supply Army detachments were notorious for their cruelty in pumping out grain from the countryside. They would take hostages until the target levy was delivered. Much of that requisitioned grain rotted in the rain at the railroad stations because there was no means to transport it. Uprisings among the frustrated peasants broke out in Samara, Simbirsk, Kazan', and Orenburg provinces and in parts of the Urals. This series of uprisings is known as the Chapan War. Local party cells and the uezd Cheka in Simbirsk province reestablished practices that could be compared only to those in effect under serfdom. For example, the Sengeleevsky CP uezd committee chairman was known to have whipped arrested peasants personally and to have taken part in dividing confiscated property. Food Supply soldiers often held drinking parties at which they fired guns aimlessly in the streets. The better-off peasants were ruined by the endless requisitions and confiscations.

On 4 March church bells rang in the village of Novodevichie, on the Volga. Peasants disarmed the Food Supply detachment and arrested the Sengeleevsky uezd Cheka chairman who was with the unit. After torturing them, they drowned them in an ice hole.[34] Insurgents disassembled parts of the railroad track to Simbirsk to prevent the arrival of punitive detachments. The insurgency quickly spread to the surrounding villages. About 25,000 peasants took part in this rebellion in Sengeleevsky uezd alone. Shortly thereafter, the insurgency spread to a large area along the Volga and the Urals. Melekessky uezd also rose up against the habitually drunken commissars. One of them would habitually whip his subordinates and then offer them 200 rubles for silence.[35] In Mamadyshsky uezd the police chief Vedernikov and the uezd Cheka chief Kuznetsov conducted illegal searches, appropriated the belongings of even the middle-income and poor peasants, listing them in the record books as if they were kulaks. They also condemned the peasants' religious attitudes and represented any manifestation of discontent as rebellion.

Peasant insurgency along the Volga mostly echoed these political slogans of the Left SRs: "Down with the Communists! Long Live Soviet power without the Communists!" but also "Down with the Jews." In Buguruslansky uezd available evidence shows direct Left SR involvement in the insurgency.[36] M. V. Frunze, who was in charge of suppressing this insurgency, reported to Lenin and Trotsky that it was a broad-based and well-organized peasant movement. The rebels aimed to seize Samara, Syzran', and Stavropol'. In the Ufa-Birsk area Frunze feared a possibility of the insurgents' contact with the advancing White troops of Kolchak.[37] The total number of peasant rebels adjacent to the front was estimated at 180,000. They killed 200 Communists altogether. In the village of Uspenskoe the rebels killed every member of a punitive detachment of 170 soldiers.[38] On the other hand, according to Frunze, 600 ring leaders and kulaks were shot in reprisal. In Syzran', division commissar Khasis reported that an order came to execute 400 rebels held as prisoners of war.[39] At least a thousand rebels were killed in combat operations.

As the Chapan War raged along the Volga, a Cossack uprising began in the Don-Kuban' area.[40] This well-known uprising was the Cossacks' response to the notorious policy of de-cossackization or mass terror against the Cossacks unleashed in March 1919 by the CP Don-buro at the instruction of the Bolshevik CC. Party policy, documented in several orders, was aimed at exterminating everyone in the upper stratum of Cossacks and launching a merciless terror campaign against all Cossacks who had directly or indirectly participated in struggle against Soviet power. The Don-buro ordered a complete disarming of the population under the penalty of summary execution. Against the 30,000-strong Cossack rebel army, the Bolsheviks deployed 39,800 infantry, 5570 cavalry, 62 artillery pieces, and 341 machine guns. On some occasions the peasant regiments deployed against the insurgent Cossacks refused to obey orders, and the Serdobsky regiment formed in Saratov province joined the side of the Cossacks.[41] The Red Army failed to defeat the Cossacks. In fact, their units devastated the Bolsheviks' southern front and cleared the way for the Volunteer Army of General Denikin to break through the front line and open its offensive, which in the end threatened Moscow itself.

Rebellions by Cossacks broke out at the same time in the Urals and in Orenburg. And in the west, a sea of peasant insurgency was raging in Ukraine. In June–July 1919, 328 peasant uprisings were registered in Ukraine alone.[42] What is less well known, however, is that peasant uprisings were just as numerous in central Russia. These were mostly mutinies of drafted peasants. According to the data of the Orel military district, which comprised agrarian provinces of central Russia except Tambov province, desertion rates or no-shows for army draft campaigns were overwhelming. By 26 May only one-fifth of those drafted actually showed up in Kursk province, and 40 percent of them deserted.[43] The desertion rate in Orel province reached 75 percent.[44] In Yeletsky uezd a rebellion of 15,000 peasants and deserters broke out.[45] The Voronezh province was swarming with deserters, and their number was growing despite measures to limit it. On 21 March the military commissar of Orel province, Makarov, reported to Moscow that martial law had been declared in the ten southern uezds. On 30 March he reported that martial law had been declared in the entire province.[46] At the end of May and in early June the concentration of deserters and draft dodgers in that area was reported as the cause of uprisings in Bogucharsky, Valuisky, Zadonsky, and five other uezds.[47] At the same time, mutinies and deserters' uprisings were engulfing seven uezds of the Kursk province. The desertion rate there was reported at 70 percent.[48] In Putivl'sky uezd the army draft failed completely: no one showed up.[49] To suppress this movement of deserters and draft dodgers in Kursk province the Bolsheviks deployed troops retreating from Ukraine.

Generally the causes of peasant uprisings in the first half of 1919 were the same as in 1918. These were requisitions of surplus grain and cattle, extraction of the Extraordinary Tax, arbitrary rule of local dictators, and army draft. In 1919, however, the Bolsheviks attempted to introduce collective farms, a concept unacceptable to peasants. The conference of Ryshkovsky canton ECs of Kursk uezd demanded in April 1919 that all collective farms be dissolved and that the word *Communist* be dropped from the official title of local government, otherwise the conference would disband the canton Executive Committee.[50] The Putivl'sky uezd peasants demanded that money taken through the Extraordinary Tax be returned. Similar demands were drafted by peasants in the northern, northwestern, and central industrial provinces.

According to the data of the Red Army Political Directorate on just three agrarian provinces of central Russia (Orel, Kursk, and Voronezh), 238 uprisings were registered for the first half of 1919. The breakdown of official causes by category follows: food supply problems, 72 uprisings, or 30 percent; army draft protest, 51 uprisings, or 21 percent; deserters, 35 uprisings, or 15 percent; requisitions, 34 uprisings, or 14 percent; land or property disputes, 17 uprisings, or 7 percent; and political mutinies in army units, 6 uprisings, or 2 percent. The remainder were set off by various other causes.[51] A great number of insurrections were protests against the Bolsheviks' antireligious policy.[52] These were particularly strong in some uezds of Tambov, Kursk, Moscow, and Kostroma provinces.

As a measure of reprisal for participation in the November 1918 draft dodgers' uprisings, the Bolsheviks imposed an indemnity on the defeated peasants of Tambov province. Their rationale was that the defeated class enemy would have to pay just as a defeated country would. The target allotment for Tambov province was set at 27 million pud. The harvest was poor, and peasants were trying to hide the remainder of their grain reserves. By June it was apparent that the peasants would not deliver grain of their own free will.[53] On 20 June the Tambov EC stated that deliveries of grain ceased altogether. On 3 July martial law was declared in eight uezds of the province.[54] Against the background of mass desertion, the coercive measures of the Food Supply Army acted as a catalyst for rebellions. On 20 July, 48,572 deserters were registered in Tambov province, and by the end of the year there were 20,000.[55] Thousands of deserters, organized in partisan detachments and supported by local populations, made requisition and mobilization campaigns impossible. On 26 June the Kirsanov uezd MRC admitted that it was powerless to combat desertion. Rural Communists and Soviet functionaries were in fact hostages in the hands of the rebels. In response, the MRC ordered CP cells and canton ECs to take hostages from among the kulaks and those who helped the deserters. These hostages would pay with their lives for every killed Communist.[56]

The report of the Central Commission for the Struggle with Desertion for 16–30 June admitted that failures at the front and anti-desertion reprisals had triggered uprisings in the majority of provinces. Particularly fierce ones arose in the rear of the southern front—Tambov, Voronezh, and Saratov provinces, where the rebels had joined the Cossacks and created a danger for the collapse of the front.[57] Peasant rebellions in these provinces indeed weakened the southern front and created conditions favorable for a breakthrough by the cavalry of General K. K. Mamontov. The Whites incited the peasant rebels to attack and rob granaries, to destroy Soviet institutions and kill the Communists. Mamontov's raid in the rear of the front line foiled the Reds' capacity to collect tribute from these areas.

Tens of thousands of deserters in Samara province likewise joined the Cossacks and paralyzed the work of soviets in the Balashov and Pugachev uezds, which became the centers of concentration of the Greens. The rebels destroyed all the collective and state farms in the area, and they called on the population to unite with the forces of Kolchak and Denikin.[58] In June, Denikin's troops entered Balashov uezd, and peasants greeted them as liberators. The Whites' rule did not make peasants' burden any lighter, however, as Denikin himself admitted. In early July, Lenin demanded in his telegrams to Saratov Communists that they root out the White Guards by the most severe measures in every canton in the area adjacent to the front line, suppressing the Greens and returning the deserters. On Lenin's recommendations, the local Communists formed special detachments for the liquidation of the Greens.[59]

Desertion and draft-dodging reached high levels among the peasants of the central industrial region as well. At the end of May 1919, 90 percent of draftees evaded the draft in Vladimir province, and in July rebellions broke out in Vladimir and Yuriev-Polsky uezds.[60] The Internal Security Troops Directorate (Vokhra) of Nizhnii Novgorod province reported systematic killings of Communists, attacks on the local soviets, and deserters' rebellions that had been provoked by mobilization, Extraordinary Tax collection, and stock-taking of grain surplus.[61] The situation was no better in Tver' province, where 85 percent of those eligible for draft did not showed up. Bands of deserters were hiding in the forests, hence the name "Greens." In July rebellions began in all fourteen uezds, and martial law was declared in the entire province.[62]

Likewise, tens of thousands of armed deserters formed the Army of the Greens, as they called themselves in Yaroslavl' and Kostroma provinces.[63] In the village of Krasnoe the Internal Security Troops engaged in combat a detachment of 600 Greens. About 1,500 peasants, armed with pitchforks and axes, joined them from nearby villages. At the end of the fighting, 300 peasants were killed, ring leaders were executed, an unspecified number of hostages were taken, and an indemnity of 500,000 rubles was imposed on the rebellious area. Six villages were burned to the ground.[64] Reporting from Yaroslavl' on another engagement, the punitive detachment commander A. F. Frenkel mentioned that 200 rebels were killed or executed.[65] A total of 35,000 rebels fought the Bolsheviks in Yaroslavl' and Kostroma provinces in the summer of 1919.[66]

In European Russia as a whole there were 266,000 deserters in July 1919, 284,000 in August, and 1,545,000 for the remainder of the year.[67] These figures suggest that a broad-based social movement of the Greens was growing in central European Russia in 1919. This was a specific form of peasant guerrilla warfare against the Communist regime. Despite its scale, this movement remained locally based and uncoordinated. There was no political party in Russia that could have channelled and organized the peasant protest movement. The Socialist Revolutionaries, the party closest to peasants, found itself in the midst of a serious internal crisis. There was no coordinating party center or local organization, which had been devastated by Communist repressions. Peasants in central Russia had not yet found their own leaders.

The internal front against peasant rebels required considerable force and resource. On 20 June 1919 the Cheka was authorized to execute "bandits," as the insurgents were called, on the spot.[68] Commissions for the Struggle with Desertion were formed in all provinces. These too had the right to execute "bandit suspects." Yet it was impossible to end the peasant war and to return 1.5 million deserters by repressive measures alone. Much more effective were economic concessions. Middle-income peasants who had failed to pay the Extraordinary Tax were pardoned, programs were launched to provide for the families of enlisted men, draft dodgers and deserters were promised pardons if they returned to the ranks voluntarily, and even peasants who had taken part in uprisings over the "lack of political consciousness" received amnesty.

Nevertheless, the turnaround in peasant attitudes occurred only when Denikin's troops were on their way to Moscow in October 1919. The real possibility that the landlords would come back blunted the intensity of the peasants' protest. The number of uprisings decreased, as did desertion rates. In Kursk province, for example, the desertion rate went down to only 5 percent, and in Tambov province it fell to 20 percent.[69] In many cities thousands of deserters returned voluntarily.[70] Village assemblies began to pass resolutions supporting the draft and asking deserters to come back. The pattern of peasant protest varied greatly throughout Russia. At the end of 1919 the provinces most unsteady in their support for the Bolsheviks were again those along the Volga and in the Urals, long since cleared from the Kolchak forces and under no threat from Denikin. In Perm' and Viatka provinces peasant rebellions resumed in December 1919.[71] Parts of Kostroma, Nizhnii Novgorod, and Yaroslavl' provinces were again put under martial law.[72] This pattern foreshadowed the course of the peasant war elsewhere: with the defeat of the Whites the civil war did not end, it just entered a new stage.

Peasant Rebel Armies—1920

As 1920 commenced, there were no Whites remaining in Central Russia, the Volga basin, the Urals, and Siberia, yet thirty-six provinces were still under martial law. Peasants were no longer willing to put up with War Communism. As early as February a large peasant insurgency had broken out in the Urals, in Ufa and Ekaterinburg provinces. That insurgency, known as the movement of the Black Eagle and the Farmer, was primarily a protest against the system of coercion, lawlessness, abuse of authority, arrests and threats to shoot those who failed to deliver the target amount of "surplus" grain.[73] The quotas, based on calculations from previous years' harvests, were impossible for the peasants to fulfill. Yet the authorities of Menzelinsk uezd still demanded that the peasants deliver the required amount within ten days, and they threatened to resort to arrest and armed force. On 20 January the plenipotentiary of the uezd Food Supply Committee, Pudov, arrested twenty men and women in the village of Novaya Yelan' for refusing to deliver 100 percent of the levy. When the peasants failed to have the arrested people set free by peaceful means, they decided to attack the Food Supply detachment. Pudov and a few others managed to flee. Peasants sent their men to nearby villages to ask for help. The uprising spread quickly, and by mid-February it engulfed Menzelinsk, Ufa, and Belebeevsky uezds. More than 50,000 men—1,500 of them cavalry—took part in this rebellion.[74] The peasants' first priority was to seize the granaries in order to prevent the removal of grain from their province. The rebels killed hundreds of Communists and Soviet functionaries. In the Menzelinsk uezd alone the Soviet losses were 145 men killed, 113 wounded, and 22 taken prisoner. In Belebeevsky uezd the rebels killed 200 Communists, and in Bugul'minsky they killed more than 100. The rebels' casualties were 544 killed, 466 wounded, and 244 taken prisoner.[75] To suppress this uprising the authorities deployed 6,376 infantry, 816 cavalry, 79 machine guns, 6 artillery pieces, and two grenade launchers.

Reports on the increasing frequency of peasants' armed resistance to the collection of the food levy were coming in to Moscow from all sides: from Vitebsk and Smolensk in the west, Viatka in the northeast, Ryazan' and Penza to the east, and Orel, Kursk, Voronezh, and Tula to the south. Peasant war was raging in Ukraine and Siberia as well. Lenin was well aware of this but refused to alter his economic policy. In a speech to the Moscow Soviet on 6 March 1920 he said that, in regard to petty proprietors and speculators, the policy was a state of war.[76] In the official documents the peasant movement was referred to as "banditry." On 19 February 1920 the Council of People's Commissars adopted a resolution,

signed by Lenin, titled "On Measures of Combating Banditry." The Cheka
and the Revolutionary Tribunals were authorized to convict without
appeal anyone guilty of armed assault, robbery, and banditry.[77] E. M.
Skliansky was put in charge of the Central Commission for the Struggle
with Banditry. Units of Special Purpose (Chon), Internal Security Troops
(Vokhra), the Cheka units and regular army troops were thrown into battle on the peasant front.

The problem the government had to face, however, was that Red Army
units were not reliable: 77 percent of the soldiers were enlisted peasants.
Clearly the army reflected the political attitudes of the peasants, who
often went over to the side of insurgents. One of the most significant Red
Army mutinies occurred in the Lower Volga-Urals area in the summer of
1920, where fighting had gone on for three years. The leader of the
mutiny was a Red Army officer, A. S. Sapozhnikov, who was from a peasant family of Novouzensky uezd, Samara province. In 1918 he served as
a chairman of the uezd soviet, by party affiliation a Left Socialist Revolutionary. In 1920 he commanded the Ninth Cavalry Division of the Second Turkestan Army. Many soldiers in his division were peasants from his
native Novouzensky uezd as well as from Buzuluksky and Samara uezds.
Like so many others, they were unhappy over the food levy, the labor
obligation, and the other burdens of War Communism. The families of
many of the enlisted men and officers had suffered at the hands of the
Food Supply detachments. Officers who served under Sapozhnikov—the
Mosliakov brothers, F. Zubarev, F. Dolmatov, V. Serov, and others—
shared the critical attitudes of enlisted men.[78] Some of them, like Sapozhnikov, were Left SRs in 1918.

The commander of the Lower Volga Military District, sensing discontent in the ranks, issued an order relieving Sapozhnikov of his duties. The
order was understood as a political act and triggered the mutiny. On 14
July 1920 Sapozhnikov and the officers loyal to him arrested all the Communists in their units and those who tried to foil their plans. Sapozhnikov
seized the township of Buzuluk and reorganized his forces into the First
Red Army of the Truth. On 15 July, Sapozhnikov had three thousand men
under his command. The 49th and the 50th Cavalry Regiments of the Second Turkestan Army made up the core of his forces. The mutiny acted as
a catalyst for peasant insurgency in the area. Very quickly the insurgency
movement spread to large areas of the grain-producing provinces of
Lower Volga: the provinces of Samara, Saratov, Tsaritsyn, Orenburg, and
Urals. Sapozhnikov, familiar with the terrain in his native land and enjoying popular support, skillfully maneuvered his troops and engaged considerable forces of the Red Army. The Red Command deployed four bat-
talions of special purpose forces against him, a detachment of infantry

school cadets, several units of Internal Security troops, and some other highly reliable Red Army irregulars, a total of 12,362 infantry and 1654 cavalry, with 46 artillery pieces and dozens of machine guns.[79] Lenin demanded a speedy and decisive action against Sapozhnikov. The main purpose was to isolate his forces from the population. To this end he advised the forces to "nip in the bud any manifestation of sympathy to let alone cooperation of local population with Sapozhnikov, relying on the full might of revolutionary authority. In those instances when cooperation did take place to demand that those guilty and the ring leaders be delivered. To forestall the possibility of cooperation, it is essential to take hostages from the villages lying on route of Sapozhnikov's detachments."[80]

The main forces of the rebels were defeated in September, and Sapozhnikov himself was killed in combat. V. Serov took command over the remainder of the rebel forces. In spring 1921 several large detachments of rebels resumed guerrilla activity in the Lower Volga provinces. Serov's detachment was not defeated until August 1922.[81]

The saga of Sapozhnikov and Serov's movement illustrates a new element in the peasant resistance. In 1920 the peasant insurgency began to embrace large areas. It became better organized and coordinated, and there appeared peasant leaders with military skills who formulated political demands. Most of them spoke against one-party dictatorship and favored democratic elections of local and central government officials. Armed and organized peasants destroyed collective farms and fought against the food levy and all the other obligations imposed on them. This effort can be defined as nothing but systematic struggle against Communist rule in the countryside.

The year 1920 was decisive in the peasant war, and the Socialist Revolutionaries were well aware of the trends. On 13 May 1920 the SR Central Committee decided to create the Unions of Laboring Peasantry. Their main objective was to organize peasant insurgency and overthrow the soviets. Colonel Makhin, a Socialist Revolutionary, worked out the tactics of peasant guerrilla warfare based on the experience of peasant rebels from Ukraine and the Black Sea coast. He pointed out that under guerrilla warfare it was essential to have a strategic objective and to seize such critical links as railroad junctions, communications, and bridges. Makhin explained, "The strategy dictates the necessity to begin popular insurrection on as large an area as possible at the same time, best of all everywhere. The power of a simultaneous action everywhere is enormous. No government is capable of coping with it. The moral impact of such a movement on the troops, defending the government, is devastating. An army which is flesh and blood of the nation would inescapably absorb the general mood and go hand in hand with the popular masses."[82]

In September 1920 a conference of SR Central Committee members and delegates from the provinces clandestinely assembled in Moscow. The SRs discussed the problem of tactics in their struggle with the Communist dictatorship. Some feared that the tactics of insurrection would clear the way to counterrevolutionaries, as in 1918. Others called for an alliance with anyone in order to overthrow the Communists. Primarily through the efforts of the SRs, the Unions of Toiling Peasantry were created in Tambov, Voronezh, Saratov, and Samara provinces. By April 1921, according to official and incomplete data, 165 large peasant insurgent detachments were active in Russia. Of those, 140 (numbering 118,000) had an SR political orientation.[83] In Siberia a powerful Peasant Union led by the SRs and People's Socialists coordinated peasant insurrections in Omsk, Tyumen', Cheliabinsk, and Ekaterinburg provinces. These were powerful peasant insurrections on a huge area and involving 100,000 rebels.[84] Peasants' political slogans were essentially identical everywhere: "Soviets Without the Communists" and "Down With State Monopoly on Grain Trade."

An example of the tactics of peasant guerrilla warfare par excellence in central Russia was the well-known insurgency in Tambov province led by an "independent" Socialist Revolutionary, A. S. Antonov. The entire male population of the area participated in this movement; the active core of rebel forces was estimated at 50,000. The Soviet government deployed against Tambov an army numbering 100,000, led by the well-known Red Army commanders M. N. Tukhachevsky and I. P. Uborevich, veterans of campaigns against Kolchak, Denikin, Wrangel, and over the rebellious Kronstadt.[85] Tukhachevsky, in his reflections on warfare against peasant guerrillas, referred to the "Tambov banditry" as a genuine peasant uprising caused by food supply policy.[86] Tukhachevsky wrote that he was conducting "not merely single operations, but a war, and not just against bandits, but against the entire local population."[87] Even though he understood the causes of this war, Tukhachevsky, as a true Communist, did not balk at using any means to suppress the insurgents. He was the author of guidelines on warfare against peasant insurgents, guidelines that called for a systematic occupation of the insurgent areas and isolation of the rebels from the population. Concentration camps for the families of the bandits were set up, and entire villages were held responsible for the actions of the partisans. In some cases, admitted Tukhachevsky, he had to resort to drastic measures, including execution, to force the peasants surrender the bandits.[88]

In May 1921 Antonov's army suffered a crushing blow. Some units escaped encirclement and went south to Voronezh province. Cavalry, armored cars, and the air force pursued them. Detachments of Nestor Makhno vainly attempted to break through and join Antonov's rebels. Peasant detachments continued their operations in Saratov, Samara, and Voronezh provinces. Yet they could not coordinate their actions. They were defeated one by one. On 20 July near the village of Yuriupinska, what remained of Antonov's army was defeated. Near the village of Kamenka the Cheka discovered the eighty leaders of the Tambov province Union of Toiling Peasantry.[89] All were executed. Antonov himself evaded arrest for another year but was seized and killed in June 1922.

As we have seen, there were two fronts of the civil war. On the external front peasants resisted a possible restoration of landlords' property. At the same time, however, the peasants never accepted the system of War Communism that the Bolsheviks tried to impose. The peasants overturned it through armed struggle. This was the second, the internal, front of the civil war. The peasants of Russia paid a hefty price for their rejection of social utopias. Thus far no one has tried to estimate peasant losses in the civil war attributable to peasant insurgencies. For the three years of the civil war the overall losses of the population, aside from deaths due to natural causes, were estimated at 10.5 million people. Of those 8.2 million were civilian casualties. The total losses of the Red Army, the Food Supply Army, the Troops for Internal Security, and Cheka troops were 900,000, including deaths from disease, casualties at the external fronts, and casualties incurred during suppression of insurgencies. One hundred thousand persons were killed by the peasant rebels, mostly civilian Soviet functionaries, Communists, and other representatives of authority.

On the other hand, the total casualties of armed peasant detachments, the Greens, deserters, and other insurgents were 1 million, counting those who were killed or executed or who died in prisons and concentration camps. The casualty rate was even higher among the civilian population in areas of the most serious insurgencies. The civilian casualties of the Red Terror in those areas were estimated at 5 million.[90] Several more million died from famine in the Volga area after the war.

The peasant war was an organic part of the civil war in Russia. In a sense it was a continuation of the peasant revolution directed against the old regime and the new Socialist order. The peasant revolution brought the Communist dictatorship to the brink of a catastrophe. It forced the Soviet regime to abandon social experiments in the countryside and to soften coercive methods of government. In this sense, the peasants won on the internal front of the civil war.

Notes

1. V. I. Lenin, *Polnoe sobranie sochinenii*, 36: 507.

2. Upravlenie delami Revoliutsionnogo Voennogo Soveta Respubliki [Military Revolutionary Council of the Republic, Directorate, hereafter MRC] in f. 4, op. 1, d. 320, p. 3, Rossiiskii Gosudarstvennyi Voennyi Archiv, [State Military Archive of Russia, Moscow, hereafter RGVA].

3. Narodnyi Kommissariat Vnutrennikh Del (NKVD) in f. 393, op. 3, d. 293, pp. 298–300, Gosudarstvennyi Arkhiv Rossiiskoi Federatsii [State archive of the Russian Federation, hereafter GARF, formerly TsGAOR].

4. O. A. Vas'kovskii, M. A. Molodtsygin, Ya. L. Nirenburg et al., eds., *Grazhdanskaia Voina i inostrannaia interventsiia na Urale* (Sverdlovsk, 1969), 169.

5. RGVA, MRC papers in f. 4, op. 1, d. 203, p. 191, and d. 236, p. 1, and d. 325, pp. 2–3.

6. Ya. M. Sverdlov, *Izbrannye proizvedeniia* (Moscow, 1959), 2: 213–215.

7. *Vestnik Narodnogo Kommissariata Vnutrennikh Del* [NKVD Courier], nos. 18–19 (Moscow, 1918), 2.

8. L. D. Trotsky, *Kak Vooruzhalas' Revoliutsiia* (Moscow, 1923), 1: 9–71.

9. *Protokoly VTsIK Chetvertogo Sozyva: Stenograficheskii Otchet* (Moscow, 1918), 301.

10. Left SRs' papers in: f. Partii Levykh Eserov, f. 564, op. 1, d. 3, pp. 8, 248, 254, 275; d. 11, pp. 16, 18, RTsKhIDNI, Moscow.

11. Cited from A. Velidov, *Shestoe Iiulia. Perepiska na istoricheskie temy* (Moscow: Politizdat, 1989), 219.

12. Cited from L. Spirin, *Krakh Odnoi Avantiury. Miatezh Levykh Eserov v Moskve 6–7 iiulia 1918 goda* (Moscow: Politizdat 1971), 81.

13. V. V. Tuliakov, *Organizatsiia, sostav i deiatel'nost' Kombedov Ryazanskoi, Tambovskoi i Tul'skoi gubernii* (Kuibyshev, diss. abstract, 1986), 11, 15.

14. Cited from *Pravda* (Moscow), 13 November 1918.

15. RGVA, f. 11, Vserossiiskii Glavnyi Shtab, op. 5, Mobilizatsionnoe upravlenie, d. 193, pp. 63–66; and GARF, f. 393, NKVD, op. 1, d. 120, p. 34.

16. RGVA, f. 1, Upravlenie delami Narkomvoendel [People's Commissar for Military Affairs Directorate], op. 1, Kantseliariia, d. 239, "Svodka Orlovskogo okruzhnogo kommissariata po voennym delam" (14 September 1918), 63. See also D. P. Selitrennikov, Miatezh v Livnakh (Tula, 1989), 28–35.

17. A. Konokotin, *Ocherki po istorii Grazhdanskoi voiny v Kostromskoi gubernii* (Kostroma, 1927), 28–30, 32–47.

18. Lenin, *Polnoe sobranie sochinenii*, 50: 149–160; and Vladimir Il'ich Lenin: *Biograficheskaia khronika: iiul' 1918—mart 1919* (Moscow, 1975), 6: 69–76.

19. *Izvestiia VTsIK* (Moscow: 15 December 1918).

20. *Iz istorii grazhdanskoi voiny v SSSR. Sbornik dokumentov i materialov* (Moscow: Politizdat, 1960), 1: 216.

21. N. I. Bukharin, *Problemy teorii i praktiki Sotsializma* (Moscow: Politizdat, 1989), 168.

22. Author's tabulation based on the materials in GARF and RGVA archives.

23. GARF, f. 1240, Materialy upolnomochennykh TsKa, SNK, i VTsIK, op. 1, d. 43, "Doklad o podavlenii miatezha v Gzhadskom uezde," 26.

24. RGVA, f. 25883, Moskovskii Voennyi Okrug [Moscow Military District] op. 1, d. 20, p. 96, and d. 148, pp. 233–234; also f. 8, Vserossiiskoe Biuro Voennykh kommissarov [All-Russian Bureau of Military Commissars], op. 1, d. 316, pp. 31–40.

25. RGVA, f. 25883, Moskovskii Voennyi Okrug, op. 1, d. 20, p. 98, and op. 2, d. 179, p. 5.

26. Ibid., d. 5, p. 149, and d. 58, pp. 20, 38.

27. M. S. Frenkin, *Tragediia krestianskikh vosstanii v Rossii, 1918–1921* (Jerusalem, 1987), 92.

28. Cited from *Neizvestnaia Rossiia. XX Vek*, no. 2 (Moscow: Istoricheskoe Nasledie, 1992), 39.

29. Ibid., 40.

30. *Pravda* (Moscow), 12 February 1919.

31. GARF, f. 393, NKVD, op. 3, d. 129, pp. 43–44.

32. Author's tabulation based on the following sources: GARF, f. 1235, op. 93, d. 33, p. 9; d. 106, pp. 72–97; d. 119, p. 4; f. 393, op. 1, d. 72, p. 248; d. 74, p. 178; d. 83, pp. 14–15; f. 1240, op. 1, d. 43, p. 26; d. 45, p. 2, 16; RGVA, f. 1, op. 1, d. 72, pp. 248–264; d. 198, pp. 233–234; d. 214, pp. 28–50; f. 2, op. 1, d. 214, p. 47; f. 8, op. 1, d. 51, p. 339; d. 55, pp. 1–27; d. 57, pp. 4–24; f. 10, op. 2, d. 1336, pp. 1–10. f. 25883, Moskovskii Voennyi Okrug, op. 1, d. 5, pp. 144–152; d. 20, pp. 2–39; 95–104; d. 51, p. 9.

33. M. A. Molodtsygin, "Rabochie i krestiane na zashchite Oktiabria. K voprosu o formirovanii vooruzhennykh sil diktatury proletariata," *Istoriia SSSR*, no. 4 (Moscow, 1987), 63.

34. M. I. Kubanin, "Antisovetskoe krestianskoe dvizhenie v gody grazhdanskoi voiny," *Na Agrarnom Fronte*, no. 2 (Moscow, 1926), 41.

35. GARF, f. 1235, VTsIK, op. 94, d. 30, pp. 24–26.

36. Ibid., d. 64, p. 112.

37. *Pod Rukovodstvom Vozhdia. Sbornik dokumentov* (Frunze, 1983), 40–43.

38. GARF, f. 1235, VTsIK, op. 94, d. 64, p. 112.

39. Ibid., d. 58, p. 44.

40. *Grazhdanskaia Voina i voennaia interventsiia v SSSR. Entsiklopediia* (Moscow, 1983), 91.

41. M. S. Frenkin, *Tragediia krestianskikh vosstanii v Rossii, 1918–1921*, 105.

42. Kh. G. Rakovsky, *Bor'ba za osvobozhdenie derevni* (Kharkov: 1920), 2, 59.

43. RGVA, f. 25887, Orlovskii voennyi okrug [Orel Military district] , op. 1, d. 106, Operativnye svodki po okrugu, p. 2.

44. Ibid., d. 183, Telegrammy iz Voronezhskoi gubernii, p. 130.

45. RGVA, f. 42, Glavnoe Upravlenie Voisk Vnutrennei Okhrany, op. 1, d. 916, p. 34.

46. RGVA, f. 25887, Orel Military District, op. 1, d. 183, pp. 64–82.

47. Ibid., pp. 44–80.

48. Ibid., d. 198, "Telegrammy iz Kurskoi gubernii," p. 69.

49. Ibid., p. 98.

50. Ibid., pp. 1, 10, 19, 41.

51. Cited from D. Kin, *Denikinshchina* (Leningrad, 1927), p. 44.

52. A. I. Klibanov, *Sovremennoe sektanstvo v Tambovskoi oblasti* (Moscow, 1960), p. 92.

53. Gosudarstvennyi Arkhiv Tambovskoi Oblasti [State Archive of Tambov Province], f. R-1, Gubispolkom, op. 1, d. 120, vol. 1, p. 480.

54. *Sovety Tambovskoi gubernii v gody grazhdanskoi voiny, 1918–1919. Sbornik dokumentov i materialov* (Voronezh, 1989), 169–171.

55. RGVA, f. 25887, Orel Military district, op. 1, d. 197, Incoming telegrams, p. 1.

56. *Sovety Tambovskoi gubernii*, 176.

57. GARF, f. 130, Sovnarkom, op. 3, d. 198, Svodki, protokoly Tsentral'noi Kommissii po Bor'be s Dezertirstvom, [Materials of the Central Commission for the Struggle with Desertion], 14–15.

58. RGVA, f. 42, Vokhr [Internal Security Troops], op. 1, d. 915, pp. 3, 97; and V. A. Radus-Zen'kovich, *Stranitsy geroicheskogo proshlogo. Vospominaniia i stat'i* (Moscow: Politizdat, 1960), 34.

59. Lenin, *Polnoe sobranie sochinenii*, 51: 4, 5, 7.

60. RGVA, f. 11, Vrerossiiskii Glavnyi Shtab, [General Headquarters], op. 8, Mobilizatsionnoe upravlenie [Mobilization directorate], d. 96, p. 21.

61. Ibid., f. 42 [Vokhra], op. 1, d. 918, p. 37.

62. Ibid., f. 25883, Moscow Military District, op. 2, d. 108, p. 149; and N. M. Filimontsev, *Trudiashchiesia Tverskoi gubernii v bor'be za ukreplenie oboronosposobnosti Sovetskoi strany v period inostrannoi voennoi interventsii i grazhdanskoi voiny, 1918–1920* (Yaroslavl', diss. abstract, 1986), 129.

63. RGVA, f. 42, op. 1, d. 915, p. 1.

64. Ibid., pp. 1–4.

65. Ibid., d. 916, p. 22.

66. Ibid., p. 28.

67. N. Movchin, *Komplektovanie Krasnoi armii, istoricheskii ocherk* (Moscow, 1926), 133.

68. *Grazhdanskaia voina i voennaia interventsiia v SSSR. Entsiklopediia* (Moscow, 1983), 53.

69. RGVA, f. 25887, Orel Military District, op. 1, d. 183, p. 178; and d. 184, p. 68.

70. Ibid., f. 42, Vokhra, op. 1, d. 915, pp. 15–22.

71. Ibid., d. 1871, "Materialy o vosstanii v raione Kazansko-Orenburgskoi zheleznoi dorogi," 1–32.

72. Ibid., d. 1872, "Vosstaniia v raione Moskovskogo sektora," pp. 2–9, 27, 34, 42.

73. Ibid., d. 1874, "Doklad operativnogo otdela shtaba Saratovskogo sektora po bor'be s dezertirstvom," 158.

74. Ibid., d. 907, p. 31; d. 1044, p. 21; d. 1893 "Menzelinskoe vosstanie," 12–16.

75. Ibid., d. 907, p. 29–31; and d. 1893, p. 16.

76. Lenin, *Polnoe sobranie sochinenii*, 40: 198.

77. V. I. *Lenin i Vecheka. Sbornik dokumentov, 1917–1922* (Moscow: Politizdat, 1987), 285–287.

78. V. K. Grigoriev, *Razgrom melkoburzhuaznoi kontrrevoliutsii v Kazakhstane, 1920–1922* (Alma-Ata: Kazakhstan, 1984), 58.

79. E. Vasina, *Banditizm v Saratovskoi gubernii* (Saratov: 1928), 5.

80. Lenin, *Polnoe sobranie sochinenii*, 51: 348.

81. V. K. Grigoriev, *Razgrom melkoburzhuaznoi kontrrevoliutsii v Kazakhstane, 1920–1922*, 169.

82. Cited from *Revoliutsionnaia Rossiia*, no. 2 (1920): 17.

83. *Otchet Narodnogo Kommissariata Po Voennym Delam za 1921 god* (Moscow, 1922), 185.

84. *Grazhdanskaia voina i voennaia interventsiia v SSSR. Entsiklopediia* (Moscow, 1983), 214–215.

85. Yu. A. Shchetinov and B. A. Starkov, *Krasnyi Marshal* (Moscow, 1990), 191–192.

86. M. N. Tukhachevsky, "Bor'ba s kontrrevoliutsionnymi vosstaniiami," *Voina i Revoliutsiia*, nos. 7 and 8 (Moscow, 1926), here no. 8, p. 4.

87. Ibid., no. 7, p. 9.

88. Ibid., no. 8, p. 13.

89. Shchetinov and Starkov, *Krasnyi Marshal*, 196–197.

90. Mikhail Bernshtam, "Storony v Grazhdanskoi voine, 1917–1922," *Vestnik Rossiiskogo Khristianskogo Dvizheniia*, no. 128 (Paris, 1979), 70.

Peasant Wars in Tambov Province 9

On 8 August 1920, A. G. Shlikhter addressed the Tambov Provincial Food Supply Conference. A longtime party member with a reputation for increasing grain procurements without inciting uprisings, he had just been appointed chairman of the Tambov provincial executive committee. In his speech opening the conference Shlikhter said that food supply workers should "work like law-abiding revolutionaries" to erase the "bitter memories of food supply workers, especially of what they were doing two or three months ago," so that they could in the future "safely walk in the countryside."[1]

This exhortation came too late. Three weeks later, an armed detachment from the Provincial Food Supply Committee entered Kamenka, a village seventy-five kilometers south of Tambov, in search of grain to requisition. The detachment was ambushed as it left the village, and annihilated. The peasants defeated several more punitive detachments sent against them. Organized by local Socialist Revolutionaries and led by a shadowy figure named Aleksandr Antonov, this rebellion soon encompassed the richest areas of the province and took tens of thousands of Soviet troops and many of the Red Army's finest commanders to suppress.[2]

This uprising was hardly unique in the civil war history of Tambov province. Tambov's Communist government was weak throughout this period and suffered many disadvantages in its attempts to rule the province, even though "rule" actually meant only collecting grain to feed the army and the cities, obtaining recruits to reinforce the Red Army, and keeping trains running through the province. Neither the provincial government nor the Communist party organization were up to the task of governance.

Government bureaucrats were ignorant, inefficient, and corrupt. Security forces executed for malfeasance the first man appointed provincial Food Supply commissar, probably the most important official after the chairman of the provincial executive committee. Lower ranking individuals were often little better: the provincial Cheka regularly arrested provincial and uezd government officials for corruption, on occasion shooting them. The Tambov government, though, had to settle for what it could get. A. Okninsky, a Petrograd bureaucrat who settled in Podgornskaia district, Borisoglebsk uezd, to sit out the civil war, writes that educated office workers were in such short supply that to keep himself from being requisitioned he had to bribe the head of the district office workers' union not to mention him to the uezd center.[3]

Even when officials were not criminal or venal, they were rarely efficient. Recruits who voluntarily showed up for enlistment often found that no preparations had been made to house and feed them. Peasants who carted grain to government collection points rather than selling it to black marketeers sometimes found the collection points full and had to bring their grain home. These experiences contributed to bad feelings among the population: as one report had it, "Dark elements used this in agitation against Soviet power."[4]

The Communist Party was not a reliable instrument, either. Total cadres were tiny, given the size of the province. In addition, as the table[5] shows, party ranks swelled and shrank enormously. Party organizations filled with poorly indoctrinated new members during membership drives, then shrank as inactive or inadequate members were purged and effective party members were promoted and drafted for work at the front or in other provinces.

Tambov Provincial Party Organization,
December 1918–December 1920

Date	Number of Party Organizations	Number of Party Members
December 1918	469	10,049
April 1919	476	9,923
July 1919	441	3,997
October 1919	156	1,676
July 1920	640	17,528
October 1920	675	11,521
December 1920	unknown	7,087

Those party members who remained in the villages developed bad reputations. Boris Shekhter, traveling in late September 1918 from Petrograd to Treskino (a village in Kirsanov uezd) was astounded at how unpopular Communists were. He blamed this unpopularity on the illegal exactions and brutal behavior of local Communists.[6]

These inadequacies spelled trouble when combined with a village population that was hostile and suspicious of the Communist government and well armed with weapons taken from the front when the Imperial Army collapsed. Violent insurrections punctuate the history of Tambov province during the civil war, starting before the October overturn. Attempts by the provincial government to collect grain by force and stop peasants from seizing nonpeasant lands led to uprisings in much of the province in September 1917, and ended with the government retreating. After the "establishment of Soviet power" the next year, the first attempt to draft peasants into the Red Army ended in a debacle in June 1918. Recruits in Tambov itself rioted, arrested most of the provincial government, looted armories, and dispersed to their villages with arms and ammunition.[7]

In November 1918 much of Tambov province exploded again in a series of rebellions. Peasant anger over the activities of the local government had been building, especially over the abuses of the new Committees of the Rural Poor (*kombedy*), but the spark that set it off was a renewed attempt to conscript peasants, an effort that coincided with the first anniversary of the October revolution. Unrest was not limited to Tambov province: peasant rebellions flared up throughout central Russia in November 1918, typically incited by recruiting.[8] Although the previous draft in June 1918 had caused serious rebellions in Tambov province, and there had been sporadic attacks on committees of the poor and Soviet officials since then, authorities were ill prepared for the widespread resistance that the new draft brought forth.[9]

The course of this rebellion is worth studying in some detail, as its suppression foreshadows the tactics that the Soviet government would use unsuccessfully against the 1920–21 uprising. The uprisings started in Morshansk, where peasants had especially suffered from committees of the poor.[10] Peasants ambushed and killed a group of uezd officials, including the chairman of the uezd party committee. The Morshansk uezd Cheka declared that peasants who attacked Soviet officials were outlaws, but this decree had little influence on peasants who soon afterward attacked local committees of the poor around the Berdy Iagodnoe railroad station. Insurgent peasants sent emissaries to other districts, where they successfully spread the rebellion over much of Morshansk uezd and parts of Kirsanov uezd. Army units supported by armored railroad cars with the machine guns were sent from Kaluga and Morshansk on 10 November to restore order. The peasants defeated them as well. The uezd authorities sent frantic telegrams to Tambov and Moscow demanding military aid "with artillery," to fight the thousands of armed peasants they reported were marching on Morshansk.[11]

The uprisings in Morshansk uezd were not unique. Tambov's provincial government received daily reports about new peasant uprisings in

November, and uprisings also occurred in Kirsanov, Usman', and Tambov uezds.[12] In Shatsk uezd mobilized men rioted in early November. Detachments sent to suppress the outbreaks met armed resistance, and an attack on the city of Shatsk by peasants was beaten off only after prolonged street fighting. The peasants then besieged the city until a large detachment of soldiers from Tambov drove them away.[13]

The life cycles of these uprisings were similar. A village assembly would organize an attack on the local soviet or committee of the poor, both to obtain weapons and to destroy tax records. In these attacks they usually arrested most soviet employees, but the peasants murdered hated officials in a variety of inventive ways.[14] The rebels would then send emis-saries to other villages or even to other districts, asking them to join the rebellion and threatening them if they did not. This level of organization seemed sufficient to peasants, who had no interest in organizing resistance in any area larger than one to three districts, or in creating a disciplined armed force. When former army officers tried to organize them to fight the punitive detachments, peasants were unwilling to follow, and the disorganized mobs that did assemble usually broke at the sound of machine guns or even heavy rifle fire. Rumors that the rebellion had been quelled in a neighboring district often were enough to persuade peasants to release arrested officials and send them to negotiate peace with Soviet punitive detachments.[15]

This vacillation, lack of wider goals, and concern over White advances meant that small detachments of Soviet troops could put down series of uprisings across large areas. Rusel'nikov, a peasant from Sosnovka in Morshansk uezd, testified to the Tambov Provincial Revolutionary Tribunal how his group (part of the thousands of peasants that so frightened Morshansk officials) melted away on the march: "Thursday morning when the church bell rang we gathered in the field. There we were put into ranks by those . . . officers. . . . I cannot say exactly how many of us were from Sosnovka, but anyhow it was not less than four hundred men. We had just marched out of Sosnovka when we heard machine-gun fire in Lamki. We got scared and we began to slip away from the column unnoticed in small groups. I went into the forest and sat there till I saw that many others were going home. Then I went home too."[16]

When punitive detachments entered a village that had supported the rebellion, they would release any imprisoned soviet or committee of the poor officials, conduct a quick investigation, and execute ten or twenty peasants as "kulak ringleaders." The detachment would also collect large fines and food products.[17]

The approach of Kasnov's Cossacks from the South in late November 1918 also hastened the end of the uprising. While Tambov peasants hated

the Soviet government, they feared the Whites more, since the latter pres-
aged the return of the hated gentry who would demand back their land.
Also, the depredations of the Food Supply detachments lessened as many
of those detachments were transferred to the front to stem the advance of
the White Cossacks.[18]

While peasant disorganization made it easy for the Soviet government
to suppress the November 1918 uprisings, the unrest did force the authorities to make concessions. On 10 November they temporarily abolished all
taxes, requisitions, and conscription. Investigations into the causes of
these rebellions exposed widespread corruption and abuse among government officials. In the weeks that followed, some officials were fired and
a few were tried. The committees of the poor, a major subject of peasant
complaints, were abolished, though only after they supervised new elections to local soviets.[19]

In July 1919 a new danger threatened Communist control of the
province as General Anton Denikin's army began to advance north. As
Red Army forces fell back, Tambov sent several drafts of party members
and Food Supply soldiers to help stiffen resistance, but the Communist
forces continued to retreat. Borisoglebsk fell to the Whites on 8 July 1919,
and on 10 August a White cavalry corps commanded by General Kontan-
tin Mamontov broke through the Red Army lines and headed straight for
Tambov.[20]

Most of the provincial government fled from Tambov to Morshansk,
leaving the defense of the city to a motley, poorly armed force of recaptured
deserters, officer candidates, and mobilized Communists. D. P. Sokolov, the
commander of this brigade, went over to the Cossacks with some of his
troops during the White assault on the city, and the rest of his command
retreated in great disorder to the north. The Cossacks occupied Tambov for
several days, destroying government offices and looting warehouses and
homes. They then turned northwest toward Kozlov, captured and looted
that town, and finally broke through the Red Army lines again near
Voronezh.[21]

The raid was especially destructive to government in the countryside.
Most reports show that peasants took advantage of the Cossacks to eliminate irritants like Food Supply requisitioning agents and detachments.
Even village and district soviets often arrested, disarmed, and robbed
Food Supply officials and then turned them over to the Cossacks to be
beaten or killed. Those Soviet officials who attempted to act differently
usually became targets for attack themselves, especially if they were
Communist Party members. Cossacks or peasants alone or in combined
groups attacked and looted collective and state farms, warehouses of
goods set aside to barter for grain, and destroyed railroad tracks and tele-

graph lines. Cossack bands trampled crops and requisitioned horses as remounts. Soviet troops in pursuit of Mamontov added to the destruction, trampling crops themselves and requisitioning grain on their own. As pro-Communist authority evaporated in the countryside in Mamontov's wake, moonshining and illegal grain smuggling reached new heights.[22]

Furious that local peasants had contributed to this destruction, the provincial government decided to make them pay for it. Just as the Food Supply Committee announced new, larger procurement quotas for the new harvest, the provincial government announced that peasants would also be assessed a 10 million ruble fine to rebuild Soviet property destroyed in the raid.[23] After Mamontov's raid, the provincial food supply organization had to be reorganized almost from scratch, but Moscow immediately demanded enormous amounts of grain and fodder. Iakov Gol'din, newly appointed Food Supply Commissar, began to exert enormous pressure to ensure that grain was collected. He ordered the heads of grain collection points shot if they allowed grain to rot. In the 1918–19 procurement campaign, the government had threatened chairmen of local soviets with fines or imprisonment if their villages did not meet procurement norms. Now, entire village soviets were arrested for this reason, soviet members were threatened with execution, and all of their grain and livestock was confiscated. All claims that the quotas were too high because of crop failures or damage by passing troops were ignored.[24] As Gol'din himself reported to the Sixth Provincial Congress of Soviets, "The tactics of the Province Food Supply Committee [Gubprodkom] differed sharply [under Gol'din] from those of previous years. . . . The [consumption] norms were established when the razverstka was compiled, and if the peasant speculated away all of his norm, it wasn't the food supply organs' fault if the peasants then had to give up even their seed."[25] He did admit that some excesses occurred in this process. By this he might have been referring to the case of Iakov Margolin, head of the Requisitioning Department, who was twenty-five at the time. According to one report, Margolin, at entering a village to procure grain, would announce ceremonially, "I bring death to you scum! Look, every one of my Food Supply Army soldiers has a hundred twenty lead deaths ready for trash like you. . . . I'll strip you sons of bitches down to your skins, just as you looted and made off with the gentry's property." Then he would get down to the business of grain procurement.[26]

The Tambov party organization did its best to support Gol'din's efforts. Local party conferences emphasized the need for propaganda explaining to the peasants the reason for grain procurements. They also spoke of the need to oversee the food supply organs to prevent abuses, although this was an impossible task without a permanent party presence in the villages. In February 1920, in the face of many complaints from local party organizations about tactics used by food supply workers, the Provincial Party Committee wrote a circular letter to all Uezd Party Committees emphasizing the need to increase procurements: "The Province Committee demands the immediate liquidation of all conflicts [with food supply organs]. You will develop food supply work to the maximum. You will answer for any decrease in procurements." The provincial party organization mobilized hundreds of its members to procure grain and to serve at the front, but it attempted to protect its image by carefully forbidding local party cells to participate directly in food procurement.[27]

Gol'din reached the logical extreme of his policy in a 10 June 1920 telegram he wrote to send to all uezd Food Supply Committees. Referring to Lenin's recent telegram demanding increased grain deliveries, he ordered all armed forces in the province to form two or three large detachments. Each detachment would descend on one village at a time, demanding immediate complete fulfillment of that village's delivery norm. If this was not forthcoming, the detachment would be ordered to arrest the entire village and confiscate all of its property. Shlikhter, the head of the Provincial Executive Committee, refused to allow this order to be carried out, writing, "Being of sound mind and body, I cannot sign this order, or allow you to do so." He then wrote to the Commissariat of Food Supply explaining that Gol'din's complaints about the Provincial Party and Executive Committees were "partly the deliriums of a sick man and partly irresponsible petty tyranny." He wrote that he had replaced Gol'din with his assistant and asked Moscow to send Gol'din's replacement immediately.[28]

Gol'din's tactics had been successful in some respects: they allowed the authorities to extract 12 million poods of grain from Tambov province in 1919–20. This achievement caused much bad feeling toward the party and government among peasants and damaged the peasant economy. Peasants planted less, not only because they saw no reason to work when the reward would inevitably be confiscated, but also because many peasants had neither the tools nor the horses to plow: the Food Supply detachments had either destroyed or confiscated them. A drought in the summer of 1920 that lowered yields drastically exacerbated the effects of this decline. This was no secret to the authorities. A Cheka report from July 1920 described the peasants' plight and their hostility to the government and the Communist Party in particular and warned, "This lays the groundwork for widespread uprisings."[29]

On 8 August, A. G. Shlikhter described the need for more intensive work to fulfill the new quota, since the harvest was going to be worse because of the drought and peasants would genuinely have difficulty meeting their quotas.[30] He did not explain how this greater intensity was to be combined with law-abidingness, but clearly the more important task was getting the grain. Another policy article published about this time reminded party members that the provincial quota for the new food supply campaign was so high that some poor and middle-income peasants would not have enough grain to plant and eat after fulfilling their quotas, and that party cells must work out plans to redistribute within the village grain left after the quotas were filled. Local party officials were not sanguine about the prospects for collecting this grain: the Ninth Tambov Provincial Party Conference in July 1920 called for strengthening armed Food Supply detachments, since the bad harvest meant that grain could be obtained only by force.[31]

This was an especially dangerous situation because of the tens of thousands of deserters and draft-dodgers who hid in Tambov's forests or in their own villages, avoiding detachments sent to find them. While many thousands reported for service when White armies approached Tambov in August and September 1919, by mid-1920 recruitment had fallen drastically and desertion was up. With the war with Poland in full swing, capturing deserters and sending them to the front was, along with extracting grain, the major task set by the provincial party committee.[32]

In spite of the Cheka's warnings and obviously tense relations with peasants, it still came as a great surprise to provincial authorities when another peasant rebellion exploded in southern Tambov uezd in August 1920. Initial attempts to quell the unrest failed, because Tambov authorities assumed that this rebellion was as unorganized as previous ones and thought that peace could be restored after a small punitive force conducted a few massacres and burned some villages. What the Tambov government did not realize was that the Communist Party now had competition in the countryside.

During 1920, hundreds of secret committees of the Union of Toiling Peasantry (*Soiuz Trudovogo Krest'ianstva*, or STK) appeared in villages throughout Tambov, Kirsanov, and Borisoglebsk uezds, and in other areas of Tambov province as well. The STK was a putatively nonparty, anticommunist organization with the goal of staging a mass organized peasant uprising against the Communists. Its origins are described in an SR Central Committee circular of 13 May 1920 that argued for a three-pronged organizational initiative. The first was the "verdict movement" (*prigovornoe dvizhenie*), in which village and district meetings would condemn the Communist government and call for a national vote of confidence. This movement would prepare the ground for the formation of the STK, a multiparty organization uniting all anticommunist forces in the countryside. The SR party organization would work simultaneously to develop itself to take the lead in the STK.[33]

In Tambov province, the work of organizing fell to hundreds of SRs who labored under enormous difficulties. The Tambov provincial Left SR party organizations were suppressed in July 1918, and performing any party work after that was perilous. In addition, rivalries still existed between Right and Left SRs. In 1920, membership in the official underground Tambov SR organization totaled only a few dozen members. Considering the great attention that the Cheka paid to organizations of other Socialist parties, it seems likely that the people who led STK committees could not have had direct connections to the SR party hierarchy, even if they considered themselves Socialist Revolutionaries. In fact, while hundreds of village STK committees existed, local cells of the STK had only limited communications with higher-level regional and uezd committees when the local village STK in Kamenka, Tambov uezd, fearing that the Cheka had discovered it, started the rebellion. Even after the Kamenka STK began fighting, SR activists in the regional STK did their best to keep peasants from indulging in what they saw as a futile rebellion. National leaders refused to support the uprising was well: the All-Russian Conference of the Socialist Revolutionary Party on 9 September rejected calls by Tambov delegates to support the uprising. These leaders were unsuccessful, though, in calming the peasants. Instead, they were carried along by the rush of events. Additional proof of the STK's independence from the SR organization is the fact that the STK network remained effective even after September 1920, when most Tambov SRs were arrested. The remainder, kept under surveillance, never dared to contact Antonov.[34]

In fact, as Antonov began to unite and organize the guerrilla bands that emerged following the Kamenka uprising, he also took steps to gain control of the village STKs. A pro-Antonov, three-man provincial STK committee replaced the less-militant regional committee. This new organization, originally based in Kamenka, the birthplace of the rebellion, transmitted orders and received information from local STK committees through a small but strictly organized bureaucracy. While their members masqueraded as peaceful, unarmed peasants when Red Army detachments came through the villages, the STK committees formed a shadow government in the countryside when the detachments left. They worked through their peasant communes to organize voluntary deliveries of supplies, recruits, and especially the remounts that gave the insurgent forces much greater mobility than Soviet cavalry. Some evidence suggests that they, like village soviets, often functioned as much as executives of the peasant commune (*obshchina*) as their leaders. Unlike the Communist-controlled village soviets, though, which depended on whatever armed detachments might be nearby to enforce orders that were against the commune's wishes, each STK committee usually had several armed guards (*vokhry*) to enforce their demands. The committees spied on large army detachments and ambushed small ones, and murdered local soviet and food supply workers and party members who did not cooperate with them. They encouraged Red Army soldiers to desert, and they apprehended deserters from the insurgent forces. The STKs also carried out more peaceful duties: keeping the peace, punishing crimes, and helping partisans' families.[35] The local committees of the STK created the higher organization that the previous peasant rebellions had lacked, and generally they were successful. A Cheka agent who infiltrated the Antonov movement wrote, "Traveling with the Antonovites I was struck by the discipline that ruled among them . . . and by the close bond Antonov's forces had with the peasants." The ideology of the STK was simple: eliminate the Communist government and end its depredations in the countryside. Various proclamations and platforms expanded this program, promising a new Constituent Assembly, personal freedom, and development of the economy through cooperation, but all of this was in the future, after the victory over the Communists. Almost all STK activities focused on the military struggle.[36]

Along with the new, better organization of peasants, the crucial element in the great 1920–21 uprising was the leadership of Aleksandr Antonov. Antonov had been active against the Soviet government starting in 1918. By early 1920 he had become successful at terrorizing soviets, destroying grain collection points and state farms, and killing soviet and party workers in Kirsanov, Tambov, and Kozlov uezds. His gang even managed to ambush and murder M. D. Chichkanov in October 1919, shortly after the latter was removed as chairman of the Provincial Executive Committee. A Cheka death squad sent after him at the time failed to find him, in part because Antonov had spies in local government, including the Kirsanov uezd Cheka.[37] His gang was small and mobile, with no more than two hundred men, but this was sufficient to keep Kirsanov uezd under martial law when it was lifted in the rest of Tambov province and to make the head of the Tambov provincial Cheka request "secret espionage forces" to fight him.[38]

After assuming command of the uprising, Antonov organized his forces much better than forces had been organized in previous uprisings. While initially he commanded mobs of poorly armed and organized peasants, as found in previous uprisings, after some defeats Antonov disbanded the large groups of *vil'niki* and sent them home to be the vokhry mentioned above. He focused his efforts on arming and organizing mounted regiments of three hundred to five hundred men, usually deserters or draft dodgers. Many guerrillas and all of their commanders had experience in the First World War. His army maintained discipline with stern punishment, especially flogging and shooting. The organizational structure mimicked that of the Red Army: each detachment even had a political officer to maintain morale and persuade insurgents to obey orders.[39]

The insurgents' tactics were simple: they used their knowledge of the region and their superb intelligence network to avoid large forces, ambush small ones, and destroy the fabric of Communist government in the countryside. They sacked collective and state farms and destroyed grain collection points and district soviet offices, often with the help of local peasants. Recognizing the importance of communications, they destroyed railroads, bridges, and telegraph lines. They tortured and murdered Communists, food supply workers, and other representatives of the Communist authorities. If Red Army soldiers were captured, they were usually released; the insurgents tortured to death officers and Communist Party members, though. Occasionally the insurgents would organize kangaroo courts to try local Communists in the villages they occupied; those found innocent of abusing their power allegedly were freed. The number of freed Communists could not have been very high, however, as hundreds of Communists died at the hands of the insurgents in the fall of 1920.[40]

N. Raivid, a member of the Military Council appointed to suppress the uprising, reminded Tambov Communists in October that they were facing not a "bandit movement" but a "real peasant uprising—a movement . . . against the Communist Party, against the grain monopoly, the labor duty and the fight against desertion." He maintained that the countryside was almost without Communist influence: there the STK ruled. Most peasants encountered only the government when detachments arrived looking for grain or recruits.[41] Throughout 1920 and early 1921, though, they could find no way to exert such influence in the villages. Instead, the Soviet strategy to suppress the uprising was based on intermittent terror. Government forces shot on the spot all captured insurgents and burned and looted villages seen as supporting the uprising. They arrested all men capable of bearing arms and sent them to concentration camps around Tambov. This strategy was both too harsh and not severe enough. It was too harsh because the government did not attempt to differentiate between peasants who supported the rebels and those who opposed them or were neutral: collective responsibility made all peasants guilty for the actions of their neighbors. This solidified commune unity against the Communist government, since waverers knew that the government would have no mercy. In addition, the Communist practice of shooting all captured guerrillas helped insurgent discipline, since the rebels were more likely to fight with desperation rather than surrender to be "chopped up like sheep." The minor attempts to reward villages (never individuals) for loyalty to the Soviet government never amounted to anything, because they also required the villages to first fulfill impossible procurement targets as well as fight the insurgents.[42]

On the other hand, the policy was insufficiently severe because the government did not have enough forces to intimidate all the peasants through this terror. In September 1920 there were only thirty-five hundred troops in Tambov province. Most were poorly armed and equipped, and many lacked even boots. These troops were largely local peasants, new draftees, or recaptured deserters who received internal-security duties because they were physically unfit to serve in the regular army. Morale was low, and entire companies of local soldiers deserted or went over to the insurgents rather than fight them. The other major support for the government, the Communist party, declined drastically. Provincial party rolls plunged from 17,500 members in July 1920 to 7,000 by the end of the year.[43]

Even as the uprising took on a larger and larger aspect, the central authorities in Moscow did not take it seriously. While sending few reinforcements they continued to demand that equal attention be paid to forced grain procurement. These commands, when not ignored, only aggravated the situation.[44]

A. S. Kazakov described the results of these policies:

> Our forces . . . concentrated more on cleaning the countryside out of all property than on clearing out and destroying bands [of insurgents]. It was not decided who was innocent and who was guilty. The entire peasantry fell into one heap and was called "bandit." The part of the peasantry that was loyal to us was in a hopeless position after it lost all its property and housing from a full *furazhirovka* [their homesteads were looted and burned]. For them there was no solution except to join a [guerrilla] band to get revenge for the destruction of their goods, obtained at such effort. Entire villages, fearing our "Red Terror," took their livestock, women and children and hid in the forests. Because of such "liquidations" the bands popped up like mushrooms, and the total number of rebels reached tens of thousands. The actions of the commanders remind us of the deeds of the person who, losing his head when he sees his house on fire, pours kerosene on it.[45]

Government reports from late 1920 and early 1921 are stereotyped. Government forces pursued guerrilla bands everywhere. They reported high body counts but low numbers of captured weapons, and in spite of their supposed successes and constant reinforcements, Antonov's forces continued to control the countryside while Communist power held only uezd capitals and other heavily garrisoned towns. Even these outposts were not always safe. Antonov's forces sacked the important market town of Uvarovo on the main Moscow-Saratov railroad after its thousand-man garrison fled, while Rasskazovo, a factory village just outside Tambov, fell to Antonov's forces both in October 1920 and in April 1921, the first time shortly after Antonov's main detachment had been reported destroyed.[46]

The crucial change came in February 1921. To eliminate the principal source of peasant discontent, on 8 February the central government also officially suspended forced grain requisitioning in twelve provinces, including Tambov. While this act did garner a certain amount of support, many peasants were suspicious, thinking that the suspension of forced procurements was temporary or that the tax-in-kind would just turn out to be forced requisitions under a new name. With the end of the war with Poland, the central government had the forces available to combat the rebellion, and Moscow sent to the province a plenipotentiary commission headed by V. A. Antonov-Ovseenko; he had full powers to suppress the uprising. As winter ended, major forces were moved into Tambov province. By the end of May there were roughly fifty thousand troops in the province, including crack cavalry brigades from Ukraine, thousands of military cadets to be used as shock troops, eight artillery brigades, and armored car and automobile detachments. These forces were heavily leavened with Communists: one source suggests that 10 percent were party members. Their commanders were heroes of the civil war, including I. P. Uborevich, G. I. Kotovskii, and M. N. Tukhachevsky, the new commander of all forces in the province.[47]

The Plenipotentiary Commission in Tambov was in charge of the entire operation, emphasizing close cooperation between political authorities, the secret police, and the military. Each uezd affected by the uprising had an uezd political commission made up of the commander of military forces, the head of the uezd party committee, the chairman of the executive committee, and the chairman of the uezd Cheka. Party organizations were strengthened and harshly disciplined, and Communists brought in from other provinces filled out their ranks. Those areas whose soviets had been destroyed or were unreliable were placed under revolutionary committees, which were appointed from above to administer their areas and backed up by the garrisons that soon arrived even in small villages to root out bandits. This permanent presence in the village struck at the root of the STK's success: before, Communist propagandists had come like circuit-riding preachers who had no effect against the STK. Now the revolutionary committees, usually headed by Communists, were a local government responsive to Tambov officials. Realizing the unpopularity of the Communist Party, the new provincial authorities launched a series of Non-Party Conferences of Peasants and published huge amounts of propaganda to convince peasants that the rebellion in no way served their interests and that those things they wanted most—an end to recruitment and forced requisitions—were already a reality.[48]

After several weeks of preparation, Tukhachevsky launched a new offensive against the main insurgent forces on 1 June 1921. When he left the province forty days later the rebellion was broken, the guerrillas reduced to small groups hiding in swamps, and Soviet power had been reestablished. Tukhachevsky's success was based on his enormous reserves of manpower, which strangled the rebellion by cutting off its life-source, the local communes. His forces occupied the entire area under rebel control, depriving the rebels of popular support while crack cavalry brigades hunted down and destroyed the two main insurgent detachments, now deprived of new recruits and supplies.[49]

In his instructions issued on taking up command, Tukhachevsky listed the basic measures to be taken.

1. Never make a threat that cannot be carried out.
2. Once given, threats must be carried through to the end.
3. Resettle families that do not surrender bandits in distant regions of the R.S.F.S.R.
4. Confiscate these families' property and divide it among Soviet-minded peasants. This will cause the division of the peasantry into layers, and on this Soviet power can lean.
5. Soviet-minded peasants must be firmly and reliably protected by our forces against bandit attacks. In general, pacification will immediately create many supports of Soviet power, since banditry is wearisome and destructive for the peasant masses.
6. Soviet-minded peasants must be drawn into Soviet work by all means, into the organization of spying on bandits, etc. This will create an insurmountable barrier between those peasants and the bandits.[50]

On 12 May the Plenipotentiary Commission issued Order 130, which put into law Tukhachevsky's third point. As codified in operational instructions, a detachment would enter a village equipped with lists prepared by the Cheka. They would arrest those men present who were on the list of suspected bandits (these included insurgents and especially STK committee members). The families of those not present who were on the list of bandits, or those who were not on the list but had no good reason for being absent, were also arrested and their property confiscated. The detachment then posted signs warning that the suspect had two weeks to surrender with his weapons. He was guaranteed his life if he did this, and his family would be freed and his property surrendered. Otherwise the family was deported to forced labor in another province, the house burned, and the property divided among "honorable peasants, especially those who suffered from the bandits." The suspect was to be shot on sight.[51]

Difficulties soon emerged when this plan was carried out. The Plenipotentiary Commission ordered uezd political commissions not to arrest as hostages people who could not work: the Tambov concentration camps were clogged with old people and children who could not be transferred to forced labor camps.[52] Also, peasants soon found a way to hinder the commissions' work: they refused to give their names. This problem was surmounted by Order 171: all those who refused to give their names to a commission carrying out Order 130 were to be summarily shot.[53]

Some detachments found two weeks too long a period to wait for bandits to surrender to free their families, and in Kirsanov uezd they pioneered a new method that the Plenipotentiary Commission soon recommended to all its detachments. A detailed report survives of how this technique worked. A detachment sealed off Osinovka, a hamlet that insurgents frequented. The peasants there claimed to know nothing of the insurgents even after Orders 130 and 171 were read, along with the list of suspected bandits. The detachment then took forty hostages and gave the villagers two hours to deliver both bandits and weapons, or the hostages would be shot. The village assembly wavered on what to do, so after two hours the detachment executed twenty-one hostages in front of the assembly "with all formalities." The horrified peasants soon came up with three rifles and five bandits. "With the goal of rendering the settlement more healthy, families of those who were shot and of bandits who were hiding were sent to a concentration camp." The detachment then moved on to the next village, where the peasants were much more forthcoming.[54]

The data used to compile the accompanying table are incomplete, but they give some idea of the scope of the campaign and of its results.[55]

Results of Order 130 Campaign

Date	Insurgents Captured	Voluntary Insurgent Surrenders	Insurgents Shot	Hostages Taken	
				Individuals	Families
June 1–9	424	201	120	920	209
June 19–25	728	479	no data	1847	308
June 26–July 2	596	507	183	683	183
July 2–9	347	476	394	432	161
July 10–16	621	796	286	942	283
July 17–23	344	768	199	642	98
July 24–30	83	508	42	327	53

The Plenipotentiary Commission publicized widely the results of the Order 130 campaign and soon added further rigor to it. A 12 June proclamation announced that families who hid weapons, insurgents, or even the families of insurgents would be arrested and sent to hard labor, except for the oldest male, who would be shot. Property would be confiscated, of course.[56]

After a district was purged of bandits and their families, the authorities appointed a revolutionary committee to govern the area. As regular military detachments were withdrawn from pacified areas for use elsewhere, they were replaced by mounted militiamen (recruited from other provinces) and local self-defense units called *druzhiny*. Drawn from the local population, these units gave the revolutionary committee armed force with which to repel insurgent incursions, spy on insurgent groups, and enforce orders on the local population. The *druzhiniki* were reliable, because any betrayal would result in severe reprisals against not only the druzhinik himself but all members of his immediate family.[57]

While most Soviet forces were thus winning over the Tambov peasantry, the elite cavalry of the Red Army, commanded by such heroes of the civil war as Uborevich and Kotovskii and reinforced with Fiat automobiles mounted with machine guns, were ordered to pursue and destroy the main insurgent armies. At this point the insurgent forces were concentrated in two armies, the First Army, with two thousand troops under Bogoslavskii, and the Second Army, with three thousand men commanded by Antonov himself. They first struck against Antonov's army. Before, Antonov's men had been able to outdistance Red cavalry by frequently changing horses. When they had lost touch with their pursuers, Antonov's forces could stop, rest, and reequip. This was no longer possible. Faster, tireless automobiles followed them constantly. Red Army commanders had trouble in coordinating cavalry units with the automobile detachments, allowing most of Antonov's forces to escape both a surprise attack on 1 June at Elan and another at Chenyshevo five days later, but the insurgents suffered serious losses both of men and especially of weapons. In addition they became intimidated by the automobiles, whose engines frightened their horses and who followed them constantly. The insurgent forces melted away, especially after Antonov received a serious head wound in Chenyshevo. Guerrillas hid in the woods along the Vorona river, attempted to return home secretly, or surrendered to the Communist forces. Antonov was left with only a few dozen men. Similar tactics were successful against Bogoslavskii's army.[58] When the remnants of the larger insurgent groups fled to forests and swamps along the Vorona river, Tukhachevsky ordered preparations to use another modern weapon, poison gas, to "smoke them out." Although Antonov-Ovseenko announced publicly this plan to encourage insurgents to surrender, it seems not to have been carried out because of technical difficulties.[59]

Such extreme measures were not necessary. The rebellion was finished by September because the insurgents found no safe base in which they could recuperate and reorganize, even though Antonov remained at large. The revolutionary committees, druzhiny, and militia had replaced the STK committees in the villages, and the insurgents could no longer count on the support of the peasants. The government had abolished forced food requisition, removed the Food Supply detachments and allowed free trade in grain. Conscription was much less pressing as the Red Army demobilized. If even some members of the Tambov uezd STK committee thought the "Bolsheviks had gone over to the STK program" with the introduction of NEP, it is not surprising that peasant support for the uprising vanished when the rebel armies were crushed and the Communist government offered real reforms. This is especially true given that the peasantry risked much greater dangers in supporting the rebels after the Communist government was firmly in place in the villages. In any case, all energies had to be focused on surviving a winter that was even hungrier than those before.[60]

Aleksandr Antonov and his brother remained at large for several more months, hiding in forests along the Vorona river or with old friends in the Kirsanov area. The Tambov secret police continued to search for them and other remnants of the uprising, using former insurgents now desperate to pay their debt to society by hunting down their former comrades. Only in June 1922 did the Cheka find the Antonov brothers. Suffering from malaria, they were recovering in a peasant hut in the village of Nizhni Shibriai. Cheka agents surrounded the hut, set it afire, and shot the men as they fled. Soviet authorities took measures to assure that Antonov would not become the subject of folklore. They distributed slides of photographs of the naked corpses of the brothers throughout the province, where activists used slide projectors to show them to peasant assemblies.[61]

The Tambov peasant uprising of 1920–21 was doomed to failure once Moscow could concentrate sufficient forces against it. Confronted with overwhelming force and swayed by the removal of many of the most galling aspects of early Soviet power, peasants weary from eight years of war returned to rebuilding their farms. But if Antonov was killed and his insurgency crushed, the Soviet government did not forget his movement. Insurgents who had surrendered to the government and redeemed themselves by fighting against their former comrades were later arrested and sent to concentration camps. Even fiction could be dangerous: Nikolai Virta's novel of the rebellion, *Odinochestvo*, led to denunciations of several peasants from Virta's village.[62]

Peasant uprisings were a constant factor in Tambov province during the civil war. The central government's policies of forced food procurement and recruiting inevitably caused discontent among the rural population. Corruption and tyranny by local government officials compounded this and led to violence. The peasant commune provided an organizing principle for expressing discontent, but only on the village or district level. This local disorganization allowed small government forces to suppress large uprisings piecemeal.

The great uprising of 1920–21 presented a new challenge to the Communist government. Still poorly armed but with a much better organization, Antonov's Insurgent Army required far greater effort to suppress, and it also forced a reassessment of the sources of peasant discontent, especially the forced grain procurement system. Military operations and cleansing of villages of "unfriendly" peasants by exile and executions ended the 1920–21 uprising, but only the abandonment of forced requisitions and the government withdrawal from confrontation with the village brought calm to the countryside. But this calm was only temporary, lasting until the new upheavals at the end of the 1920s.

Notes

1. Speech by A. G. Shlikhter to Gubernskoe prodovol'stvennoe soveshchanie, 8 August 1920, Gosudarstvennyi Arkhiv Tambovskoi oblasti (hereafter GATO), f. R-1236, op. 1, d. 765, l. 8.

2. V. V. Samoshkin, "Miatezh. Antonovshchina: kanun i nachalo," *Literaturnaia Rossiia*, no. 23 (8 June 1990): 19.

3. Uezd was a political subdivision of a Russian province (Tambov province had twelve uezds). "Kazn' komissara Seremiagina," *Izvestiia Tambovskogo gubernskogo soveta*, 12 September 1918, 1; GATO, f. R-1236, op. 1, d. 746, l. 10; Gosudarstvennyi Arkhiv Rossiskoi Federatsii (formerly Tsentral'nyi Arkhiv Oktiabrskoi Revoliutsii; hereafter GARF), f. 393, op. 13, d. 463, l. 338; report of Tambov Revision Commission, 14 February 1919, GATO, f. R-394, op. 1, d. 392, ll. 128–128ob; Instructor Gados to Gubernskii otdel upravleniia, 6 January 1919, ibid., ll. 90–93; A. Okninskii, *Dva goda sredi krest'ian* (Riga: M. Didkovska Izdvnieciba, 1936), 38.

4. *Izvestiia Narodnogo komissariata po prodovol'stviiu*, nos. 1–2 (January 1919): 57; Protocol 30 of Tambov Gubprodkollegiia, 31 March 1919, Rossiiskii Gosudarstvennyi Arkhiv Ekonomiki (formerly Tsentral'nyi Gosudarstvennyi Arkhiv Narodnogo Khoziaistva; hereafter RGAE), f. 1943, op. 3, d. 293, l. 344ob; also Protocol of 6 May 1919 instructors' meeting, ibid., l. 485ob.

5. S. L. Protasov, "Volostnye i sel'skie organizatsii RKP(b) Tambovskoi gubernii," in *Voprosy partiinogo stroitel'stva v tsentral'nom chernozem'e* (Tambov: n.p., 1988), 52, 62; *Lichnyi sostav RKP(b) v 1920 g.* (Moscow: n.p., 1921), 62; S. L. Protasov, personal communication.

6. Boris Shekhter to VTsIK, stamped 27 January 1919, GATO, f. R-1, op. 1, d. 138, ll. 122–122ob.

7. E. A. Lutskii, "Krest'ianskoe vosstanie v Tambovskoi gubernii v sentiabre 1917 g.," *Istoricheskie zapiski*, no. 2 (1938), 72–75; P. Kroshitskii and S. Sokolov, eds., *Khronika revoliutsionnykh sobytii v Tambovskoi gubernii (1917–1918)* (Tambov: Tipografiia "Prole-

tarskii svetoch," 1927), 60; "Tambovskie motivy," *Izvestiia Tambovskogo gubernskogo soveta,* 7 July 1918, 2; Kolosov, *Put' bor'by,* 35–37; V. Vasil'ev, "Iz istorii antonovshchiny," in *Antonovshchina* (Tambov: Izdatel'stvo Tambovskogo gubkoma partii "Kommunist," 1923), 11; Provincial Commissar of Labor B. Vasil'ev, report to Narkomtrud, 19 June 1918, GARF, f. 393, op. 3, d. 378, l. 134ob.

8. T. V. Osipova, "Krest'ianskie vosstaniia v gody grazhdanskoi voiny," 1990, Manuscript, 13.

9. V. V. Aver'ev and S. Ronin, "Kulatskie vostaniia v epokhu kombedov," *Bor'ba klassov,* no. 3 (1935): 87; Gubernskii otdel upravleniia report to NKVD otdel mestnogo upravleniia, 16 October 1918, GARF, f. 393, op. 3, d. 378, l. 146.

10. Protocol 37 of the Morshansk uispolkom, 23 October 1918, GATO, f. R-20, op. 1, d. 30, l. 204.

11. Glavnyi Komissar s.v. dorogi Kudriavtsev to Gubispolkom, 10 November 1918, GATO, f. R-1, op. 1, d. 31, l. 218; Deputy Chairman of Gubispolkom Monaenkov [*sic*] to Sovnarkom, VeCheKa, etc., 10 November 1918, GARF, f. 130, op. 2, d. 631, l. 39.

12. Krotshitskii and Sokolov, *Khronika revoliutsionnykh sobytii v Tambovskoi gubernii,* 70.

13. A. Komarov and P. Kroshitskii, *Revoliutsionnoe dvizhenie: Khronika 1918 goda* (Voronezh: Izdatel'stvo "Kommuna"), 150; N. P. Zybko, *Tambovskaia partiinaia organizatsiia v gody grazhdanskoi voiny i inostrannoi interventsii (1918–1920 gg.)* (Tambov: Tambovskoe knizhnoe izdatel'stvo, 1961), 16; "Doklad o vazhneishikh sobytiiakh v Kirsanovskom uezde za god sotsialisticheskoi revoliutsii," GATO, f. R-1, op. 1, d. 138, l. 21ob; Gubinstruktor V. Zheladnov report to Gubprodkom, 23 November 1918, GATO, f. R-1236, op. 1, d. 94, l. 105; Tambov Voenkomat to the Commander of the Southern Front, 12 November 1918, GATO, f. R-1, op. 1, d. 31, l. 239.

14. Zybko, *Tambovskaia partiinaia organizatsiia,* 16; Aver'ev and Ronin, "Kulatskie vostaniia v epokhu kombedov," 87.

15. Aver'ev and Ronin, "Kulatskie vostaniia v epokhu kombedov," 94.

16. Quoted in ibid., 94.

17. Gubinstruktor V. Zheladnov, report to Gubprodkom, 23 November 1918, GATO, f. R-1236, op. 1, d. 94, l. 105; *Bor'ba rabochikh i krest'ian pod rukovodstvom bol'shevistskoi partii za ustanovlenie i uprochenie Sovetskoi vlasti v Tambovskoi gubernii (1917–1918 gody)* (Tambov: n.p., 1957), 90.

18. A. Morozov, "Doklad-Otchet o prodarmii," n.d., RGAE, f. 1943, op. 11, d. 204, ll. 62, 69.

19. Margolin to the Provincial Requisition Department, 15 November 1918, GATO, f. R-1236, op. 1, d. 155, l. 160; Protocol of Gubcheka Collegium, 28 April 1919, GATO, f. R-1, op. 1, d. 120, l. 6ob; Report to Gubprodkom from Gubinstruktor V. Zheladnov, 23 November 1918, GATO, f. R-1236, op. 1, d. 94, l. 105; Telegram from Tambov Voenkomat to the Commander of the Southern Front, 12 November 1918, GATO, f. R-1, op. 1, d. 31, l. 239.

20. N. E. Kakurin, *Kak srazhalas' revoliutsiia* (Moscow: Gosudarstvennoe Izdatel'stvo, 1926; reprint, Moscow: Politizdat, 1990), 2: 261; *Ocherki istorii Tambovskoi,* 110.

21. "Delo o sdache g. Tambova," *Vestnik Tambovskogo otdela upravleniia,* nos. 30–31 (27 September 1919), 44; V. Verkhovykh, "Shest' let partraboty v Tambovskoi gubernii," *Kommunist* (Tambov), no. 11 (1923): 19.

22. Lipetsk Zarekviotdel to Gubrekviotdel, 21 September 1919, GATO, f. R-1236, op. 1, d. 578, l. 33ob; *Zhurnal* no. 69 of the meeting of heads of state farms of Kozlov uezd, 16 September 1919, GARF, f. 4390, op. 7, d. 44, l. 9; Shmidt to Gol'man, report, September(?) 1919, RGAE, f. 1943, op. 1, d. 439, l. 7; Gol'man to Tsiurupa, August

1919, ibid., l. 16; Tambov Gubotdelupravleniia to Militia chiefs, 12 November 1919; GARF, f. 393, op. 13, d. 463, l. 140; Head of Kirsanov uezd administration department, Report on 1919, ibid., d. 472, l. 5.

23. Minutes of the 28 October 1920 meeting of the Collegium of the Tambov Provincial Finance Department, GATO, f. R-1, op. 1, d. 137, l. 962. This tax was abandoned in December; see ibid., l. 963.

24. Telegram from Gol'din to all Uprodkomy, 17 February 1920, GATO, f. R-1, op. 157, l. 129; Telegram from Shpunt to Smirnov, December 1919 and note from Gol'din to all heads of collection points, RGAE, f. 1943, op. 1, d. 576, ll. 2, 20.

25. *Izvestiia Tambovskogo gubernskogo soveta*, 23 May 1920, 2.

26. Report to the Gubispolkom by Chairman of the Borisoglebsk uprodkom, 9 February 1920, GARF, f. 1235, op. 95, d. 430, l. 34ob. Margolin was arrested by the Cheka on direct orders from VTsIK February 1920 (see ibid., l. 35) but was not brought to trial until November. He was found guilty of exceeding his power, but his prison term was suspended due to his services to the revolution. See *Kniga registrasii sudebnykh del prodovol'stvennykh rabotnikov Tambovskoi gubernii za dekabr' 1920—ianvar' 1921*, GATO, f. R-1236 op. 1, d. 798, l. 2.

27. A. L. Avrekh, "Partiinye organizatsii Chernozemnogo Tsentra Rossii v bor'be za khleb v period inostrannoi voennoi interventsii i grazhdanskoi voiny" (Cand. diss., Tambovskii gosudarstvennyi pedagogicheskii institut, 1978), 76, 86, 98.

28. Telegram to all Uprodkomy, 11 June 1920, GATO, f. R-1, op. 1, d. 234, l. 501; Telegram to People's Commissar Tsiurupa from Shlikhter, 15 June 1920, RGAE, f. 1943, op. 1, d. 576, l. 112.

29. Weekly Report of the Secret Department of the VeCheKa, 1–16 July 1920, GARF, f. 130, op. 3, d. 414, l. 31; protocol of 23 April 1920 meeting of Usman' uispolkom) GATO, f. R-1236, op. 1, d. 849, l. 32; Vladimir Samoshkin, "Miatezh. Antonovshchina: kanun i nachalo," *Literaturnaia Rossiia* 1990, no. 23 (8 June 1990), 18–19; Sergei Pavliuchenkov, "Pochemu vspykhnula 'Antonovshchina,'" *Nedelia*, no. 44 (1989): 10–11.

30. Speech by A. G. Shlikhter to Gubernskoe prodovol'stvennoe soveshchanie, 8 August 1920, GATO, f. R-1236, op. 1, d. 765, l. 8.

31. R., "Dve boevye zadachi," *Kommunist* (Tambov), no. 1 (1 September 1920), 3; Avrekh, "Partiinye organizatsii," 94.

32. "Perelom sredi dezertirov," *Vestnik Tambovskogo gubernskogo otdela upravleniia*, 26 July 1919, 339; R., "Dve boevye zadachi," 4.

33. *Obvinitel'noe zakliuchenie po delu tsentral'nogo komiteta i otdel'nykh chlenov inykh organizatsii partii s.-r.* (Moscow: VTsIK, 1922), 40–41.

34. For the clearest exposition of the murky issue of SR collaboration in the uprising see S. A. Esikov and V. V. Kanishchev, "'Antonovskii NEP' (Organizatsiia i deiatel'nost' 'Soiuza Trudovogo Krestianstva' Tambovskoi gubernii: 1920–1921 gg)." *Otechestvennaia istoriia*, no. 4 (1993): 60–71. See also Oliver H. Radkey, *The Unknown Civil War in Soviet Russia* (Stanford: Hoover Institution Press, 1976), 120, 143–146; V. P. Antonov-Saratovskii, ed., *Sovety v epokhu voennogo kommunizma* (Moscow: Izdatel'stvo Kommunisticheskoi Akademii, 1928–29), 2: 447–448; A. Kazakov, *Partiia s.-r. i Tambovskoe vosstanie 1920–1921 gg.* (Moscow: n.p., 1922), 7–8; Petitions of Kirsanov ex-SRs, arrested in July 1920, GARF, f. 1235, op. 95, d. 432, ll. 54–57; GARF, f. 393, op. 22, d. 340, l. 51; [Iurii Podbelskii], "Po Rossii."

35. "Vosstanie tambovskikh krest'ian," *Volia Rossii*, 22 April 1922, 3–4. Esikov and Kanishchev, "'Antonovskii NEP,'" 65; B. Leonidov, "Esero-banditizm v Tambovskoi gubernii i bor'ba s nim," *Revoliutsiia i voina*, nos. 14–15 (1922): 156; M. Tukhachevskii, "Bor'ba s kontrrevoliutsionnymi vosstaniiami. Iskorenenie tipichnogo banditizma (Tambovskoe vosstanie)," *Voina i revoliutsiia*, no. 8 (1926): 8; E. F. Murav'ev, "O likvidatsii Antonovshchiny," 1964, Manuscript, Pokaliukhin folder, Tambovskii Oblastnoi Kraeve-

cheskii Muzei, 34; V. Andreev and S. Kulaev, *Oktiabr'skaia revoliutsiia i grazhdanskaia voina v Tambovskoi gubernii* (Tambov: n.p., 1927), 45.

36. Esikov and Kanishchev, "'Antonovskii NEP,'" 63–64; Murav'ev, "O likvidatsii Antonovshchiny," 29.

37. Osipova, "Krest'ianskie vosstaniia v gody grazhdanskoi voiny," 64–65; M. I. Pokaliukhin, "Razgrom kulatsko-eserovskogo miatezha na tambovshchine," in *Krai, preobrazhennyi oktiabrem*, 1: 38–39 (Tambov: Izdatel'stvo Tambovskaia Pravda, 1967); Ezhenedel'naia svodka sekretnogo otdela VeCheKa za vremia s 1–7 fevralia 1920 g., GARF, f. 130, op. 3, d. 414, l. 1ob. See also GARF, f. 1235, op. 95, d. 429, ll. 502, 506, 510ob for the unsuccessful petition for amnesty of a member of the Inzhavino rairevkom, condemned to death for spying for Antonov.

38. Svodka #170/op voisk vnutrennei okhrany respubliki za 27 dek. 1919, GARF, f. 130, op. 3, d. 428, l. 129; *Sovety Tambovskoi gubernii*, 227 (Gubispolkom decree dated 12 January 1920).

39. M. I. Pokaliukhin, "Ob Antonovshchine (vospominaniia chekista)," 1964, Manuscript, Pokaliukhin folder, Tambovskii Oblastnoi Kraevecheskii Muzei, p. 20; V. Mokerov, "Kursantskii sbor po bor'be s antonovshchinoi," *Voina i revoliutsiia*, no. 1, (1932): 65–66; Jan M. Meijer, ed., *The Trotsky Papers, 1917–1922* (The Hague: Mouton, 1964–71), 2: 500–502; B. Leonidov, "Esero-banditizm v Tambovskoi gubernii i bor'ba s nim," 159–160.

40. RTsKhIDNI Rossiiskii Tsentr Khraneniia I Izucheniia Dokumentov Noveishei Istorii (formerly Tsentral'nyi Partiinyi Arkhiv; hereafter RTsKhIDNI), f. 17, op. 84, l. 138 (I thank D. A. Nalitov for this citation); Telegram from Gubispolkom to Lenin, 8 September 1920, GATO, f. R-1, op. 4a, d. 83, l. 702; I. P. Donkov, *Antonovshchina: zamysly i deistvitel'nost'* (Moscow: Izdatel'stvo politicheskoi literatury, 1977), 29, 39.

41. N. Raivid, "O rabote v derevne," *Kommunist* (Tambov) nos. 2–3 (15 October 1920), 2; see also *Trotsky Papers*, 2: 507.

42. V. V. Samoshkin, "Miatezh. Antonovshchina: protivostoianie," *Literaturnaia Rossiia*, no. 43 (26 October 1990), 18. The quotation is from N. Raivid in his report to the 5 October 1920 Gubispolkom meeting, GARF, f. 393, op. 22, d. 340, l. 50, *Sovety Tambovskoi gubernii v gody grazhdanskoi voiny 1918–1921 gg.* (Voronezh: Tsentral'no-Chernozemnoe Knizhnoe Izdatel'stvo, 1989), 265–266, 307–308.

43. Gubprodkom Protocol 57 for 16 December 1920, GARF, f. 393, op. 22, d. 341, l. 96; Samoshkin, "Protivostoianie," 18; Verkhovykh, "Shest' let partraboty v Tambovskoi gubernii," 21; Reports from A. G. Shlikhter to Revvoensovet and Tsentroevak, 11 September 1920, GATO, f. R-1, op. 1, d. 137, ll. 713, 716; *V. I. Lenin i VeCheKa* (Moscow: Izdatel'stvo Politicheskoi Literatury, 1972), 403.

44. *Vnutrennye voiska Sovetskoi respubliki (1917–1922 gg.)* (Moscow: Iuridicheskaia Literatura, 1972), 524–525.

45. Quoted in Samoshkin, "Protivostoianie," 18.

46. Pokaliukhin, "Ob Antonovshchine," 40; *Vnutrennie voiska*, 539; Telegram from Tambov Gubotdeltekstil' to VTsKVPS Tekstil'shchikov, dated 20 April 1921, GARF, f. 1235, op. 96, d. 590, l. 5; Tukhachevskii, "Bor'ba s kontrrevoliutsionnymi vosstaniiami," no. 9, p. 7. For typical reports see *Vnutrennie voiska*, 520–522, Operativnaia svodka za 13 maia 1921, GARF, f. 130, op. 5, d. 712, l. 13 or Operativnaia svodka za period 13 marta po 16 marta 1921 ibid., d. 713, l. 2.

47. S. A. Esikov and L. G. Protasov, "'Antonovshchina': Novye podkhody," *Voprosy istorii*, nos. 6–7 (1992): 51; Mokerov, "Kursantskii sbor po bor'be s antonovshchinoi," 61; V. V. Samoshkin, "Posledniaia krest'ianskaia voina," *Trud*, 21 October 1990, 4; *Vnutrennie voiska*, 596.

48. "Otchet Tambovskogo Gubernskogo Komiteta R. K. P. za mai 1921 g." *Kommunist* (Tambov) 1921, no. 5, p. 9; "Otchet Gubkoma XII Gubpartkonferentsii," *Kommunist* (Tambov) 1921, no. 7, p. 4; *Trotsky Papers*, 2: 520; Radkey, *Unknown Civil War*, 244–245.

49. Tukhachevskii to Military District Commanders, 30 May 1921, GARF, f. R-8415, op. 1, d. 122, l. 44; Leonidov, "Esero-banditizm v Tambovskoi gubernii i bor'ba s nim," 167–168.

50. Quoted in Leonidov, "Esero-banditizm v Tambovskoi gubernii i bor'ba s nim," 171.

51. *Sovety Tambovskoi gubernii,* 319–320 (Prikaz 130); Prikaz 14, GARF, f. 8415, op. 1, d. 122, l. 55; Tukhachevskii, "Bor'ba s kontrrevoliutsionnymi vosstaniiami," no. 8, p. 8.

52. GARF, f. 8415, op. 1, d. 122, l. 125.

53. D. Fel'dman, "Krest'ianskaia voina," *Rodina,* no. 10 (1989): 57; Tsentral'nyi Gosudarstvennyi Arkhiv Sovetskoi Armii f. 235, op. 3, d. 13, l. 14 (my thanks to D. A. Nalitov for this citation).

54. Report by Shchekoldin, chairman of a Polnomochnaia Piaterka, dated 8 July 1921, GARF, f. 8415, op. 1, d. 122, ll. 103–103ob; Telegram to Predupolitkomissii of all military districts from Antonov-Ovseenko, Tukhachevksy, Lavrov, dated 23 June 1921, ibid., l. 94. See also Tsentr dokumentatsii noveishei istorii Tambovskoi oblasti (formerly Partiinyi Arkhiv Tambovskoi Oblasti; hereafter TsDNITO), f. 840, op. 1, d. 1048, ll. 9–10ob.

55. Guberniia Reports by the Plenipotentiary Commission, GARF, R-8415, op. 1, d. 121, ll. 30–33ob, ibid., d. 122, ll. 82–83, TsDNITO, op. 1, d. 1048, ll. 9–16ob (my thanks to S. A. Esikov for this reference and that from TsDNITO in previous note).

56. "Krest'ianstvu Tambovskoi gubernii," 12 June 1921, GARF, f. R-8415, op. 1, d. 122, l. 79.

57. Leonidov, "Esero-banditizm v Tambovskoi gubernii i bor'ba s nim," 171; Tukhachevskii, "Bor'ba s kontrrevoliutsionnymi vosstaniiami," no. 9, p. 10; Instructions on Re-Establishing Soviet Power, GARF, f. R-8415, op. 1, d. 116, ll. 18–19ob; Instructions on organizing district druzhiny, ibid., d. 122, ll. 63–64.

58. Combined Cavalry Group Combat Report, 28 May–8 June 1921, GARF, f. R-8415, op. 1, d. 122, ll. 49–52; I. I. Trutko, "Takticheskie primery iz opyta bor'by s banditizmom: Unichtozhenie bandy Boguslavskogo," *Krasnaia armiia* nos. 3–4 (1921): 35–37.

59. I. I. Trutko, "Takticheskie primery iz opyta bor'by s banditizmom: Primenenie aeroplanov kak rezervov," *Krasnaia armiia,* nos. 5–6, (1921): 41–43; GARF, f. 8415, op. 1, d. 122, ll. 70, 80 (Order from Tukhachevsky to use poison gas dated 12 June 1921, and proclamation from Antonov-Ovseenko dated 11 June 1921 threatening its use); Mokerov, "Kursantskii sbor po bor'be s antonovshchinoi," 79; Fel'dman, "Krest'ianskaia voina," 57.

60. B. V. "Partiia na prodrabotu," *Kommunist* (Tambov) 1921, no. 6, p. 2; Kazakov, *Partiia s.-r. i Tambovskoe vosstanie 1920–1921 gg.,* 10; Vasil'ev, "Iz istorii antonovshchiny," 16.

61. Boris Ileshin, "Posle pozhara," *Krest'ianskie vedomosti,* no. 15, (1991): 13; Ser. Polin, "Poslednie dni esero-bandita Antonova. (iz zapisnoi knizhki chekista)," in *Put' bor'by* (Tambov: Izdatel'stvo Tambovskogo gubkoma R. K. P. "Kommunist," 1923), 51–53.

62. Ileshin, "Posle pozhara," 13.

Four

Representations and Actions

Unpublished Lenin 10

P eople who have never worked in archives regard them with a mystical awe. Viewing published sources as biased if not deliberately falsified, prone to seeing conspiracies behind every historic event, they seem to think that it is impossible to know what really happened unless one has access to the unpublished sources. During the years I worked on my history of the Russian Revolution, I was often asked whether I had located "new materials," the unspoken assumption behind the question being that only such materials justified still another book on the subject.

This opinion rests on a misconception. The historian judges the motives and intentions of historical actors by their deeds: actions speak for themselves. We need not see, black on white, the resolution of the Bolshevik Central Committee setting the date of the October coup d'état to know when it happened.[1] Nor do we require a written order by Hitler to murder all Jews to know that this is what he intended and nearly accomplished. In fact, the most important governmental decisions are often not committed to paper because statesmen, mindful of their place in history, prefer either not to spell out their intentions or to conceal them behind spurious motives. Lenin in particular, having spent his entire early life in the underground, made certain that the orders with which he did not want to be identified were either communicated orally, or, if committed to paper, promptly destroyed.[2]

To say this is not to belittle the value of historical archives. In fact, nothing is more reassuring to the historian than to see contemporary records. Merely to hold them in one's hands gives a sense of communicating with the past that no printed source can convey. They provide the scholar with all kinds of important details, and, if he has studied printed sources conscientiously, ultimate confirmation of hypotheses.

Having done research in what used to be known as the Central Archive in Moscow (now clumsily renamed Russian Center for the Preservation and Study of the Documents of Modern History, or RTsKhIDNI) on papers dealing with the history of Soviet Russia under Lenin's rule (1917–24), I have to state that they did not compel me to alter views which I had formed on the basis of published materials. They proved of great value in confirming intuitions and clarifying certain otherwise baffling events. But there were no startling revelations; no document came to light that required me fundamentally to revise any part of my narrative.[3] On balance, the greatest value of these researches was to give me confidence that the facts presented in my histories will not be upset by information from currently unknown sources.

According to I. Smirnov, the director of the Institute of Marx-Engels-Lenin, his archive, the predecessor of RTsKhIDNI, in December 1990 held 6,724 unpublished Lenin documents.[4] Nearly one-half of them bore only Lenin's signature (for example, the minutes of the Council of Peoples' Commissars). The remaining 3,724 documents, however, were either written by Lenin or have Lenin's marginal annotations. The bulk of this material was held in the "Secret" part of the Lenin archive (f. 2, op. 2). All unpublished Leniniana at RTsKhIDNI is said to have been "declassified" in the winter of 1991–92, gradually transferred to the open part (f. 2, op. 1), and made available to Russian and foreign scholars. I have been shown, however, only about one-third of this material.[5] The reason why the Communists had kept some Lenin documents secret is not always apparent. A high proportion of them deal with the Soviet government's subversive activities abroad, activities that gave lie to the pretense that it scrupulously respected international law. Others expose internal Bolshevik disagreements which the party preferred to shield from public view. Documents that attest to Lenin's cruelty and exercise of indiscriminate terror also were likely to end up in the secret archive.

In addition to the Lenin deposits (f. 2, op. 1 and 2), I have seen parts of fond 5 (Lenin's Secretariat), fond 17 (the Central Committee), and several personal archives (of Stalin, Dzerzhinsky, and others). Some of this material I managed to incorporate in *Russia Under the Bolshevik Regime*.[6] The remainder came too late to my attention to be cited. Below I summarize some of the most important archival materials that I have found at RTsKhIDNI bearing on Lenin and the early history of Soviet Russia.

Access to the archives has not altered the picture I had formed of Lenin's personality. No newly released documents have revealed an unsuspected dimension of Lenin's psyche or mind; rather, they brought out even more forcefully his familiar traits.

There is nothing surprising in this, of course: the Communist authorities had no need to hide texts that cast a favorable light on Lenin. If, for instance, Lenin had taken the trouble to invite a few hundred *besprizornye* (the homeless waifs who in his day roamed Moscow like wild animals) to be fed by the Kremlin kitchen, this fact would have been made public long ago. So would other acts of kindness and generosity. Hidden was evidence of inhumanity, misanthropy, cynicism, vulgarity, and brazen lying. Lenin's admirers will find little comfort in these materials.

Some reviewers have criticized my work for failing to bring out Lenin's alleged idealism and for overstressing his obsession with power. Not a single document of the hundreds that I have inspected gave any hint of Lenin's idealistic propensities: on the contrary, they confirmed his utter indifference to human lives and human suffering, and his all-consuming concern with holding on to and expanding his power.

A few examples must suffice. One receives a jolt reading a report from late 1920 to Lenin from Dzerzhinsky, the head of the Cheka, an establishment not known for compassion, that tens of thousands of White prisoners of war as well as Cossacks who had been expelled from their homelands and confined to internment camps in Ekaterinburg were living in "inhuman" conditions. Dzerzhinsky requested that steps be taken to improve their lot. In the margin stands Lenin's terse "Into the Archive." On another occasion, when Dzerzhinsky suggested that the sailors and soldiers taken prisoner after the suppression of the Kronstadt mutiny in March 1921 be interned in the Crimea and Caucasus, Lenin told him that "it would be more convenient" to have them sent north.[7] In accord with his wishes, the Cheka incarcerated the prisoners in concentration camps in the barren wastes of the White Sea, from which few ever returned. In no unpublished document did I find a trace of humanity except where Lenin's own family and close associates were concerned.

The same callousness is revealed in Lenin's attitude toward the victims of anti-Jewish pogroms. That he did not react to the massacres of Jews in the Ukraine by White Cossacks can be justified—if one is charitably inclined—by his inability to do anything about them. But how can one justify his indifference to similar atrocities committed by the Red Cossacks? The archive contains an urgent appeal to Lenin from the Jewish Section of the Communist Party's Central Committee (*Evsektsiia*), dated July 1920, informing him that on its retreat from Poland Budennyi's cavalry was "systematically exterminating" Belorussian Jews. The Evsektsiia requested that local workers be allowed to arm themselves. On the margin of this document stands Lenin's dismissive "Into the Archive of the Central Committee." Aware that Lenin was untainted by anti-Semitism, I was shocked to read in the draft of his resolution dating from late 1919 on the structure of the Soviet government about to be installed in the reconquered Ukraine, a clause calling for the exclusion of Jews. (As an afterthought, Lenin added, in the margin, "Put it more politely: Jewish petty-bourgeoisie."). This is a classic example of his obsession with power politics, for, aware of the intensity of anti-Jewish feelings in the Ukraine, he did not want to make his regime even more unpopular there by employing Jews. The same consideration, of course, had lain behind the much-criticized policy of the White Armies to dismiss and exclude Jews from all government posts in the Ukrainian areas under their control.

Total lack of concern with human suffering permeates the entire collection of unpublished Leniniana at RTsKhIDNI. Sources sometimes speak as eloquently by what they pass over in silence as by what they say. Nowhere did I find expressions of regret or sorrow over the deaths from disease and hunger that the Revolution, civil war, and the famine had inflicted on Russia—deaths that demographers estimate at 10 million, a figure equal to all the casualties of World War I. The condition of their people interested Soviet leaders only insofar as it affected state security: quite typical is a warning from Dzerzhinsky from July 1921 to the Cheka staff that the famine (which ultimately afflicted some 30 million people, of whom more than 5 million died) might encourage counterrevolution, and that called for harsh preventive measures.

The unpublished sources shed much light on the relationship of Lenin with both Trotsky and Stalin. Trotsky liked to depict himself as an intimate of Lenin's and Stalin as a nonentity laboring in the shadows until Lenin's illness enabled him to grab power. He also made a great deal of the disagreements that broke out between Lenin and the general secretary in the winter of 1922, claiming (falsely) that they caused Lenin to break relations with Stalin. Trotsky's version gained wide credence abroad because it enabled those who wanted to disassociate Lenin from Stalin to blame all that was odious in Communism on his successor. No one propagated this version more assiduously than Trotsky's worshipful biographer, Isaac Deutscher.

Archival sources do not lend support to Trotsky and his apologists. Lenin valued Trotsky as a colleague and dedicated Communist, which is evident from his angry reaction in 1922 to the proposal of Lev Kamenev, acting on behalf of himself as well as Stalin and Grigorii Zinoviev, to expel Trotsky from the party for his unwillingness to accept the post of Sovnarkom deputy chairman that Lenin had offered him.[8] (Trotsky's handwritten "Categorically refuse" on the Politburo motion gives one a jolt, since in the Bolshevik militarized political culture such refusal was akin to mutiny.) But there was neither personal nor intellectual intimacy between the two men. Trotsky showered Lenin with verbose memoranda in which he subjected government actions to scathing criticism and suggested alternative policies. Lenin usually disposed of them with a curt "V *arkhiv."* There are almost no Trotsky memoranda, whether bearing on political, military, or economic matters, that Lenin thought worthy of acting upon. It seems also that in 1922–23, when Lenin was forced, for reasons of health, to retire to Gorki, his suburban country estate, Trotsky rarely if ever visited him there.

Trotsky's reputation as organizer of the Red victory in the civil war does not find substantiation in the archives. Especially damaging is a memorandum that Trotsky sent to Lenin at the end of September 1919 criticizing the deployment of troops facing General Anton Denikin's army and predicting further reverses. Lenin noted at the bottom: "Nothing but bad nerves."[9] Indeed, a month and a half later the Red Army crushed Denikin. This compromising text lends credence to what otherwise would be a suspect claim by Viacheslav Molotov that during the civil war "Trotsky did not have much power."[10] It seems that in 1919–20, as in October 1917, his main contribution was to serve the party as peerless orator, uniquely capable of galvanizing the masses.

That the Bolsheviks held Trotsky in low esteem even when, to all appearances, he stood at the pinnacle of power is attested to by unpublished records of elections to the Central Committee at the Eighth Party Congress (March 1919). Trotsky came in ninth place, far behind Stalin and Bukharin (who shared second place after Lenin), right behind Mikhail Tomsky. The materials in the Russian archives on Trotsky are likely to do further damage to his reputation as Lenin's partner and alleged heir-presumptive, as well as the popular image of him as second only to Lenin in popularity and contribution to the Communist cause.

By contrast, there is a great deal of evidence of Lenin's affection for Stalin and respect for his judgment. Unlike Trotsky, Stalin never questioned Lenin's decisions (at any rate, not until the very end—that is, the fall and winter of 1922). The archives contain numerous notes from Lenin requesting Stalin's opinion on current questions, including issues of foreign policy. Stalin's responses were invariably crisp and to the point: the advice of a politician concerned not with the objectives—these he left to Lenin—but the best means of attaining them. Stalin also visited Lenin more frequently than any other member of the Politburo during his forced retirement at Gorki and provided the main conduit of instructions from the sick leader to the Politburo.[11]

That Lenin had grave doubts about his potential successors is confirmed by a startling note to the Central Committee from March 1921 in which he asked that a visiting German specialist on "nervous diseases" examine Chicherin, Trotsky, Kamenev, Stalin, and other high Soviet officials. (Not himself, however.)

The archives contain just enough material on Lenin's relations with

Inessa Armand to confirm that the two were not merely friends, as some historians have maintained, but lovers. The bulk of their correspondence seems to have been destroyed on Lenin's initiative. (In one communication he requests that she bring along his letters.) But the available exchanges provide solid evidence of an intimate relationship. The most revealing is an emotional letter from Armand to Lenin from December 1913 when she lived in Paris and he in Austrian Poland. Using the second person singular (as he also did in his letters, addressing her as "My dear & dearest friend") Armand speaks of her longing, adding that she would "manage without the kisses" if she could only be near him.[12]

The archives also confirm Lenin's abiding faith in Roman Malinovskii long after his trusted associate had been unmasked as a police agent. Postcards that Lenin had sent to Malinovskii between November 1915 and November 1916 at a prisoner-of-war camp in Germany were friendly and solicitous. They help explain why Malinovskii ventured to return to Russia in late 1918, at the height of the Red Terror, apparently confident that Lenin would protect him. But the Soviet leader, either because he had seen new evidence implicating Malinovskii or had no more use for him, refused to testify at his trial and had him shot.

The preoccupation with power, the pervasive fear of subversion, the tendency to see everywhere hidden enemies, afflicted Lenin with something akin to political paranoia. It expressed itself in a police mentality similar to but even more intense than the obsessive concern with security prevalent among officials of the tsarist regime.

One of the most striking documents I found at RTsKhIDNI was an undated memorandum of Lenin's to N. N. Krestinskii, the secretary of the Central Committee, ordering the immediate launching of a campaign of terror.[13] Russian archivists, for no apparent reason, have assigned this document the year 1920, although no campaign of terror was launched at that time. Internal evidence suggests that it was written during or after March 1918, the month the Soviet government moved from Petrograd to Moscow, because it is written on Kremlin stationery. While it is difficult to date it with any certainty, the document most likely was written early in September 1918, as Lenin was recovering from the wounds inflicted by a would-be assassin. This was the time when the government, in reprisal for the assault on Lenin, formally launched the Red Terror, which was to claim the lives of thousands of people, a high proportion of them hostages.

Several documents illustrate Lenin's police mentality. He went to extraordinary lengths to persecute intellectuals who refused to fall in line, going to the trouble of drawing up detailed lists of those he wished exiled to Siberia or expelled abroad. In September 1922 he asked the Chekist I.

S. Unshlikht to mark on an attached list which of the regime's opponents had been exiled, which imprisoned, and which (and on what grounds) were still left at liberty. Several times he raised before the Politburo the case of the Menshevik historian N. A. Rozhkov. In December 1922, following repeated strokes that would soon put him permanently out of commission, he still mustered the energy to ask Stalin to have Rozhkov deported.

Then there were detailed instructions for the infiltration and surveillance of foreigners that might have come from the director of the Okhrana. In 1920 a fact-finding British Trade Union delegation visited Soviet Russia at Moscow's invitation. Lenin issued confidential orders that the Soviet press undertake a systematic campaign to "unmask" the visitors as "social-traitors, Mensheviks, accomplices in the English looting of colonies," and that they never leave sight of "reliable" interpreters.[14] In anticipation of the arrival of Americans working for Herbert Hoover's Relief Administration, whose mission was to feed starving Russians, Lenin ordered Molotov to mobilize the "maximum number of Communists familiar with the English language to introduce them into Hoover's commissions and employ for other forms of surveillance and information-gathering."[15]

The patrimonial mentality—the tendency to view the land with its people and resources as the ruler's private property—is reflected in several documents. In one, dated March 1921, Lenin ordered Communist authorities in Astrakhan to "mobilize" on behalf of the local fishing enterprise 3,000 men and 8,000 women. He gave similar orders to the authorities in Saratov and the Kalmyk Autonomous Region. These were acts reminiscent of Muscovite *tiaglo*, forced labor routinely resorted to by the tsarist authorities. (Peter I built St. Petersburg in this manner.) In another document Lenin asks Saratov to inform him about a shipment of a few hundred sheep and pigs. In a third, he listed the precise quantities and dimensions of lumber that Tsaritsyn was to deliver to Baku. These instructions were undoubtedly written by subordinates and submitted for Lenin's signature, but it is doubtful whether any other head of a major state would waste time on such trivia. Baku, incidentally, figures in another secret Lenin order from June 1918 that in the event of an invasion (presumably by the Turks) the city was to be burned to the ground. In February 1920, Lenin threatened to "slaughter" all the inhabitants of Maikop and Groznyi should their oil fields be sabotaged.[16] There is no way of knowing how many orders of this nature are still kept secret.

Resort to unrestrained brutality was not counterbalanced by reverence for Marxism. Historians who seek to explain Communist behavior in terms of ideology will be as disappointed by the archival evidence as will those who believe in Lenin's idealism. Nowhere do Communist leaders in their internal communications propose to act or to refrain from acting with reference to Marxism. In none of the documents I have inspected were there allusions to doctrine: the problem of ideology simply did not exist. What did exist was desperate anxiety about the regime's survival in an overwhelmingly hostile environment.

The secret archives are rich in documentation on the foreign relations of Soviet Russia, both on the diplomatic and subversive levels.

One of most startling documents to come to light is a secret address that Lenin delivered to a conference of Communists in September 1920 in an attempt to explain and justify the debacle which had just befallen the Red Army in Poland.[17] It is a rambling, often incoherent speech even by Lenin's standards, by a man unwilling to face the fact that he had made a disastrous misjudgment in ordering the Red Army to advance on Warsaw and yet unable to shirk responsibility for it. He did not mean for the speech to be published, and at one point he interrupted himself to admonish the stenographers not to "write so much." Fortunately, they did record nearly his every word, producing a document that illuminates the reasons behind the Communist invasion of Poland. The sovietization of Poland, we now learn, was intended as the first phase of a general assault on the West aiming at nothing less than the conquest of Europe as a prelude to the conquest of the world.[18]

Lenin explained that with the defeat of the main White forces in late 1919 the Soviet leadership had decided that the time had come to launch a general offensive against capitalism: "We arrived at the conviction that the Entente's military assault against us was over, that the defensive war against imperialism war was over; we had won it. . . . We could and should take advantage of the military situation to begin an offensive war." And by that he meant an armed invasion of Western Europe for the purpose of linking up with the revolutionary forces in Germany, England, and Italy. Impressed by the emergence in England of the Trade Unions' "Council of Action," whose purpose was to prevent military supplies from being shipped to Poland, he concluded that England was already in the throes of a revolution, power being split between the bourgeoisie and the proletariat, exactly as it had been in Russia in 1917. He spoke of "hundreds of thousands" of German Communists volunteering to link up with the advancing Red troops.

These remarks elucidate actions otherwise difficult to explain, namely Tukhachevsky's decision to detach troops from the army besieging Warsaw and send them into the Polish Corridor, a maneuver that contributed materially to the Red Army's defeat. This operation, it transpires, was intended to carry the revolution into Germany. The failure of the southern army, whose political commissar was Stalin, to join Tukhachevsky's main force, which enabled Pilsudski to pierce the thinly held Red Army front south of Warsaw and force the enemy into a general retreat, seems to have been due not to Stalin's insubordination, as Trotsky would claim, but to Lenin's desire to keep the southern army in reserve for the planned invasion of Hungary, Czechoslovakia, and Romania.[19] The speech reveals Lenin's complete misunderstanding of conditions in Western Europe and his wildly exaggerated expectations of its revolutionary potential.

RTsKhIDNI holds documents on the earliest Allied landings in northern Russia. They consist of tapes of teleprinter conversations held in late March and early April 1918 between Lenin and Stalin and the chairman of the Murmansk Soviet. The latter asked for permission to request British military assistance against an anticipated German-Finnish assault. Lenin and Stalin authorized the Murmansk Soviet to solicit Allied help, provided secrecy was observed.

Much archival information is coming to light on Lenin's dealings with the Germans after 1917, especially on Soviet-German military cooperation, which began in earnest in 1921 and continued until September 1933. These data are especially valuable because in the 1930s the Germans systematically destroyed documentation bearing on this sensitive subject.[20] The political background of this collaboration is illuminated in documents scattered in several deposits at RTsKhIDNI; the strictly military aspects are reflected in materials held by the Russian State Military Archive (RGVA).[21] They indicate in detail how close was the cooperation between the two countries, how much the Germans benefited from Soviet collusion in circumventing the provisions of the Versailles Treaty to develop on Russian soil the weapons and tactics of Blitzkrieg warfare, and how much the Red Army, in turn, profited from German training in these weapons and tactics. One of the most interesting of these documents is a report from Leonid Krasin to Lenin from September 1921 on the progress of his negotiations with the Germans for economic and military assistance. Krasin, who had excellent connections with German business circles antedating World War I, wrote that he had given up trying to deal with German businessmen because they thought of nothing but profits and feared Allied reprisals. He much preferred negotiating with those Germans who "thought seriously about revenge"[22]—that is, right-wing nationalist and military circles. Systematic analysis of these materials will reveal the extent to which the Reichswehr and the Red Army collaborated in laying the groundwork for World War II, which both devoutly desired: the Germans in order to restore their position as a world power, the Russians to achieve the final victory of Communism.

A note from Lenin to Chicherin from February 1922—so secret that

Lenin insisted on it being destroyed and never mentioned—urged that the forthcoming Genoa Conference be "wrecked" but that this not be done by the Soviet delegation. The ploy, which Chicherin carried out by persuading the Germans to sign at Rapallo a separate treaty with Soviet Russia, was designed to forestall a rapprochement between Germany and the Allies.

I have not studied the records of the Communist International, but I did see some materials of fond 495, which holds the archive of its Executive (IKKI). I found especially instructive the Comintern's financial records. They indicate that the Comintern generously financed Communist parties and publications abroad, including those in France, which French Communists liked to depict as financially independent of Moscow. Second, they show that these financial operations were conducted in a slipshod manner, with large amounts of money unaccounted for. Lenin, as we know from the memoirs of Angelica Balabanoff, the first secretary of the Comintern, forever urged its functionaries "not to spare money." The documentary evidence indicates that his wishes in this matter were respected.

And, finally, mention may be made of a message, in English, that Lenin had sent to a Danish newspaper in response to its inquiry whether it was true that Nicholas II had been killed: "Rumour not true exczar safe all rumours are only lie of capitalist press." It was dated 16 July 1918, mere hours before the Ekaterinburg Cheka, on Lenin's orders, would murder the ex-tsar along with his family and servants.

Access to the archives of Lenin and his regime produces an effect not unlike that obtained by cleansing a photographic portrait of the retoucher's work. The face that emerges is the same—only more so.

Notes

1. Indeed, the handwritten text of the minutes of the Central Committee on the night of 10 October 1917, when the decision to topple the Provisional Government was taken, gives no date—an omission explainable by Lenin's conspiratorial habits. In my *Russian Revolution*, written before I had the chance to inspect the original, I mistakenly attributed the absence of such information in the printed edition of these minutes to editorial tampering (*The Russian Revolution* [New York, 1990], 472n).

2. Thus, for example, in a secret speech to a Communist conference in September 1920, first published in 1992, in which he revealed that the decision to invade Poland in July 1920 had been intended as the opening phase of a general campaign against the West (see below), Lenin admitted that this objective had not been spelled out in the protocols of the Central Committee (*Istoricheskii Arkhiv*, no. 1 [1992]: 16).

3. It must be noted, however, that there exist unpublished materials on the early history of Soviet Russia still closed to outside scholars. They are stored in the Archive of the President of the Russian Republic (APRR), which contains, among other materials, minutes of Politburo meetings and the archive of the Cheka and its successors. Judging by the publications of Dmitrii Volkogonov, who had access to both, they also contain no sensational revelations.

4. *Rodina*, no. 1 (1992): 81.

5. I first gained access to them as a private scholar and subsequently as editor of *The Unknown Lenin* (New Haven: Yale University Press, 1996).

6. Richard Pipes, *Russia Under the Bolshevik Regime* (New York: Knopf, 1994).

7. Ibid., 386.

8. Ibid., 467.

9. Ibid., 126.

10. F. Chuev, *Sto sorok besed s Molotovym* (Moscow, 1991), 200.

11. All through the Soviet period it was believed that Lenin had approved of but not initiated Stalin's appointment as general secretary. Trotsky's claim that it was done over Lenin's objections was never taken seriously (*Moia zhizn'* [Berlin, 1930], 2: 202–203). It has become known from the recently published recollections of Molotov that Lenin personally selected Stalin for the new post of general secretary (Chuev, *Sto sorok besed s Molotovym*, 181). The relevant document has not yet come to light.

12. This letter has been published in *Svobodnaia mysl'*, no. 3 (1992): 80–83.

13. RTsKhIDNI, f. 2, op. 2, d. 492.

14. *Russia Under the Bolshevik Regime*, 203–204.

15. Ibid., 417–418.

16. Ibid., 58.

17. Deposited in RTsKhIDNI, f. 44, op. 1, d. 5, it is reproduced in *Istoricheskii arkhiv*, no. 1 (1992): 14–29.

18. Those who still doubt that such was the ultimate objective of the Bolsheviks are referred to a letter of Lenin's to the Central Committee dated 14 September 1917—on the eve of the October coup—and of course not meant for publication, in which he wrote that securing an armistice with the Germans would make it possible "to conquer *the whole world*" (V. I. Lenin, *Polnoe Sobranie Sochinenii* [Moscow, 1962], 34: 245 (emphasis in the original).

19. *Russia Under the Bolshevik Regime*, 177.

20. Hans Speidel in *Vierteljahreshefte für Zeitgeschichte* 1, no. 1 (1953): 9.

21. The International Security Program at Yale University has under way a joint project with RGVA to reproduce and, eventually, to publish many of these documents.

22. *Russia Under the Bolshevik Regime*, 426–427.

Mobilization, Utilization, and the Rhetoric of Liberation: Bolshevik Policy Toward Women 11

One of the greatest fallacies in the mythology of the Bolshevik revolution concerns the experience of women. The Bolshevik revolution is almost automatically associated with the liberation of women. True, it did not come overnight, and the actual conditions women faced may have in fact deteriorated in the aftermath of Bolsheviks' coming to power; and the plight of bourgeois women was unenviable. But as Elizabeth Waters put it, "Nonetheless, commitment to the principle of equality for women remained, and as the regime consolidated itself, a wide range of policies was implemented to improve the status of women."[1]

The discussion usually focuses on Aleksandra Kollontai and other Bolshevik party women, who concentrated on improving the lot of women.[2] Scholars cite the travails of the Women's Departments under the party committees as evidence that the Bolsheviks took women's issues seriously—that they, unlike the preceding regime, even had a women's policy, let alone one that was aimed at liberation.[3] Women were to be drawn into the political process, given a political voice, and offered opportunities to achieve upward mobility.[4] The Bolsheviks' intention to accomplish all these objectives was never questioned by scholars. But critics of Bolshevik policies toward women say too little was done too late. Because the Bolsheviks could not overcome the cultural constraints of their time, their male-dominated culture failed to produce real equality for women.[5] Nevertheless, the argument goes, women definitely benefited from the Bolshevik rule in terms of civil rights and job opportunities.

According to Richard Stites, one of the founders of Russian women's studies in America, the Bolshevik government had an unprecedented desire to involve women in bettering their own lives. The Bolshevik women enthusiasts carried on almost a sort of missionary work among the "dark women's masses," trying to involve women, wake them up to state tasks, draw them away from their "backwardness," and grant them social and political rights. According to Stites, the Bolshevik Women's Departments succeeded in "raising the consciousness of poor and backward women."[6] Like the Bolsheviks, Stites sees the traditional culture of worker and peasant women as backward, and he shares the Bolsheviks' patronizing and modernizing attitude toward women. As a result of mobilization efforts, he argued, thousands of women gained employment access that was unthinkable under the old regime. For the first time many women were hired to be commissars, commanders, and skilled workers. Stites concludes that the cause of women's liberation under the Bolsheviks was much more advanced than in the West, where suffrage was the modest objective of the liberation movement.[7]

There are three problems with this rosy picture of the achievements of socialist construction. First, the Bolsheviks' publicly articulated intention to liberate women cannot be taken at face value. What they meant by *liberation* needs to be defined and analyzed. The work of the Women's Departments must be examined as a cultural phenomenon revealing the values and cultural practices of its leaders. Second, Women's Departments were not the only organizations whose policies had a direct bearing on women. Moreover, they were not even the most important ones. To limit Bolshevik women's policy to the pronouncements of the Women's Departments would be tantamount to limiting the U.S. policy toward Indians to the pronouncements of the Bureau of Indian Affairs. Third, it is essential to distinguish between Bolshevik policies to different categories of women: bourgeois women, working women, and peasant women. Even though these categories do not exactly correspond to social reality, they point to the fact that Bolshevik policy differed depending on which class women belonged to. And policy toward women in each of these categories differed markedly from that toward men of the same social group, and from policies to women in other social groups.

Any attempt to re-create women's experiences under the Bolsheviks would be incomplete without listening to the women's voices. What did the peasant women think was going on? How did they relate to Soviet power? What did such notions as Soviet power and liberation mean to them? The voices of working women, Cossack women, and intelligentsia women would provide different perspectives on the same polices. But reconstruction of women's history during the civil war cannot be done on the basis of Bolshevik myths and carefully selected policies of Women's

Departments. All of the polices affecting women must be examined in conjunction with the diverse experiences of various groups of women.

Women's Departments

The creation of Women's Departments within the CP is a manifestation of the mobilization efforts of the Bolshevik regime. Every part of the population had to be involved in strengthening the new regime, and Women's Departments were charged with mobilizing the female masses. It was not until 1919, after much soul-searching and several delays, that the Bolshevik Central Committee agreed to set up Women's Departments. As R. C. Elwood convincingly argues, the departments were not created to promote women's rights or the feminist agenda in Russia. The party had shown almost complete indifference to women's issues from the beginning, and party leaders resisted creating separate organizations for women or for any other group. But the pressure of the Whites in 1919 made effective use of female labor necessary, and Women's Departments were better suited to reaching the female constituency than were the agencies run by men. As Elwood explained, the departments were to operate "as a transmission belt but a transmission belt downward only, a way of conveying the party's objectives and instructions to a hitherto inaccessible constituency."[8]

The Bolsheviks' aim was to extract maximum use from women with minimum effort and compensation. The Bolshevik women leaders of the Women's Departments hoped that, in the end, women would benefit. The understanding was that the leaders would help to bring women under the influence of the party and that in return the party would help the leaders improve women's social and political conditions. They accepted the underlying principle of women's subordination to the party, even though Kollontai made feeble attempts to turn the Women's Departments into organs representing women's interests in the party. Nevertheless, Women's Departments became what they were conceived to be: party organizations that channeled women into the hospitals, factories, and other agencies useful for the war effort which were vacant for the lack of men. Women's Departments were mobilization agencies whose recruits were women, not organizations promoting affirmative action for women. The demise of Women's Departments was of course inevitable. As soon as their mobilizational and utilitarian value declined they were perceived as interest groups. They faced the same fate as the Jewish Communist Bund, Proletkult, and any other Communist organizations that tried to maintain autonomy from the CP.

Women Workers

Mobilization

The set of ideas that women workers were to internalize focused on the party as a source of power and authority, the proletariat as a social group into which women could be admitted if they developed the proper consciousness, and Socialism, the ultimate goal, as producing a superior and just society. The problem with this message was that women's admission to the "ruling class" was conditional. They were first to abandon their supposed backwardness. Women were regarded as inferior partners of male workers, a sexist and patronizing attitude that was an essential ingredient in official Bolshevik culture. In fact, Women's Departments were derogatorily referred to by men as *Babkom* or *Tsentrobaba*. And Bolshevik feminists themselves had maintained that women workers could not separate themselves from their male comrades and that liberation could be achieved only in the context of "proletarian dictatorship."[9] The role of women workers was that of an auxiliary detachment of the proletariat, a group that would follow men workers and the party in fulfilling state tasks. Bolshevik women leaders willingly defined women's role in these terms for years, contributing to the stereotypical thinking that women were to be guided and led by a superior male authority.

Under ideal circumstances, working women who chose to accept that role for the sake of a better future theoretically would have received positive reinforcement in their daily contact with Bolshevik authorities and would have seen a rationale for their own contribution and change. Yet for most women workers, idealized visions of the proletariat and the party marching toward a bright future had nothing to do with reality. In daily life they faced old cultural practices.

For a woman working on the factory floor, the material situation deteriorated sharply after the Bolshevik revolution. One worker wrote to the newspaper *Pravda* that she was humiliated every day by the men guards at her factory, who searched women workers (they were regarded as potential thieves).[10] She was constantly urged to grow out of her backwardness and develop a "proletarian consciousness." Although women could see that Bolshevik propaganda was aimed at undermining their self-confidence, they still confronted Cheka detachments at the railway stations when the soldiers confiscated from them the food that they had bought with great difficulty in the countryside. At the factories they encountered gun-waving Bolshevik commissars who demanded obedience and hard work. Elevated expectations met disappointing reality.

Most women workers displayed varying degrees of opposition to the Communists in 1919 and 1920. In general they were more ardent and vociferous in their discontent than the men were. The proof is in *Pravda*'s fourth-page column "Workers' Life," in which Communist functionaries repeatedly complain that the Mensheviks speculated on the temporary difficulties of Soviet power and enjoyed success among the masses "lacking political consciousness." A Factory Committee member in Moscow lamented, "In our district the Mensheviks are beginning to rear their head. Using the industrial and food supply crisis, they incite against Soviet power and the Communist party, masses lacking political consciousness. . . . They began to incite the masses especially of women."[11] The Bolsheviks perceived the political protests of women workers as yet another manifestation of their petty bourgeois consciousness and backwardness.

In June 1920 the Tula authorities ordered the wives of the workers of the armaments plant to show up for a public work project on a Sunday. (Women were now subject to universal labor conscription.) Most women perceived this as an additional burden in their hard lives, yet Bolshevik women leaders praised this measure as another step on the path of women's liberation.[12] The Tula conscription happened to fall on a religious holiday, and Sundays were the only days when women could go to the villages to buy food from peasants. So the women of Tula did not show up for the work project. The Bolsheviks denounced this as sabotage, and men workers went on strike at two large plants in Tula.

The strikes show that the local Bolsheviks regarded the wives of their workers as a reserve labor force at their disposal. They considered the women's refusal to appear as an act of political sabotage, and they reported it as such to Moscow. The women's actions demonstrate that they had remained indifferent to Bolshevik exhortations to work harder for Soviet power. The priority in their lives was to feed their families, and when this priority was threatened, they refused to comply with the order.

As the strike escalated, Bolshevik authorities in Tula resorted to intensifying the repressions. Women responded in a way that surprised both the Bolsheviks and their husbands. It started in the streets of Tula when groups of arrested men workers were led along the street by the Cheka. Some women ran up to the Cheka guards and, when pushed aside, pleaded that they be arrested too. This movement, dubbed "self-arresting," grew enormous as hundreds of women were joined by men. In three days the Cheka held more than ten thousand prisoners. Today we would call this behavior nonviolent resistance. For the Tula women it was an act of defiance and desperation. They were telling the Bolsheviks that when they deprive them of food and a religious holiday and of their husbands, they might as well take them too. Again, women's defense of their traditional life and family was labeled by the Bolsheviks as backwardness, petty bourgeois consciousness, and political sabotage.

Attitudes

The typical information on working women gathered by the Women's Departments focused on their numbers, their productivity, the number of participants in the Red Army recruitment week, the number recruited to become nurses, and the number enrolled in other educational or propaganda activities. Never would one learn what kind of dresses the young workers wore, whether they used makeup, what kind of plays or books they preferred, what kind of songs they sang, or any other information that would reveal their cultural preferences, their tastes, and their worldview. The picture of working women depicted in the reports of the Women's Departments ignored all aspects of behavior that did not fit the stereotype, brushing them aside as manifestations of "petty-bourgeois consciousness."

Mentality—a set of attitudes and beliefs shared unconsciously and automatically by a certain social or cultural group—reflect the mainstream beliefs and responses of a given time and place. An episode describing a scene on a street corner or in the theater or in a small village can be held as a representation of that groups' mentality. The mentality of women under the Bolsheviks is illustrated in the following discussion.

Orekhovo-Zuevo was in many ways a typical industrial town of central Russia. Its core was made up of textile mills, and as in most textile towns of central-northern Russia, women traditionally constituted the majority of the population, because men often left the area for jobs in the bigger cities. So in many ways this was a women's kingdom (*bab'e tsarstvo*), with its own subculture. What is most striking about the cultural atmosphere in Orekhovo-Zuevo of mid-1918 was its detachment from the national agenda. The daily concerns of men and women had little to do with intervention, civil war, the Czech front, nationalization, War Communism, or any other issue dominant in the capitals. Socialism and dictatorship of the proletariat were concepts about which most women had but the vaguest notion. They had of course heard of nationalization of factories, but they understood it to mean that a commissar was the boss instead of an owner. They had heard of dictatorship of the proletariat, but they did not quite understand who the proletariat was. They had heard of Soviet power and that it was supposed to be better than the old regime, but they often complained that some commissars who represented Soviet power had requisitioned pillows and blankets and samovars. Orekhovo-Zuevo women could not comprehend why Soviet power prohibited private trade, which they saw as a natural activity. Through newspaper reports, one senses no urgency on women's part to understand great political issues of the day. One is left with an impression that women considered these questions to be not their concern. They showed no interest in Bolshevism.[13] They focused not on Socialist construction or the needs of the Red Army but on their community and their role in it. They took advantage of new conditions to enhance their own lives as best they could.

Working women were interested not in factory life but in "real life"— life outside the factory. Theaters and tea parlors, the centers of local social life in Orekhovo-Zuevo, were always full. According to one perceptive observer, women borrowed ostentatious habits from the old bourgeoisie. They liked to dress beyond their means and occupy front-row seats in the theater. They liked to be noticed. They used garish makeup and went out of their way to show off their new and elevated position in society. Consumption of alcohol was widespread, and sexual promiscuity was commonplace. In this sense it is possible to draw a connection between the change in social relations after the Bolshevik seizure of power and the cultural milieu in a provincial town. As a local correspondent observed, "Many speculate with cloth instead of wages from their factories. The majority of speculators are women. Moral decay has reached unprecedented proportions. Marriages for a month or three are an everyday occurrence. Faithful couples are jeered at. To cheat, to dupe somebody is considered up to the mark. Vulgarity, crassness, and rudeness are considered to be at the top of the democratic heap. The girls try to get a guy as soon as possible. For the lack of local 'fiances' they 'marry' prisoners of war en masse. The general mood is loot the looted."[14]

The Bolsheviks' repeatedly stressed that the old propertied classes had been overthrown and dispossessed. Now the working class was in power, they said, and all the good things in life would henceforth be the reward of the workers. It is plausible to suggest that women workers in a town like Orekhovo-Zuevo perceived that the Bolsheviks' were encouraging them to assert themselves in the community. Their social standing was enhanced, and they could go to the theater—to the front row—without being afraid of what anyone would say. It seems that their garish clothes were a sign of self-affirmation, and their presence in the tea parlors (where vodka was sold) could be seen as affirmation of their freedom to do what men did. Their sexual promiscuity can likewise be seen as a liberation from tradition. Bolshevik propaganda encouraged the destruction of the bourgeois morality of marriage and social hierarchy. As Roger Chartier explains it, ordinary people appropriate the ideas and beliefs of their time in ways that may distort or even mutilate them.[15] The key here is that the response of Orekhovo-Zuevo women to this liberation from restraint did not take the shape of Socialist consciousness—whatever that means. Through their cultural practices the women rejected the norms propagated by the Bolsheviks. They modeled these practices on those of the social group they perceived as superior to their own: the merchants. The "new elite" imitated and tried to outdo the old one.

Peasant Women

Unlike working women, peasant women did not even in theory belong to the new ruling class. Like all peasants, they were labeled as "backward"— even more backward than working women.[16] Peasant women's contact with the new regime was more limited than that of working women. Bolshevik propaganda reached them only occasionally, and often only in bits and pieces. As a result, peasant women never had clear ideas on what Soviet power was and what they were supposed to do. In the first year of proletarian dictatorship the Bolsheviks had no message addressed specifically to peasant women. Not until 1919 and 1920, when the peasant war against the Bolsheviks intensified, did the Bolsheviks formulate a policy for peasant women as a social group. Before then, peasant women encountered Soviet power only in the context of grain requisitioning and committees of the poor, the main planks of Bolshevik agrarian policy in 1918.

The cultural norms held by the peasant women on the eve of this upheaval has been studied in some detail.[17] The peasant woman's world rotated around her village, church, and family. Peasant women were at the center of village life, and they served as links between families. They were a part of the social hierarchy and of the hierarchy of authority as well.[18] They were aware that their role was subordinate to that of men, and yet a "conservative, religious and illiterate *baba* found support in the oppressive world she was a part of."[19] Now that world was going to be shattered.

Like all peasants, women suffered from poaching by the army, and the Red Army was no exception. We learn from a classified Red Army report that "Red Army soldiers, having no money, take foodstuffs from the local population without paying, causing by this hatred by peasants."[20] In addition to regular Red Army units, all kinds of special detachments robbed the population, as a classified report attests: "The punitive detachment, without bothering to investigate the behavior of the locality during the attack of the partisan bands, robbed the population under the guise of a search, taking horses, clothing, and breaking the closets by force."[21]

The arrival of requisition detachments in Russian villages in June 1918 created a permanent infrastructure of robbery, from the peasant women's point of view. Poor peasants were encouraged to denounce richer ones and receive a share of requisitioned goods for their services. It was a policy designed to divide the peasant community and to explode traditional authority structures. As is well known, peasants responded with a series of insurrections. What is often ignored is that women were often the instigators. Report after report describes peasants assembling at the main square, church bells ringing, women shouting and clamoring and inciting to violence. Finally a commissar would be killed or a requisition detachment ambushed or a soviet building set on fire.[22]

The arrival of Soviet power in the countryside disturbed the traditional flow of the life cycle, disrupted informal authority ties, challenged community structure, and threatened the social hierarchy. Women were the most ardent defenders of what for them was security and stability— that is, old structures of authority. From the Bolsheviks' point of view, peasant women were loudmouthed troublemakers who cared only about their own family, cow, and village and did not comprehend the state tasks of the proletarian revolution. From the point of view of peasant women, the new local authority was that of thieves, of village scum who helped themselves to the property of others. The women also had little regard for the central Bolshevik government. Anton Okninsky spent the civil war in Tambov province, where he collected remarkable evidence of peasant attitudes. He overheard and recorded a conversation between two peasant women:

> "Tell me who these Lenin and others are? I just cannot understand. Are they spies or something?"
>
> "I don't know myself. Even men are saying all kinds of different things but how should we women [baby] know? . . . Some say that Lenin and the comrades had killed the Tsar and his entire family and now they themselves instead of him rule over all of Russia. But who they are nobody knows exactly. Some say they are German spies, others that they are former convicts, and some that they are hooligans like our Peter [volost ispolkom chairman], only they are a little more literate, you know, like teachers."[23]

The nature of rural government changed profoundly in 1918. Control of formal government passed from leading families and village assemblies to the Bolshevik appointees, local upstarts who were willing to risk their lives to serve the provincial Bolshevik authorities. An invisible and informal peasant government remained, however. It was busy supplying Green rebels, who hid in the forests and ambushed Bolshevik detachments. In this context peasant women came into contact with a new social type: a local dictator who called himself a Bolshevik. In fact, there were still few party members at the village level, but there were people who could be described as agents of the center. According to a report of a Red Army commander who was to pacify insurgents in Smolensk province in the summer of 1919, peasants judged Soviet power by the actions of these local rulers. "But the local population testifies that it has been terrorized by the actions of local power holders to such an extent that children are frightened upon hearing the name of Antip."[24]

Antip and his relatives exercised complete control of the village. Local people hated the Soviets, especially Antip. Arbitrary arrests, confiscations, and requisitions were practiced systematically. Antip and his cohorts confiscated not only grain but also personal belongings, including samovars and dishes. "The people are terrorized by the actions of the local Communist cell." When one woman asked Antip why he was taking property, he answered promptly that it was for his personal use. His time had come to live well, he said. Despite this evidence that support for the Greens was justified, the commander reported that he took hostages (that is, women) from the families of suspected rebels.

The rise of local cliques that abused local peasants and celebrated their upward mobility by exercising ruthless and unbounded dictatorship is a cultural phenomenon that deserves study in its own right. Suffice it to say here that this cultural type was all too familiar to peasant women: a gun-waving, shouting, and often drunken dictator who demanded obedience and craved unlimited power. He was a well-known social type in the village, only now he was acting on behalf of the state. And his theft was called "construction of Socialism." Traditional tools of village authority, available earlier to restrain an unbound dictator, were no longer available.

Hostility and *hatred* were the words used to describe peasant attitudes in thousands of reports from local Bolshevik officials and, most important, from the Cheka departments, which monitored popular attitudes and reported to Lenin weekly.[25] Peasant women's response to this new power structure seems to have been to retreat into the familiar world of community, family, and church and to hold on to these bonds more strongly than ever. Bolshevik dictatorship unified the peasant community as a whole and it strengthened rather than weakened traditional values and practices.

Peasant War: Women as Object

In 1919 and 1920, Bolshevik authorities had to fight the Green rebels on at least one front in every province. And in many outlying provinces they had to fight on a second front against advancing or retreating White armies. Peasants' support of the Green rebels or of the Whites was a matter of serious concern for the Bolsheviks. War with thousands of deserters, Green partisans, and bands affected every town and village in Russia. It touched the lives of virtually every family. Bolshevik social policies toward women during that war were vastly more effective than were the mobilizations of the Women's Departments, which were unknown in most rural areas. During that war fought on internal fronts, the Bolsheviks' enemies were the peasants, mostly men, who were hiding in the forests. They were hard to trace and even harder to defeat. Women, on the other hand, stayed at home, where they were reachable and vulnerable. As the war against peasant rebels intensified, policy toward women—civilian noncombatants—was formulated.

In a special study on the nature of peasant insurgency in Ukraine, Cheka officials concluded that every rebel detachment was connected with a cluster of villages called a nest. To undercut the rebels one had to deal with the nests—that is, with the women, children, and old men who had stayed at home and provided supplies to the rebels. The main methods the Bolsheviks employed were taking of hostages from the families of suspected rebels, deportation of women and children, and outright destruction of a suspect village by artillery fire. An order to the troops signed by Lenin instructed: "To announce a seven-day grace period for the return of the deserters. Upon completion of this term, to strengthen repressions to unreturned deserters and to their families and to those who protect them since they are unrepentant traitors of the laboring people."[26]

Lenin advocated dealing with the families of rebels as a part of overall war strategy. In a document from the Viatka province the local authorities reported on the measures they undertook to combat peasant insurgency. They admitted that bands of deserters had grown since 1919. By the end of 1920 the situation had deteriorated even further. The attitude of the population toward the Soviet authorities was negative, but toward the bands of deserters it was positive. Viatka comrades reported that beginning in July 1920 they kept food rations from 28,879 families of deserters. There were 5,185 families of deserters fined for systematic complicity with the deserters and 3,082 families whose property was confiscated for the same offense.[27] Special detachments were dispatched to seize hostages.[28]

In Voronezh province the official instructions to the plenipotentiaries of the Province Party Committee ordered that the activities of the Cheka, the Anti-Desertion Committee, and special departments be coordinated "to combat insurrections of the counterrevolutionary elements. One should not balk at adopting the most repressive measures. . . . It is ordered to declare a state of emergency and seize hostages [October 1919]."[29] Hundreds of cases like these can be cited from every corner of Russia. Women were fined, seized as hostages, and exiled because they were related to rebels. Women were targeted to discourage their sons and brothers and husbands from participating in anti-Bolshevik insurgency. Male councils would decide whether to fight the Bolsheviks, and peasant women were expected to provide support whatever course of action was chosen. The Bolshevik authorities knew that they were punishing people who had no say in the actions for which they were being punished.

A announcement posted publicly in the North Caucasus and Kuban' in 1920 read:

1. *Stanitsy* [Cossack villages] and villages hiding the Whites and the Greens will be destroyed [*unichtozheny*], adult population executed, and property confiscated.
2. All persons who have rendered aid to the bands will be shot.
3. The majority of Greens in the mountains have left behind relatives in the villages. All of them have been registered [*vziaty na uchet*], and in case of an offensive of the bands, all adult relatives of those fighting against us will be shot and minors will be exiled to central Russia.
4. In cases of mass insurrection of certain villages, *stanitsy,* and cities, we will apply mass terror: for every Soviet official killed, hundreds of residents of these places will pay. Our warning is not an empty threat. Soviet power possesses adequate means to implement all this. October 1920, [K. I.] Lander[30]

In Petrograd province the Bolshevik authorities announced that relatives of the Green insurgents had been taken as hostages and that troops would shoot without warning anyone older than twelve found in the forests without authorization.[31] In the Volga basin, North Caucasus, and Ukraine the Bolshevik authorities went even further. They publicly threatened to annihilate villages.

2. Closest relatives of insurgents will be taken hostage and placed in concentration camps. . . .
3. Villages which had rendered assistance to the insurgents by providing horses, carts, and reinforcements are declared to be under martial law and will be subjected to the following reprisals: a) confiscation of food supply stocks, b) monetary indemnity, c) confiscation of property, d) bombardment of the village, e) final annihilation of the village [*unichtozhenie*].
4. All chiefs of the rear and all officials of Soviet power in the localities are to draft a list of villages which are centers of counterrevolution and to apply the above listed measures in regard to these villages.[32]

Several villages were in fact burned in retaliation for attacks on the Reds by the Ukrainian partisans.[33]

Revenge

In all practices examined so far, Bolshevik authorities used women as tools to enforce compliance of the population. Fines, confiscations, and even hostage-taking were implicitly conditional on the actions of Bolshevik opponents. It was clearly communicated repressive measures against the local population would stop if guerrilla activity in a given province ceased. Outright atrocities against women, if they were reported before 1919, were usually violations of official policy by the troops or Cheka units. Rape and plunder were dismissed as undesirable but unavoidable by-products of war. In spring 1920, however, a new phenomenon began to unfold: officially sanctioned revenge on the entire population, including women, in areas deemed hostile to Soviet power. These were not simply the violations of passing drunken troops with the connivance of Red commanders but were part of a well-planned large-scale operation of revenge by the occupation army on the defeated land of the Cossacks.

The Bolsheviks subjected Kuban and Don to a bloody purge. Special party/Cheka units arrived in every settlement and summarily executed anyone even suspected of serving in the White army. As the special functionary of the local Cheka reported, "These Troykas were going to execute active elements on the spot, and their families would be taken as hostages and their property confiscated and dispatched to Ekaterinodar."[34] It was considered a preventive cleansing of the population from hostile elements. The special plenipotentiary wrote, "The operation went through quickly and efficiently." The death penalty had been officially abolished and the Whites defeated, but the statute on Punitive Troykas reintroduced mass executions without trial of those considered "active elements," exactly as a year earlier, during the de-cossackization campaign. The Bolsheviks were thorough in their cleansing. The widows of the executed men, who were suspect by association, were herded into a makeshift camp. They were not told about the investigation, nor was there even an inquiry on their involvement in anti-Bolshevik activity. The question of their participation really did not matter, however. The purpose was to decimate the Cossacks "as a class." In his report, the Cheka boss A. N. Latsiss calmly described the executions and the taking of hostages. One paragraph suggests that even he was moved by the suffering of the hostages: "Brought over to Maikop by various Troykas, the hostages: women, children, and old men lived in terrible conditions. In October, they were living in mud and frost, some in a barrack at the station, and some under the open sky. There they were giving birth and contracting disease, and there they were dying."[35]

There were several camps for the widows and daughters of the executed Cossacks. These women, continued Latsiss, would do anything to obtain release. Red Army soldiers asked permission to marry some of them, but first they made inquiries regarding the property of the prospective wife to pay for the marriage and possible release. The chairman of the Maikop Political Bureau asked Lander what to do. Lander waived his hand and said, "All right. Let Russian blood mix with Cossack blood." According to Latsiss, this was understood as a license: "The bacchanalia of trade with hostages took off. The women agreed to marry anyone in order to have a chance to break out of the camp. There was a case when a young girl, who had already been released, refused to marry a Red Army soldier. And he pulled her back into the camp."[36]

Hostage women paid Red Army soldiers for their release with whatever possessions they still had, and the soldiers in turn paid the camp officials a bribe for the release of their "slaves." In his report Latsiss did not condemn the atrocities: sexual exploitation, degradation, and trade with hostage women in the death camp; he matter-of-factly listed them among the activities conducted by the Cheka. The only "crime" committed by these women was being the wives and mothers and daughters of men who may have fought with the Whites.

Class Enemy Women

Female workers endured humiliating searches and labor conscription, and peasant women suffered fines and deportation in areas affected by rebellion. The fate of bourgeois women was much worse. These members of the overthrown propertied classes and the intelligentsia had to endure a double burden, as class enemies and as women. In the first months of the Bolshevik rule the propertied classes in Russia already were dispossessed. Land estates, factories, and bank accounts were seized in the name of the proletariat. In Petrograd the former bourgeoisie received the lowest food ration. Bourgeois men and women were evicted from their apartments in the name of social justice, and many of them were conscripted to dig trenches at the approaches to Petrograd.

The bourgeoisie was considered a defeated enemy in the class struggle. And as a defeated party in war, the bourgeoisie was to pay an indemnity to the victorious proletariat. The pattern was repeated again and again. As soon as the Red Army entered a city in Russia or Ukraine, the Bolsheviks imposed an indemnity on the bourgeoisie. They took hostages and threatened to execute them if their families failed to raise the funds. In a typical scene of the time a Cheka detachment would burst into the apartment of a lawyer, doctor, businessman, or an officer, with guns pointed at the owner, and, after a search, confiscate valuables, and take hostages. It was common knowledge that Cheka agents kept much of the booty for themselves.[37] Some reports indicate that bourgeois women were drafted for "hard work"—a euphemism for rape.[38] In Odessa, the Bolsheviks imposed an indemnity of five hundred million rubles.[39] The Red Guards and the Cheka began searching block after block, apartment after apartment, confiscating clothing, food, and valuables. By mid-May 1919, the Bolsheviks in Odessa decided to regularize this mass expropriation, and they published this order: "In accordance with the decision of the workers' Soviet, today on 13 May registration of property will begin according to a special questionnaire with the aim of expropriating from the propertied classes foodstuffs, shoes, clothing, money, valuables, and other items which are needed by the entire working people. . . . Everyone is obligated to render assistance in this sacred task. . . . Those who will not abide by this directive must be arrested immediately, and those who render resistance must be shot."[40] There followed a list of items subject to confiscation: men's suits, bicycles, blankets in excess of one per bed, sheets in excess of two per bed, and so forth. The only problem the commissars encountered was that the workers' wives protested when their soup bowls were expropriated, and the men workers staged a rally to urge that they be allowed to keep their property.[41] Systematic searches of apartments and confiscation of furniture and clothes was also reported from Kharkov.[42] This policy of mass robbery did not distinguish between men and women, but there were other elements in Bolshevik revenge on the propertied classes that were aimed specifically at women. Odessa *Izvestiia* wrote, "If we shoot several dozen of these scoundrels and fools, and if we force them to sweep the streets and their wives to wash Red Army barracks (an honor for them), then they will understand that our authority is firm and they should not pin their hopes on the English."[43]

Making the wives of the bourgeoisie wash the barracks apparently was a widespread practice, as there were references to it in Kharkov, Kiev, and even Perm' provinces.[44] There is an element of sadistic jubilation among the Bolsheviks over having the power to force former society women to do their dirtiest jobs. A recurring theme in many reports is that bourgeois women were systematically raped by the Red Army soldiers. These incidents of humiliation and rape were the result of a policy designed to enhance the soldiers' commitment to the proletarian revolution and bolster their self-esteem as members of the ruling class.

Bourgeois women conscripted to dig trenches or wash the barracks typically were random victims simply seized in bourgeois neighborhoods or conscripted on the basis of food ration class lists. Another category of class enemy women were singled out. In dozens of cases, wives of officers were held as hostages to dissuade their husbands from serving the White cause. For example, in July 1919 a Red Army regiment in Tambov defected to the Whites, a frequent occurrence in those days. The political Commissar Tkachenko sent a telegram to the headquarters of the Ninth Army: "Primarily the officers of the Tambov regiment were the initiators of surrender [to the Whites], i.e., instigators of treason. Therefore you have to apply the most severe measures in regard to their families."[45] The word *family* here stands for wives, mothers, sisters, and children. Their class position as bourgeois removed any moral or legal restraint, and they could be treated as class enemies.

In some cases, however, Bolsheviks could not easily label the families of their opponents as bourgeois. The wives of men who were involved in legal political activity were protected by law. This protection applied to women of the intelligentsia and to the families of prominent Socialists. Increasingly, however, Bolshevik authorities ignored these laws.

The most flagrant abuse of the law was that of the family of Victor Chernov, the leader of the Socialist Revolutionary Party, which was theoretically a legal political party in Soviet Russia. In spring 1920, Chernov, fearing arrest, went into hiding. The Cheka did everything in its power to capture him but consistently failed despite ambushes, raids, and provocations. Chernov made a sensational appearance at the printers' rally, which was attended by the British Trade Unions delegation. The furious Bolsheviks finally adopted measures that had hitherto been reserved for the class enemy. The Cheka seized Chernov's wife and daughters as hostages. They were interrogated persistently on Chernov's whereabouts, and Cheka agents were placed in their cell, pretending to be friends who could pass a message to Chernov. These methods led Chernov to write a bitter, sarcastic letter to Lenin:

> I congratulate the Council of Peoples' Commissars on the occasion of its great success on the internal front. A few days ago your agents arrested my wife and three daughters, the oldest being seventeen and the youngest, seven years of age. . . . I realize, of course, that maddened by repeated failures and embittered by the futile hunt for me, that worthy institution has to vent its spleen on someone. I also realize that sick women and children make a fitting object of vengeance at the stage of moral development to which it is but natural for the minions and gendarmes of degenerating regimes to fall. I congratulate you on this manifest proof, this vivid illustration of that state to which your rule and its bearers have sunk.[46]

Chernov's friend Ida Germus asked Lev Kamenev and Anatoliy Lunacharsky to help release Chernov's family. She reported Kamenev as saying, "They will be kept as hostages." Kamenev's wife, Olga, had been well acquainted with Chernov's in Paris before the war. She decided to take Ariada, the youngest of Chernov's daughters, to stay with the Kamenevs' in their apartment in the Kremlin. That moved Chernov to write another indignant letter, this time to Kamenev, demanding that all of his children be handed over to the International Red Cross.

Chernov was of course not the only one whose family was taken hostage. In a letter to the British Trade Unionists, arrested Socialists wrote that the wife of another Socialist Revolutionary, Kuznetsov had been seized as well "and flogged in prison for refusing to divulge her husband's whereabouts."[47] This practice was standard procedure until 1953. Special camps were created for the family members of the "enemies of the people." The wives of many high-ranking Communist officials were arrested or exiled or deprived of their civil rights. Women were not legally separate from their husbands in the land of victorious proletariat.

Red Terror

Finally, there was a category of women whose own social position, property, status, or political activity caused them to be repressed. Among them were women active in the opposition parties of the SRs, Left SRs, and Mensheviks. Several of them were in the highest party leadership. Sofia Zaretskaia was the Menshevik Central Committee member, and Mariya Spiridonova was the leader of the Left Socialist Revolutionaries. The Bolshevik rhetoric and actions against them were particularly vicious. During numerous political campaigns against the Mensheviks, SRs, and Left SRs the Bolsheviks introduced an entirely new political vocabulary: "traitors, servants of the capital, informers of Lloyd George, yellow lackeys of the bourgeoisie, White Guards' agents, Black hundreds in disguise," and so forth. These labels were used with varying intensity in regard to each of the three opposition parties. When an opposition political leader was a woman, however, and additional and specifically sexist and humiliating vocabulary was used. Mariya Spiridonova, after being released from prison in January 1919 after six months' confinement, began speaking at factories and plants, a perfectly legal and legitimate activity. Her fiery speeches generated enthusiastic support, leading one Communist functionary to demand that she "shut her mouth, so that she does not talk too much [*mnogo ne rasprostranialas'*] and let her get out of here to her own company, the camp of General Krasnov. But here in Soviet Russia, there is nothing to do for all kinds of whores from the White Guardists' camp."[48]

Women of the aristocracy or landowning class were class enemies by definition. In August 1919, on the eve of the departure of the Reds before the advancing Whites in Kiev, the Bolsheviks launched the Red Terror campaign. The account of Red Terror in Kiev, made by the Red Cross Sisters of Mercy, reiterates many of the essential reports from Kharkov. "Continual executions took place. They went on every night during June, July, and August. But this last week was one of wholesale slaughter."[49] As in Kharkov there was a concentration camp for counterrevolutionaries, with several hundred inmates, in addition to those kept at the Cheka headquarters itself. Beginning 8 August, the terror intensified as the Bolsheviks began to fear that they would have to abandon Kiev. A special commission was set up to review cases and to pass verdicts quickly. According to the Sisters' testimony

> the examiners—two men and one woman—arrived at the concentration camp. They were quite uneducated people. The prisoners were called out in alphabetical order and presented to these individuals who had the right to liberate them, transfer them to the category of hostages, or shoot them. There existed no preliminary examination minutes, no statement of the case to guide these revolutionary examiners. They were only in possession of the prisoner's identity card. It contained name, age, class, profession of the prisoner, and the category to which he had been previously assigned, sometimes a brief qualification of the crime. . . . The commission worked from 12 to 5 and reviewed 200 people, consequently giving only one or two minutes to each. The sentences were pronounced with lightning rapidity. There was no one and nowhere to appeal to. The sentence was final.[50]

To the Red Cross Sisters it appeared that the decisions were made arbitrarily. The Sisters could not understand that the Communists applied not the criterion of individual guilt but their own "class criteria." It was irrelevant what one did or did not do. By definition he or she was class enemy. A typical case was that of Mrs. Bobrovnikova, a landowner from the Chernigov province. The Sisters described her last days: "She was informed on by her servant and imprisoned together with her infant child. When Mme. Bobrovnikova realized that death was inevitable, she flung herself on the floor weeping, tore her hair, and implored mercy for her child's sake."[51] Some victims were executed not on the basis of class origin but simply out of revenge: "One was a Soviet employee, Mariya Gromova, a young and intelligent woman. She was a Socialist, but probably not a Bolshevist. Her honesty rebelled against the cupidity and corruption of the commissars. Apparently she had attempted to bring charges against someone and was imprisoned for that. During the last few days she was terribly agitated. Her forebodings proved correct. She was shot by the Communists."[52] In the last days of Bolshevik rule a huge trench was dug behind the house at No. 5 Sadovaia street. According to the Sisters' report, "the prisoners were led out stark naked in batches of ten, placed on the edge of the ditch and shot."[53] The same procedure from a different source was reported from Kharkov.[54] When the Whites entered Kiev, they found 123 bodies in that ditch.[55] One thousand eight hundred people were executed in Kiev in the last weeks of Bolshevik rule, and the total number of those executed from February to August was estimated at three thousand.[56]

Conclusion

The history of women under the Bolsheviks is a sad one. It is a combination of radical feminist legislation that blinded and impressed Western observers and the patronizing and sexist mobilization and utilization of women as laborers for state projects. The rhetoric of liberation, decrees and proclamations, laws and constitutions achieved the main objective of Bolshevik propaganda: to create an impression that proletarian women were equal to men. In theory they had constitutional rights that far exceeded those of women in the capitalist West.

What the Bolsheviks meant by liberation of women was not liberation at all but utilization as a labor pool. They did not mean true equality of opportunities for men and women. Their record has consistently been that of patronizing sexist bosses who assumed the pose of taking care of the oppressed female masses. In the CP itself and in the CP's policy toward women workers the pattern is repeated and reinforced: that of male chauvinist domination and exploitation sweetened by the rhetoric of liberation. The activities of the Women's Departments demonstrate that women were looked upon as objects of action. No one cared about what women themselves wanted or strived for. They were treated as children who had to be educated and were used as a cheap resource for all kinds of projects, mostly auxiliary service for the Red Army.

Most Russian women probably had never heard of the Women's Departments. They came into contact with Soviet power through regular Bolshevik institutions, party committees, military commanders, the Cheka, and other police authorities. These Bolshevik institutions had a policy for women as well: to use women as a group to leverage the actions of men. Officers' wives, Socialists' wives, and peasants' wives were all hostages of the Bolsheviks.

The story of Bolshevik policy toward working women is one of indoctrination and utilization, abuse at the factories, humiliating searches at the rail stations and factory gates. Women were treated as fundamentally inferior to male workers since they ostensibly lacked political consciousness. Bolshevik policy toward peasant women was equally utilitarian. They were used as an instrument of social control to combat the male rebels. Being defenseless, they were used as objects of revenge for the actions of men. They were herded into camps, raped, traded, and abused just because of who they were: mothers, sisters, and daughters of the Bolsheviks' opponents. Perhaps the worst treatment was that received by bourgeois and aristocratic women. They were regarded as people without any rights at all. Elements of class stigmatization and sadistic revenge were combined in incidents of rape by Red Army soldiers or when they were forced to do the dirtiest jobs just because of their social origin.

The echoes of women's own voices briefly presented here suggest that women from various social groups responded vigorously to the challenges of the new regime and the civil war. Working women wrote to *Pravda* in protest and volunteered to be arrested in Tula. Peasant women, the backbone of the traditional rural society, perceived the Bolsheviks as thieves and convicts in power. Women of the educated classes plunged into political life, and many were prominent in several political parties. All of these women acted in defense of their dignity, family, community, religion, and political convictions.

The much talked about upward mobility of women in Soviet society was granted on condition of political loyalty. If one were willing to be an obedient servant to the party state, one had career opportunities. If one refused to obey or wanted to choose another political or religious creed, one would have no job opportunities—and one's life would be in danger. Bolshevik missionaries told women what they ought to do, what they should believe, and how they should live. Women's professional, religious, and family life was determined by the party without their participation or consent. In the end, women had to carry a double burden: full-time job, and family and child care.[57] In the decades to come women would be forced to experience horrendous conditions in the notorious communal (*kommunalki*) apartments, simply because the party decided that communal living was superior.

The worst legacy of Bolshevik policy toward women during the civil war was that cultural practices established then did not disappear. Until 1953 women were still held hostage for the actions of their men. In the middle of the twentieth century in the country of the "victorious" proletariat women were still treated as an extension of their husbands. They were imprisoned for the actions of their husbands. They had no inviolability of person or a fair trial or any recourse to law. They were victimized because of who they were: mothers, sisters, and wives.

Notes

1. Elizabeth Waters, "The Female Form in Soviet Political Iconography," in Barbara Clements, Barbara Alpern Engel, and Christine D. Worobec, eds., *Russia's Women: Accommodation, Resistance, Transformation* (Berkeley: University of California Press), 232.

2. Beatrice Farnsworth, *Aleksandra Kollontai: Socialism, Feminism, and the Bolshevik Revolution* (Stanford: Stanford University Press, 1980).

3. See, for example, Robert H. McNeal, "The Early Decrees of Zhenotdel," in Tova Yedlin, ed., *Women in Eastern Europe and the Soviet Union* (New York: Praeger, 1980), 75–87, esp. 76.

4. For a positive assessment of the work of the Women's Departments see Beatrice Brodsky Farnsworth, "Communist Feminism: Its Synthesis and Demise," in Carol R. Berkin and Clara M. Lovett, eds., *Women, War, and Revolution* (New York: Holmes and Meier, 1980), 145–165.

5. Barbara Clements, "Impact of the Civil War on Women and Family Relations," in Diane Koenker, ed., *Party, State, and Society in the Russian Civil War* (Bloomington: Indiana University Press, 1988), 105–123.

6. Richard Stites, *The Women's Liberation Movement in Russia* (Princeton, N.J.: Princeton University Press, 1978), 345.

7. Richard Stites, "Zhenotdel: Bolshevism and Russian Women, 1917–1930," *Russian History/Histoire Russe* 3 (1976): part 2, pp. 174–194.

8. R. C. Elwood, *Inessa Armand: Revolutionary and Feminist* (Cambridge: Cambridge University Press, 1992), 242. See also Stites, *Women's Liberation Movement*, 335.

9. Linda Edmonson, "Russian Feminists and the First All-Russian Congress of Women," *Russian History/Histoire Russe* 3 (1976): part 2, pp. 123–150.

10. This appears to have been a deeply rooted practice; see, for example, Rose Glickman, *Russian Factory Women: Workplace and Society, 1880–1914* (Berkeley: University of California Press, 1984), 212–218.

11. "Rabochaia Zhizn. Prekrasnaia taktika," *Pravda*, 11 March 1919, 4.

12. Farnsworth, *Aleksandra Kollontai*, 188–189.

13. The view of proletarian women as "hostile to revolution" and as "outside politics" is perceptively discussed by Alix Holt, "Marxism and Women's Opression: Bolshevik Theory and Practice in the 1920s," in Tova Yedlin, ed., *Women in Eastern Europe and the Soviet Union* (New York: Praeger, 1980), 104.

14. "V Rabochem Kotle," *Zaria Rossii* (Petrograd), 24 May 1918, reprinted as "Among the Workers," in Vladimir Brovkin, ed., *Dear Comrades: Menshevik Reports on the Bolshevik Revolution and Civil War* (Stanford, Calif.: Hoover Institution Press, 1991), 75.

15. Roger Chartier, *Cultural History: Between Practices and Representations* (Oxford: Polity Press, 1988), 36.

16. Beatrice Farnsworth, "Village Women Experience the Revolution," in Beatrice Farnsworth and Lynne Viola, eds., *Russian Peasant Women* (New York: Oxford University Press, 1992), 145–166.

17. Cathy Frierson, *Peasant Icons: Representations of Rural People in Late Nineteenth Century Russia* (New York: Oxford University Press, 1993), esp. chapter entitled *"Baba*: The Peasant Woman—Vigaro, Eve, or Victim?"

18. Richard Stites, "Equality, Freedom, and Justice: Women and Men in the Russian Revolution, 1917–1930" (Research paper no. 67, Hebrew University, Jerusalem, 1988), 6.

19. Barbara E. Clements, "Baba and Bolshevik: Russian Women and Revolutionary Change," *Soviet Union/Union Sovietique* 12 (1985): part 2, pp. 162, 163, 173.

20. Politsvodka 9oi armii 29 July 1919, f. 192, op. 1, d. 53 TsGASA.

21. Svodka No. 127 Informatsionno-Instruktorskogo Podotdela Kubansko-Chernomorskogo Otdeleniia Upravleniia (7 October 1920) Politotdel 10oi armii f. 192, op. 1, d. 240 TsGASA.

22. See, for example, such incidents described in Vladimir Brovkin, *The Mensheviks After October: Socialist Opposition and the Rise of the Bolshevik Dictatorship* (Ithaca, N.Y.: Cornell University Press, 1987).

23. A. L. Okninsky, *Dva Goda sredi krestian. vidennoe, slyshannoe, perezhitoe v Tambovskoi gubernii s noiabria 1918 goda do noiabria 1920 goda* (Riga, 1936; reprint, Newton, Mass.: Oriental Research Partners, 1986), 120.

24. Donesenie Roslavl'skomu Uezdvoenkomu, WKP No. 119, Smolensk Archive, Harvard University.

25. Ezhenedel'nye svodki tovarishchu Leninu. Cheka. GARF, f. 130, op. 3.

26. Prikaz Voiskam Kavkazskogo Fronta No. 779 (18 May 1920) Rostov-on-Don. TsGASA f. 193, 10aia armiia, op. 1, d. 66.

27. "Otchet o deiatel 'nosti Viatskoi Kommissii po Bor'be s Dezertirstvom za 1920 god." RTsKhIDNI, f. 17, op. 12, d. 110.

28. "Doklad ob otriadakh osobogo naznacheniia," TsKa RKP(b), RTsKhIDNI, f. 17, op. 12, d. 110.

29. "Voronezh: Instruktsiia dlia otvetstvennykh upolnomochennykh Gubkompart, RKP(b), RTsKhIDNI, f. 17, op. 6, d. 48, p. 212.

30. "Krovozhadnyi manifest," *Revoliutsionnaia Rossiia*, no. 7 (May 1921): 30.

31. "Ot Chrezvychainogo Komiteta revoliutsionnoi okhrany Korel'skogo uchastka," *Izvestiia Petrogradskogo Soveta* (Petrograd), 12 July 1919, 1.

32. The text of the order is in "La Terror en Russie Contre Les Paysans," *Pour La Russie* (Paris), 29 December 1920, 1.

33. The names of the burned villages are in "Povstancheskoe dvizhenie na Ukraine," *Revoliutsionnaia Rossiia*, no. 11 (August 1921), 23–25.

34. A. N. Latsiss: "Doklad o deiatel'nosti upolnomochennykh VeCheka i Osobykh Otdelov VeCheka na Severnom Kavkaze i o sostoianii Cheka i Osobykh Otdelov na mestakh" (25 December 1920) [Report on the Activity of the Plenipotentiaries of the Cheka and the Special Departments of the Cheka], RTsKhIDNI, f. 17 TsKa RKP(b), op. 84, Biuro Sekretariata TsKa, d. 75, p. 56.

35. Ibid., p. 57.

36. Ibid., p. 58.

37. That is clear from the Latsis letter. M. Latsis, "Vsem Chrezvychainym Kommissiiam po bor'bes kontrrevoliutsiei na Ukraine," in "Rabota Cheka," *Na Chuzhoi Storone*, no. 5 (Berlin, 1924), 170.

38. Ibid., 22.

39. "Ot Odessy do Tiflisa," *Borba*, no. 146 (July 1919, Tiflis), 2. Also Andreas Nieman, *Fünf Monate Obrigkeit von Unten. Erinnerungen Aus den Odessauer Bolschewistentagen. April bis August 1919* (Berlin: Der Firn, 1920), 10.

40. "Den' mirnogo vosstaniia," *Izvestiia Odesskogo Soveta Rabochikh deputatov*, no. 36 (13 May 1919, Odessa), 1.

41. "Ot Odessy do Tiflisa," *Borba*, no. 146 (July 1919, Tiflis), 2.

42. This is an exceptionally detailed and well-documented account of industry, politics, and civil war entitled "Khar'kov." The author is not identified. It is clear from contents, however, that the document was written in the summer of 1919 after Kharkov was taken by Denikin's army and that the document was an attempt to survey economic and political situation in the area. A copy was sent to the Allies. Cited here from a copy in the National Archives. State Department, Dispatch No. 861 00 7791, *Records of the Department of State Relating to the Internal Affairs of Russia and the Soviet Union*. Washington, D.C.

43. Mel'gunov: *Krasnyi Terror v Rossii*, 49.

44. "Siberia Today," *The Times* (London), 12 February 1919. This has also been reported from Mr. Alson to Balfour, Vladivostok (14 January 1919), d. 22, in *Collection of Reports on Bolshevism in Russia: Abridged Edition of Parliamentary Paper, Russia No. 1* (London: His Majesty's Stationary Office, 1919), 32.

45. V Shtab 9oi armii. Telegramma (18 July 1919), TsGASA, f. 192, 9th army, op. 1, d. 26.

46. Wiktor Tschernow (Viktor Chernov), *Meine Schicksale in Sowiet-Rußland*, 33. See also the text of the letter in "Victor Chernov's Family Taken as Hostages," *Information Bulletin*, nos. 10–12 (October 23 1920), 6–7.

47. The appeal of the imprisoned Socialists "to the British Workmen and to the Members of the Labor Delegation to Russia," in Samuel Gompers, "Labor Victims and the Serfs of the Soviets," *American Federationist* 28 (28 March 1921): 213.

48. "O Vystuplenii Marii Spiridonovoi," *Pravda*, 4 February 1919.

49. *In the Shadow of Death: (A Document) Statement of Red Cross Sisters on the Bolshevist Prisons in Kiev*, 44.

50. Ibid., 46.

51. Ibid., 47.

52. *In the Shadow of Death*, 46.

53. Ibid., 47.

54. "Kharkov Under Red Terror," *Bulletins of the Russian Liberation Committee* (London), no. 35 (18 October 1919), 3.

55. *In the Shadow of Death*, 48.

56. "Eshche o Kievskikh CheKa v 1919 godu," letter dated 13 January 1921, *Na Chuzhoi Storone* (Prague), no. 10 (1925): 220–221, and *In the Shadow of Death*, 23. See also reprints from a variety of Ukrainian newspapers on Red Terror: "Les Tchrezvytchaikas (Commission Extraordinaires Bolchevistes)," *La Russie Democratique* (Paris), no. 8 (17 December 1919).

57. Clements, "Impact of the Civil War on Women and Family Relations," 105–123.

JONATHAN W. DALY

"Storming the Last Citadel": The Bolshevik Assault on the Church, 1922 **12**

I n this chapter I propose that the Bolshevik confiscation of movable church property in the first half of 1922 was both a major attack on Russian society and the first practical development in peacetime of what Joseph Goebbels would later term the "big lie." The policy sought to weaken the church as the last bastion of organized resistance to the new regime while increasing the wealth of the state primarily at the expense of ordinary people. Unlike monastic latifundia, which diverse rulers since Henry VIII have seized with little popular resistance, the chalices, ciboria, crosses, embellished Bibles, and church adornments expropriated in 1922 had served chiefly to brighten the lives of the majority of Russians who were at least occasional churchgoers. The Bolshevik leaders knew this and sought to win acceptance for the unpopular policy by falsely presenting it as a means to alleviate the effects of a famine then raging in southeastern Russia. Bolshevik innovations in the uses of propaganda have received little scholarly attention.[1] Until the Soviet archives recently opened, historians could do little more than speculate about the divergence between official pronouncements and the voiceless opposition. In this chapter I seek to lay bare that divergence in the campaign of 1922 against the Russian Orthodox church.

On 26 January 1918 the new Bolshevik regime decreed the separation of church and state and nationalized all church property, including movable objects, which the religious could continue to use only with government permission.[2] During the second half of 1918 the government closed many churches, seized and inventoried church property and valuables, conducted antireligious campaigns (for example, unsealing fifty-eight relic repositories), and executed at least ten church hierarchs as well as many priests and other clergy. When Patriarch Tikhon inquired in November 1918 and again in February 1919 as to why the government had ordered Bishop Lavrentii's execution, a Cheka official asserted that

"Soviet power will keep shooting these lords until we smash and crush the criminal counterrevolutionary activity of church leaders."[3]

As militant atheists and materialists, the leading Bolsheviks viewed religion and all religious organizations as mechanisms for the oppression of the masses. They assumed that religious faith resulted from both harsh oppression and popular ignorance. Consequently, many Bolsheviks expected religion to disappear following the abolition of capitalism and through the education of believers.[4] As early as 1909, Lenin warned Social Democrats against committing Bismarck's error (*Perebismarkit' samogo Bismarka*) of strengthening "militant clericalism through police persecution of Catholics."[5] Thus a decree of December 1918 stated that "against religious prejudice and the blindness of popular superstitions, one must struggle not with punishment and repression, but with good schools, Communist propaganda, and socialist economics." The decree instituted a temporary truce that held until early 1922 and made eminent practical sense. For example, in August 1920 the Petrograd Soviet refused to launch an antireligious campaign: Given the current shortages of food and fuel, the war against Poland to the east, and Russian anti-Bolshevik forces under General P. N. Wrangel to the south, who needed another front? Yet this tactical "retreat" on the "ecclesiastical front" did not prevent the regime from launching in 1919 a journal designed to prepare antireligious agitators for combat.[6]

Indeed, the truce could not last long, as the Bolshevik regime aimed at destroying all centers of independent authority and political power, whether institutional or informal, capable of challenging the legitimacy of the new regime. Some of these "intermediary bodies" and associations were left over from prerevolutionary Russia, such as the nobility, the officer corps, the state structure, and the church. Others had developed under the nurturing but restrictive autocratic order—for example, mercantile and industrial entrepreneurs and educated elites—so necessary for modernization yet so subversive and difficult to control. Still others the autocracy had created almost in spite of itself in an effort to rationalize the machinery of state (the *zemstva* and Town Councils and the independent court system) or under pressure from public opinion (the Duma). Finally, some arose and developed spontaneously as expressions of the growth of civil society: a flourishing press and publishing industry, philanthropic organizations, and diverse nongovernmental organizations and associations.[7] According to Marxism-Leninism, all nonproletarian institutions and associations were counterrevolutionary by their very nature. This, coupled with the Bolsheviks' utopian ideal of unified political, economic, social, and culture control, compelled them to destroy or bridle every element of Russia's Old Regime and incipient civil society.

The most resilient and dangerous intermediary body, from the point of view of the Bolsheviks, was the church, just as the most indomitable social class was naturally the largest: the peasantry.[8] It had been relatively simple to close newspapers, courts, unions, and philanthropic associations, the zemstva and town councils; to persecute specific social groups; to assassinate the imperial family, individual nobles, officers, and clergy; and to nationalize businesses and church property. It had proved impossible, however, to confiscate the fruits of peasants' labor without gravely undermining the most fundamental element of the Russian economy: agriculture. Likewise, the Bolshevik leadership, having separated church and state, prudently avoided launching a frontal assault on the church.[9] After all, in 1914 the Russian Orthodox church was the most extensive and formidable institution in Russia, apart from the state itself, embracing over 200,000 parish and monastic clergy, 31,000 parishes, more than 75,000 churches and chapels, over 1,100 monasteries, some 37,000 primary schools, 57 seminaries and four university-level academies, and thousands of orphanages, old people's homes, and hospitals. It was also an eminently *popular* institution, for, as Lenin himself admitted in 1909, Russian Orthodoxy had retained the allegiance of many urban industrial workers, of large numbers of semiproletarians, as well as of the majority of peasants.[10] The regime ultimately succeeded in crushing the independent peasantry and in bringing the church to heel, although the church has outlived both the Bolshevik and the Soviet regimes.

By late 1920 the Bolsheviks had won the civil war, but the country lay in ruins. In March 1921, in the face of widespread social discontent and massive popular revolts, the party instituted the New Economic Policy (NEP). Although willing to compromise with the peasants economically, the Bolshevik leadership remained determined both to crush those institutions capable of representing the peasants politically, namely the Socialist Revolutionary Party and the Russian Orthodox church, and to weaken all independent forces in both society and the party.[11] As Lenin wrote on 2 March 1922, "It would be the greatest mistake to imagine that NEP has put an end to terror. We will return to terror, indeed to economic terror." For a time, however, Lenin preferred to avoid confrontation with the church, and in mid-April 1921 he warned Molotov that the government must give "absolutely no offense to religion." This became official policy on 21 April.[12] Yet in 1922 most of the church's remaining valuables were confiscated, many religious leaders were tried and executed, and efforts were made to provoke a schism in the church, all accompanied by a massive antichurch propaganda campaign. What had happened?

The Bolshevik leaders fully expected religion to disappear in Russia entirely; however, they feared it as a current social force and hesitated before striking at the church. The famine of 1921–22 served to justify an assault. Without the famine, the Bolshevik government surely would not have called for the confiscation of the church's treasures in 1922. The confiscation campaign in turn provided a pretext for an antichurch propaganda offensive, since many church leaders and laypeople balked at surrendering the church's valuables to a state they distrusted. Finally, the schism between clergy loyal to the patriarch and the "progressive" clergy, who supported the regime, permitted the government to declare the former "counterrevolutionaries" and therefore to bring them to trial.

The government itself bore some responsibility for the poor harvests. In 1919–20 the government expropriated (practically without compensation) a significant proportion of the peasantry's food and seed stores. As a result, winter and spring plantings were greatly reduced in 1921. This, coupled with a terrible drought in the spring of 1921, led to massive peasant uprisings and famine. NEP immediately diminished popular discontent and eventually sparked an economic revival, but not before famine had ravaged much of the country.[13]

On 26 June 1921, the government warned that 25 million people in the Volga region faced starvation. Three days later the Interior Ministry (NKVD) asked local organs to inventory church property. In July and August, Russian social activists and church leaders attempted to organize collections for the hungry, but the government soon restricted and finally prohibited their efforts. Bolshevik diplomats appealed for aid to governments and private organizations in nearly every country of Europe, while the VTsIK (the All-Russian Central Executive Committee) created a triumvirate of Kamenev, Molotov, and Trotsky to manage the dangers to the Bolshevik state that opening the country to foreign philanthropists would present.[14]

During August and September 1921 the state-controlled press (in this chapter I draw on *Pravda, Izvestiia,* and *Petrogradskaia pravda*) devoted considerable attention to the crisis, calling on the people to give freely and to mobilize all resources against this "enemy," the famine. Yet, since the government did not wish to tap the potential energies that initiatives outside the bureaucracy could have unleashed, the campaign produced meager results. Moreover, throughout the fall and into the winter, press coverage of the famine diminished, until by December it was scarcely mentioned. This neglect continued through most of January. An exhaustive analysis of Politburo *protokoly* (dockets of topics discussed and decisions reached) indicates that the leadership paid little attention to the crisis during this period. But for *Pravda*'s New Year's wish of a "triumph over the famine," one might have supposed that it had come to an end.

Indeed, as late as 31 January *Pravda* disingenuously complained that the issue of aid to the hungry had disappeared from view.[15]

Meanwhile, preparation for the confiscation of church valuables was under way. On 12 November 1921 the Scvnarkom appointed Trotsky to head a commission to unify and accelerate the confiscation of valuables of all sorts. Trotsky already headed Goskhran, the agency created to administer expropriated movable property, and in December he joined Litvinov in directing efforts to sell such property abroad. Moreover, and perhaps most important, Lenin had placed Trotsky in charge of the regime's antireligious policy in late 1921 or early 1922 (a position he was to occupy until October 1922). In late November 1921, the Economic Administration of the Cheka demanded that Glavmuzei (the Main Administration of Museums) send information on valuables in museums, palaces, churches, and monasteries. On 2 January 1922, the VTsIK decided to liquidate all remaining church property and immediately circulated a secret instruction on conducting inventories of movable property in monasteries and churches. Not only did the instruction fail to mention the famine, it also provided for the delivery of objects of historic or artistic value to Glavmuzei for distribution to museums.[16] In other words, from the beginning the campaign centered on despoiling the church, not on combating famine.

In late January 1922, *Pravda* and *Izvestiia* began to remind their readers of the extreme gravity of the famine, and *Pravda* called for placing the antihunger campaign on a military footing. Although one reporter in *Pravda* argued that the food situation in Russia was less a catastrophe than a crisis, the propaganda campaign was soon raised to a high pitch. On 26 January, *Izvestiia* first mentioned the possibility of using church valuables to help the hungry. The following day, *Izvestiia* reported widespread cannibalism and demanded that donations to fight the famine be made obligatory, but it did not mention church valuables.[17]

By 26 January, Trotsky had already laid the groundwork for the confiscation of church valuables and reported so to the Politburo. He suggested that details of the campaign be worked out at an "absolutely closed" session of the Sovnarkom on 31 January.[18]

Yet sometime before this, orders must have gone out to local Cheka departments, since on 24 January the Tatarstan Oblast Committee approved an elaborate project that the local Cheka had drafted for the confiscation of church valuables. The Tatarstan project would never have come to my attention had it not been found, in the words of a Politburo resolution, "politically illiterate and tactless." The Politburo distinguished four major flaws in the project. First, to permit selected clergymen to initiate the process would "increase the clergy's authority" in the eyes of the people. Second, the Politburo considered it "unacceptable" to draw an analogy with the legendary grass-roots movement led in 1611–12 by Kuz'ma Minin and Dmitrii Pozharskii, presumably because such a movement would escape party control. Third, the suggestion that "various sorts of raids (*nalety*) and attacks (*napadeniia*)" be launched against individual churches would, according to the Politburo, alienate believers. Finally, the thought of violating private correspondence in search of money would "legalize theft, which cannot be considered a method of operation of Soviet power at the present moment."[19] In other words, the party leadership planned to launch a carefully orchestrated, minutely regulated, and astutely presented campaign.

For example, the Bolshevik authorities preferred that the call for the confiscation of church treasures appear to come from nongovernmental sources, and throughout the campaign they employed this oblique method of promoting the policy. Thus, on 31 January *Izvestiia* noted that the bishop of Saratov (a city located in the hunger-stricken Volga region) expressed no objection to using a part of the church's valuables to buy food for the hungry. Simultaneously the press apparently invented appeals from model citizens. For example, on 1 February 1922, *Izvestiia* printed the impassioned letter of a certain "N," who described himself as a peasant and the son of a weaver, neither a member of any party nor a "godless *intelligent*," who had never finished primary school, now worked in a factory, and, with his wife and five children, ate mostly potatoes yet gave 1,000 rubles monthly for famine relief. A marvel of prescience for a humble worker, the letter encapsulates the official justification of the confiscation campaign as it was to unfold, namely that 1) the government disposed of insufficient resources to deal with the famine; 2) the church in collaboration with the autocracy had kept the people in a state of ignorance which promoted the outbreak and spread of the famine; 3) the more "progressive" parish clergy would support the government's efforts in alleviating the famine; 4) but since the parish clergy feared Patriarch Tikhon's excommunication, 5) a revolution had to occur in the church. The author pointed out that "Peter [the Great] did not ask permission to take church bells, nor Catherine [the Great], to take church lands."[20] It seems likely that the secret meeting of the Sovnarkom, to which Trotsky referred, agreed on this strategy. As throughout the entire campaign, however, government officials proceeded with extreme caution.

Thus, the major dailies printed more letters supporting the confiscation of church valuables; they allegedly received thousands of missives from workers, soldiers, peasants, and others. Since the government used professional agitators to bring people together to pass resolutions in favor of the campaign and encouraged editors to publish them, I cannot affirm that all such documents arose spontaneously.[21]

Responding to the implicit threat, on 6 February 1922, Patriarch Tikhon encouraged believers to donate valuables not consecrated for use in religious ceremonies to state agencies for famine relief, and the Politburo approved the publication of his appeal. But on 11 February, *Pravda* complained that the "progressive" clergy had been too slow in lending their support to the plan and declared that the VTsIK had decreed the immediate removal of all sacred vessels and other valuables from churches, monasteries, and other church institutions. In reality, the government had decided on this policy on 16 February and had issued a detailed instruction to local officials on its implementation. Simultaneously, Archpriest Vvedenskii, the future leader of the Renovationist movement, chided the church leaders for their hardheartedness. A secret police report (on 8 February the State Political Administration, known as GPU, replaced the Cheka) noted that Vvedenskii's appeal had fooled many clergy (*proizvelo na nikh odurachivaiushchee vpechatlenie*).[22] His advocacy of the confiscation of church valuables won valuable support for the Renovationist movement, which he would lead.

The major dailies constantly stressed the need for militancy and enthusiasm. The party leadership seemed to fear that NEP was "perverting the perspective of workers and peasants" and deflecting them from "struggle, building, exploits, and martyrdom." *Petrogradskaia pravda* on 10 February tied this call for militancy and enthusiasm to the confiscation campaign, calling it the "final battle, the decisive battle to save revolutionary Russia."[23]

At the same time, however, the leadership feared provoking popular animosity toward the government. Thus a 24 February article in *Izvestiia* stated that the confiscation campaign should not be turned into an affront to religion, and that there would be plenty of time afterward for exposing "religious prejudice and the roots of religion."[24] Indeed, after the above-mentioned *Petrogradskaia pravda* article, official press rhetoric about "decisive battles" against religion ceased until mass resistance to the confiscation campaign began in mid-March.

In response to the 26 February decree on the confiscation of church valuables, Patriarch Tikhon on 28 February issued an epistle in which he, citing canon law, declared sacrilegious even the voluntary surrender of consecrated vessels and warned that the penalty for sacrilege was excommunication. But the wheels of the state machine were turning and would render inevitable a confrontation, for on the same day the VTsIK issued a general instruction to local officials on how to confiscate the valuables.[25]

In late February and early March press coverage of the famine was still overshadowed by other issues, including the Genoa Conference, the diplomatic recognition of Soviet Russia, the state of the economy, the merits of the "united front" tactic in European politics, and various elections and plenums in Soviet Russia. Therefore, *Pravda*'s sudden declaration on 21 February that the struggle with hunger should take on a "mass character" probably sounded hollow.[26]

From 24 February to 4 March 1922 the quantity of relief supplies unloaded in Russian ports that had to be stored for lack of rail transport rose from 13,621 to 98,940 metric tons. A shortage of space in warehouses, especially in the Baltic, required the American Relief Administration (ARA) to curtail its shipments of supplies. In other words, the Soviet transport system could not, until August, have handled any more shipments of grain and other supplies even had they been purchased with gold or silver expropriated from churches, and by August the famine was all but over. This did not, however, prevent foreign relief organizations from providing more and more people in Saratov Province (in the heart of the famine-stricken Volga region) with one meal per day: from 24 percent of the population in April to 44 percent in May and 60 percent in June and July.[27]

In late February and early March 1922, GPU reports chronicled popular discontent, which had been running high since before the first of the year, especially in the regions where the mortality rate peaked between February and April (147 percent above normal in Saratov Province). The same police reports noted only sporadic and minor agitation for and against the decree on confiscation in Russia at this time, though they also indicated that in a few provinces most sentiment ran against it.[28]

On 5 March 1922, Metropolitan Veniamin of Petrograd reiterated the patriarch's condemnation of the confiscation decree of 26 February. Yet he also intimated that the church would nevertheless surrender all its valuables on receipt of three assurances: that all available resources had been exhausted, that the proceeds would truly benefit the hungry, and that the Russian Orthodox church leaders would "bless the sacrifice."[29] It is unclear which of the conditions was least acceptable to the Bolshevik leadership.

Also on 5 March the Politburo discussed a secret intelligence report warning that counterrevolutionaries both within Russia and abroad were planning to launch a coordinated assault against the Soviet state in mid-March or early April. The Politburo resolved to heighten vigilance in all sensitive organizations, especially the military, and to order the deputy commissar for defense, Mikhail Frunze, to concentrate on this issue. In addition, the major newspapers were to be instructed to publicize the imminence of a "White guard" offensive.[30] I have found no further references to this supposed conspiracy, and prosecutors failed to mention it at the trials against church leaders in May and June 1922. Indeed, it seems unlikely that the members of the Politburo would have chosen to broadcast such sensitive information had they actually received and believed it. Perhaps one may conclude that in early March party officials expected popular resistance to the enforcement of the decree on the confiscation of church valuables and *in advance* sought to link all potential resistance to an alleged counterrevolutionary conspiracy. Whatever the explanation for the mysterious police report, resistance soon broke out.

On 11 March 1922, a large crowd in Rostov-on-the-Don violently opposed attempts to strip the major churches. That day Trotsky proposed that the Politburo create a secret shock commission (*udarnaia komissiia*) in Moscow to prepare the ground for the confiscation of church valuables and then to direct the campaign. On the following days (12–16 March) crowds fiercely opposed state officials in Smolensk, Shuia (Ivanovo-Voznesensk Province), and Staraia Russa (Novgorod Province), forcing authorities to call out military reinforcements. Clashes left several dead and dozens wounded. Minor confrontations occurred in Petrograd and in numerous other places across Russia at this time. Yet the press not only failed to report on the violence, it mentioned only those localities where the campaign encountered no resistance. Although the Bolsheviks later claimed that the church hierarchy had organized these incidents, secret police reports suggest that they occurred spontaneously.[31]

Trotsky and the Politburo responded swiftly to them. On 12 March, Trotsky declared to the Politburo that "our entire strategy at the present moment must be calculated to provoke a schism among the clergy on the concrete issue of the seizure of church valuables."[32] On 16 March the Politburo ordered local officials to prepare the ground thoroughly before proceeding to strip the churches, and a second instruction directed officials to begin with large towns or with localities where popular opinion supported the decree.[33] The following day Trotsky proposed a detailed plan, which the Politburo adopted on 20 March and issued as an instruction to local police and party authorities on 21 March. Trotsky's plan called for, first, secret party-controlled commissions to direct the confiscation in each city, beginning with the most important, behind the cover of official bureaus that were staffed primarily by Russians ("to give no grounds for chauvinistic agitation"); second, massive press campaigns focusing on aid to the hungry (without mentioning the struggle against the church or religion); third, an effort to seek to divide the clergy by actively supporting those openly in favor of the confiscation policy and by depicting leading opponents as "inhuman and greedy 'princes of the church'"; fourth, a secret warning to well-known priests that they would bear direct responsibility for any acts of resistance to the decree; fifth, mass agitation (showcasing famine victims) in support of the confiscation; and, finally, the stationing of loyal Communists near churches during the removal of valuables.[34]

Lenin had been ill in January and again beginning about 1 March 1922. Consequently, on 6 March he and his wife, Krupskaia, had retired to a dacha in the village of Korzinkino outside Moscow, where they stayed until the 25th. There he completed (on 12 March) a lengthy article calling for a more active propaganda campaign against the "ruling religious obscurantists [*gospodstvuiushchie religioznye mrakobesy*]."[35] As a result, two antireligious journals, *Ateist* and *Nauka i religiia*, began appearing in May.[36]

But in the meantime, popular resistance to the confiscation campaign had broken out across Russia, and Lenin responded on 19 March 1922, with his now-notorious letter to the Politburo. If Trotsky's proposal for action was eminently practical and aimed at finishing the confiscation campaign as successfully as possible, Lenin's letter was primarily an ideological diatribe demanding an all-out assault on the church. He deduced from the existence of both popular and official church resistance to the decree the existence of a "black hundred" ecclesiastical conspiracy to engage the Soviet government in a "decisive battle precisely at this moment."[37] But, according to Lenin, this was "precisely the moment, the only moment when we can count on nearly absolute success to smash the enemy on the head and to assure for ourselves for many decades the position we need. Precisely now and only now, when in the famine-stricken areas cannibalism is rampant and roads are strewn with hundreds (if not thousands) of corpses, can we (and therefore must we) carry out the confiscation of church valuables with the most furious [*beshenoi*] and merciless energy, not stopping before any opposition." Not only did Lenin consider it essential to strike mercilessly and with lightning speed so that the "enemy" (the church) would not forget the attack for several decades, he hoped that a "very large number of the most influential and dangerous reactionaries in Shuia and, as far as possible, in other cities" would be tried and executed. While considering it imprudent to harm Patriarch Tikhon, he suggested that "the larger the number of reactionary clergy and bourgeois we are able to execute on these grounds, the better."[38] Lenin expected the operation to yield several hundred million (or even billion) gold rubles, which could be used for state-building and would place Soviet Russia in a strong bargaining position at the Genoa Conference (which met from 10 April to 19 May, to discuss the Russian problem and general international economic issues).[39] By contrast, he failed to even mention the needs of the hungry.

In alleging the existence of a church-directed counterrevolutionary conspiracy against the Soviet state, in his letter to the Politburo of 19

March, Lenin cited reports issued by the Russian Telegraph Agency (ROSTA) but referred to no secret police reports. What had become of the secret report referring to an imminent counterrevolutionary attack on Soviet Russia, which the Politburo had discussed on 5 March? Collections of secret police reports now available to researchers contain no warnings of counterrevolutionary conspiracies then in preparation. Can one infer that none existed? That is, is it possible that some members of the Politburo fabricated the report in order to stimulate support for a harsh policy against the church among the remaining members of the Politburo?

Even more perplexing is Lenin's failure to denounce the Russian Orthodox Church Abroad, headquartered in Sremski Karlovci, Yugoslavia, which repeatedly denounced the new regime after the Bolshevik coup. As recently as 29 January 1922, for example, Metropolitan Antonii (Khrapovitskii), a well-known reactionary, had publicly advocated the restoration of the Romanov dynasty, and on 1 March 1922 he had called on the prospective delegates to the Genoa Conference to urge their governments to help overthrow the new Russian regime. The Russian church Synod in Moscow denounced the Karlovatskii Sobor on 8 April 1921 and 30 January 1922, and both times ordered the sobor (council) to subordinate itself to Evlogii, Metropolitan of Volynia, whom Tikhon had appointed as his representative in Europe in spring 1921. The sobor in Sremski Karlovci refused to comply. The resulting struggle spawned a heated polemic that has complicated the work of historians.[40] Yet whatever the true relations between the two branches of Russian Orthodoxy, in mid-March 1922, concerned with "black hundred ecclesiastical campaigns," Lenin would surely have mentioned the Russian Church Abroad had he believed it a threat.

On 20 and 21 March 1922, local officials received government orders to continue to delay implementation of the decree if necessary, but on 22 March Trotsky recommended that the Politburo launch a major offensive against church leadership. He proposed to loose a violent flood (*beshenyi tok*) of information about clerical "mutinies" in Smolensk, Petrograd, and elsewhere, and then to publicize the events in Shuia. A trial of church leaders was to begin within one week in Shuia, leading to the execution of the "ring-leaders" (*konovodov*). Following this, he advocated arresting Patriarch Tikhon and the Synod.[41]

By this point, anger at the confiscation campaign had diminished in Smolensk and Shuia, though popular opinion evidently remained divided on the issue all across Russia and general discontent remained acute.[42] No further incidents of violent resistance to the decree would occur, however, and for this the regime would seem to have been beholden primarily to Trotsky's leadership, both in organizing prudent implementation of the decree and in orchestrating a massive propaganda campaign to justify it.

On 23 March the Politburo adopted Trotsky's proposal for the immediate allocation of 1 million paper rubles to Pomgol as the first installment of hunger relief procured in exchange for confiscated church valuables. At the same time, Trotsky requested 10 million rubles to finance the confiscation campaign. Whereas this disbursement remained secret, the former, smaller one was to receive wide publicity.[43] President Mikhail Kalinin would simultaneously announce (and the press would broadcast) that the campaign was not at all a struggle against religion but rather against the counterrevolutionary "princes of the church" who hoped to destroy Soviet power, and that (unspecified) church representatives would, "of course," be allowed to monitor the whole process.[44]

The state-controlled press did not mention the incidents of militant resistance until 28 March 1922, but in the meantime it had begun to devote more space to the famine. For example, on 15 March *Izvestiia* ran a special five-page edition on the hunger problem. Various articles exhorted all Russians to redouble their efforts to help the hungry, and a caricature depicted a resplendent Patriarch Tikhon denying a starving man the chalice he pleads for. Of course few people could just ride off to the "hunger front," as adventurous as that might have seemed to militant Communists of civil war vintage. They could, however, march on the "confiscation front," and that was apparently what the government was calling them to do.[45]

On 21 March 1922, in accordance with Trotsky's 17 March proposal to the Politburo, *Pravda* declared a two-week campaign to aid the hungry and devoted its front pages each day to the issue. On the first day, amid a plethora of articles on assistance to the hungry provided by trade unions, workers, the Comintern, individuals, and foreigners, one finds a tiny notice concerning the administration of the confiscation program. But surely the question of the confiscation of church valuables was foremost in the minds of the editors of *Pravda*. Perhaps they wished to insinuate that the church had done little to help the hungry, save under pressure from the state, so that the ultimate disclosure of information about the events at Shuia would provoke feelings of indignation. The press soon began a vituperative campaign that placed the blame for resistance to the confiscation program squarely on the church hierarchy.[46] This campaign continued into the summer.

On 24 and 25 March 1922, *Izvestiia*, in fulfillment of Trotsky's proposal of 17 March, presented the official version of the events surrounding the confiscation campaign: the government's resources were limited, foreign aid had been insufficient, and "bourgeois" governments had refused to extend credits; therefore the "broad masses" had petitioned the government to use church valuables to help the hungry. The government had acceded to the people's entreaty and assured clergy and laypeople that they would be allowed to monitor the confiscation process, but a handful of "princes of the church" in collaboration with ex-merchants and ex–tsarist officials had sought to use this legitimate action as a pretext for launching a counterrevolution—even though the campaign had never been directed against the church or religion as such.[47]

Actually, each of these claims is false. The government had not used all of the resources at its disposal in famine relief, and it had refused to allow autonomous associations to participate in the antihunger campaign. Moreover, it clearly had chosen to alienate the church hierarchy and many believers instead of enlisting their support in battling the famine. Likewise, Soviet Russia could have obtained foreign credits had its leaders agreed to assume responsibility for the repayment of debts incurred by the imperial regime. The "broad masses" of Russia certainly did not provide the impetus leading to the implementation of the confiscation decree (the press did not begin to call attention to resolutions in support of confiscation until early March; and police reports indicate that few were adopted before mid-March, and that popular opinion remained divided throughout the campaign). Nor were religious leaders permitted to monitor the confiscation process. Finally, the proposals to the Politburo by Trotsky and Lenin of 17 and 19 March, respectively, make it clear that the party directed the campaign precisely against the church and religion.

In accordance with Trotsky's proposal of 17 March 1922, this antichurch campaign had two elements: to isolate the ecclesiastical hierarchy and to win over the lower clergy. Thus the GPU secretly warned the patriarch that his failure to prevent violent opposition to the confiscation campaign would result in severe punishment for him and other church leaders.[48] Meanwhile, on 24 March, *Pravda* called the higher clergy "parasites living off the blood of workers," and on 26 March the same newspaper urged militants to isolate the higher clergy from the mass of believers and from the lower clergy by accusing them of both selfishness and participation in a "definite counterrevolutionary organization." On 28 March, *Izvestiia* linked the resistance to the confiscation campaign to the "Rothschilds and international capital," the alleged "masters of the church hierarchy," and on the same day *Pravda* warned the "princes of the church" that they risked being crushed like the other remnants of the old regime. It is curious that during this intensive anticlerical propaganda campaign the press hardly mentioned the alleged relations between the church hierarchy in Russia and the Karlovatskii Sobor (the seat, as mentioned, of the monarchist Russian Orthodox Church Abroad). Only in mid-April—by which time the confiscation campaign was nearing completion—did the press begin to link the two.[49]

In the interest of avoiding conflict, some local state and party authorities apparently conducted only a superficial and perfunctory confiscation of local church valuables. Trotsky denounced such "criminal" negligence and urged the Politburo to demand that in such cases the officials return and complete the confiscation of *all* valuables from each church. By contrast, the Smolensk Gubkom presumably hewed to the spirit of the Politburo directive when it ordered local authorities to strip the churches only when "the enemy has been, by means of the enumerated methods, sufficiently terrorized."[50]

The government's policy toward the lower clergy resembled its stance vis-à-vis some non-Communist intellectuals. In 1921 a group of émigré intellectuals in Harbin, Paris, and Prague welcomed the NEP as a softening of Bolshevism, a sign that all patriotic Russians could rally to the new regime as the legitimate government of Russia. Their movement bore the name Smena Vekh, which played on the title of the famous compendium *Vekhi*, published in St. Petersburg in 1909. Beginning in November 1921 the Bolsheviks supported the movement financially, eventually turning it into a powerful magnet for drawing Russian intellectuals (both abroad and within Russia) into the service of the government.[51]

The movement, after all, further divided the émigré intelligentsia, which had never achieved anything resembling unity. Lenin understood well the dictum *divide et impera,* and in his tactical handbook of 1920, *"Left-Wing" Communism: An Infantile Disorder,* he wrote that in order to defeat their more powerful enemy (the bourgeoisie) Communists were "obligated" to exploit, "in the most painstaking, cautious, careful, and skillful fashion, any, even the smallest, fissure [*treshchiny*] among [their] enemies, [to exploit] any conflict of interests among the bourgeoisie of different countries and among various groups and types of bourgeoisie within individual countries, as well as [to exploit] any, even the slightest, possibility of acquiring a mass ally, be it temporary, vacillating, unstable, unreliable, conditional."[52] As with the émigré intelligentsia, so with the church. Already in late 1917 the Bolsheviks had begun to discriminate between "higher" and "lower" clergy and, in an effort to demoralize their ecclesiastical opponents, had begun to receive collaborators from among the "progressive" clergy.[53]

The Renovationist (*obnovlencheskoe*) movement, which Trotsky called the "Smena Vekh in the church," began with Archpriest Vvedenskii's appeal of 18 February 1922, in which he urged his ecclesiastical superiors to surrender the Orthodox church's treasures. A few other priests and bishops timidly joined Vvedenskii in urging the surrender of church valuables. Mikhail Gorev lectured in early March on "Hunger, the church Valuables, and the Karlovatskii *sobor,*" after which well-known "progressive" clergy and antireligious activists exchanged ideas.[54] Only after the incidents of resistance in Shuia, Smolensk, and elsewhere on 11–16 March 1922, however, did the embryo of a movement appear. A number of clergymen, including Frs. Aleksandr Boiarskii, Evgenii Belkov, and Vladimir Krasnitskii, and Archbishop Evdokim of Nizhnyi Novgorod, soon began to support the Bolsheviks' policy on church valuables. It will be remembered that on 12 March Trotsky recommended making every effort to provoke a schism among the clergy. It is probable that government agents contacted the above-mentioned clergymen and encouraged them to form a "pro-Soviet" ecclesiastical movement. At any rate, these clerics incessantly urged compliance with the governmental decree, criticized the ecclesiastical leadership, and actively participated in the campaign to confiscate church valuables. Some Renovationists later testified against the clergymen tried for obstructing the confiscation process.

On 25 March 1922, *Izvestiia* urged propagandists to appeal to the patriotic feelings of the lower clergy and lay leaders in order to win them over just as agitators had won over "specialists" and officers during the civil war. The same day, in Petrograd, twelve Renovationist priests were reported as advocating full cooperation with the confiscation campaign and as accusing "many church people" of "heartlessness" and of bringing politics into the church. The letter of the "twelve" became a sort of manifesto of the "progressive" clerical movement. Some official propagandists drew on the central elements of Christian moral teaching (for example, "If you have two shirts, give one to the needy") in order to persuade believers to support the confiscation campaign, and a few authors went so far as to capitalize the name "God," which usually appeared only in lowercase type.

On 30 March the VTsIK urged local officials to support the "loyal" clergy who had defended the campaign, and Bishop Antonin encouraged Patriarch Tikhon to accept President Kalinin's assurance that there would be "no persecution of religion or the religious, only a battle of ideas." It is unclear how many clergy actually believed these promises, although Vvedenskii seems to have distrusted the church hierarchs more than he did the Bolsheviks. The latter did not reciprocate: on 26 March, Trotsky warned the Politburo that the press had mistaken the Renovationists' opportunistic professions of loyalty for genuine support of the regime.[55] In other words, the Renovationists could expect no brighter a future with the Bolsheviks in power than could the patriarchal church.

In a report on Petrograd of 25 March 1922, the GPU noted that in a pastoral letter Metropolitan Veniamin had again condemned the confiscation campaign, citing Patriarch Tikhon's epistle of 28 February. The same report pointed to widespread popular discontent with living conditions and agitation against the confiscation campaign even among workers. By early April, active resistance to the confiscation campaign had diminished (but had not disappeared), although dissatisfaction with the overall material conditions of life persisted in most parts of Russia.[56] Thereafter the confiscation proceeded relatively smoothly, thanks to a shift in Bolshevik tactics.

On 3 April, for example, the VTsIK (following a letter from Trotsky) ordered officials conducting the confiscation of church valuables to avoid behavior insulting to believers, such as spitting, smoking, or failing to remove headgear or galoshes within a church. The directive also recommended appointing for this duty people raised in the religion of the church to be stripped of valuables, and it suggested beginning in a specific locality with synagogues, then proceeding to Orthodox and then to Roman Catholic churches. Also, Bishop Antonin received permission on 13 April to join the Central Committee of Pomgol.[57]

Yet the government continued to maintain pressure on the religious. On 6 April, for example, the Politburo "proposed" to the Supreme Tribunal to ensure "extraordinarily severe punishment" of the defendants in the impending trial of clergy and lay people in Saratov accused of obstructing the confiscation campaign, but added that nothing of this should come out in the press. The major dailies echoed the Politburo by demanding the punishment of those clergy who had allegedly incited people to obstruct the campaign in Shuia, Smolensk, and Moscow. This too, presumably, was meant to discourage further resistance to the decree. The combination of threats of retribution and a more diplomatic implementation of the confiscation decree seem responsible for weakening the resolve of key church leaders. Thus, on 4 April Veniamin appointed Archpriests Vvedenskii and Boiarskii (both Renovationists) as his plenipotentiaries, and the next day they signed an agreement to cooperate with Pomgol officials, who also adopted a more conciliatory attitude—at least ostensibly. The agreement gave believers the right to participate in and monitor the confiscation process. It also stated that items needed for worship, and for which ready replacements of lesser value could not be found, could remain in small number in places of worship during the time required for locating substitutes. The church could also conserve certain relics and icons, if their monetary value was slight, and a list of such items was appended. The agreement was to take effect from the moment of Veniamin's appeal to the faithful of the Petrograd Diocese (10 April), which appeared in full in *Petrogradskaia pravda* on 14 April. It should be noted, however, that despite numerous official statements to the contrary, government policy strongly and consistently discouraged local officials from permitting the substitution of various items for church valuables. One directive, for example, disallowed the substitution of food for church valuables while permitting the substitution of gold or silver.[58]

By 9 April, Patriarch Tikhon ordered church leaders to prevent resistance to the decree. Pointing out that the use of violence contradicts Christian teaching, he warned that dissatisfaction with the decree could be used to incite the Russian Orthodox faithful against ethnic minorities, especially Jews. The patriarch sent a copy of this letter to President Kalinin. He also informed the GPU in another letter that he had ordered the suppression of the Russian Church Abroad. Veniamin, in his address of 10 April to the Petrograd diocese, opposed surrendering such objects as chalices, crosses, and the like but felt obliged to comply with the more powerful state's wishes, albeit without giving his blessing to the enterprise. Nevertheless, he called on the faithful to renounce the use of violence or harsh expressions in and around churches, saying, "The Lord furnished us with beautiful objects for our churches, now He is taking them away. Hallowed be His name. Let us pray that the hungry will benefit." Archpriest Boiarskii, one of the "twelve Renovationist priests," also called on believers to surrender church valuables, asking whether believing Russians could refuse to give one hundred rubles if there was a chance that one would actually reach a starving man. In other words, none of these clergyman asserted that the valuables would actually serve to feed the hungry, yet they all chose to submit themselves, and the rest of the church, to the demands of the state. The Renovationist Boiarskii was simply more unequivocal.[59]

A large portion of the valuable objects seized from churches found their way not to the hungry but into museums. Only the staff of the Main Administration of Museums (or Glavmuzei) had the necessary expertise for appraising the valuables. Beginning in early April, Narkompros (the Commissariat of Enlightenment, or Education Ministry, its parent agency) began requesting funds to finance the added burden redounding to Glavmuzei. While Sovnarkom and VTsIK generally approved these requests, some tension did arise among these institutions. For example, on 19 April VTsIK complained that Glavmuzei had acquired a massive quantity of treasures through the confiscation of church valuables and therefore should foot the bill itself.[60] For its part, Glavmuzei repeatedly reproached clumsy and inexperienced officials for carelessly damaging priceless objects in their haste to seize them. Trotsky rejected these charges and warned that "by their very profession" many archaeologists at Glavmuzei "have close ties to church circles, possess counterrevolutionary attitudes, and seek to undermine the confiscation process." Thus, although he noted that vandalism must be avoided, Trotsky was primarily concerned with completing the confiscation campaign as quickly as possible.[61]

On 22 April, *Petrogradskaia pravda* reported that the confiscation program in Petrograd had met almost no resistance and was being carried out in an extremely peaceful manner with the cooperation of the higher clergy, including Metropolitan Veniamin. Police reports corroborate this assessment, and by the end of April the campaign had nearly been completed throughout Soviet Russia. This is significant because Veniamin was later charged with "counterrevolution" for his alleged part in the resistance to the implementation of the confiscation decree, and he was sentenced to death on that basis. Also on 22 April, *Petrogradskaia pravda* noted that the "ecclesiastical counterrevolution" had turned into a "church revolution"[62]—in other words, the alleged attempts by Orthodox clergy to overthrow the Soviet regime not only had failed, but they had brought about in a schism in the church. This was, of course, precisely what the Bolshevik leadership had hoped for.

Public "agitation" trials, where "enemies" of the new order—illiteracy, religion, Wrangel, superstition—were found guilty, mocked, and burned in effigy, became a fixture of Soviet public life. Trotsky attempted to render antireligious propaganda more effective by lending it theatrical attributes. Lenin went even further. Aware that it was not enough merely to destroy religion and that the new regime had to offer a suitable replacement, he suggested to Kalinin that perhaps only theater was capable of filling the void. A theatrical artifice to which the new Russian regime would have repeated recourse in its effort to discredit opponents and win popular support for its policies was the political trial. The resistance to the confiscation of church valuables provided the government with a suitable pretext for an all-out assault on the church, and the trials of church leaders furnished a means to legitimize that assault.[63]

On 13 April 1922, thirty-two clergy and lay leaders were summoned for hearings in Moscow on charges of obstructing the confiscation campaign. That the trial would be far from impartial is apparent from *Izvestiia*'s statement that in order to "destroy the remnants of reaction" it was best to bring them to court, for "no other propaganda (oral or written) can be as effective." Hearings soon began in Shuia as well. By midsummer, court proceedings had been or were being carried out against religious leaders in many cities throughout European Russia. The main charge against the religious leaders was "counterrevolution"—that is, activity directed at overthrowing the Bolshevik governmental order. On 25 April the Supreme Tribunal ordered local courts, in areas where resistance to the decree had broken out, to arrest church leaders "as consciously having permitted" such agitation, whether or not their direct participation could be demonstrated.[64]

At the Moscow trial (29 April to 9 May), testimony by Renovationist clergymen, including that of Bishop Antonin and Father Kalinovskii, according to whom Patriarch Tikhon's appeal not to surrender the church's valuables had had no canonical basis, was critical.[65] Equally important, however, were numerous unsubstantiated assertions that began appearing in the major dailies following Trotsky's appointment by the Politburo (on 4 May) to instruct newspaper editors to devote more coverage to the trial and to "explain the role of church hierarchs."[66]

Izvestiia reported on 9 May 1922 that eleven of the fifty-four defendants had been sentenced to death and explained that the church had carried out a systematic counterrevolutionary battle against the Soviet state.[67] These defendants were not high-ranking religious leaders but district or parish priests and laymen who allegedly had distributed Patriarch Tikhon's epistle of 28 February 1922. Following an unspecified proposal made by Bishop Antonin to President Kalinin, the Politburo on 11 May ordered the Tribunal to commute five of the eleven death sentences.[68] Almost two weeks later the Archbishop of Canterbury appealed to the Bolshevik government on behalf of Patriarch Tikhon, and similar letters from other Western church leaders followed.[69]

The trials were accompanied by an ecclesiastical coup d'état, which began in mid-May when the confiscation campaign was drawing to a close and the press had nearly ceased providing information about the famine. On 7 May, *Pravda* had noted with pleasure that the church "schism" was deepening, but it cautioned that the lower clergy still did not have an organizational center. By mid-May the Bolshevik authorities permitted the "progressive" clergy to publish a journal called *Zhivaia tserkov' (Living Church)*, a rare privilege in a country where no religious publications had appeared since 1917, and particularly given the Bolsheviks' fervent belief in the power of the printed word. The editors of the new journal did not disappoint the Bolshevik leadership—*Izvestiia* praised the "tougher, more decisive tone" and "staunch anticapitalism" of the third issue, which appeared in June. It is noteworthy that one of the new antireligious journals, *Nauka i religiia*, whose first issue appeared on 10 May, excoriated the "princes of the church" and lent support to the "progressive" clergy.[70]

Four of the Petrograd clergy (Archpriest Vvedenskii and Frs. Belkov, Kalinovskii, and Krasnitskii) succeeded in persuading Patriarch Tikhon, whom the Bolshevik authorities had arrested soon after 4 May, to renounce his office and to transfer his authority to Metropolitan Agafangel of Iaroslavl'. The four also publicly accused the entire church hierarchy of waging a "civil war" against the state. Trotsky expected this accusation to provoke a "complete schism between the democratic *smenavekhovskii* part of the church and its monarchist counterrevolutionary elements." He advocated increasing the propaganda campaign in support of the lower clergy against the higsher, "neither hiding our materialistic attitude toward religion nor proclaiming it, however, *for the current* moment."[71]

On 20 May, Renovationist clergy set up a "Temporary Higher Church Administration" (VVTsU, or VTsU) in Patriarch Tikhon's former residence at Troitskoe Podvor'e in Moscow. *Petrogradskaia pravda* pointed out that the "progressive" clergy had denounced the Karlovatskii Sobor and capitalism and that it was *"because of this* that Patriarch Tikhon had gone into retirement and church authority had passed into the hands of the VTsU" (emphasis added). Vvedenskii on 31 May stated that the entire transfer of authority had gone smoothly and without recourse to pressure tactics, and *Petrogradskaia pravda* immediately hailed the move as extremely progressive. In a 24 May report to the Politburo, Trotsky anatomized the "schism," pointing out that the "center (Antonin) and leftists (a few young priests [*popy*]) now head the church." He considered it probable that the new leaders would either elect a "loyal" patriarch or a "loyal" synod without a patriarch, or that the church would become fully decentralized without a patriarch. In order to promote further discord among the church leadership, Trotsky proposed to disallow the immediate convocation of a church sobor (which did not meet until April 1923). He expected this to divide the church between those supporting a "loyal" patriarch and those refusing to support him, leading to a fuller and more irreparable schism.[72]

Thus, with strong government backing the schism was consummated. The Living Church avoided persecution while the patriarchal church was all but outlawed. In exchange for state support the Renovationists had served the interests of the regime by fostering a schism within the church by overtly supporting the Bolshevik government and by corroborating Bolshevik claims that the higher church leaders were in league with counterrevolutionary elements in Russia and abroad. Their testimony decisively bolstered the government's case against those clergy and laypeople tried for obstructing the confiscation campaign. It also permitted the government to claim that it attacked not the church itself but only those clergymen who had broken the law. In return, many leading Renovationists obtained important positions within the church hierarchy.[73]

The last major obstacle to the consolidation of the Renovationists' authority was Metropolitan Veniamin of Petrograd, a popular, liberal prelate. On 19 May 1922, *Izvestiia* reported that Veniamin had received a summons to appear in court, and on 24 May the VTsU appointed Archpriest Vvedenskii to try to enlist the metropolitan's support for the establishment of its organization in Petrograd, the cradle of the "progressive" movement. Far from offering his blessing, however, Veniamin temporarily excommunicated Vvedenskii and other Renovationists. On 30 May, *Petrogradskaia pravda*'s headline read: "Petrograd Veniamin Lights Fire of Civil War in Country, Openly Moving Against the Part of Clergy Closest to Masses. The Punishing Hand of Proletarian Justice Will Put Him in His Proper Place." An editorial called the prelate's actions more outrageous than those of Patriarch Tikhon and warned that the whole church, with Tikhon at its head, would answer for this before the Revolutionary Tribunal. That very day the VTsU retired the prelate and replaced him with Bishop Aleksei of Iamburg, who immediately nullified his predecessor's excommunication of Renovationist clergy. The press applauded these changes; *Izvestiia* considered it "high time to finish off the princes of the church." Next the VTsU reorganized the Petrograd diocesan administration, naming Vvedenskii and other Renovationist clergy to important positions. The antireligious activist Mikhail Gorev warned that if the Renovationists could not halt the "counterrevolution in the church" the government would do so at the trials (slated to begin soon in Petrograd) against clerical and lay leaders who allegedly had obstructed the confiscation campaign in Petrograd. Of what "counterrevolution" Gorev spoke is unclear, since church leaders had cooperated with the government on the confiscation issue from late April. Likewise, it is unclear why Veniamin's resistance to the Renovationist bid to seize power within the church should be considered "counterrevolutionary." Especially since the Bolsheviks considered the Renovationists merely tolerable temporary allies to whom, as Central Committee member and antireligious activist I. V. Skvortsov-Stepanov wrote in early autumn 1922, the Bolsheviks owed nothing.[74]

On 1 June the GPU ordered its Petrograd branch to arrest Veniamin and his collaborators. Obviously, Metropolitan Veniamin's "illegal" excommunication of the Renovationists provided the Bolshevik leaders with the only pretext on which to charge him with "counterrevolution." The essence of the policy, then, was that it suited the Bolshevik leadership's purposes to support a group of clergymen for whom it felt, insofar as they were clergymen, great contempt. Yet, in the words of Skvortsov-Stepanov, the church schism, if rightly manipulated, might become as important as the defeat of Wrangel.[75]

Unlike the confiscation campaign and the church schism, which the Bolshevik press never ceased extolling as positive events, one finds no consistent picture in Bolshevik writings of the "progressive" clergy or of the Living Church. Like the Smena Vekh movement, the church Renovationists represented for the Bolsheviks an enemy that had temporarily become a tactical ally. In both cases Bolshevik propagandists portrayed these movements in two lights, now praising their support for the Bol-

shevik regime, now cautioning that they were not Communists but opportunists. In early June 1922, for example, *Izvestiia* both asserted that true
reformation would require "complete liberation from the church" and
greeted the church coup d'état (or "schism") with enthusiasm.[76]

Skvortsov-Stepanov probably spoke for most Bolsheviks when he referred to the Renovationists as clerical "Nepmen" and wrote that "religion in the pure state would still be counterrevolutionary." Yet tactically it
made sense to seek to exploit any rift among the clergy. Bolshevik propagandists even encouraged their temporary allies to develop methods of
agitation and propaganda, for the "new movement needs, as any mass
movement [does], clear, precise organization and slogans." This official
support was a small price to pay. For as *Petrogradskaia pravda* remarked
on 8 June 1922, the five-year-old Bolshevik regime, thanks to the church
schism, was finally "storming the last citadels."[77]

The second major trial of religious leaders, in which Metropolitan
Veniamin was the central figure, began on 10 June 1922 in Petrograd.
During the course of the trial eighty-nine defendants, including many
highly educated people and several important clergy and laymen, appeared
before the court. In this trial, as in the earlier trial in Moscow, the prosecution accused the defendants of using their religious authority among
backward peasants and workers to foment opposition to the government's confiscation of church valuables and ultimately to overturn the
Bolshevik regime and reinstate the monarchy. The Petrograd trial ran
parallel to the first political "show trial" in Soviet Russia, in which Socialist Revolutionaries were also accused of counterrevolution.[78]

The trial of the church opposition, which began on 10 June 1922 at
the grand State Philharmonic building in central Petrograd, was apparently the culmination of over one month's analysis of the case by six legal
researchers. Although one of the prosecuting attorneys, Petr Krasikov,
asserted that "innumerable documents" proved that the church leaders had
sought to use the famine to "stifle the revolution," according to both published and unpublished official records no such documents were introduced. The prospects for a fair trial appeared bleak: on 11 June, *Petrogradskaia pravda* carried the headline: "No Pity for Blackhundred Clergy."[79]

The state's case rested on four supports. First, it was alleged that
Veniamin's resistance to the confiscation campaign had been uncanoni-
cal. Krasikov called this a "decisive element" in the state's case against the
religious leaders in Petrograd. Yet the question of canon law was inher-
ently irrelevant, since the prosecution attributed no validity to canon law.
Second, Father Krasnitskii asserted that Veniamin had been in contact
with the Russian Church Abroad in Karlovatskii (a charge not confirmed
by other witnesses). Third, the prosecution alleged that the Society of

Orthodox Parishes of Petrograd, which Veniamin chaired, was a "counterrevolutionary . . . united front of ordinary people and the international
bourgeoisie against the existence of the Worker-Peasant regime." Fourth,
the prosecution argued that because in March 1922 believers violently
resisted implementation of the confiscation decree in several locations
simultaneously, Veniamin and other religious leaders must have organized
and inspired them.[80] In other words, none of the prosecution's major allegations could withstand intensive scrutiny.

Metropolitan Veniamin's attorney, Iakov Gurovich, submitted eloquent
briefs in defense of the prelate, arguing that Veniamin had always been
entirely apolitical, that he was widely popular, and that the patriarch had
opposed his patronage of young "progressive" clergymen. He also noted
that since Petrograd was not under martial law, the death penalty could
not be invoked. Other defense attorneys (most eloquently Professor
Zhizhilenko, who declared himself an atheist) argued that the prosecution had failed to demonstrate that the Society of Orthodox Parishes of
Petrograd had engaged in "illegal activity," that Veniamin had in any way
associated himself with the Karlovatskii Sobor, or that the defendants had
instigated popular resistance to the confiscation campaign. The official
accounts of the trial exclude any mention of these arguments and portray
the defendants as sneaky, cowardly, and bungling, and the prosecutors as
competent, clever, and fair.[81]

On 5 July the Petrograd Revolutionary Tribunal sentenced ten of the
fifty-four defendants to death, while a number of others received prison
terms of various lengths. Numerous people appealed for clemency on
behalf of the ten; one petition held 286 signatures. Even Vvedenskii oppor-
tunistically pleaded for leniency, arguing that the prelate's execution would
make him a martyr and thus "harm our [the Renovationist] cause." As a
concession to the Renovationists, the Politburo consented to spare six of
those condemned to death, but not Veniamin. Metropolitan Veniamin and
three others were shot secretly during the night of 12–13 August 1922 at
Porokhovye Station on the Irinovskii Railroad. Official notice of the execution was never issued. In all, from May 1922 to spring 1923, fifty-five
tribunals in Russia tried 231 cases involving 732 people accused of obstructing the confiscation campaign, of whom 44 were executed and 346
received prison sentences of one to five years. This of course excludes summary executions and murders, on which I have found no reliable information. It should be noted that the presidium of the Supreme Court of the
RSFSR on 31 October 1990 declared innocent of any criminal activity all
of the defendants in the Petrograd trial of 10 June to 5 July 1922.[82]

On 6 July 1922, the day after the Petrograd Revolutionary Tribunal
had sentenced to death ten defendants in the trial of the church opposi-

tion, the Politburo resolved to prepare a campaign to "collect as much grain as possible remaining in the possession of the peasants" for export.[83]

By this time both the confiscation campaign and the famine had nearly drawn to a close, though the operation had netted many fewer valuables than the authorities had expected. Indeed, an official Pomgol report admitted that the government had grossly exaggerated the quantity of valuables at the church's disposal. Another official report attributed the disappointing results to Patriarch Tikhon's alleged campaign of resistance to the confiscation decree, but, as mentioned, the resistance was short-lived, and by late April had dissipated completely. Trotsky was convinced that church officials had hidden most of the valuables during the civil war, and on 25 April 1922 he ordered an assistant to look for discrepancies in church records and for evidence of foreign bank accounts. This seems to have yielded no results. At any rate, Kalinin himself had admitted in May that most church valuables had been seized during the civil war.[84]

By August 1922 the campaign had yielded 17,000 poods (one pood equals thirty-six pounds) of silver and fourteen of gold worth a total of 1.4 million gold rubles. These figures reached 24,565 poods of silver and twenty-six of gold by April 1923, for a total value of 6,067,970 gold rubles. These were surely discouraging figures for Lenin, who, as noted above, had hoped for a yield of several hundred million or even a *billion* gold rubles. In mid-September Pomgol itself was replaced by "Posledgol," or the Committee for Struggle with the After-Effects of the Famine. Also in mid-September the press began to refer to the export of foodstuffs, and on 7 December 1922 the Politburo resolved to export up to 900,000 tons of grain. Yet the government predicted continuing hunger and therefore requested that the ARA carry on its program of feeding 3 million children through 1923. The ARA, after some difficulties with public opinion in America, complied with this request until June 1923.[85]

The Bolshevik campaign to confiscate church valuables in 1922 only partially achieved its objectives. It dealt a harsh blow to the last institution remotely capable of resisting the Bolsheviks' revolutionary designs and in the process raised much-needed capital. Moreover, the church leadership split over the issue of submitting to the demands of the state. True, the campaign met with resistance, but far less than one might have expected. It seems likely that the portrayal of the confiscation of church valuables as a means to bring aid to the hungry paralyzed potential opposition to the campaign. It is also true that the quantity of valuables seized was far smaller than the Bolshevik leaders had hoped, but even 6 million gold rubles was a significant sum for the fledgling regime.

In May 1923, Patriarch Tikhon, still under house arrest in the Don Monastery, was stripped of his monastic orders (*san*) and his patriarchal title by the Renovationist sobor. Then on 12 June an antireligious commission chaired by E. Iaroslavskii presented Tikhon an ultimatum: publicly repent of his "opposition to the Soviet state" or face trial on charges of counterrevolution. On 16 June he chose the former, and in July 1923 he declared himself a "friend of the Soviet state." So ultimately the schism in the church forced even the initially defiant patriarch to sue for peace. The government finally dropped its case against Patriarch Tikhon in March 1924, and he presided over the Russian Orthodox church until his death in April 1925. As a result of Tikhon's rehabilitation, most Living Church parishes returned to the patriarchal fold.[86]

For several years the Bolshevik government would undertake no new assaults on the church, and the latter would exist uneasily alongside the hostile Soviet state. Persecution of the church did not cease, but it would not reach its paroxysm until the collectivization drive and the Terror of the 1930s. The 1922 Bolshevik assault on the church weakened and chastened that institution, leaving no powerful centers of potential opposition in Soviet Russia.

The story of the Bolsheviks' assault on the church cannot be properly recounted without mention of their policy of spuriously presenting that assault as a popularly inspired means to alleviate hunger in Russia. The extent of the regime's misrepresentation of this issue bespeaks a profound fear that its policy utterly lacked popular support and would surely fail without the attendant propaganda campaign. Obviously governments had previously inaccurately represented their policies, especially during war time, and the word *propaganda* had first appeared in 1689 in the name "congregatio de propaganda de fide" (Congregation for the Propagation of Faith) instituted to propagate the Catholic faith. But was not the Bolshevik leaders' policy of presenting so egregiously fraudulent a picture of their policy on church valuables somehow unique and innovative among modern governments in peacetime? Alas, our twentieth century would see other flagrant misrepresentations of the course of governance, but was this not the first? We need to study this phenomenon in order to understand both its development worldwide and the role it played in the formation of Soviet political culture.

Notes

In preparing this study I benefited from the advice and criticism of Richard Stites, James Cracraft, and Richard Pipes, and I received material support from the Campus Research Board of the University of Illinois at Chicago and from the International Research and Exchanges Board (IREX), with funds provided by the National Endowment for the Humanities and the U.S. Information Agency. None of these organizations is responsible for the views expressed.

1. On Soviet propaganda as a tool of foreign policy see Frederick Barghoorn, *The Soviet Cultural Offensive: The Role of Cultural Diplomacy in Soviet Policy* (Princeton, N.J., 1960), 28–59. Peter Kenez's study concentrates on Bolshevik efforts to use propaganda to found a new culture and society, but it does not analyze critically their egregious falsifications of reality (*The Birth of the Propaganda State: Soviet Methods of Mass Mobilization, 1917–1929* [Cambridge: Cambridge University Press, 1985]). See also Richard Pipes, *Russia Under the Bolshevik Regime* (New York: Knopf, 1994), 282–336.

2. See "Ob otdelenii tserkvi ot gosudarstva i tserkvi ot shkoly" in *Kommunisticheskaia partiia i sovetskoe pravitel'stvo o religii i tserkvi* (Moscow: Gos. izd., 1959), 42–43. On the Bolshevik assault on religion see Pipes, *Russia Under the Bolshevik Regime*, 337–368.

3. GARF, f. A-353, op. 3, d. 731 and others; ibid., op. 4, d. 379, l. 3; ibid., op. 2, d. 520, l. 2. The Cheka report related to the February 1919 letter (see ibid., op. 4, d. 383, ll. 44, 46).

4. V. I. Lenin, "Ob otnoshenii rabochei partii k religii," in *Polnoe sobranie sochinenii*, 5th ed. (hereafter *PSS*]) (Moscow: Gos. izd. politicheskoi literatury, 1961), 17: 419–420. See also M. I. Shakhnovich's impressive study *Lenin i problemy idealizma. Kritika religii v trudakh V. I. Lenina* (Moscow: Izd. Akademii nauk SSSR, 1961), 9–69, 157–169, 278–356, 527–645. See also V. I. Lenin, *Religiia, tserkov' i partiia* (Moscow: Gos. izd., 1926). Lenin conveyed his personal opinion of even liberal forms of religious experience to Gorky in no uncertain terms: "Every flirtation with even an apparently decent god [*bozhen'ka*] is the most inexpressible abomination [*nevyrazimeishaia merzost'*] . . . the most dangerous abomination and the vilest contagion [*samaia gnusnaia 'zaraza'*]" (Lenin, "Pis'mo A. M. Gor'komu," November 1913, in *PSS*, 48: 226–227).

5. Lenin, "Ob otnoshenii rabochei partii k religii," 416–417.

6. The December decree is in "Tsirkuliar po voprosu ob otdelenii tserkvi ot gosudarstva," December 1918, in *Kommunisticheskaia partiia*, 45–50. For disagreements among the Bolsheviks on this question see Zenovia A. Sochor, *Revolution and Culture: The Bogdanov-Lenin Controversy* (Ithaca, N.Y.: Cornell University Press, 1988), 163; Shakhnovich, *Lenin i problemy idealizma*, 623. See the Petrograd Soviet's letter to Sovnarkom (10 August 1920, GARF, f. A-353, op. 4, doc. 379, ll. 8, 10, 33). See the programmatic issue of *Revoliutsiia i tserkov'. Ezhemesiachnyi zhurnal*, no. 1 (1919).

7. Among recent studies see Edith W. Clowes, Samuel D. Kassow, and James L. West, eds., *Between Tsar and People: Society and the Quest for Public Identity in Late Imperial Russia* (Princeton, N.J.: Princeton University Press, 1991); Charles A. Ruud, *Russian Entrepreneur: Publisher Ivan Sytin of Moscow, 1851–1934* (Montreal: McGill-Queens University Press, 1992); Louise McReynolds, *The News Under Russia's Old Regime: The Development of a Mass-Circulation Press* (Princeton, N.J.: Princeton University Press, 1991); Alfred J. Rieber, *Merchants and Entrepreneurs in Imperial Russia* (Chapel Hill: University of North Carolina Press, 1982).

8. Since both the church and the Socialist Revolutionary Party enjoyed more support and popularity among the peasantry than any other organizations, it was probably not a coincidence that the government launched massive show trials simultaneously against both church leaders and the Socialist Revolutionary leadership in 1922. On the latter trial see Marc Jansen, *A Show Trial Under Lenin: The Trial of the Socialist Revolutionaries, Moscow 1922*, Jean Sanders, trans. (The Hague: Martinus Nijhoff, 1982).

9. On Russian church-state relations at this time see John S. Curtiss, *The Russian Church and the Soviet State* (1953; reprint, Gloucester, Mass.: Peter Smith, 1965); Johannes Chrysostomus, *Kirchengeschichte Russlands der neuesten Zeit*, vol. 1: *Patriarch Tichon, 1917–1925* (Munich: Anton Pustet, 1965); A. Levitin (Krasnov) and Vadim Shavrov, *Ocherki po istorii russkoi tserkovnoi smuty* (Kusnacht, Switz.: Institut Glaube in der 2. Welt, 1977); Francis McCullagh, *The Bolshevik Persecution of Christianity*

(London: John Murray, 1924); Pipes, *Russia Under the Bolshevik Regime*, chap. 7; Mikhail Pol'skii, *Novye mucheniki rossiiskie* (Jordanville, N.Y.: Holy Trinity Monastery Press, 1949); Dmitrii Pospielovskii, *The Russian Church Under the Soviet Regime, 1917–82*, vol. 1 (Crestwood, N.Y.: St. Vladimir's Seminary Press, 1984); Lev Regel'son, *Tragediia russkoi tserkvi, 1917–45* (Paris: YMCA Press, 1977); Matthew Spinka, *The Church and the Russian Revolution* (New York: Oxford University Press, 1927); I. Stratonov, *Russkaia tserkovnaia smuta, 1921–31* (Berlin: Parabola, 1932); B. V. Titlinov, *Tserkov' vo vremia revoliutsii* (Petrograd: "Byloe," 1924).

10. On church institutions see Igor Smolitsch, *Geschichte der russische Kirche, 1700–1917* (Leiden: E. J. Brill, 1964), 359, 380; Ia. E. Bodarskii, "Zemlevedenie russkoi pravoslavnoi tserkvi i ee khoziaistvenno-ekonomicheskaia deiatel'nost' (XI-nachalo XX v.)," in A. I. Klibanov, ed., *Russkoe pravoslavie: vekhi istorii* (Moscow: Izd. politicheskoi literatury, 1989), 554–557. For Lenin's recognition of the popularity of Russian Orthodoxy see his "Ob otnoshenii rabochei partii k religii," 418–419.

11. This policy included the expulsion from Russia of Menshevik leaders, the June 1922 trial of right SR leaders, the Tenth Party Congress curtailment of dispute within the party, and the 1921–22 party purge (E. H. Carr, *The Russian Revolution, 1917–1923* [London: Macmillan, 1950–53], 1: 176–177, 180–182, 199–200).

12. Lenin to Kamenev, 2 March 1922, *PSS*, 44: 428; Lenin to Molotov, 9 to 21 April 1921, *Leninskii sbornik*, 35: 233; *Pravda*, 21 April 1921 (cited in Shakhnovich, *Lenin i problemy idealizma*, 623).

13. S. N. Prokopovich, *Narodnoe khoziastvo SSSR* (New York: Izd. im. Chekhova, 1952), 1: 156–162; H. Fisher, *The Famine in Soviet Russia, 1919–1923* (New York: Macmillan, 1927), 481–490, 497–500; Orlando Figes, *Peasant Russia, Civil War: The Volga Countryside in Revolution (1917–1921)* (Oxford: Oxford University Press, 1989), 268–273.

14. Fisher, *Famine*, 51; NKVD to Gubispolkomy, 29 June 1921 (GARF, A-353, op. 6, d. 10, l. 113). Several social activists were arrested and exiled in September and October (RTsKhIDNI, f. 17, op. 3, d. 196, l. 2; ibid., d. 219, l. 5). Regarding Bolshevik appeals for aid see GARF, f. 1235, op. 2, d. 12; ibid., d. 24, ll. 1–10.

15. 1 January 1922, p. 1; "Spasaite golodnykh," ibid., 31 January 1922.

16. On the confiscation policy see GARF, f. A-2307, op. 3, d. 131, l. 9; ibid., f. 1235, op. 2, d. 36, l. 16; RTsKhIDNI, f. 17, op. 3, d. 244, l. 5. On the efforts to sell valuables abroad see ibid., d. 242, l. 2; GARF, f. A-2307, op. 3, d. 131, l. 58. Trotsky mentions his role in Lev Trotsky, *Moia zhizn'. Opyt avtobiografii* (Berlin: izd. "Granit," 1930; Moscow: Kniga, 1990), 2: 213. The order to inventory valuables is in GARF, f. A-2307, op. 3, d. 131, l. 27. For the directive on liquidating church property see ibid., f. 1235, op. 39, d. 85, l. a-2; ibid., A-353, op. 6. d. 10. l. 113.

17. "Ocherednye zadachi Pomgol," *Pravda*, 14 January 1922, p. 1; "Ne katastrofa, a krizis," ibid., 22 January 1922; "Pomoshch' golodaiushchim i dukhovenstvo," *Izvestiia*, 26 January 1922, p. 2; "Dobraia volia i tverdaia volia," ibid., 27 January 1922, p. 1. See also ibid., 28–29 January 1922; "Intelligentsiia i golod," *Pravda*, 26 January 1922; "Neobkhodimo vypolnit' plan obshchepitaniia v golodnykh raionakh polnost'iu," ibid., 27 January 1922.

18. RTsKhIDNI, f. 17, op. 3. d. 255, ll. 1–7; Trotsky to Lenin, 30 January 1922, Trotsky Archive, Houghton Library, Harvard University, Cambridge, Mass., T-728.

19. GPU to TsKRKP, 2 March 1922, RTsKhIDNI, f. 5, op. 2, d. 48, l. 1; "Proekt iz"iatiia iz ruk chastnykh lits i ne gosudarstvennykh organizatsii zolotoi i serebriannoi valiuty i dragotsennykh izdelii iz zolota i serebria," Tatarstanskaia oblastnaia Cheka, 24 January 1922, ibid., l. 3ob; Iakovlev to Molotov, n.d., ibid., l. 4.

20. 31 January 1922, p. 1; "O bogatstvakh tserkvi," ibid., 1 February 1922, p. 3.

21. References to "popular demands" for the confiscation of church valuables

began to appear sporadically in *Pravda* between 11 February 1922 (p. 3) and 5 March (p. 2) and then became a regular feature until the end of the campaign. On government use of professional agitators see GARF, f. 1064, op. 5, d. 194, l. 48; RTsKhIDNI, f. 17, op. 3, d. 286, l. 4.

22. For the patriarch's appeal see RTsKhIDNI, f. 17, op. 3, d. 261, l. 6, 13–14; GARF, f. A-353, op. 5, d. 254, l. 4; "Bor'ba s golodom," *Izvestiia*, 15 February 1922. The immediate official response is in "Golod i tserkovnye sokrovishcha," *Pravda*, 11 February 1922. The confiscation decree was made public on 23 February (GARF, f. A-2307, op. 3, d. 131, 220–1, 289; "Khotiat otdelit'sia piatkom?" *Izvestiia*, 22 February 1922, 1; *Pravda*, 23 February 1922, 1). For Vvedenskii's appeal see "Tserkov' i golod," *Petrogradskaia pravda*, 18 February 1922, 2; RTsKhIDNI, f. 17, op. 84, d. 381, l. 10.

23. "Dva goda agit-teatra Terevsat," *Pravda*, 14 February 1922, 1; "Khleb iz zolota," *Petrogradskaia pravda*, 10 February 1922, 1.

24. "Vserossiiskaia nedelia tserkovnykh tsennostei," *Izvestiia*, 24 February 1922, 2.

25. See Tikhon's appeal in GARF, f. A-353, op. 5, d. 254, ll. 5–6. The text has been published in A. A. Valentinov, *Chernaia kniga (Shturm nebes)* (Paris: Izd. russkogo natsional'nogo studencheskogo ob"edineniia, 1925), 253–254. The VTsIK general instruction is found in GARF, f. 1235, op. 1, d. 59, l. 7. It is impossible to ascertain which—if either—of the documents was a reaction to the other, since it is unclear which appeared first.

26. 21 February 1922, 3.

27. Fisher, *Famine*, 173–194. *Izvestiia* admitted the existence of some problems, but not a crisis. "Pomoshch' golodaiushchim i transport," 16 March, 1. On the brightening agricultural indices see "Urozhai i Gaaga," *Pravda*, 8 July 1922, 1; "Sbor urozhaia," ibid., 27 July 1922, 5. *Izvestiia* predicted that some grain would be exported ("Tov. Briukhanov o novom urozhae," *Izvestiia*, 21 July 1922, 1). See also "Urozhai i perspektivy," *Pravda*, 11 August 1922, 1. On foreign aid see S. G. Wheatcroft, "Famine and Epidemic Crises in Russia, 1918–1922: The Case of Saratov," *Annales de demographie historique* (1983): 345–347. By 1 April the ARA alone had delivered more food and fodder to the famine-stricken areas than had the government itself (GARF, f. 1064, op. 3, d. 39, ll. 35, 39).

28. The mortality rate had reached 169 percent above normal by June 1921 (Wheatcroft, "Famine and Epidemic Crises," 336–341). For police reports see RTsKhIDNI, f. 17, op. 84, d. 381, ll. 14–15, 20–23; ibid., d. 340, l. 4; ibid., f. 5, op. 1, d. 2629, ll. 9–100. See also the police reports in the National Archives, Washington, D.C., "Records of the All-Union (Russian) Communist Party, Smolensk District, Records Group 1056" (hereafter Smolensk Archive), WKP 273, pp. 4, 13, 15, 22, 25, 33, 35, 40–42, 49, 50, 70, 73, 74, 80, 94, 98, 101, 103–106, 109, 114, 116, 118, 120, 126, 160.

29. 5 March 1922, GARF, f. A-353, op. 6, d. 11, l. 1.

30. RTsKhIDNI, f. 17, op. 3, d. 277, l. 3.

31. Concerning the popular resistance on 11 March see RTsKhIDNI, f. 17, op. 3, d. 286, l. 7; Iona Brikhnichev, *Patriarkh Tikhon i ego tserkov'* (Moscow: Kransnaia nov', 1923), 15; RTsKhIDNI, f. 17, op. 3, d. 280, l. 19; Trotsky Archive, T-736. Only on 22 March did *Pravda* begin to warn that "dark forces" were working to obstruct the campaign; the events in Shuia were reported only on 28 March, and those in Rostov-on-the-Don were alluded to only on 4 April. See 22 March 1922, *Pravda;* ibid., 28 March 1922, 3; "Pravitel'stvennoe soobshchenie o sobytiiakh v gorode Shuia v sviazi s iz"iatiem tserkovnykh tsennostei," *Izvestiia*, 28 March 1922, 1; ibid., "Vesennie nastroeniia," 28 March, 1; 4 April, 1922, *Pravda*, 3; 4 April 1922, *Izvestiia*, 1. Curiously, *Pravda* had also mentioned "dark forces" on 11 March ("Na golodnom fronte," *Pravda*, 11 March 1922, 2). On other confrontations see GARF, f. 1235, op. 1c, d. 60, ll. 644–646, 921–924; RTsKhIDNI, f. 17, op. 84, d. 349, l. 59; Brikhnichev, *Patriarkh Tikhon*, 17–19. Several

authors refer to 1,414 incidents of violent resistance to the decree. The first and only official reference to this number appeared in *Izvestiia*, which quoted a polemical speech by the Renovationists, Metropolitan Petr Blinov and Archpriest Vvedenskii (see "U tserkovnikov [K protsessu byvsh. patriarkha Tikhona]," *Izvestiia*, 15 April 1923, 6). Archival research has not corroborated their assertion. See the laconic press reports in *Izvestiia*, 11 March 1922, 1; *Pravda*, 12 March 1922, 3; *Petrogradskaia pravda*, 14 March 1922. For official denunciations of "church-organized conspiracies," see, for example, "Politika vysshei ierarkhii po voprosu ob iz"iatii tserkovnykh tsennostei," *Petrogradskaia pravda*, 27 May 1922, 2; "K predstoiashchemu sudu nad tserkovnikami," 9 June 1922, 4; V. D. Bonch-Bruevich, *Na boevykh postakh fevral'skoi i oktiabr'skoi revoliutsii* (Moscow: Federatsiia, 1931), 219. For the true version of the incidents of resistance see the police reports in Smolensk Archive, WKP 273, p. 128 (11 March), p. 129 (14 March), p. 130 (15 March), p. 150 (28 March), pp. 154–155 (29 March).

32. Trotsky to Politburo, 12 March 1922, RTsKhIDNI, f. 5, op. 2, d. 48, l. 10.

33. RTsKhIDNI, f. 17, op. 3, d. 282, l. 2; GARF, f. 1064, op. 5, d. 194, l. 7. See also "Iz arkhivov partii," *Izvestiia TsK KPSS*, no. 4 (1990): 195.

34. RTsKhIDNI, f. 17, op. 84, d. 381, ll. 59–60, 66; ibid., op. 3, d. 283, l. 1 (also in "Iz arkhivov partii," 194–195).

35. vol. 36: 441–412, 447; *PSS*, 45: 663; V. I. Lenin, "O znachenii voinstvuiushchego materializma," *PSS*, 45: 23–33. The essay appeared in *Pod znamenem Marksizma* (March 1922), which was created as an organ for materialist and atheistic propaganda in January 1922 (Lenin, *PSS*, 45: 504).

36. Shakhnovich, *Lenin i problemy idealizma*, 633. Two more atheist journals, *Bezbozhnik* and *Bezbozhnik u stanka*, began publication in December 1922 and early 1923, respectively. Between 1922 and 1924 more than three hundred antireligious titles were published as part of a cultural offensive that Richard Stites has termed "rather unsuccessful" (*Revolutionary Dreams: Utopian Visions and Experimental Life in the Russian Revolution* [Oxford: Oxford University Press, 1989], 105–109). The exile beginning in August of more than one hundred professors and intellectuals, many of whom were idealists and not unfavorable to religion, was surely connected with this cultural offensive (see Roger Pethybridge, *One Step Backwards, Two Steps Forward: Soviet Society and Politics in the New Economic Policy* [Oxford: Oxford University Press, 1990], 218).

37. "Blackhundreds" were prerevolutionary members of various monarchist, antirevolutionary organizations, such as the Union of Russian People (*Soiuz russkogo naroda*).

38. RTsKhIDNI, f. 2, op. 1, d. 22947, ll. 1–4. See the brief description of this document in Lenin, *PSS*, 45: 666–667. Originally revealed (but inaccurately dated) in *Vestnik russkogo studencheskogo khristianskogo dvizheniia*, no. 68 (1970): 54–63, the text appeared with commentary and archival citation in *Izvestiia TsK KPSS*, no. 4 (1990): 190–197. Curiously, n. 4 of that publication fails to indicate that Trotsky's proposal to the Politburo of 17 March antedates Lenin's (ibid., 194).

39. As it turned out, the total value of the confiscated valuables scarcely exceeded 6 million gold rubles. See below.

40. *Novde vremiia* (Belgrade), 29 January and 1 March 1922 (cited in GARF, f. A-353, op. 16, d. 10, ll. 38–40, and Stratonov, *Russkaia tserkovnaia smuta*, 46). In spring 1921, Evlogii was an archbishop; he was appointed metropolitan in January 1922 (Curtiss, *Church*, 110). Regarding the Patriarchal-Sobor controversy see N. E. Markov, *Pravda o smute tserkovnoi* (Paris: n.p., 1926), Petr I. Popov, *Karlovatskaia smuta* (Iur'ev: Tip. Ed. Bergman, 1927), and N. D. Tal'berg, *Tserkovnyi raskol* (Paris: Izd. "Doloi zlo," 1927).

41. GARF, f. 1235, op. 1, d. 59, l. 89; RTsKhIDNI, f. 17, op. 84, d. 381, l. 66; ibid., op. 3, d. 284, l. 9.

42. RTsKhIDNI, f. 5, op. 1, d. 2630, ll. 19–66; GARF, f. 1235, op. 2, d. 47, ll. 1–53;

Smolensk Archive, p. 140 (15 March), p. 143 (22 March), pp. 158, 160 (March 31), p. 176 (8 April), p. 208 (24 April).

43. Publicity was in fact slight (see *Izvestiia*, 1 April 1922, p. 2). Only on 20 May did *Petrogradskaia pravda* report that the first sixteen railroad cars full of food for the hungry had been purchased with the proceeds of the confiscated church treasures and had left Finland on route for Moscow.

44. RTsKhIDNI, f. 17, op. 3, d. 285, l. 13.

45. "Ruka daiushchego da ne oskudevaet," "Itogi borby s golodom i perspektivy," "V shtabe Golodnogo fronta," and "Dukhovenstvo i golod," *Izvestiia*, 15 March 1922, 1–5.

46. *Pravda*, 21 March, 1–2; see also *Izvestiia*, 21 March 1922, 2–3; "Khleb nasushchnyi dlia golodaiushchikh" and "Zoloto tserkvi na pomoshch golodaiushchim," ibid., 21 March 1922, 1. *Petrogradskaia pravda* began this campaign earlier ("Nashi khristiane," 16 March 1922, 1).

47. "K voprosy ob iz"iatii tserkovnykh tsennostei," *Izvestiia*, 24 March 1922, 1. See also the interview with Kalinin (ibid., 25 March 1922, 2).

48. Letter of 28 March 1922, KGB Archive (cited in M. I. Odintsev, "Delo Patriarkha Tikhona," *Otechestvennye arkhivy*, no. 6 [1993]: 59).

49. "Zhestokovinost' dukhovnaia," *Pravda*, 24 March 1922, 1; "K iz"iatiiu tserkovnykh tsennostei," *Pravda*, 26 March 1922, 1; "Sviateishaia kontrrevoliutsiia," *Izvestiia*, 28 March 1922, 2; *Pravda*, 28 March 1922, 3; P. A. Krasikov, "Pozitsiia ierarkhov," *Pravda*, 11 April 1922, 1. A *Pravda* editorial on 12 May recounted a new version of the events surrounding the confiscation campaign, this time with the Karlovatskii group as an integral actor ("Pod sudom," 12 May 1922, 1).

50. Trotsky to Politburo, 26 March, RTsKhIDNI, f. 17, op. 3, d. 286, l. 9; Kamenev to VTsIK, 30 March, GARF, f. 1235, op. 1, d. 59, l. 18; Smolensk gubkom directive, 26 March 1922, RTsKhIDNI, f. 17, op. 84, d. 354, l. 3.

51. On "Smena vekh" see Robert C. Williams, *Culture in Exile: Russian Emigres in Germany, 1881–1941* (Ithaca, N.Y.: Cornell University Press, 1972), 263–275. For a critique of "Smena vekh" by one of the original *Vekhi* authors see A. S. Izgoev, "Vekhi i Smena vekh," in *O smene vekh* (Petrograd: Logos, 1922), 7–24. For documents concerning Bolshevik government support of "Smena vekh" consult RTsKhIDNI, f. 17, op. 3, d. 233, l. 1; ibid., d. 260, l. 3; ibid., d. 261, l. 1; ibid., d. 278, l. 4. In November 1921 the press spoke favorably of the movement, noting that Marx and Engels had foreseen a "part of the old ruling class coming over to the class to whom history belongs" ("'Smena vekh' v mirovoi istorii," *Petrogradskaia pravda*, 20 November 1921, 1; see also "Eshche o 'Smene vekh'," *Pravda*, 19 November 1921, 1).

52. The leader of Smena vekh, the erstwhile Kolchak partisan N. V. Ustrialov, wrote that it behooved the group to divide the emigration and "reconcile [it] to the Soviet government" (Williams, *Culture*, 265–267). Lenin's strategy of "divide and rule" is formulated in *Detskaia bolezn' "levizny" v kommunizme* (Lenin, *PSS*, 41: 54).

53. Father M. Galkin (Gorev), who became one of the major Bolshevik antireligious activists, was the first such convert. He joined the Justice Commissariat's Eighth Department (for the liquidation of institutions of the old regime) in 1918 (Shakhnovich, *Lenin i problemy idealizma*, 565, 626).

54. Trotsky to Politburo, 15 May 1922, RTsKhIDNI, f. 2, op. 1, d. 27072 (cited in "Iz arkhivov partii," *Izvestiia TsK KPSS*, no. 4 [1990]: 196–197; see also I. I. Skvortsov-Stepanov, *Zadachi i metody antireligioznoi propagandy* [Moscow, 1925], 17–28). V. N. Lvov, Ober-Prokurator under the Provisional Government, was both a *smenavekhovets* and a Renovationist (*Izvestiia*, 29 April 1922, 2, 23 June 1922, 5); "Vserossiiskii s"ezd 'Zhivoi tserkvi'," *Pravda*, 10 August 1922, 4. For Vvedenskii's appeal see "Tserkov i golod," *Petrogradskaia pravda*, 18 February 1922, *Izvestiia*, 18 February, 2, and *Pravda*, 19 February 1922, 1. *Izvestiia* reported on Gorev's lecture (7 March 1922, 2).

55. See the "Twelve's" appeal in "Ob agitatsii v sviazi s iz"iatiem tserkovnykh tsennostei" (*Izvestiia*, 25 March 1922, 2; *Petrogradskaia pravda*, 25 March 1922, 1–2). *Pravda* had printed Bishop Evdokim's appeal in part on 22 March 1922 (p. 2). *Izvestiia* reprinted both on 29 March (p. 2). The term *progressive* was used primarily by Bolshevik propagandists, whereas both the latter and the clergy who supported Bolshevik policy on the confiscation of valuables employed the term *Renovationist* (*obnovlencheskoe*). The Renovationist movement arose after the turn of the century and enjoyed significant influence during the 1917–18 Church Sobor, but it became especially influential thanks to Bolshevik support beginning in May 1922 (see James W. Cunningham, *A Vanquished Hope: The Movement for Church Renewal in Russia, 1905–1906* [Crestwood, N.Y.: St. Vladimir's Seminary Press, 1981], and Catherine Evtuhov, "The Church in the Russian Revolution: Arguments for and Against Restoring the Patriarchate at the Church Council of 1917–8," *Slavic Review* 50 [Fall 1991]: 497–511). For an official reference to Christian moral teaching see, for example, "Na golodnom fronte," *Pravda*, 26 March 1922, 3. See the VTsIK directive of 30 March 1922, in GARF, f. 1235, op. 1, d. 59, l. 20. Antonin's letter is published as "Obrashchenie k patriarkhu Tikhonu," *Izvestiia*, 30 March 1922, 3; "Privlechenie ep. Antonina k rabote v TsKPomgol," ibid., 29 March 1922, 2.

Regarding Vvedenskii's views see A. I. Vvedenskii, *Tserkov' i gosudarstvo. Ocherk vzaimo-otnoshenii tserkvi i gosudarstva v Rossii, 1918–1922* (Moscow: Krasnyi proletarii, 1923), 244–246. Trotsky's letter to the Politburo is in RTsKhIDNI, f. 17, op. 3, d. 286, l. 9.

56. GPU report, 22 March 1922, GARF, f. 1235, op. 2, d. 47, l. 53. For GPU reports in April see RTsKhIDNI, f. 5, op. 1, d. 2631, ll. 1–64; GARF, f. 1235, op. 2, d. 47, ll. 1–53; Smolensk Archive, WKP 273, p. 172 (6 April), p. 189 (15 April), p. 191 (15 April).

57. VTsIK directive, 3 April 1922, GARF, f. 1235, op. 1, d. 59, ll. 16, 37–38. Roman Catholics seemed to offer the most tenacious resistance to the decree. The VTsIK's order concerning Antonin is in GARF, f. 1064, op. 5, d. 194, l. 34.

58. Politburo order, 6 April 1922, RTsKhIDNI, f. 17, op. 3, d. 287, l. 9. For press demands for the punishment of implicated clergy see "Dovol'no," *Izvestiia*, 2 April 1922, 1; "Kak oni boriatsia," *Izvestiia*, 4 April 1922, 1. On Veniamin's appointment of Vvedenskii and Boiarskii see GARF, f. A-353, op. 6, d. 11, ll. 56–56 ob. The text of their agreement with Pomgol is printed in "Soglashenie ob iz"iatii tsennostei iz tserkvei," *Petrogradskaia pravda*, 14 April 1922, 2. Veniamin's appeal is found in "Vozzvanie mitropolita Veniamina petrogradskoi pravoslavnoi pastve," ibid., 14 April 1922, 2. For the official policy on substitutions see the directive of 12 May 1922, in GARF, f. 1064, op. 5, d. 194, l. 7.

59. See Tikhon's letters in GARF, f. A-353, op. 6, d. 11, ll. 124–126. The major dailies did not print Veniamin's appeal (ibid., ll. 57–58, and "Soglashenie ob iz"iatii tsennostei iz tserkvei," *Petrogradskaia pravda*, 14 April 1922, 2). See Boiarskii's appeal in ibid., 14 April 1922.

60. GARF, f. A-2306, op. 1, d. 1140, ll. 3–5, 17–21; ibid., f. 2307, op. 3, d. 131, l. 100–102.

61. Discord continued from March through August: GARF, f. 1235, op. 1, d. 59, l. 98; ibid., f. A-2307, op. 3, d. 131, l. 114–115; ibid., op. 8, d. 23, ll. 99, 118.

62. "Iz"iatie tsennostei," *Petrogradskaia pravda*, 22 April 1922, 1. For a similar assessment see "V Petrograde," *Pravda*, 23 April 1922, 2. For police reports see RTsKhIDNI, f. 17, op. 83, d. 349, l. 47; ibid., f. 5, op. 1, d. 2631, ll. 117–181.

63. On Bolshevik agitation trials see Claudine Chevrel-Amiand, "Méthodes et formes spécifiques," in *Le Théâtre d'agit-prop de 1917–32*, vol. 1: "URSS Recherches," edited by "Equipe moderne" of the CNRS (Paris: La Cité-l'Age d'homme, 1977), 49–61, esp. 52–54. On Trotsky and antireligious propaganda see Rene Füllöp-Miller, *The Mind and Face of Bolshevism: An Examination of Cultural Life in Soviet Russia* (New York:

Harper and Row, 1965), 135–151, 190–192. For Lenin's views on the matter see *Lenin i iskusstvo* (Leningrad: Izd. pisatelei, 1934), 169 (cited in Shakhnovich, *Lenin i problemy idealizma*, 595). For an example of the official assault on the church see "Kontr-revoliutsiia pod tserkovnym flagom," *Izvestiia*, 13 May 1922, 2.

64. GARF, f. A-353, op. 6, d. 6, l. 12.

65. "Na golodnom fronte," *Pravda*, 22 April 1922; "Sudebnyi otdel," *Izvestiia*, 29 April 1922, 3; "Sudebnyi otdel," *Izvestiia*, 3 May 1922, 4.

66. RTsKhIDNI, f. 17, op. 3, d. 291, l. 2; "Genshtab kontrrevoliutsii," *Izvestiia*, 6 May 1922, 1; "Kontrrevoliutsiia pod tserkovnym flagom," *Izvestiia*, 9 May 1922, 3; "Zagovor i sud," *Pravda*, 6 May 1922, 1; "Sudebnyi otdel," *Pravda*, 6 May 1922, 4; "Raskol v dukhovenstve," *Pravda*, 7 May 1922, 1. See also "Komu pomogaiut te, kto protivitsia obmenu tserkovnykh tsennostei na khleb dlia golodaiushchikh," in P. A. Krasikov, *Na tserkovnom fronte (1918–1923)* (Moscow: "Mysl' pechatnika," 1923), 217; Krasikov, "Pozitsiia ierarkhov," in *Pravda*, 225.

67. "Kontrrevoliutsiia pod tserkovnym flagom," *Izvestiia*, 9 May 1922, 3. This became a regular column beginning 6 May; *Pravda* carried a similar rubric ("Sviateish-aia kontrrevoliutsiia") beginning 7 May.

68. RTsKhIDNI, f. 17, op. 3, d. 292, l. 4; "Kontrrevoliutsiia pod tserkovnym flagom," *Izvestiia*, 12 May 1922, 2.

69. The *Times* (London), 29 May 1922, p. 9, 1 June, p. 10, 8 June, p. 7, and 20 June, p. 9.

70. On the church "coup d'état" see Levitin, *Ocherki*, 77–119; Spinka, *Church*, 207; Curtiss, *Church*, 129–156. Regarding official support for the schism see "Raskol v dukhovenstve," *Pravda*, 7 May 1922, 1. For official assessments of *Zhivaia tserkov'* see "Kontrrevoliutsiia pod tserkovnym flagom," *Izvestiia*, 13 May 1922, 2; P. A. Krasikov, "Golod i khristianstvo," *Na tserkovnom fronte*, 199. On 13 September 1921, Lenin had approved a Politburo decree ordering local officials to pulp religious and pornographic books seized after October 1917 (*Leninskii sbornik*, 36: 319). For *Izvestiia*'s assessment of the journal's third issue see "Tserkovnye dela," *Izvestiia*, 4 June 1922, 2. For *Nauka i religiia*'s excoriation of the "princes of the church" see "Tserkovnoe zoloto golodaiushchim," no. 1 (1922).

71. On Tikhon's arrest see RTsKhIDNI, f. 17, op. 3, d. 291, l. 2; "Kontrrevoliutsiia pod tserkovnym flagom," *Izvestiia*, 9 May 1922, 3. On his transfer of authority see "Schel za blago," *Petrogradskaia pravda*, 17 May 1922, 1. The four Renovationists' public condemnation of the church hierarchy is printed as "Veruiushchim synam pravoslavnoi tserkvi Rossii," *Pravda*, 14 May 1922, 1. An editorial note warned that the appeal contained "religious prejudice" yet urged all believers to read it. Trotsky's recommendations are in Trotsky to Politburo, 14 May 1922, RTsKhIDNI, f. 2, op. 1, d. 27072 (cited in "Iz arkhivov partii, *Izvestiia TsK KPSS*, no. 5 [1990]:196–197). Emphasis in the original.

72. On the takeover of the patriarchal church offices see *Petrogradskaia pravda*, 20 May 1922, 1; *Izvestiia*, 21 May 1922, 1; *Pravda*, May 21, 1922, 1. *Pravda*'s initial reaction to this was guarded (ibid., "Kem i zachem byl izbran patriarkh," 19 May 1922, 1), but *Petrogradskaia pravda*'s was not (*Petrogradskaia pravda*, 20 May 1922, 1; "Perelom v tserkvi," ibid., 31 May 1922, 1; "Peredacha Patriarkhom Tikhonom upravleniia tserkvi," ibid., 20 May 1922, 2). Trotsky's report to the Politburo is available in RTsKhIDNI, f. 17, op. 3, d. 294, ll. 9–10. On the sobor see Curtiss, *Church*, 154–158.

73. S. V. Troitskii, *Chto takoe "Zhivaia Tserkov'?"* (Warsaw: Sinodal'naia tip., 1927), 11. Joseph Douillet met many Roman Catholic and Orthodox clergy in Bolshevik prisons, but no Renovationists. Many of the former had been imprisoned for refusing to swear allegiance to the Living Church movement (Joseph Douillet, *Moscou sans voiles [neuf ans de travail au pays des Soviets]* [Paris: Spes, 1928], 146). See also Mikhail

Pol'skii, *Polozhenie Tserkvi v Sovetskoi Rossii. Ocherk bezhavshego iz Rossii sviashchen-nika* (Jerusalem: Izd. avtora, 1931), 12–13. Vvedenskii became metropolitan of Siberia on 16 July, and the Living Church Congress in August retired thirty-six ecclesiastical hierarchs (for a total of sixty retired since the creation of the Living Church) (*Pravda*, 18 July 1922, 6; *Pravda*, 16 July 1922, 4; "S"ezd Zhivoi tserkvi," *Pravda*, 17 August, 2).

74. Skvortsov-Stepanov, *Zadachi i metody*, 24.

75. GPU order, 1 June 1922, GARF, f. A-353, op. 6, d. 11, l. 127; I. V. Skvortsov-Stepanov, *O "Zhivoi tserkvi"* (Moscow, 1922), 5 (cited in Chrysostomus, *Kirchen-geschichte*, 192).

76. Trifonov's characterization of the church schism as having been caused by an "anti-religious movement of the popular masses coupled with a blow by the Soviet government against religion" is typical (I. Trifonov, *Ocherki istorii klassovoi borby v SSSR v gody Nepa [1921–37]* [Moscow: Gospolitizdat, 1960], 35). For official Bolshevik portrayals of the "Smena vekh" and the Living Church movements see "Russkaia intelligentsiia, emigratsiia, 'Smena vekh'," *Izvestiia*, 29 June 1922, 4; *Pravda*, "O 'smene vekh'," 28 June 1922, 1; Iaroslavskii, *Razvernutym frontom*, 37–38; Vladimir Bonch-Bruevich, *"Zhivaia tserkov" i proletariat*, 2nd ed., (Moscow: Zhizn' i znanie, 1924), 15–19; Skvortsov-Stepanov, *Zadachi i metody*, 17–18; P. A. Krasikov, "Golod i khristianstvo," 198. For press advocacy of church renovation see "V. I. Belavin (patriarkh Tikhon)," *Izvestiia*, 2 June 1922, 2, and "Tserkovnaia revoliutsiia, ee vragi i druz'ia," *Izvestiia*, 4 June 1922, 2.

77. Skvortsov-Stepanov, *Zadachi i metody*, 19–20, 28. Bonch-Bruevich declared that the proletariat needed "neither a living, nor dead, nor new, nor old church" (*Zhivaia tserkov*, 63). For the official discussion of the Living Church's need for propaganda see *Pravda*, "Tserkov na novykh putiakh," 17 May 1922, 1. The reference to "storming the last citadels" is in "Sud nad tserkovnikami," *Petrogradskaia pravda*, 8 June 1922, 1.

78. For a detailed eye-witness account, recently published from a manuscript in the Russian State Archive of Literature and Art (RGALI) see *"Delo" Mitropolita Veni-amina (Petrograd, 1922 g.)* (Moscow: "Rossiiskii Arkhiv," 1991). During the height of the Petrograd church trial even *Petrogradskaia pravda* devoted far more space to information concerning the concurrent Socialist-Revolutionary trial in Moscow (which ran from 8 June to 7 August). Three Socialist lawyers were permitted to represent the SR leaders. This fact assured intensive coverage of the trial in the West European press, thus opening up the new Bolshevik order for inspection abroad. The Bolshevik press in turn devoted massive coverage to the trial in an almost frantic effort to justify the case against the defendants.

79. Krasikov, "Golod i khristianstvo," 195. Krasikov was head of the Fifth Section of the Commissariat of Justice, which was charged with implementing the decree on the separation of the church and state (A. M. Gindin, *Petr Krasikov. Zhizn i revoliut-sionnaia deiatelnost'* [Krasnoiarsk: Knizhnoe izd., 1972], 257–258). The official record of the trial is in "Protsess Petrogradskogo dukhovenstva (mitr. Veniamin i dr.) v sviazi s iziatiem tsennostei" (*Revoliutsiia i tserkov'*, 1–3 [1923]). For unpublished materials see GARF, f. A-353, op. 6, d. 11. The condemnatory headline appeared in *Petrogradskaia pravda*, 11 June 1922, 3. The same newspaper noted on 1 June that, while the trial of the SRs had not yet begun, the working class had already passed judgment" ("Ognen-nye slova," 1 June 1922, 1).

80. "Protsess Petrogradskogo dukhovenstva," *Revoliutsiia i tserkov'*, 62–68, 72, 79–80, 97; *Izvestiia*, 13 August 1922; "K predstoiashchemu sudu nad tserkovnikami," *Petrogradskaia pravda*, 7 June 1922, 4; "Sud nad tserkovnikami," ibid., 13 June 1922, 3; *"Delo" Mitropolita Veniamina*, 54–63.

81. GARF, f. A-353, op. 6, d. 11, ll. 12–13 ob, 86–87, 108–114, 131–139, 161;

"Protsess Petrogradskogo dukhovenstva," *Revoliutsiia i tserkov'*, 79–97; *"Delo" Mitropolita Veniamina*, 64–79.

82. On the court sentences see *"Delo" Mitropolita Veniamina*, 84–88; "Protsess Petrogradskogo dukhovenstva," *Revoliutsiia i tserkov'*, 101. See the appeals for clemency in GARF, f. A-353, op. 6, d. 11, ll. 12–13 ob, 42–47, 64–65 ob, 78–78 ob, 131–136, 140–161. The Politburo decision may be found in RTsKhIDNI, f. 17, op. 3, d. 303, l. 9. Regarding the executions see *"Delo" Mitropolita Veniamina*, 93; Polskii, *Mucheniki*, 56–57; McCullagh, *Persecution*, 52. Also executed were Archimandrite Sergei (V. P. Shein), a former member of the State Duma; Professor Iu. L. Novitskii of Petrograd University; and I. M. Kovsharov, a former attorney, and legal counsel of the Alexander Nevskii Lavra. For trial statistics see Brikhnichev, *Patriarkh Tikhon*, 19. A few cases were still pending as the latter book went to press in 1923. Reference to the posthumous exoneration is in *Nauka i religiia*, no. 5 (1991): 5–9.

83. RTsKhIDNI, f. 17, op. 3, d. 302, l. 1.

84. S. Ingunov, "Agitatsionnaia kampaniia Pomgola," *Itogi borby s golodom v 1921–1922 gg. Sbornik statei i otchetov* (Moscow: Izd. TsK Pomgol, 1922), 155; TsK Posledgol, GARF, f. 1065, op. 4, d. 31, ll. 139–141; Trotsky to Unshlikht, 25 April 1922, ibid., f. 1235, op. 1, d. 59, l. 57; "Rech' pri otkrytii 3-i sessii VTsIK, IX sozyva, 12 maia 1922 g.," Kalinin, *Stat'i i rechi*, 84–85. Patriarch Tikhon had also cautioned that the church valuables, being mostly of silver, were worth less than was generally supposed ("Tserkovnye tsennosti dlia pomoshchi golodaiushchim," *Izvestiia*, 15 March 1922, 5).

85. See these statistics in "Khronika," *Pravda*, 9 August 1922, 5. This was just over 330 million paper rubles at the current official rate of 220 paper to one gold ruble (M. B. B., "Der misslungene Versuch zur Vernichtung der Russisch-Orthodoxen Kirche in den Jahren 1922–1923 und die Niederlage des linken Kommunismus," *Ostkirchliche Studien* 22 [September 1973]: 129). The second set of statistics is available in GARF, f. 1065, op. 4, d. 33, l. 34; *Itogi bor'by*, 435–436. It is unclear what happened to the bulk of the valuables. By July 1922, apparently none had yet been sold abroad (GARF, f. A-2307, op. 3, d. 266, l. 97). On the institutional reorganization see Politburo order, 7 September 1922, RTsKhIDNI, f. 17, op. 3, d. 311, l. 1. Reference to the export of grain may be found in "Bor'ba s posledstviiami goloda," *Izvestiia*, 14 September 1922, 4; "Ekonomicheskii front," ibid., 14 September 1922, 2 (on this see also Pethybridge, *One step Backwards*, 116–117). See the Politburo resolution to export grain in RTsKhIDNI, f. 17, op. 3, d. 325, l. 2; ibid., d. 327, l. 2. Fisher concluded that the Bolshevik government had fabricated the idea of a continuation of the famine in order to ensure continued ARA grain shipments. William N. Haskell, ARA director for Russia, cabled a message to New York in early 1923 urging the suppression of Soviet correspondence concerning the grain exports, since he felt it might turn public opinion against the program (Fisher, *Famine*, 315–329, 352, 373).

86. The Commission for (*po provedeniiu*) the Separation of the church from the State was created in October 1922 (see Odintsov, "Delo Patriarkha Tikhona," 51). On Tikhon's exoneration see VTsIK order, 21 March 1922, GARF, f. A-353, op. 5, d. 254, ll. 11–12, and Odintsov, "Delo Patriarkha Tikhona," 64–7. On the withering of the Living Church movement see Gregory L. Freeze, "Counter-Reformation in Russian Orthodoxy: Popular Response to Religious Innovation, 1922–1925," paper presented to the AAASS National Convention, November 1993. This paper appeared in *Slavic Review* 54 (Summer 1995): 305–339.

Five

Ideology, Mentality, and Culture

DMITRY SHLAPENTOKH

Bolshevism, Nationalism, and Statism: Soviet Ideology in Formation

13

T
he glue that holds any society together is its ideological paradigms. The cohesive nature of these paradigms perhaps lies in the fact that they invariably take on the overtones of religious dogma. In fact, one could say that all the great ideological paradigms of modern times are rife with certain dogmatic principles, whether the paradigm is eighteenth-century liberalism and its "All people are created equal" or Marxism and its "Proletariat of all countries unite." Moreover, at the time when a political ideology is born, there is usually no difference between the sacred shibboleth of the faith and its pragmatic application to life—that is, to what extent the particular ideology can be made to fit the strain of changing reality. Later—and the moment usually comes soon after the political movement's victory—the ideological paradigm undergoes a transformation, a fracturing into layers.

The first layer contains the most cherished paradigms, the sacred symbols of the movement. Even though they may become detached from real political and economic discourse, they may be preserved in their purity indefinitely, for no one dares to challenge their validity. They constitute "pure" ideology in the sense that they provide a link to the founding fathers and legitimize the political reality that develops over time.

The second ideological layer could be called "functional" ideology. While the ideological paradigms of the founding fathers tend to stay the same and, in some cases, ossify to the degree of religious dogma, every society developing and changing. Thus, a split from the pure aspects of the ideology develops as soon as those who have carried out the principles of the ideological paradigm have come to power. The leader of the movement needs to explain and justify his political activity to the media, so he calls on the ideological paradigms inherited from the founding fathers. Of course some of these paradigms might well suit the explaining of the political reality; however, quite a few have little to do with the real development of events. The initial paradigm must evolve, then, and this evolution can take several different routes.

The first way (definitely the easiest route for the movement's leaders) is merely to modify the initial paradigm to fit the changing reality. A second method would be to attempt to incorporate the tenets of the old paradigm into a new one. Though the new paradigm that results might seem to be absolutely at odds with the old one, they could coexist until a new ideological synthesis could emerge. The history of the incorporation of nationalism into the Soviet brand of Marxism serves as a good example of this sort of ideological cohabitation. The ideological child it finally produced could be called National Bolshevism.

From Worldwide Revolution to the Revolutionary State

Nationalism is a complicated and diversified phenomenon. Since its emergence in the modern era, the term itself has been interpreted broadly. Yet regardless of its particular political context, nationalism is inseparable from the idea of the state. Thus the emergence of nationalism in the historical context of Soviet Russia is inseparable from the restoration of the state to its legitimate right. The history of the French Revolution, which had fascinated Russian revolutionaries for generations, provided the Bolsheviks with the historical backdrop needed for understanding how to restore the state to its paramount position.

Marxism, the Bolsheviks' political and quasi-religious doctrine, originally had an ambiguous vision of the state and downplayed its role in any social upheaval. As Marx believed that a "dictatorship of the proletariat" was a prerequisite for a proletarian victory in the Socialist revolution, he can hardly be accused of ignoring the role of the state. Yet the state was secondary in Marx's overall picture of history, especially in his vision of the coming worldwide revolution.

His deemphasis of the state's role had several reasons. Marx considered the state tightly connected to the ruling social group and bound to civic society. While it would be unfair to ignore Marx's understanding that the state had a certain independence from civic society, it would be wrong to assume that Marx saw the state as powerful enough to force its change. The state could change civic society only to a limited degree; in general it had to follow orders, so to speak, from the the ruling class. Another reason Marx disregarded the role of the state as important to the historical process was his vision of the party. As in the case with the state, Marx's vision of the party was certainly ambiguous. On one hand, Marx—in his teaching and even more so in his political activity—emphasized the role of the party, seeing it as the means to educate the proletariat about its mission: to become the class "for itself." On the other hand, Marx deemphasized the role of the party, for he believed that once the proletariat reached its social maturity there would be no need for a party, at least not as a body distinct from the masses. The party would naturally dissolve into the proletariat. Second, the party was never meant to become tightly structured and bureaucratically rigid. Indeed, the stress was on the free unity of fellow communists bound together by common ideological strands. It was here that Lenin, who emphasized the need for a strong political party as a prerequisite for victory, differed from Marx. And it was the idea of a strong party that provided Lenin with an appreciation for the state. Lenin's contribution, if not to Marxist theory then at least to the tactics of revolutionary struggle, was his theory of party. Lenin made the idea of the party into the cornerstone of Bolshevik doctrine. Lenin's teachings about its role were a reflection of the Bolsheviks' and other revolutionaries' position in imperial Russia.

Marx's ambiguity about the role of the state and the party was due to the spread of democratic tradition in late-nineteenth-century Europe. At the time, the fate of an increasing number of Western European governments was being defined by civic society—that is, by forces from below rather than from above. Lenin lived in a country cast from an opposite mold entirely. The authoritarian streak running through Russian political tradition, which had always enhanced the state's paramount position, had a profound effect on the nature of the revolutionary movement. This authoritarian streak was certainly passed along to Russian revolutionaries, but in their case it developed into a sort of embryonic statism. Russian revolutionaries naturally assumed that the state would play an important and a perhaps decisive role in any social upheaval.

The imperial regime's strong statist element also influenced the revolutionary movement in other ways. First, the absence of political freedom in Russia either precluded or at least seriously hindered the development of legal social-democratic parties. This lack certainly provided the inducement to create a strong bureaucratically regimented underground party. Second, the very nature of the Russian state, its ability to mold civic society to its own liking, inspired some Russian revolutionaries, Lenin included, to see the revolutionary party and, consequently, the revolutionary state as a powerful force in future changes. One could even argue that Lenin's strong party and his belief in its leading role was a transmutation of the imperial government's statism. This imperial tradition was perhaps behind the revolutionary government's stress on patriotic ardor and military tradition and helped transform Bolshevism into a sort of patriotic Jacobinism, a development that became the first step in transforming the internationalism of Marxism into its Nationalist Bolshevist modification.

From National Jacobinism to National Bonapartism

Though the idea of a strong government had occurred to Lenin long before the victory in 1917, it took time to materialize. The Bolsheviks had come to power in the wake of a social upheaval that had strong antistatist and, in many cases, anarchistic overtones. Thus, the Bolsheviks' leaders had followed the masses' lead and denied any attachment to strong government and the tradition of military conquest in the Jacobinic fashion of the French Revolution. Their antistatist and antimilitary remarks were a sort of revolutionary shibboleth. Instead, it was the Provisional Government, the Bolsheviks' enemy, that tried to don the clothing of revolutionary Jacobins.

Indeed, many supporters of the Provisional Government looked for a Russian Napoleon to restore the glory of the army (Alexander Kerensky and Lavr Kornilov were seen as the most likely candidates). Jacobins were praised not for their revolutionary activity but for restoring discipline in the army. In short, many people were willing to welcome terror from any side and under any slogan if it would restore order in the army and save Russia from disintegration or make it safe from foreign conquest, or both. By the autumn of 1917, however, ideas about a strong nationalistic government were out of favor entirely. The Bolsheviks came to power behind slogans calling for the discarding of the standing army and for universal peace as the prerequisite for worldwide revolution. During the first months of the Bolsheviks' regime the general anarchy and the disintegration of the army continued unabated. The humiliating Brest Litovsk Treaty signed by Lenin was a sign of the new regime's weakness. To many Russians the Bolsheviks seemed willing to betray the national interest and turn Russia into a German colony while hiding behind utopian slogans of worldwide revolution. The new rulers also seemed either unwilling or unable to stop the anarchic behavior spreading throughout the country. But then came the Red Terror, and everything changed drastically.

The Red Terror was officially aimed at organized counterrevolution. But it was members of the middle and upper classes who were dubbed the enemy. Several hundred were shot in Petrograd alone during the first few days of the terror. Political parties opposed to the regime (and they included all parties in Russia) were also decimated. Yet the terror had an even broader implication: it was also seen as the means to curb the antisocial proclivities of the populace in general. After their ascendance to power, along with their move against organized opposition and the crackdown on the local separatists, the Bolsheviks put down the drunken riots in Petrograd and attempted to eradicate the drunkenness and crime spreading throughout the country. They increased this emphasis on order after the inauguration of the Reign of Terror in August and September 1918, when they suppressed the workers' movement, reinstituted the military draft, and introduced harsh discipline in the army. In the eyes of the military officers and others, the Bolsheviks were now no longer the party of radical change but rather the party of order. Indeed, their conflicts with workers and fellow Socialists (the Mensheviks) were fairly close to what Kornilov and those on the right had wanted. Some observers of the Bolsheviks—for example, B. Maklakov, a prominent liberal—even saw them as conservative forces with a harsh disciplinary nature. He wrote that the "new government [has] started to restore the state apparatus, to recreate order. In this realm they exhibit energy and even talent."[1] Such thinkers as Maklakov viewed the radicalism symbolized in the Bolsheviks' claim to represent workers and peasants and their supposed goal for a worldwide revolution as perhaps merely slogans. At the very least, their harsh disciplinary nature could be seen as a temporary aberration in Bolshevik policy. Some even thought that this harshness, overlaid with apparent patriotism, was a manifestation of the regime's very essence. Further developments in the Soviet system, as well as the course of time, seem to favor the latter opinion.

Among those who saw the Bolsheviks as a nationalistic force were many officers of the old imperial army.[2] This was the case with Aleksei Brusilov (1853–1926), one of the most talented generals of the imperial army and the army of the Provisional Government. He cooperated with the Bolsheviks because he saw them as foremost a nationalistic force. (It should be added that information about the reasons for Brusilov's collaboration with the Bolsheviks is conflicting enough. There is some evidence that he was involved in an anti-Bolshevik plot.)[3] The feeling that there was a nationalistic implication to the civil war, both for the Bolshevik elite and for those who supported the Bolsheviks because of nationalist considerations, became apparent in 1919.[4]

When World War I ended, the Western allies sent troops to Russia to assist the White Army, which relied heavily on their support. Foreign observers saw the bellicose slogans of the Bolsheviks' leaders as merely another brand of revolutionary nationalism. Watching the increasing power of the Red Army and Trotsky, its leader, they believed that Red Russia was turning out to be a nationalistic power and, following the script of French Revolution, would soon be under the control of a dictator and out looking for conquests. The underlying nationalistic intent of the civil war became apparent when, toward its end in 1920, the Bolshevik government confronted Poland. At that point the civil war was transformed into a regular war between states. And it was at this point that Bolshevism was finally blended into nationalism in the eyes of those members of the old elite who had managed to join the regime, as well as in the eyes of some members of the emerging Bolshevik elite—mostly Red Army officers who perceived the nationalism inherent in Bolshevism and felt that the Bolsheviks would protect Russia better than the other contending political parties.

One episode recorded by survivors of the civil war is characteristic of their attitude. Two Russians, both enemies of the Bolshevik regime, were having a conversation while observing Red Army troops. One of the Russians observed that "we won"—that is, that the White cause had actually won. His interlocutor was puzzled because he could find no logic in the statement, for the soldiers they were observing were not White troops but Red troops. The other man disagreed, pointing out that the external symbols that inspired the Red Army (such as the red star) or even their political affiliation were not important. The most important thing was the White idea: Russia must remain a powerful state backed by a strong, disciplined military force. And it was precisely this quality that he saw before him. He remarked that he had not seen such well-disciplined troops with such fighting spirit in the Russian army since the beginning of World War I.[5]

While old-time nationalists, mostly officers of the imperial army, drew close to the Bolsheviks, however, the opposite thing happened within the emerging Bolshevik elite, who were, for the most part, military commanders themselves. Though the Bolsheviks' leaders saw the Red Army as a force that would help the international proletariat—recently published reports show Lenin urging the Red Army to ready itself for a deep penetration into the heart of Europe to assist the international proletariat[6]—some commanders of the army, and not necessarily only those who had been drawn from the imperial army, saw an entirely different role for the Red Army: they saw the military as a force that would preserve the unity of Russia and implicitly upgrade the country's military standing. In their eyes the major justification for the civil war, and the paramount goal of the Red Army, was the slogan "Russia United and Indivisible."

There was of course a good reason, at least according to Russian nationalists, for why they could not fight with the Red Army. They believed that the Bolshevik regime, for all its victories and its success in preserving the basic unity of the state, had failed to protect Russia's national interest. First, the Bolshevik revolution and the following civil war had led to the intolerable loss of many of the empire's most important territories, including the Baltic states, Finland, and Poland. Second, and this was regarded as more important, the Bolsheviks still were viewed as the representatives of international Communism or of certain minorities, specifically the Jews. Even some of its supporters felt that the militant nature of the regime's Communism made the leaders of Soviet Russia different, less than "normal," in the sense that it was felt they would never really bring Russia to prosperity or ensure its military might. In the context of this political paradigm it was believed that the Bolsheviks, on finishing their role as Jacobins in disciplining the army and society, were to be replaced by a "normal" regime, one to which Europeans and Russians were accustomed. Such a scenario implied the end of Bolshevism, with its disregard of the country's national interest; and the final legitimation of private property, including the right to own land as a basic right.

At the same time, the new economic, political, and ideological makeup of Russia would not be merely a returning to the prerevolutionary past. Rather, the new Russia would be a synthesis of the past and present. This new synthesis was called postrevolutionary ideology, and in a broader context it reflected the ideological developments in post–World War I Europe, national-socialism being the most prominent example. And indeed, postrevolutionary ideology in fascism combined revolutionary radicalism with the most ferocious nationalism, which long was viewed as essentially the ideology of the right.

From National Bonapartism to Eurasianism

Postrevolutionary Bolshevism, despite all its specifics, also reflected this general trend. A variety of émigré intellectuals, who spoke for a much broader audience and who reflected the views of a large segment of the Bolshevik elite, became the spokesmen for this ideological synthesis in Russia. At the same time, the increasingly nationalistic trend in Bolshevik ideology also reflected the mood of the Soviet populace (mostly ethnic Russian). From the inauguration of the New Economic Policy (NEP) onward, nationalistic feelings were on the rise, with the people instinctively looking for a sort of postrevolutionary synthesis—that is, a way to place the Russian revolution in the context of Russia's traditional confrontation with the West.

One resident of NEP Russia provided the following description of the mood of the populace: "The people from the street discard various class and social divisions, and all of their oppositionist energy translates into nationalism. The Communist Party and international Communism try to root out this healthy instinct of the masses to juxtapose internationalism with nationalism, which for some time has taken an ugly, chauvinistic turn." Though the Soviet elite tried to preserve their outlook, the pressure from below led them to evolve in the direction of being Russian nationalists rather than Marxist internationalists. "The Soviet power takes into account the rising nationalist feeling and tries to channel it into an anti-Western direction, not without the assumption that it could benefit from the rising feeling of hatred toward the West."[7]

The postrevolutionary ideologies typically could be divided into two types. First were those émigré intellectuals who thought that many elements of the Bolshevik regime were artificial and tended to see the future regime in Russia as moving toward the tradition of European liberal capitalism. They wanted to retreat as far away from the principles of world Communism as possible. They could be identified with the right wing, which later emerged as the right of the party. They wanted to move away from the state's ownership of the economy and toward a free competition of ideas; yet at the same time they praised the revolution for putting forward a vigorous political elite that eventually would raise the country's international standing. Believing that Russia was a European power, these people viewed the country in the context of the French Revolution, with a Bonaparte-style dictatorship looming in the future. Moreover, their feeling was that an authoritarian rule of a post-Bolshevik Napoleon was necessary to secure the country's international standing, though it would be replaced in the future by a democratic regime. Nikolai G. Ustrialov (1890–1938), the leading figure in the Change Landmarks Movement, was this group's most representative spokesman. Members of this group assumed that in the long run Bolshevism represented the national interests of Russians but not of the international proletariat.

A second postrevolutionary group consisted of those émigré intellectuals who stressed the importance of the changes brought on by the revolution. Their ideology tended to be indistinguishable from official Soviet propaganda, as they emphasized the importance of government involvement in society's economic life. More important, though, they emphasized the indefinite reign of a totalitarian regime under a dominant ideology. This strain of postrevolutionary thought, more than any other, demonstrated the deep connection between the émigré ideological process and the same process within Russia. These émigrés' ideology, then, represented more than the thoughts of a small band of outsiders. It represented the ideological trends within Russia proper.

These intellectuals were anti-Bolsheviks, but only in name. Their only major difference from the Bolsheviks was their open promulgation of the thesis that the goal of the revolution was to benefit Russia, not to be a harbinger of a worldwide proletarian revolution. To underscore the nationalistic nature of the Russian Revolution they separated all of Russian history from the West, instead emphasizing the historical unity of the various ethnic groups that made up the Russian empire. While the ideological premises of this group were popular among those on the right, it was their extreme hatred of Western democracy and their belief that Russia was generally different from the West that appealed to the ruling elite. The Soviet elite saw this group of émigré intellectuals, the Eurasianists, as best representing their opinions about the country's political direction.

It goes without saying, however, that whether the National Bolsheviks (a term used in its broadest sense) were right in their vision of history in general and the Bolshevik Revolution in particular, that most of the postrevolutionaries hardly envisaged many of the crucial features of the emerging Stalinism. Indeed, although Ustrialov and scores of others had envisioned the coming of the Russian Thermidor, with the restoration of private property as the cornerstone of Russian society, the opposite happened. Stalin's revolution from "above" put an end to private property. Even the majority of Eurasianists, who more than any other of the postrevolutionaries saw the country in the context of an authoritarian model, hardly understood the totality of the Stalinist regime, which in many aspects exceeded even Oriental despots in the completeness of its control over society.

The Eurasianists' assertions about Russia's uniqueness were also rather far-fetched. Their emphasis on the goodness of the orthodoxy and Russian spirituality as making the country superior to the "rotten" West were hardly different from the old Slavophile illusion. Most of those "postrevolutionaries engaged in political activity—or, more correctly, quasi-political activity. Ustrialov and his political allies as well as the Eurasianists, especially those on the left, were eager to be involved in Soviet politics. Moreover, they sincerely believed that Soviet leadership—Stalin, of course, first of all—would be lost without their personal guidance. They had visions of being invited to take an active leadership role in the country, and they believed that various political and ideological crises would help them to achieve this goal. Their inspiration for these ideas came from the Bolsheviks themselves, for hadn't they risen from the humble position of starving émigrés to the pinnacle of power on the crest of revolutionary upheaval? Their dreams of a triumphant return were certainly understandable but not unique among postrevolutionaries. Indeed, such dreams were common in émigré communities with a sufficient number of intellectuals. In such communities there was never a shortage of would-be leaders.

Their belief in their coming personal triumphs was erroneous. How-

ever, Soviet leaders, Stalin included, were eager to incorporate postrevolutionary paradigms into the regime's ideology. Stalin even occasionally
employed some postrevolutionaries. This was the case with Alexei Tolstoy,
who started his political career as a supporter of the Change Landmarks
Movement. He later became one of Stalin's most trusted lieutenants and
the regime's official writer, glorifying Stalin as the new embodiment of
Peter the Great. Tolstoy was sent to western Europe during the Great
Purges to convince the Western European public that the regime's official
version of the events was indeed accurate.

Other postrevolutionaries were incorporated into Soviet officialdom,
too. Some even managed to survive and die in their own beds, yet even the
most successful among them played the secondary role. They were essentially servants to the regime, skillful, well-paid mouthpieces of the official
point of view who never were among those who set the country's political
and ideological direction. It should also be added that only a few of those
who returned from exile ended up as lucky as Tolstoy. Most, including the
intellectual stars, such as Ustrialov, were either consumed by the purges
or ended up in the camps.

Although the postrevolutionaries were wrong in quite a few of their
assumptions about the nature of the Stalinist regime, their view of history
in general and Russian history in particular had many sound observations. First, the postrevolutionaries, especially the Eurasianists, were correct when they foresaw the Bolshevik Revolution as a powerful force that
would eventually lead the country to become an authoritarian-totalitarian
state. They were also correct in their assumption that the push to authoritarian-totalitarian regimes was a worldwide phenomenon. This important observation made the postrevolutionaries different both from the
majority of Bolsheviks and from Western European intellectuals. The Bolsheviks, despite the authoritarian-totalitarian seeds in their ideology, still
assumed that their revolution was the beginning of an era of real democracy. Lenin's "State and Revolution" was a clear indication of this state of
mind. Most Western European intellectuals saw the Bolsheviks as dictators but assumed that this was only a brief setback for democracy, which
was considered the future for all of mankind. But the postrevolutionaries,
together with some other European intellectuals (Oswald Spengler) and
Russian intellectuals (Mikhail I. Rostovtsev), saw the Bolshevik Revolution as the beginning of a global push for totalitarianism. And, according
to them, this was not to be a short-lived aberration.

Second, the postrevolutionaries were right when they emphasized the
importance of historical tradition and implicitly stressed the authoritarian
roots of Russia's political culture. Third, they rightly foresaw the inevitable
blend of Marxist doctrine with nationalism in the case of a Marxist vic-

tory. Here they implicitly saw Marxism as following the road of the me-
dieval Catholic Church, which was "international" in the Middle Ages but
which became "nationalized" later—that is, integrated into the political
and ideological settings of particular nations upon the strengthening of
the European state at the beginning of the modern era.

The representatives of the so-called Change Landmarks Movement
were the first group of postrevolutionaries. The movement emerged in
1921 and was centered on a publication of the same title. Ustrialov was
undoubtedly the ideological leader of the group, and it was he, more than
any other member of the movement, who represented those believing that
the Bolshevik Revolution was no accidental event and would benefit the
country in the long run.[8] According to Ustrialov, after certain modifica-
tions the regime would lay the foundation that would lead to the upgrading of the country's international standing. As was the case with other
émigré intellectuals, he represented not only the émigré community but
also a broader constituency: the Soviet elite. Indeed, Lenin himself found
the ideas of Ustrialov appealing and wished to see him among the members of the Soviet elite. Lenin made this desire clear enough by sending
another émigré the following message: "Tell Ustrialov that Il'ich [suppos-
edly V. I. Lenin] is fascinated by him, and his book *In Struggle for Russia*
is on Lenin's desk." Il'ich ordered him to send Ustrialov a letter and
"thought to bring him [Ustrialov] to the Center with great pomp."[9]

About a year later, Ustrialov received another letter indicating Lenin's
strong interest in his National Bolshevism: "Matveev said that he had discussions with Lenin about the new direction of émigré thought. He had the
impression that Lenin paid considerable attention to the movement and
selected you among those intellectuals who are well disposed to the Soviets (*primirentsy*) and probably knows your publications not only in *Change
Landmarks*, but in *News of Life* as well."[10] Lenin definitely appreciated
Ustrialov's call for all Russian intellectuals to work for the Bolsheviks, yet
this was not the only reason for his appreciation. Despite their political
and ideological differences, Lenin saw a kindred spirit in Ustrialov, a
man who also wanted a mighty Russia that could rise up and confront the
West.[11]

Ustrialov was fairly well known before the Bolshevik Revolution. He
taught at Moscow University and, according to accounts by those who
knew him there, had quite a bizarre personality. Yet it seems that no one,
not even those who failed to appreciate his ideas or his future political
activities, denied his erudition and brilliance. This was certainly the
impression of those who took his courses or associated with him as a colleague, and it is certainly the impression of Nicholas Riasanovsky, of the
University of California, Berkeley, whose father worked with Ustrialov.[12]

As with many other players in world history, Ustrialov held contradictory viewpoints, or at least viewpoints so complicated that they do not fit into any one historical model. One could characterize him as a conservative Westernizer (for lack of a better term—those who thought Russia would follow the Western political model of development) when he started his professional career at Moscow University. One could even argue that at the time he was intellectually close to the right wing of the Constitutional Democrats (Kadety), who emphasized political liberty as essential to upgrading Russia's international standing. He was in Moscow during the early months of Bolshevik rule, and he hardly could have appreciated the political developments. Like many other Russian nationalists, he saw Bolshevism as catering to the populace by appealing to its anarchical tendencies, which were bound to lead the country to ruin. This was the main reason he rushed to join Aleksandr Vasil'evich Kolchak, the recognized leader of the anti-Bolshevik movement.

Ustrialov, like most Westernized intellectuals of late imperial Russia, saw Russian political development in the context of the French Revolution. In the context of this historical model, Kolchak could certainly be construed as a possible Russian Napoleon. Ustrialov believed that Kolchak was the man who would lead the victory over the Reds and restore Russia, "United and Indivisible," to its imperial splendor while guaranteeing basic liberty for all citizens. Kolchak made it clear, as did all the anti-Bolshevik pretenders from Lavr Kornilov onward, that his dictatorship would be a temporary measure. It was needed only to restore order in society and in the army and to ensure victory in the war. As soon as these goals were achieved, he would surrender his power to the Constitutional Assembly, which could then decide the country's fate. And indeed, the idea that a dictator, deprived of the charisma of royalty, or at least of its historical prestige, could survive for a long period was basically foreign to pre–World War I European political thought.

In the context of this political paradigm, Ustrialov believed that Kolchak or some other successful White general would ensure the final triumph of political liberty in Russia. Political liberty, though not a goal for Ustrialov in itself, was definitely the major reason he joined Kolchak. From the beginning of his intellectual career Ustrialov certainly thought that political liberty was inseparable from the rejuvenation of Russia as a great nation enjoying international prestige. He saw in Kolchak the feverish spirit of the true nationalist and the strength to restore the country's international standing, sorely needed because of the humiliation suffered during the Russian-Japanese War. Ustrialov blamed the inept and cumbersome Russian monarchy for leading the country to this fate.[13]

For Ustrialov, it was England, with its imperial domain, solid and vast, that personified the benefits of political liberty in a successful foreign policy. From this perspective, Ustrialov was indeed close to Peter B. Struve and others like him, who saw the glory of the state and personal political liberty as interconnected. Yet political liberty was viewed as an instrument of ensuring the glory of the empire. Since it was not human rights but the glory of the state that was the paramount goal, a liberal government of the English type would not serve as well as a harsh dictatorship. One could abandon the liberal principles of its philosophy altogether or at least strongly modify them in response to political events. And this seems to have happened to Ustrialov, when in the midst of the civil war his political philosophy developed along two avenues.

First of all, even when Ustrialov was a member of the Kolchak government he undoubtedly was already questioning the applicability of liberal principles in Russia, especially as far as the might of the state was concerned. Indeed, White leaders, as did their Red counterparts, confronted the same patterns of antisocial behavior in various forms—drunken riots, crime, and the mutiny of their troops, who often defied the White authorities and joined with the Reds or engaged in plain and simple banditry. As a matter of fact, the bandits' rank and file comprised soldiers and ex-soldiers of both the White and Red armies. Both sides, albeit White more than Red, engaged in numerous pogroms. Many liberal politicians thus concluded that only a strong regime could save the country from anarchy. This was certainly the view of Struve, who stated that the anti-Jewish pogrom in which Denikin's army was involved was owing not to the commander in chief's encouragement but to the fact that he was soft. Only a strong dictatorial power could save the Jews and, implicitly, any other residents of Russia who were the victims of spontaneous violence.[14]

Although Kolchak seemed to be tougher than Denikin and tried to curb the cases of spontaneous violence that had an antisocial bent, Ustrialov's experience in Kolchak's government, especially its cruel dealings with the opposition, probably left him with the belief that liberal institutions would hardly work in Russia. Moreover, they were even less appropriate for maintaining Russia's international standing and the stability of its state. Indeed, the several democratic governments that did develop in the territories controlled by the Whites had a very short lifespan. Kolchak himself came to power as the result of a coup that overthrew one of them. It became apparent to Ustrialov that Russia's political reality made any sort of liberal institution unfit for the country. The country's very survival depended on choosing the right man to be dictator. One could of course assume that the choice ran the scale from most brutal to least brutal. But the level of brutality is hard to measure, and Ustrialov was unconcerned with this problem. His primary concern was the strength of the state, thus the choice was who could strengthen it the most.

But by 1921 there was no choice to be made, at least not for Ustrialov. The civil war was over, and the White armies, including that of Kolchak, had all suffered a similar fate. Kolchak and his prime minister Pepeliaev were shot to death. The Reds' victory was certainly a sign to Ustrialov that they were the party fit to lead Russia. After the civil war he settled in Harbin, the capital of Manchuria and the home of numerous Russians who worked for the Chinese Eastern railroad. There he joined the faculty of the local university. Even though he was willing to accept the Bolsheviks as victors, Ustrialov was still reluctant to preach the new variant of the well-known expression of Hegel, that everything that exists is reasonable and everything reasonable exists. Ustrialov was still a Westernizer; he still placed Russian history in the context of Western capitalism. This was indeed one of the major reasons Ustrialov continued to see the country's development in the context of the French Revolution. In his view, Bolshevism had quite a few "odd" elements that impeded the country's development and its transformation into a great power. At the same time he hoped that the inauguration of the NEP, which had slackened government control over society, meant that the country was now on the right track.

During the early years of his emigration Ustrialov saw the Soviet regime as having the following agenda. First, it must move further toward unleashing market forces and restoring private property rights. Ustrialov was convinced that Russia was, and would be for the foreseeable future, a country of peasants. In order to prosper, peasants must not simply lease the land but become its proprietor. In this respect he definitely followed the lead of Arkadii Stolypin, whose dissolution of the commune theory was aimed at creating a strata of rich peasants as a major source of government support. Second, even with his worship of the use of force to ensure success and his understanding that Russia needed a strong government, Ustrialov still did not completely sever his ties to his liberal past. Ustrialov loathed the repression and the unbridled government control over the country's political and intellectual life. And, while hailing the signs of Soviet moderation, he assumed that the government needed to move further in this direction. Third, and most important, the basic ideological transformation should come from within the Soviet elite. Indeed, he felt that the Soviet elite was not cognizant of the nationalist essence of the revolution and entertained what could be called a false consciousness.

For Ustrialov this false consciousness was evidenced in the Bolsheviks' pronouncements about the nature of the revolution after the civil war. The Bolshevik leaders had come to the conclusion that their hope of seeing the revolution ignite a worldwide conflagration would not materialize. Instead, the capitalist world had entered what was dubbed a "temporal stabilization," and the intensity of its class struggle was subsiding. However, Bolshevik leaders continued to maintain that the setback was temporary; eventually the economic and political problems of the capitalist world would lead to an eruption in the class struggle. And when it came, the Bolsheviks would honor their obligation to the European proletariat. After all, it was in hopes of spurring an international workers' uprising that the Bolsheviks had launched their own uprising in Petrograd in 1917 in the first place. Indeed, the Bolsheviks had preached from the start of the revolution and on through the civil war that they would not be able to survive if they were merely the party of the Russian proletariat, as the country was made up of mostly peasants and was too backward for socialist remodeling.

And it was this approach to the nature of the Russian Revolution, Ustrialov stated, that had to change. Bolsheviks needed to understand that their revolution was not started to benefit the international proletariat, but Russia. Furthermore, he said, they should spend less time thinking about foreign workers, and more time thinking about Russian ones. Ustrialov implied that the slogan "Proletariat of All Countries Unite" should be changed, in response to the present-day Russian leaders' need, to "Unite All Russians." The regime was still not cognizant of its national goal, the state's control over the economy needed to be lifted and a full-fledged market economy put into effect. The regime needed to abandon its overly repressive policies and its control over the spiritual life of society. Indeed, more needed to be changed in the regime than preserved. From this perspective, then, Ustrialov did not see the regime as truly nationalistic, and he dreamed of a Russian "Thermidor" that would, as in France's case, preserve the positive elements of the regime while purging it of its negative ones. This uneasiness with the Bolshevik regime indicated that despite his generally positive vision of it, Ustrialov still did not fully identify it with a nationalist cause.

Other Russian intellectuals began to see Bolshevism in a different light, however. Instead of viewing it in the context of European tradition, they saw the Bolshevik Revolution as following the totalitarian path of Russian history. This transformation implied not only a change in the historical paradigm—that is, a transition from the French Revolution as the model that explained Russian national history—but also a definite appreciation for the totalitarian principles that the Bolshevik regime had brought to Russian life. This was the case with a variety of intellectual trends in postrevolutionary Russia, which could be dubbed in rather awkward terms as "orientalist" or "Easterner." These terms indicated that they could easily be distinguished from other intellectual trends with a National Bolshevist flavor by their historical paradigms. While for Western-izers it was the French Revolution that provided the historical framework for understanding Russia's present and future, for the Easterners it was non-Western history that was viewed as the historical framework for understanding the meaning of the Russian revolution.

Eurasianism was one of the best examples of this type of postrevolu-tionary intellectual current.[15] In fact, Eurasianism was crucial to the ide-ological evolution that lead to the emergence of National Bolshevism as a distinct ideological paradigm. First of all, it placed the Bolshevik Revo-lution outside of its international context and firmly in the context of Russian history. The Eurasianist vision of Russian history was different from the majority of Russian nationalists of the late imperial regime. While the late imperial nationalists (for example, Slavophiles) maintained that Russia was a uniquely Slavic cultural and ethnic entity, Eurasianists emphasized the unity of Russians with other non-Russian peoples of the empire and later of the USSR. The Eurasianists thus not only placed Rus-sia outside of Western European tradition but outside of Eastern Euro-pean tradition as well.

Secondly, Eurasianism, especially in its leftist version, saw the Soviet regime's authoritarian drive as a rather positive element firmly embedded in Russian culture. From this perspective, they believed that the Soviet regime needed to make few changes to represent the country's national aspirations. Indeed, with their emphasis on dictatorial government, sin-gle ideology, and the necessity of government regulation of economy as permanent elements of Russian culture, the Eurasianists were nothing but Bolsheviks. And it was not accidental that their program was actually reduced to the simple replacement of "bad" Bolsheviks with "good" Eur-asianists who would be able, contrary to the Bolsheviks, to recognize the revolution's true purpose: the making of Russia-Eurasia into a strong nation, into the actual leader of humanity. The strong similarities between Bolshevism and Eurasianism made it quite easy for Eurasianism to blend with Bolshevism. Eurasianism represented more than the beliefs of a small community of émigrés. It also represented the values of a broad sec-tion of the ruling elite in Soviet Russia. From this perspective Eurasianism certainly provided the final synthesis between nationalism and Bolshevism regardless of whether the Bolsheviks were aware of this themselves.

The ideology was the brainchild of several individuals, but Petr Niko-laevich Savitsky is regarded as the movement's founding father.[16] It was probably Savitsky who started to conceive of the basic ideas of the move-ment, probably toward the end of the civil war, which he spent in the Crimea—the last area of control for the White forces led by General Petr Nikolaevich Wrangel.[17] At the time, Savitsky was quite close to Struve, who by then was both his intellectual mentor and his employer. When Savitsky managed to escape to Bulgaria, it was Struve who provided him with a job at his magazine *Russian Thought*.[18] By then Savitsky's Eurasianist inclinations were firmly shaped, and in a letter to his parents he stated that he "diligently proselytized Eurasianism" and that "virtuous Europeans listen to the Eurasianist maxims in horror."[19] By 1921, Savitsky was acquainted with Peter P. Suvchinsky, at the time one of the managers of a Russian-Bulgarian publishing house. Suvchinsky became not only the cofounder of the movement but also later was the leader of the leftist Eurasianists and a major ideological rival of Savitsky. Savitsky was also joined by Nikolai S. Trubetskoi and Georgii V. Florovsky, the other cofounder of the movement. Later the group published the brochure "Turn to the East," which became the movement's manifesto. From then on Eurasianists comprised a small but loyal group of followers who continued to preach the movement's teachings to the public.

By April 1921 the first public meeting of Eurasianists took place. Savitsky wrote about the event to his parents: "Yesterday the Eurasianists gave their first public meeting under the blessing of the religious-philosophic circle. There were around 40–50 members. I did not speak out, but Trubetskoi and Florovsky [did]. We did not recruit any new followers."[20] Later that year Savitsky moved to Prague, which, with Paris, became the leading center of Eurasianist activities in the years ahead. There Savitsky enrolled as a graduate student at a local university, later becoming a professor. While working on his dissertation he continued to propagandize the movement, and on 21 August 1921 he read his first public lecture, "The Justification for Eurasianism."

The popularity of Eurasianism was on the rise. It had a certain following among the general public and aroused the interest of the foreign Slavists and representatives of other émigré groups. The Socialist Revolutionaries were among those who found the Eurasianists to be kindred spirits. In Prague, the "Russian House" affiliated with the Socialist Revolutionaries staged a presentation by Mark Slonim, a well-known émigré intellectual, on Eurasianism, during which he criticized some premises while finding others "marvelous."[21] Savitsky became a local celebrity in Prague, and barely a year after his arrival in the city, he was invited to a "five o' clock tea" in the apartment of Carel Kramar (1867–1937), who had led the fledgling Czechoslovak Republic in 1918–1919. In a letter to relatives, Savitsky proudly announced that the people who attended the party were small in number but represented the elite.[22]

The movement steadily gained an international reputation, attracting a growing number of members of the émigré community, including some of its more prominent members. Pavel Iv. Novgorodtsev (1866–1924) was one of the more important early catches for the Eurasianists. He was a prominent liberal scholar who wrote extensively on law and modern Western European philosophy, mostly on Kant and Hegel. Novgorodtsev seemed to be firmly steeped in the Kantian ethic that the human being was always a goal in itself, certainly one of the major principles of Western liberalism. He was also a leading figure in the Kadet Party. His conversion to Eurasianism could, of course, be attributed to various reasons, but his contemporaries mostly attributed it to the religious crises Novgorodtsev underwent in the last years of his life.[23] This recognition of Savitsky's spiritual and intellectual leadership by a famous writer and scholar was a great success for Savitsky, at that time only a graduate student and much younger than Novgorodtsev.

Other prominent Russian writers and poets followed suit. Nikolai Al. Berdiaev (1874–1948), one of the founders of existentialism and undoubtedly one of the more influential of all Russian émigrés, also fell under the spell of Eurasianism. One sign of this was the Eurasianist Il'in's (not to be confused with the philosopher Ivan Al. Il'in, who hated the movement) invitation to speak out in Berdiaev's circle (1923), undoubtedly to elaborate his Eurasianist views.[24] Representatives of belles lettres also flocked to the Eurasianist camp. Andrei Belyi (1880–1934), one of the poets of the Russian Silver Age, "became fascinated with Eurasianism."[25] This was also the case with Fedor A. Stepun (1884–1965), the prominent Russian émigré writer, essayist, and philosopher. His work *Life and Creativity* (*Zhizn' i tvorchestvo*, Berlin: Obelisk, 1923), in which he discussed Spenglerian ideas about the decline of Europe, indicated that he was influenced by the movement. Later, Savitsky elaborated on Stepun's interest in one of his private letters: "He [Stepun] had gravitated very much to Eurasianists and came to me for a detailed discussion."[26] All of this certainly indicated Eurasianism's growing influence.

By 1923 the Eurasianists were numerous enough, or at least confident enough, to contemplate the creation of a Eurasian Party. A meeting held in Berlin in March 1923 was an important step in this direction. It was later called the "meeting of the three": Savitsky, Suvchinsky, and P. S. Arapov. According to Arapov's account, the meeting was a "big step in the broadening of publication activity, as well as a launch for practical Eurasian work."[27] On 6 December 1924 a sort of Eurasian Party was hammered out by the Council of Five in Vienna. That group—Trubetskoi, Suvchinsky, Savitsky, Arapov, and Malevich—was the leading organ in the movement, and it retained the same members until 1928, when the movement underwent its first split. Later it was said that "for the years of 1924–28 there were many organizational changes, yet throughout all of these years the Council functioned as the leading Eurasian organ."[28]

By the middle of the 1920s, Eurasianists had continued to strengthen their hold on the Russian Diaspora scattered over the globe. One of the reasons for the movement's success was its active recruitment of new members. In 1925 an emissary was sent to establish Eurasianist groups in America. The journey lasted from 8 December 1925 to 31 March 1926 and resulted (so the emissary claimed) in the establishment of several Eurasianist groups in various American cities, including New York, Chicago, and Boston.[29] The rise in membership and the large amount of publicity among émigrés definitely helped the Eurasianists to obtain funding from foreigners interested in Russia, an important prerequisite if the movement were to continue its growth.

By the second half of the 1920s the Eurasianists were entrenched. They had their own publishing house, which published periodicals and engaged in other similar enterprises. And not only did the Eurasianists emerge as a force in other countries, but they also became a force back in the USSR itself and became incorporated into the Weltanschauung of the Soviet elite. The major premises of Eurasianism were linked to the Soviet reality of the post–civil war period and collaterally the mentality of the Soviet elite of that time.

Eurasianism was certainly a complicated and controversial intellectual and to some degree quasi-political movement. Some of the founders of the movement ironically admitted that there were as many brands of Eurasianism in the movement as Eurasianists. And indeed, from the very beginning of Eurasianism, Savitsky acknowledged that it represented all shades of political opinion "from my National Bolshevism to the orthodox anti-Bolshevism of Florovsky."[30] Personal rivalry and the desire to assert personal importance (a phenomenon prevalent in the emigration), the proclivity for intellectual play, the use of ostentatiously difficult language to assert its individual elitism—certainly a Russian intellectual proclivity resulting from the influence of German philosophy in the nineteenth century—all of these might have obscured the central idea of the movement. Yet an intellectual kernel did exist, and it was what made Eurasianism into the ideal vehicle for the development of National Bolshevism. The Eurasianists' success in integrating Russian nationalism into Communist ideology was due to three major premises:

1. Its complete separation of Russia from not only the West but also from any people outside Soviet borders, while stressing the basic unity of all peoples in the USSR.
2. Eurasianism looked on the totalitarian system prevailing in Russia not as a temporary hiatus but rather as a permanent element of the country's life.

3. Though they stressed the absolute separation of the country from the rest of the world, Eurasianism, especially in its leftist version, made eschatological claims asserting that Russia would have the leading role in transforming humanity. Eurasianism was the perfect intellectual breeding ground for blending Bolshevism into Konstantin Leont'ev's promethean brand of nationalism.[31]

While the juxtaposition of Russia to Europe was hardly an innovation of the Eurasianists, their view on the subject was drastically different from the Slavophile perspective. According to the Eurasianists, the true allies of ethnic Russians were not other Slavs but rather other non-Slavic and Asiatic peoples of the empire. Even though each nationality of the Russian state preserved its own characteristics, together they constituted a sort of aggregate unity of nations that in turn had created a sort of transethnic unity or a new type of "Eurasian nation"—what was in fact later called the Soviet people. As such, their unity was deeply organic and natural, not merely the product of Russian conquest. The Russian empire, they argued, could not be viewed in the context of a regular European empire. Since each ethnic group had become an organic part of the "Eurasian nation," each part of the nation had no desire for separation. And it is precisely this that made the difference between the Russian empire and regular European empires.

In spite of their emphasis on the uniqueness of the Russian (Eurasian) culture, Eurasianists from the beginning were more predisposed to the East than to the West. The Asian parts of Eurasian nations, of course, naturally gravitated to the east, but even ethnic Russians had more in common with their Asian cultural heritage than Europe's (Eurasianists emphasized the cultural link rather than the ethnic link, and here they were different from European and Russian fascists). The Asiatic roots of Russians and the creation of the cultural unity of the peoples of what was the Russian empire and now the USSR was attributed to the Mongols, specifically, Ghengis Khan and his successors, who had spread their domination throughout Eurasia.

In their praise of the Mongols as being the only real contributors to the well-being of the Russian empire and as those who were responsible for Russia's great future, Eurasianists were definitely unique. Konstantin Leont'ev, even with all his reverence for the Asiatic heritage that ran through Russian culture, never praised the Mongols openly. Even the radical poets of the revolutionary era, who espoused revolutionary violence as a way of preparing society for the building of a new edifice of social harmony, did not see the Mongols as a creative force. The Mongols, despite their revolutionary "goodness" (as the poets might fancy it), were regarded as a destructive force, not a constructive one. Their image in the Russian national psyche was too negative; they were mostly remembered for their onslaught on Russia. And on top of this, while the barbarians of the Great Migration could be credited (at least in the eyes of the Marxists) for the destruction of an outmoded method of production (they replaced the slave owners' society with a feudal one), the Mongols did not bring any changes of this sort to the society they had invaded.

In their insistence on the Mongolian roots of Russian culture, many Eurasianists, such as Trubetskoi and George Vernadskii, saw the Mongols as the political force that had united Eurasia, actually the territory of the Russian empire, forged out of what was originally ethnically and culturally diverse territory. At the beginning of the movement the Eurasianists did not stress the totalitarian-authoritarian traditions of the Mongols, and they even fulminated against the Soviet regime for its brutality and despotism. Yet as time passed the authoritarian aspects of Eurasian teaching became apparent and perhaps constituted a logical derivation of their praise of the Mongol heritage. This authoritarian-totalitarian implication in their praise for the Mongols had been well gauged by some in the movement, who wondered about the group's direction. For example, this was the case with the Eurasianist Sadovskii, who was outraged by the publication of the Trubetskoi brochure "Ghengis Khan's Heritage." In a letter to Savitsky (26/VII-1925) he complained that regardless of the author's intention the work not only praised despotic rule but actually asserted that this sort of brutal despotism was the best government for Russians. He found the book full of "praise for our disgusting and most shameful slavery and the Tatars under whose rule we were the most down and out, unless of Khan, and we were from this respect quite similar to the position of the Senegalese vis-à-vis the French."[32] And, indeed, it was their vision of Russia as being permanently in the grip of totalitarian regimes, and the clarity of their totalitarian design for society, that made Eurasianists different from most other postrevolutionary movements. And it was these totalitarian proclivities that made for an easy integration of Eurasianism into Bolshevik ideology, in some cases even supplanting it.

The Eurasianists' totalitarian proclivities could be seen in their approach to Orthodoxy. Although they were certainly different from traditional Slavophiles, Eurasianists preserved their high regard for the Orthodoxy. The classical Slavophile viewpoint said that the Orthodoxy, owing to its stress on love for fellow human beings, was the only true manifestation of Christianity. It was also regarded as the very essence of the Slavic soul and its inborn gentleness and nobility. In the view of the Slavophiles, Orthodoxy was to be preserved as the foundation of the

Russian state and supported by the authorities as the only state religion. Eurasianists followed the model of the Slavophiles with, of course, some amendments. As the Slavophiles, they saw collectivism as the kernel of the Orthodoxy. But for the Slavophiles this collectivism implied Christian love and, collaterally, the willingness to sacrifice for fellow human beings. In the Eurasianist model the collectivism of the Orthodoxy was merely a tool that could be used to unite the entirety of Russian society. There was no mention of Christian love and kindness. The approach of the Slavophiles and Eurasianists to the relationship between the state and society was also vastly different.

Though the Slavophiles regarded the Orthodoxy as a crucial ideological paradigm, they did not emphasize coercion as the way to enforce the Orthodoxy. Coercion was also not in the design of the Slavophiles' vision of relations between state and society. The Slavophiles believed that the Russian czar was not meant to be a West European type of ruler, who dealt with his subjects through cold judicial formalities or enforced his laws by means of brutal coercion, but rather he was to be a father to the people. In essence, then, they believed that Russian society should be a gemeinschaft society rather than a gesellschaft one. Eurasianists had a differing opinion.

The Eurasianists believed that Russian society was different from its Western counterpart, for Eurasian society did not have strict, legally defined boundaries between members of the society and between society and the state. From this perspective Eurasian society could indeed be defined as a Gemeinschaft society. The Eurasianists believed that the Gemeinschaft elements of the society—that is, the absence of legal definitions of the rights of citizens and the state—implied that the state was not obligated to have any restraint in dealing with its subjects. Thus it did not matter whether the ruling elite was made up of people of conscience with a real concern for the well-being of their subjects.

Their view of the Orthodoxy as the ideological framework for the future post-Soviet society also revealed their deep-seated totalitarian proclivities. The Eurasianists stated quite openly that not only would the Orthodoxy be the kernel of the ideological framework of the future society but also that there would be only one ideology. Only those who supported it would be allowed to become members of the elite. There were intimations that the ideology would be strictly enforced, by government intervention if necessary, and that the future regime would tolerate no adverse ideological movement—that is, ideas of Western liberal capitalism.

The Russian state, however, was composed both of members of the Orthodoxy and of Moslems. This problem was to be solved in the following way. Eurasians asserted that the Moslems, because of the collectivistic nature of their faith, were already quite close to the Orthodoxy. Some Eurasianists even claimed that Moslems were closer to the Orthodoxy than Catholics and Protestants. And besides, the fact that these nations lived together with Russians led to certain mutual ideological penetrations. This call for ideological and political control over society and praise for cooperative political and economic institutions made Eurasianism a more or less accurate reflection of the post–civil war Soviet society. Indeed, the fact that the USSR was a country with a centralized party bureaucracy that thought of itself as a permanent element of the country's political landscape, that the Soviet interpretation of Marxist ideology emphasized the unity of the Soviet people in confronting the West, the country's cooperative social and economic structure—fit the Eurasianists' philosophy exactly. The similarity between Eurasianism and the Bolshevik post–civil war ideology was evident in the Soviet leaders' stressing that the hoped-for worldwide proletarian revolution had never materialized and that now Socialism was going to have to be built "in one country." In this context, Socialism had become nothing more than a Russian phenomenon and entrenched in the context of Russian history. Eurasianism could have been renamed Bolshevism with a stress on nationalism.

Savitsky, echoing Alexander Ivanovich Herzen's famous letter to Jules Michelet, stated that Russia was different from Europe in various ways, but what made Russia most different from Europe was that Russia would not "follow the middle road"—that is, would not become a country of Western philistines. Russia would either perish or accomplish "some extraordinary historical achievements." Following Herzen, and to some extent the Slavophiles who believed that Christian-type suffering was the essential element of the nation's spirit, Savitsky stated that one of the greatest achievements of the Bolshevik Revolution was that it was able to assert the uniqueness of the Russian national character and that it would make Russia the leader of nations. "Revolution is nothing but the smithy of the spirit," he wrote. And the very fact that the Russian revolution was grander than anything seen before assured the country's special place in history. Elaborating on this, Savitsky wrote: "Each global people's suffering is nothing but smithy of the spirit." From this perspective there was nothing empirically (*empiricheski*) right about the messianic prophets of the French Revolution or the prophets of the Polish national disaster. Yet the downfall of Russia was qualitatively different from the catastrophe of the French Revolution and the Polish national disaster; it definitely exceeded the latter by its span." Thus, even the suffering that the Bolshevik Revolution brought to Russian society had a positive effect, for it reasserted the country's difference from the West. Seeing in the nation's religious exclusiveness its greatest treasure, Savitsky was horrified by the possibility of Russia winning World War I, because Russians would then "have to betray our religious calling." All of this proves that Eurasianism acknowledged the positive aspects of the Bolshevik Revolution from the beginning and thus had a sort of love-hate attitude toward the regime. Later the evolution of some Eurasianists, namely their leftist variant's move toward Soviet officialdom, became an indication of a similar process on the part of Soviet officials and of Soviet ideology's increasing nationalism.

The affinity between Soviet ideology and, in general, authoritative, fascist types of ideologies was apparent to many early observers of Eurasianism. They detected the pro-Soviet inclination of Eurasianism, despite its representatives' insistence that Eurasianists were the mortal enemy of the Kremlin. Peter Struve was one of the first to make this point clear. Though Struve had been Savitsky's academic mentor and employer,[33] by the time Savitsky was elaborating on Eurasianism their relationship had begun to cool. In May 1921, Savitsky was thinking about quitting his job with Struve.[34] That summer Savitsky complained in a letter to relatives that Struve called Eurasianists "babblers" and "cowards" and that Struve was doing his best to "excommunicate me from the church of pious struviats (*struvisty*)" because of Savitsky's attachment to Eurasianism.[35] By the time he arrived in Prague, Savitsky had made an irreparable break with Struve. Struve then turned into Savitsky's intellectual enemy and remained so throughout his career. His rancor was such that Struve attempted to prevent Savitsky's admission to graduate school in Prague.[36] Savitsky also had conflicts with other groups of émigrés, especially wi   ose on the right and later the liberals. For example, he engaged in a   ter conflict with *Rul'* (*Helm*), which was edited by the prominent liberal politician Iosif Vl. Gessen (1865–1943) and was the leading liberal newspaper in Berlin, at the time the center of the Russian emigration.[37]

Struve's break with Savitsky could be rooted in personal conflicts, of course, or perhaps in the problems that all émigrés (not only Russians) encounter while living in a foreign country. Yet this cannot be the only explanation. Struve was among the first to detect the similarities between the Eurasianist and Change Landmarks movements.[38] He saw in both ideologies an attempt to nationalize, to domesticate Bolshevism. The process was intended to transform that foreign phenomenon into an ideology embedded in Russia's history and, therefore, legitimize it. And this is precisely what Struve could not stand. Though Struve was wrong in seeing Eurasianism as an intellectual and political trend foreign to Russian tradition, he was definitely right in gauging the striking similarities between Eurasianism and the ideological premises of NEP Russia. Indeed, in the end it took the reconciliation of both sides to make the final ideological

synthesis of the Bolsheviks' radicalism, the growing totalitarian ossifica-
tion of Soviet society and die-hard Russian nationalism. This type of synthesis is hardly unique, as Germany's fascists (with due reverence to their
own nationalist traditions) were to achieve the same sort of synthesis in the
near future. In the process of possible ideological and political amalga-
mation, Eurasianism and other postrevolutionary groups made the biggest
steps in this direction—that is, in acknowledging that the Bolshevik regime was an organic part of Russian history. Over time, the feeling grew
that the regime would actually require few changes if it were to become a
nationalist power, and, in such a capacity, benefit the Russian state.

Conclusion and Postscript

The Bolshevik ideology began to "nationalize" from the first months of
Soviet rule, when the emphasis started to shift from a worldwide proletarian uprising to a concentration on the revolutionary state. Bolsheviks
originally assumed that the mighty Soviet state was the only tool necessary for keeping the country afloat until the start of the world revolution;
however, they slowly started to realize that the state was a goal in itself.
This was the reason many people who were originally anti-Bolshevik enemies changed sides from the outbreak of the civil war onward. For them,
the Bolsheviks were first of all nationalists crushing foreign intervention
in Russia's affairs. The members of the Change Landmarks Movement,
notably Ustrialov, and the Eurasianists, finally shaped the ideology of National Bolshevism, in which they emphasized the revolution's role stressing the country's difference from the rest of the world (especially the
West). The revolution was also credited with forging a mighty Russian
state. From this perspective, then, Ustrialovism and Eurasianism were
more than the ideologies of a narrow circle of outsiders, émigrés. They
represented the beliefs of a broad constituency within Soviet Russia itself.
And this was the reason some stubborn anti-Bolsheviks, such as Struve,
saw Eurasianism as merely a modification of Bolshevism. By the beginning of the 1930s, National Bolshevism was fully incorporated into the
official doctrine. Nationalism became the functional ideology of the
regime, although Marxism-Leninism (transformed into Stalinism) continued to be the official rhetorique of the regime.

Notes

The research for this chapter was funded by a grant from the Hoover Institution and by
several grants that I received from Indiana University (Bloomington and South Bend).
I also owe gratitude to my colleagues at the Harvard Russian Research Center, the Hoover

Institution, and the department of history at Indiana University at South Bend. Their discussions contributed greatly to the ideas found in this article.

1. Hoover Institution Archive, B. Maklakoff-Basis A. Collection, box 20, acc. 57005, Maklakov article, p. 17.

2. Ibid., p. 18; *Novye Vedomosti*, 20 April 1918.

3. Hoover Institution Archive, Peter B. Struve Collection, box 028, no. 26–86, A. Erdman's letter to Peter Struve, n.d.

4. Some observers of present-day Russian life believe that the Bolsheviks began to actively employ nationalism as early as 1917. See Dmitry Rogozhin, "V kakoi oppozitsii nuzhdaetsia Rossiia," *Nezavisimaia Gazeta* (Moscow), 10 December 1992.

5. Iu. K. Rapoport "U krasnykh i u belykh," *Arkhiv Russkoi Revoliutsii* 30 (1930): 242–247.

6. Anatolii Latyshev, "Dva sokola iasnykh veli razgovor," *Rossiiskaia Gazeta*, 27 March 1993.

7. GARF, Savitsky Fond, ed. khr. 359, 25 February 1925, Trubetskoi letter to Savitsky.

8. On the early work of Ustrialov see N. Ustrialov, *Rossiia u okna vagona* (Harbin: Tipografia Kitaiskoi Vostochnoi Zheleznoi Dorogi), 1926; *Pod znakom revoliutsii: sbornik statei* (Harbin: Izdatel'stvo; "Russkaia zhizn'," 1925); *V bor'be za Rossiiu: sbornik statei* (Orange, Conn: Antiquary, 1987). For the history of National Bolshevism and Ustrialov's role in the development of this ideological trend see the work of the late Mikhail Agursky. I had a chance to meet with Agursky in Israel and at several scientific conferences, and many of the ideas in this chapter were inspired by our conversations. The following works by Agursky are most pertinent to this study: *The Third Rome: National Bolshevism in the USSR* (Boulder: Westview, 1987); *Contemporary Russian Nationalism: History Revisited* (Jerusalem: Hebrew University of Jerusalem, Soviet and East European Research Centre, 1982); *Ideologiia natsional-bol'shevizma* (Paris: YMCA Press, 1980).

9. Hoover Institution Archive, Ustrialov Collection, Moia perepiska s raznymi liud'mi, Iakov Dunin letter to Ustrialov, 26 May 1921.

10. Ibid., Letter of A. F. Bonch-Osmolovskii to Ustrialov, 2 May 1922.

11. As early as 1918, some Bolsheviks thought Lenin was actually a great Russian patriot. This was the case with Bonch-Bruevich, who accused Sergei P. Mel'gunov and others of a similar ilk of "not understanding the patriotism of Il'ich" (S. P. Mel'gunov, *Vospominaniia i Dnevniki*, 2 vols. [Paris: n. p., 1964], 2: 39).

12. I received this information from Nicholas Riasanovsky during the summer of 1993. While a fellow at the Harvard Russian Research Center in 1990–1991, I met other people who had studied under Ustrialov. They essentially corroborated Riasanovsky's information.

13. According to Richard Pipes, "Russia's defeat at the hand of the Japanese was to have grave consequences for the whole of Europe by lowering the esteem in which whites had been held by the non-Western people: for it was the first time in modern history that an Asiatic nation defeated a great Western power" (*Russian Revolution* [New York: Knopf, 1991], 35).

14. Hoover Archives, Peter B. Struve Collection, Box 004, no. 4–20, Letter of P. B. Struve to N. I. Astrov, 12 April 1921.

15. On Eurasianism see Otto Boss, *Die Lehre Der Eurasier* (Wiesbaden, 1961), and Nicholas V. Riasanovsky, "The Emergence of Eurasianism," *California Slavic Sudies* 4 (1967). Important information can also be found in Robert C. Williams, *Culture in Exile: Russian Emigres in Germany 1881–1941* (Ithaca: Cornell University Press, 1972).

16. P. N. Savitsky's personal archive, deposited in GARF, was originally located in the Prague Archive, one of the biggest depositories of émigré-related materials. The

archive, still practically unresearched by Western scholars, contains a wealth of information about the rise of the movement and its ideological transformation.

17. Ibid., ed. khr. 326, Savitsky letter to his parents, 21/IV-4 V, 1920.

18. Ibid., 4/VII-1920. Savitsky letter.

19. Ibid., 19/VII-1920, Savitsky letter.

20. Ibid., 4/IV-1921, Savitsky letter.

21. Ibid., 21/8–1921, Savitsky letter.

22. Ibid., ed. khr. 326, 8/III-1922, Savitsky letter.

23. Ibid., ed. khr. 326, 3/I-1922, Savitsky letter.

24. Ibid., ed. khr. 403, 18/V-1923, anonymous letter to Suvchinsky.

25. Ibid., ed. khr. 388, 20 January 1922, Suvchinsky's letter to Peter Ivanovich? and Georgii Ivanovich?

26. Ibid., ed. khr. 356, 1 April 1932, Savitsky's letter to Alekseev.

27. Ibid., ed. khr. 403, undated note.

28. Ibid., ed. khr. 403, undated note.

29. Ibid., ed. khr. 363, undated "Amerikanskaia Poezdka."

30. Ibid., ed. khr. 358, August 1921, Savitsky's letter to Struve.

31. Leont'ev was a late-nineteenth-century Slavophile who emphasized the non-Slavic elements in Russian ethnicity and culture. He also viewed socialism as developing along totalitarian lines, and he was one of the first European thinkers to envision the rise of twentieth-century European totalitarianism.

32. GARF, f. 5783, kh1, ed. khr., 26/VII, Sadovsky's letter to Savitsky.

33. Ibid., 4/VII-1920, Savitsky letter.

34. Ibid., 14/V-1921, Savitsky letter.

35. Ibid., 15/VII-1921, Savitsky letter.

36. Ibid., 20/XI-1921, Savitsky letter.

37. Ibid., 8/III-1922, Savitsky letter.

38. Ibid., ed. khr. 326, 3/I-1922, Savitsky's letter to relatives.

Values, Substitutes, and Institutions: The Cultural Dimension of the Bolshevik Dictatorship

14

In recent years a number of historians have pointed to the gap in scholars' understanding of the cultural dimension of the Russian Revolution. Moshe Lewin, in his pathbreaking study of the cultural component of the Revolution, stated that "'what makes Russia tick' is not the simple mechanism located in the Politburo but the country's history, traditions, culture, economy, social structure, international environment. Also leadership—in that order."[1] One might add geography to the list, but the sentiment expressed remains valid. Dan Orlovsky has argued that "any theory of revolution that seeks to explain both the breakdown of the old regime and ultimate historical outcomes must take into account society's cultural dimension."[2] He expands on this in the following terms: "Explanations of revolution that embrace culture must consider both structure and event; they must go beneath the formal institutions and laws to grasp their dynamics as cultural repositories and artifacts."[3] He also produces a yardstick—which has added poignancy since it was written—by which to measure the Revolution: "If revolutionary theory and practice are to produce desired transformations, they must take account of the collective mentality and how to communicate with it, mobilize it and change it."[4]

The themes opened up in the cultural area are enormous. To what extent did the tsarist environment make Bolshevism what it was? Did the Revolution fail in the long run because the revolutionaries, instead of persuading Russia to absorb the new values, were swallowed up by "traditional" values of low productivity, drunkenness, mistrust of the state, what Lenin called an "Asiatic" trading mentality, attachment to religious practices, and so on? Above all, wasn't the baneful cultural influence of serfdom still to be traced in the revolutionary years and, arguably, down to the present? After all, the rational working practices of serfs—doing as little as possible for landowner or state and as much as possible on one's own plot—are not dissimilar from attitudes toward work in Russia noted by a multitude of observers down to the present. The inward-looking, defensive self-sufficiency of, especially, the peasant community was rational under serfdom and survived well beyond 1917. Indeed, for many peasants 1917 seemed to be the triumph of their own values and communities over the hated oppressor state. One aspect that certainly seems to have survived to affect popular views of politics and politicians in the post-Soviet period is the defensive mistrust of central authority. Bolshevism itself took over many of the worst aspects of tsarism—exile, prison camps, political repression, censorship, a would-be "totalitarian" official ideology, and nationalism and militarism—and built them into a monstrosity way beyond tsarist means though probably not tsarist aspirations, if the behavior of some Whites and monarchists in the civil war are anything to go by.

The Soviet system also built on some of the more "positive" features of prerevolutionary society, notably the interest in science of the intelligentsia, the collective values of the ordinary people, not to mention their abhorrence of violence and enduring patience, which limited popular rebelliousness. One cannot overlook that many of the achievements of the Soviet period came about through the ingenuity, initiative, and determination of the ordinary people, sometimes despite the state as much as because of it.

Clearly this is not the place to follow up all these vital themes. My aim here is more limited. Part of the recent explosion of historiography of the Revolution has, especially since the early 1980s, been devoted to questions of Bolshevik culture and values. There have been many contributors to this debate, among them Sheila Fitzpatrick, Richard Stites, Peter Kenez, Abbott Gleason, William Rosenberg, Zenovia Sochor, Lyn Mally, John Biggart, Jane Burbank, and Katerina Clark. These authors have elucidated many aspects of the period, and their works are essential to an understanding of it. But there is, perhaps, an underlying weakness to some of this literature (including my own contributions), which we are now in a better position to put right. Most of us taking part in the debate have tended to see the cultural dimension of the Revolution as fascinating but secondary. By and large, detailed examination of interesting fringe groups and engaging marginal figures—notably Proletkul't and A. A. Bogdanov—have been more common than analyses of the effects of cultural presuppositions on mainstream policymaking.

As a result, it sometimes looks as though the debate assumes that social and economic forces are deemed to be the primary base and that culture (and, more ambiguously, politics) is a part of the secondary super-structure. However, especially in an ideologically driven movement like Bolshevism, the cultural dimension has to be seen as an important part of the movement's core. Without its transforming cultural objectives, Bolshevism makes no sense at all. Its goals and assumptions percolate into all areas of its institutional and economic construction and cannot simply be confined to a separate ideological or cultural sphere. Bolshevism was, ultimately, a mechanism for transforming values and, in the longer term, human nature, not just ordering society better. In the words of one recent account, "Bolsheviks wanted to change the world, not manage it."[5]

In understanding Bolshevism, we must make the cultural dimension central. It should be placed alongside the more familiar trinity of social, economic, and political factors as at least an equal partner. In the revolutionary period itself, cultural assumptions contributed greatly to a breach between the Bolsheviks and a large part of the active revolutionary forces of Russia. The cultural dimension may help explain the reasons for early Bolshevik institutions taking the form they did as well as Bolshevism's profound problems and ultimate failures.

In broad terms, culture is assumed to mean those aspects of life acquired through learning and developed through creativity—in other words, that part of our personality and behavior that is not biologically or genetically determined, that is not purely instinctive. In this chapter I frequently use the term in a rather narrow sense. Here culture is taken to mean ideas and values, the intellectual and spiritual side of the activities of the Bolshevik leadership. Ultimately, these were the elements that constituted for them the meaning of what they were doing.

Cultural Revolution and the Transition to Socialism: Theory

At first sight, Lenin seems an unlikely utopian. The concerns expressed in his multitude of writings are overwhelmingly practical and immediate. He rarely muses about the final goal of the movement. In at least one respect, however, culture was crucial to his outlook, especially in 1917. In particular, ideas and values played a key part in Lenin's understanding of the way in which Socialism would triumph in Russia in the form of rising consciousness. Lenin often uses this phrase in terms similar to the way that a religious person uses the term *enlightenment*. The level of consciousness (rather like levels of enlightenment in some religions) was a measure of the degree to which an individual had traveled along the road to truth.

Although we cannot examine all the implications of consciousness for

Lenin, we can consider its importance to one of his most fundamental assumptions in 1917. Lenin thought that there would be a "cultural" or "spiritual" revolution—based on will, voluntarism, change of heart, conversion—which would be a vital underpinning of the material, structural, political, economic, and institutional revolution that we normally associate with the Bolsheviks. The failure of this "spiritual" revolution, of this conversion to Bolshevik ideas and values, was of enormous significance for the Revolution. In the end the absence of such a transformation of values led to the search for organizational and institutional substitutes for it.

It has often been pointed out that, in 1917, the Bolsheviks had no detailed plans for the transition to Socialism. An examination of key texts of Lenin shows that a revolution of values and consciousness was assumed as a prerequisite for, or at least an essential adjunct to, all other major aspects of the Revolution. This seems all the more surprising given the fact that Russia's problems appeared to be of a very material nature.

At the time of the overthrow of the tsar in February, Russian cities were already suffering a deepening economic crisis. Prices were rising faster than wages. Food and fuel supplies for key regions, notably Petrograd, were hopelessly inadequate. The crisis steadily worsened through the year, threatening total economic collapse. An awareness of the depth of this crisis, a knowledge of the extent of shortages of key human and material resources, led many on the left, including the Socialist Revolutionary and Menshevik leaderships, to decide it was necessary to support the liberal-dominated Provisional Government in order to stave off a political and economic crisis of potentially apocalyptic proportions. In their view, a deepening of the Revolution could result only in famine and bloody civil war.

Lenin, however, would have none of this. He consistently argued that the opposite was true. Only a deepening of the Revolution could *avert* the looming catastrophe. Lenin's opinion was based on political eschatology rather than economic analysis. Consider the following sentences written on 14 September: "Only the dictatorship of the proletariat and poor peasants is capable of smashing the resistance of the capitalists. . . . *Power to the Soviets—this is the only way to make further progress gradual, peaceful and smooth.* . . . Power to the Soviets means the complete transfer of the country's administration and economic control into the hands of workers and peasants, to whom *nobody* would dare offer resistance and who, through practice, through their own experience, *would soon learn* how to distribute land, products and grain properly" (emphasis in original).[6] Only Soviet power, he wrote at about the same time, could "make the country secure against military and economic catastrophe." A takeover would get the support of nine-tenths of the population of Russia, who would manifest the "greatest revolutionary enthusiasm . . . without which victory over famine and war is impossible." Firmness of the Soviets would overcome resistance: "No class will dare start an uprising against the Soviets, and the landowners and capitalists, taught a lesson by the experience of the Kornilov revolt, will give up their power peacefully and yield to the ultimatum of the Soviets. . . . Such measures of punishing the recalcitrants as confiscation of their entire property coupled with a short term of arrest will be sufficient."[7]

The overcoming of shortages was, for Lenin, only a matter of expropriating goods from those who had too much. For instance, in the event they would have to continue the war, "we shall conduct it in a truly revolutionary manner. We shall take all the bread and boots from the capitalists. We shall leave them only crusts and dress them in bast shoes. We shall send all the bread and footwear to the front."[8] Underlying this was the assumption that the "resources both spiritual and material for a truly revolutionary war in Russia are still immense."[9]

It was not only in September that Lenin was turning to such themes. They go back to the discussion on the key Theses of April 1917 and are rooted even deeper in Lenin's ideas on the war. In April he had argued in similar terms:

> The workers, soldiers and peasants will deal better than the police with the difficult *practical* problems of producing more grain, distributing it better and keeping the soldiers better supplied etc. etc.
>
> I am deeply convinced that the Soviets will make the independent activity of the *masses* a reality more quickly than a parliamentary republic. . . . They will more effectively, more practically and more correctly decide what *steps* can be taken towards socialism and how these steps should be taken. . . . The Soviet will be able to take these steps more effectively for the benefit of the people if the whole state power is in its hands.
>
> What *compels* such steps? Famine. Economic disorganisation. Imminent collapse. The horrors of war. The horrors of the wounds inflicted on mankind by the war. (Emphasis in original.)[10]

For our purposes one theme stands out. In order to fulfill these prophecies a real cultural revolution would be required, because they imply rapid, harmonious, near-unanimous action by the masses in conjunction with the Bolshevik leadership. The only institutions called on to perform this feat are the soviets. Once liberated, Lenin assumes that people will work together instinctively. No further complications ensue about exactly how the boots will be taken from the capitalists or even how the capitalists will be identified. Nor is there any suggestion as to how the supposedly vast hidden reserves of the country will be mobilized. The power of what Lenin calls the immense spiritual resources of the country is presumed to be sufficient. The independent activity of the masses will do the job.

It appears from these ideas that Lenin consistently believed that the Revolution he envisaged would lead to rapid healing and harmony in Russian society, that resistance would be confined to a hopelessly outnumbered minority. If anything this vision is "populist" in that Lenin usually assumes united joint action between all sectors of the ordinary population. There is no word here of major divisions between workers and peasants, or even within the peasantry itself though he did, of course, make an issue of these things on many other occasions.

In 1917, a great deal of what Lenin wrote was propaganda intended to put a favorable gloss on Bolshevik policy and aims, and one must be on watch for those occasions on which Lenin was being economical with the truth. One cannot, however, dismiss the above views as mere propaganda for two reasons. First, they were initially expressed at a crucial party meeting at which genuine strategy was being hammered out. Second, they are consistent with Lenin's major practical and theoretical writings of the time. One can find similar implications in the April Theses, in which he famously posits "abolition of the police, army and bureaucracy" without any but the sketchiest provisions about how they might be replaced. Here, too, a massive cultural revolution is implied. In *State and Revolution*, written between the July Days and the Bolshevik Revolution, Lenin is also musing on the ease of transition. The routinization of capitalism and state administration was thought to have brought the tasks of political and economic management within the compass of the ordinary person possessing an average level of education. Let that individual get on with it and he or she would run society in a harmonious, conflict-free fashion.

At this crucial time of preparation for the Bolshevik Revolution, Lenin's ideas about the postrevolutionary world lacked detail. In some ways this is understandable, but that doesn't make the consequences any less profound. There was no hint of an economic policy. Would the market continue to function on the day after the takeover? If so, for how long? How would Soviet power deal with inflation? Would the stock exchange be shut down? Who would own which enterprises, and for how long? Would Russia's international trade continue? Lenin's only response to detailed questions was general principles. Banks alone would be nationalized as a first step. (How? Who would run them?) Implicitly, a form of market capitalism "supervised" by the soviets would be the backbone of the transitional period. But how would soviets exercise their supervision? What skills would they be able to call on? Who would resolve the inevitable conflicts? Where would the personnel come from in "backward" Russia?

While Lenin was aware of the problem, his solutions—workers and peasants who *"would soon learn* how to distribute land, products and grain properly"—implied a simple transition and a sudden and all-embracing cultural revolution. Even the war effort would be reversed, not by breaking through material constraints first but by mass efforts of will, through the application of the "greatest revolutionary enthusiasm," which would release "immense resources both spiritual and material, for a truly revolutionary war." To ignore this aspect of Lenin would be to misunderstand one of his most important characteristics. Throughout his career he had given politics a primacy scarcely compatible with the economic deterministic understanding of Marx that he shared with most of his contemporaries. Time and again Lenin met economic and related problems with political (that is, organizational and institutional) solutions. The communist movement inherited this characteristic. One can see in these pre-October writings a clear link between Lenin's belief in the potential explosion from below of mass revolutionary action along the lines he desired and later similar phases in the history of the Communist movement. Not only did Stalin's second revolution revert to "voluntarist" expectations, but Mao's Great Leap Forward of the late 1950s and Great Proletarian Cultural Revolution of the 1960s and 1970s had a generic link. In his pre-revolutionary thinking Lenin was at his most Maoist.

Cultural Revolution and the Transition to Socialist Practice

From the early days in power the transition proved infinitely tougher than Lenin had expected. Economic organization had deteriorated further. The country was collapsing into a series of disconnected regions. Fighting had broken out in many places. The Bolsheviks had increasingly resorted to force, not only to quell the right but also to crush groups on the left who didn't quite see things the Bolshevik way. By early 1918 Lenin's argument that only a soviet takeover could prevent civil war, famine, and economic collapse had been shown to be detached from reality. Far from unleashing a massive surge of unconditional support for Bolshevik goals, October had above all consisted of limited, conditional support on the part of workers and peasants. By early 1918 the popular movement was continuing to pursue its own goals of taking over the land, widening local democracy, and fighting for more humane living conditions. Only a minority pursued the full Bolshevik dream. As a result, Lenin and the Bolshevik leadership were left with unexpected problems. Why hadn't the near-universal upsurge of support happened? How could it be nurtured? Could the Bolshevik Revolution survive without it?

In October Lenin had continued, in public at least, to propose full creative freedom of the masses as the driving force of the Revolution.[11] However, the tone soon changed. Lenin's postrevolutionary discourse quickly began to take into account the fact that correct consciousness was, as yet, insufficient. In place of arguing that the support of nine-tenths of the population would make the transition "gradual, peaceful and smooth," Lenin reverted to other themes. In particular, consciousness became linked with "iron discipline" and was backed up by an increasingly menacing discourse of "harmony" and the rediscovered "backwardness" of Russia, conveniently overlooked in the optimistic belief in a smooth transition. In April 1918, Lenin, in "The Immediate Tasks of the Soviet Government," set out from the assumption that the most important feature of the situation was the "ruthless struggle against chaos and disorganisation."[12] Of course, the Lenin of September 1917 had dismissed fears of chaos and disorganization and proposed the Soviet takeover as a way of avoiding them. Now, however, the reality, which had always been apparent to his critics, had become central to Lenin. He still argued that the Revolution "can be successfully carried out only if the majority of the population, and primarily the majority of the working people, engage in independent creative work as makers of history."[13] But this discourse of free creativity is bound in with another on class-consciousness and discipline. Discussion centers on a "big word"—*dictatorship*, which is "iron rule, government that is revolutionarily bold, swift and ruthless in suppressing both exploiters and hooligans."[14] Lenin argues that, since large-scale machine industry requires "absolute and strict *unity of will*" and that it is also the "foundation of Socialism,"[15] it follows that Socialism also requires "that the people *unquestioningly obey the single will* of the leaders of labour."[16] Can dictatorship be linked to creative freedom? "Given ideal class-consciousness and discipline on the part of those participating in the common work, this subordination would be something like the mild leadership of a conductor of an orchestra." But, Lenin goes on, "it may assume the sharp forms of a dictatorship if ideal discipline and class-consciousness are lacking."[17] Given the fact that the entire article was aimed at the indiscipline of the situation, it follows that, for Lenin, ideal conditions were absent. Thus, it becomes clear that Lenin attributed the ruthlessness of the dictatorship to the absence of "ideal class-consciousness and discipline," not simply to the ravages of war and class struggle.

Lenin continued to believe that, somehow, the contradictory halves of his discourse on creative freedom and iron discipline could be brought together. "We must," Lenin concludes, "learn to combine the 'public meeting' democracy of the working people—turbulent, surging, overflowing its banks like a spring flood—with *iron* discipline while at work, with *unquestioning obedience* to the will of a single person, the Soviet leader, while at work." Not surprisingly, Lenin says, "we have not yet learned to do this."[18] Indeed, earlier in the article he had commented that, far from being dictatorial, "our government is excessively mild, very often it resembles jelly more than iron."[19]

In this way, subordination to a single will, supposedly limited to when a person was at work, though this was a purely artificial distinction, opened up a more "Stalinist" set of propositions. They were also being put forward before the civil war proper had begun. Nowhere in the article does Lenin argue that the deepening civil war is shaping the system. To the contrary, he argues that "the nearer we approach the complete military suppression of the bourgeoisie, the more dangerous does the element of petty-bourgeois anarchy become,"[20] which seems to mean that the nearer one is to victory the greater the need for discipline and dictatorship, a thought analogous to Stalin's view that the closer the state came to withering away the more it had to assert itself. He does, however, revert to a quite different law of revolution from the one he had been promoting in autumn 1917. "Every great revolution, and a socialist revolution in particular, even if there is no external war, is inconceivable without internal war, i.e., civil war, which is even more devastating than external war, and involves thousands and millions of cases of wavering and desertion from one side to another, implies a state of extreme indefiniteness, lack of equilibrium and chaos."[21] So much for gradual, peaceful, and smooth transitions.

If we turn from Lenin's ideas to the policies being implemented in the increasingly dangerous situation of 1918 and 1919 we can see how Lenin's principles were being applied. In particular, far from a wave of ever-mounting support—as consciousness and enlightenment grew in the population—the Bolsheviks faced desertion by large parts of the popular movement, partially counterbalanced by the fact that the White threat itself imposed some self-discipline on workers and peasants who saw the Bolshevik government as the only vehicle that could defend them.

As the tide of support receded in early 1918 the Bolshevik ship of state risked being beached. However, efforts to get out of danger were not simply measures designed to keep the craft afloat, they were also intended to point it toward its destination. Every major aspect of Bolshevik policy shows the profound influence of its cultural objectives, in the forefront its desire to win over the ordinary population not just to its policies but, equally important, to its values. The propagation of its values and the need to succeed in this crucial sphere are an essential, fully integrated, shaping influence on even the most "practical" institutions of the Bolshevik system as it emerged. If we take up Orlovsky's invitation to "go beneath the formal institutions and laws to grasp their dynamics as cultural repositories and artifacts" we will find that cultural aims were not confined to the Education Ministry. They were at the heart of the party, the army, the trade unions, and even the Cheka. On one level, the whole Bolshevik state apparatus was designed to revolutionize the value systems of Russia and then of the world. The Communist movement in the revolutionary years had taken on not only tasks of management but also of transforming values. In both areas the Bolshevik leaders were adopting a "war-fighting" mode that predated the civil war and even October and was rooted in Lenin's interpretation of Marx's concept of class struggle and his own views on civil war. Even without the Whites and foreign intervention the Bolsheviks would still have had major conflict on their hands. And even before the civil war they had begun to take on the forms of minority dictatorship and coercion. I will look briefly at the party, the army, the unions, the legal system, and the Cheka to illustrate the importance of taking Bolshevik determination to spread their values very seriously in understanding how these key institutions came to take the shape they did. I will then look at the party's most detailed self-definition of the period, the 1919 Party Program and its associated explanatory primer *The ABC of Communism*, with a view to showing the deeply integrated element of cultural revolution present in them. But, first, the party.

Let us start with a short journey into the obvious and, one hopes, indisputable. From its origin in 1903 the Bolshevik party had been chiefly a repository for correct consciousness and a means for its propagation. After all, in these years the party was little more than an organization devoted to the production and clandestine distribution of a newspaper. Lenin's celebrated argument with the Mensheviks centered on this question, with Lenin insisting on reserving party membership for people with the right level of consciousness rather than opening it to less committed sympathizers. His career in the wilderness of exile is remarkable for the relentlessness with which he attempted to build up party orthodoxy and drive out heretics. There is nothing to suggest that he had substantially changed his approach in 1917. After the seizure of power the goal of preserving the correct ideological outlook, values, and consciousness was pursued with as much ruthlessness as it had been while the party was only a tiny sect. Despite the extraordinary turnabout in the party's fortunes, which had brought it to be sole head of the postrevolutionary state, its culture of sectarianism, orthodoxy, and pursuit of heresy remained unchanged and was given enormous scope for its expression, not least because the absence of spontaneous rallying of the nation to Bolshevik principles meant that the nurturing of the right ideas and values was seen as one of the most important strategic issues essential to the party's very survival.

This led to two sets of problems for the party leadership. First, while it was a small sect of leaders, many of whom knew one another personally, it was relatively easy to ensure orthodoxy. However, the Revolution had brought an avalanche of new members to the party. The most reliable estimates would suggest that the party had gone from some 10,000 members in January 1917 to some 250,000 by the end of the year—that is, twenty-five members for every one member ten or eleven months earlier. Inevitably, the new members were by no means as committed to or even aware of the party's ultimate goals as those who had been in the party for many years. The leadership's first task, then, was to educate the party itself, and the evidence suggests that a great deal of scarce time and energy were spent on this during the civil war. Naturally, as party membership grew, the problem continued to exercise the leadership. However, when one bears in mind that even the expanded party constituted only 1 percent or so of the entire population, we begin to see the immensity of the second cultural task facing the leadership. It was essential to the leadership to keep control not only of the party but also of society in the hands of the most reliable, "conscious" members, those most imbued with the culture and values they expected to spread to the rest of the population. Remembering that only some 10,000 reliable members were in the party in early 1917 we can see that it follows that from the beginning the Bolsheviks were trying to evolve institutions which ensured that this tiny minority would keep control over a society of nearly 120 million people. This fact is surely at least as important as any other in explaining the authoritarianism of the Bolsheviks. Institutions and arrangements to keep control in the hands of this tiny minority can be found in its new approaches to forms of government, the role of the party, and so on.

Innovations began within the party itself. The best known was the process of "purging" or cleansing the party membership to rid it of cadres who were below even the much-reduced quality threshold that opened the way to membership. Much less well known but an equally ingenious way of keeping the "enlightened" old guard in control was the use of length of party service as a guide to reliability. Responsible posts began to be reserved for the longest-serving and therefore presumably the most dedicated party members. One of the first formal implementations of the principle was spelled out in the decree on control commissions passed in March 1921 at the Tenth Party Congress. "Not less than ten years' party membership" was specified for the Central Control Commission, five years for oblast' level and pre-February membership for guberniia level. Thus all these key posts were specifically reserved for the dwindling band of 10,000 or so who were in the party on the eve of the February Revolution. While this was one of the first times that party seniority had been explicitly linked to important posts, it had, none the less, been informally applied earlier and continued in force for many years to come.

Taken together, the two institutions of purging and party seniority illustrate a vital aspect of Bolshevism in power. Authority was to be confined to a tiny elite of prerevolutionary party members. When it conflicted with democracy, in the sense of the opinion of the majority, authority did not hesitate to assert itself wherever it had the power to do so. In any case, following the wishes of the workers rather than leading them to enlightenment had been, since the early days of the party, a designated heresy known as *khvostizm* (or "tailism" in English, meaning hanging on to the tail of the workers' movement rather than controlling it, presumably by means of the bridle and reins). The implication is clear. In its very essence the party was set up to ensure continuing control by the most reliable, correctly thinking, self-appointed elite. In this respect it bears more comparison with, say, the Catholic Church than with a conventional political party. The Central Committee became a kind of College of Red Cardinals, the party apparatus was the Curia. The leadership claimed teaching and administrative authority and circulated a multitude of encyclicals defending absolute values. Eventually the cult of personality was to produce an "infallible" leader to outdo the pope. The party soon evolved its own inquisitorial apparatus in the form of institutions, such as the Orgburo, Rabkrin, and the Control Commissions, which put the most trusted party members in the position of overseeing the political rectitude of party and state and, as such, clearly checking to ensure that the correct consciousness was being implemented. For both the Vatican and the Kremlin, undemocratic structures were justified by the desire to preserve the purity of the faith and to spread it as the main task and, only secondarily, to govern in a practical sense.

Provisions to implement the hierarchical relationship can be found in many areas. It was one of the main shaping elements in the forms of the new Soviet state. In the first place, the privileged position of the party in the soviets at all levels (and hence of the tiny minority of party leaders) was justified in the eyes of those who constructed it that way by cultural and ideological objectives, not by purely pragmatic aims of controlling the country in the material interests of the elite. The Party Rules, adopted in December 1919, made the organizational arrangements clear. The tasks of each party body, starting at the top with the Central Committee, were defined in similar terms. They were charged with organizing party institutions, directing their activities, appointing editors of party publications, organizing and directing significant enterprises, allocating party funds and personnel, and controlling the treasury. Their tasks extended beyond the party into the state, where they were charged with directing the work of soviet and social organizations through the party fractions.[22] The guberniia committee was charged more explicitly with directing the activities of the soviet, the trade unions and the cooperatives through the corresponding party fractions.[23]

At the grass-roots level the party relied on cells and fractions to spread its values to the overwhelmingly nonparty masses. The rules made their role explicit. The first task of the party cell was that of "bringing the party's slogans and decisions to the masses." To spread party influence fractions were to be formed in nonparty institutions, defined as "soviets, executive committees, trade unions, communes etc." Their task was "the comprehensive strengthening of party influence, implementation of its policy in the non-party environment, and the establishment of party supervision over the work of all these institutions and organizations."[24]

Although the tasks defined here went well beyond the cultural sphere, it remains the case that culture and values were an important part of them. Much of the supervision and directing was ideological and involved spreading the fundamental ideas of the party and its hopes for transforming Russia. The same concern for ideological rectitude and cultural transformation can be seen in even more prosaic state institutions like the army and the trade unions.

As far as the army was concerned, two aspects in particular bear out this argument. These are the transition to Lenin and Trotsky's view that only a regular army with an authoritative center rather than a people's militia was an efficient means of fighting the Whites, and, second, the institution of political commissars.

There is a vast debate about the first of these issues. In the party's own words the decision to abandon the militia idea was taken for purely pragmatic reasons. The decree on the military question of the Eighth Party Congress in 1919 argued that "guerilla methods of struggle were imposed on the proletariat in the early period because of its oppressed position in the state, just as the use of primitive underground printing presses and secret meetings were imposed on it." The resolution went on to say—in conformity with the discourse of a single, central will, introduced above—that the capture of state power allowed the proletariat "to use the state apparatus for the planned construction of a centralized army, whose unity of command alone can assure the achievement of the greatest results with the smallest losses." To ensure that there were no lingering doubts it emphatically concluded that "to preach the doctrine of guerilla forces as a military program is tantamount to recommending a return from large-scale to cottage industry."[25] In other words, it was deemed to be the most effective way to fight a war.

Whether it actually was the most efficient way is, however, far from clear. Given the degree of success enjoyed by the guerrilla bands, notably that of Makhno, operating with the skimpiest of resources and against the hostility of both Reds and Whites, it looks at least possible that a properly supported militia army backed up by the full resources of the new state might have been at least as effective as the Red Army in its more conventional form. Clearly we cannot have a definitive answer to this question. However, the adoption of the more authoritarian model seems inevitable, not from the immediate exigencies of the struggle against the Whites, which might have been conducted in other ways, but from the whole cast of mind of the Bolshevik leadership and Lenin's tendency, going back long before the Revolution, let alone the civil war, to centralize as much power as possible in key areas for fear of letting power slip into the hands of the "backward" part of the population.

The role of the political commissar was to be the political conscience of the unit to which he was attached. The idea had developed from the Provisional Government practice of having commissars sent out to explain the political rationale of the war to those who had to fight it. However, they had nothing like the powers of a Soviet political commissar. The latter was usually the most politically powerful individual in the unit, exerting more authority than the commander. The commissar was the one who had a hot line to the party and Cheka to enforce his will. The actual army officer was, with the exception of a few trusted Bolsheviks, reduced to the technical role of running the army and organizing it as a fighting force. Nowhere else did armies have personnel quite like this. Part army chaplain on behalf of the new Communist religion he was supposed to promulgate and part security policeman, political spy and, sometimes, judge and jury, the political commissar was a key figure. The decree on the military question stoutly defended commissars as "carriers of the spirit of our party" and praised their "heroic work," although it did concede that the political sections of the army should maintain the quality of commissars and eliminate "any who were appointed by accident." Party cells in the army were exhorted to work directly with commissars, and "rapid numerical growth of communist cells" was described as an "extremely important guarantee that the army will be permeated by communist ideas and discipline."[26]

Here was a classic example of substituting new institutions for the missing consciousness. Instead of an enthusiastic mass of conscious Leninist soldiers and sailors, the armed forces had a thin network of political commissars who were supposed, with the help of political departments, to build up the troops' knowledge of Bolshevism and enthusiasm for revolutionary transformation. As an institution they are a clear sign of the Bolsheviks' political weakness. Where correct consciousness was lacking, the

commissars were supposed to compensate, to act as the "advanced" interpreters of party will in the specific circumstances in which they found
themselves. The party's difficulty in finding suitable candidates for the
role of commissar and its growing concern about the poor quality and
potential careerism in these key institutions is additional testimony to the
thin spread of "advanced" values.

Elsewhere, the transformation of trade unions can only be understood
in the light of the Bolsheviks' cultural aims. Before the Revolution the
unions had been defenders of the immediate interests of workers and
were responsible to them. Many workers and trade unionists had even
understood the Bolshevik revolution as a prelude to unions and other
workers' organizations taking direct control of production, and in the
early months of Soviet power there were many such takeovers. By 1920,
however, the role of unions had been redefined. According to the decree
on trade unions of the Ninth Party Congress, "The tasks of the trade
unions are principally organizational-economic and educational." They
were to be "schools of communism" linking the party as proletarian vanguard with "the most backward masses of the proletariat. . . . The trade
unions must educate, organize culturally, politically and administratively,
must raise these masses to the communist level and train them for the
role of creators of the communist order which the Soviet state is bringing
into being."[27]

Wherever we look we find the consciousness gap being plugged by, in
many cases, original institutions. The judiciary and the legal system are a
case in point. It was unthinkable that tsarist law should be applied in the
new revolutionary conditions, but at the same time there was no opportunity to build up a new code of law. Similarly, tsarist judges had to be
removed (when they had not fled), and there were no qualified personnel
to replace them. The solution was to set up a network of informal people's
courts under magistrates charged with applying Socialist law where it
existed and, where it did not, deciding cases in light of "socialist conscience."[28] In this area, as in so many others, the only barrier against
arbitrariness was a thin line of Bolsheviks with the wisdom of a socialist
Solomon. Needless to say, few men and women were able to fit this bill.

All the basic institutions of the developing Soviet system had the fundamental problem of culture and values rooted in them. It was not just
special departments of education and, later, agitation and propaganda
that devoted attention to them. The Bolsheviks knew that their real battle was not for the immediate support of the population but to win over
their minds to the Bolshevik vision and Bolshevik values. The clearest
expression of this came in the party program and associated "catechism"

of the new religion, the *ABC of Communism*. They were published in 1919. The centrality of the cultural dimension of the Revolution is reinforced by the fact that considerable time and effort were spent on them at the lowest point in the civil war, when the existence of the Soviet order was on the line. They were intended, above all, to provide a basic focus for the educational and propaganda work being conducted in the country. While it was relatively easy to set up institutions like political departments, reading groups, and so on, it was much more difficult to find reliable books, pamphlets, and other materials to develop the required consciousness. The Party Program and the *ABC of Communism* were intended to explain what the party was about and how it situated itself not only in Russia but in the global context.

Since the Russian Revolution we have become accustomed to documents like the Party Program, but in its day it was unprecedented and provided a model for its successors. Much of it was taken up with mundane, highly practical objectives. It promised an eight-hour day, a forty-two-hour period of continuous rest once a week and free medical attention. Child care and communal eating and laundries were proposed to release women from housework. There were schemes to help peasants improve their land. While some of these proposals smacked of utopianism, interwoven with them were even more speculative propositions, such as the future abolition of money and the goal of attaining Communism.

The document opened with several pages of complex Marxist-Leninist analysis of the current world conjuncture. Its opaque language, all too familiar to those who have read subsequent official documents from the communist movement, would have been as impenetrable to the ordinary Russian toiler as theological arguments are to the average churchgoer. Deeply entwined within its heavy prose was the apocalyptic expectation of the "victory of the world proletarian revolution" to be attained by the "closest brotherly unity and co-ordination of all revolutionary activities of the working class in all advanced countries." The purpose of the proletarian revolution was no less than "to lead mankind out of the blind alley" created by imperialism and war. Readers were no doubt comforted to learn that "in spite of all the difficulties . . . the final victory of the proletariat is inevitable." This was no ordinary party manifesto. Most of the major themes of Communist ideology at the time were represented. The elitism of the party was stressed in its self-definition, for example, which stated that the aim of the international Communist party was "to make the proletariat capable of fulfilling its great historic mission." The party, it says, "organizes," "reveals to," and "explains to" the proletariat. The choice of language suggests that the party is the active element, the class passive. The class principle of positive discrimination in favor of proletarians and, sometimes, semi-proletarians, on the one hand and deprivation of exploiters' rights on the other is fully entrenched throughout. Far-reaching ideological aims can also be found in all sections, from the role of army commissars in establishing an "internal ideological bond" in the Red Army to turning schools into instruments "for a communist regeneration of society."[29] The whole document combines practical detail with breakouts into the most sweeping vision of the transformation of humanity.

The ABC of Communism was designed to underline the main points and be circulated widely, particularly in the party, as an educational aid to explain the party's purpose to its own members, who were mostly unaware of its long-term goals on anything other than a sloganistic level. If anything, The ABC of Communism was even more utopian than the party program, particularly when it came to gazing into the not-too-distant future. Consider the following: "The Communist method of production presupposes in addition that production is not for the market, but for use. . . . In consequence of this change, we no longer have *commodities*, but only *products*. These products are not exchanged for one another; they are simply stored in communal warehouses, and are subsequently delivered to those who need them." The objection that some people would take too much is brushed aside by saying that "perhaps for twenty or thirty years it will be necessary to have various regulations," but that when there is a sufficiency of products (an unlikely concept in itself) people will only take what they need. After all, "today, for example, no one thinks it worth while when he wants one seat in a tram, to take three tickets and keep two places empty. It will be just the same in the case of all products." Arguing by analogy with free tram tickets seems barely adequate to the complexities of the problems skated over in these few lines. The simple statement, "Money will then have no value" calls forth a host of cultural implications, not to mention the immense difficulties of transition that are normally solved by the benevolent supervision of an enlightened bureaucracy as the communist form of the not-so-hidden hand. The above quotations do, after all, come from the chapter on "The Dictatorship of the Proletariat."[30] They open up not only deep questions about the fundamental cultural revolution needed to achieve the goals set but also cultural questions about the source of this eschatological type of argument, which would take us way beyond our present scope. The ABC of Communism was pointing out no more than the truth when it claimed that the party was committed to the proposition that "within a few decades there will be quite a new world, with new people and new customs."[31]

Bolshevism as a Mechanism for Revaluing All Values

The emphasis on a new world and new people runs through Bolshevism as an ultimate goal. Even at his more pragmatic stage Lenin had mentioned in *State and Revolution* that Socialism required more than the "present ordinary run of people" (*obyvatelia*) if it was to succeed.[32] Even more ambitiously, Trotsky concluded his pamphlet on *Literature and Revolution*, written in 1924, with the sweeping, Chernyshevskian view that, under Socialism the "average human type will rise to the heights of an Aristotle, a Goethe, or a Marx. And above this ridge new peaks will rise."[33] The Stalin period, too, was famous for posing the ideal of the "new Soviet person." To forget that this is ultimately what leading Bolsheviks thought their movement was about is to miss a key dimension. At its very heart, Bolshevism was a kind of Nietzschean project for the revaluation of all values by an elite. It produced mechanisms that impinged on cultural questions of transformation in two ways. They were substitutes for the absence of transforming values or correct consciousness and were, as much as anything else, intended as a means to nurture and create it.

Three particularly important conclusions arise from seeing Bolshevism in these terms. In the first place, it follows that the Bolsheviks imposed their own vision and values not only on the obvious counterrevolutionary enemy but also on the main driving force of the radical revolution of 1917, the popular movement. For the Bolshevik leadership the real, vibrant, popular revolution was at best half-baked, at worst counterproductive. In their view it was their own vision of the Revolution that should prevail over the aims and aspirations of those out there actually making the Revolution. The Bolsheviks distrusted peasants as potentially petit-bourgeois, market-oriented, proprietorial capitalists. Soldiers' and sailors' demands for democratization of the armed forces were swept aside in the construction of the Red Army. Even workers were not trusted. Many of them were deemed "backward" and unreliable. The Bolsheviks became prisoners of their own discourse.

Many of the Bolsheviks' assumptions are quite extraordinary given the fact that the peasants were liquidating private ownership by landowners and Stolypin separators in favor of the commune, that workers were experimenting with a wide variety of forms of collective ownership and that soldiers and sailors were setting up self-governing military units much closer to the supposedly sacred principles of the Paris Commune, praised by Lenin in *State and Revolution*, than was the Red Army. Bolshevik imposition of their own vision of transition—via the instruments of party, soviets, tame trade unions, political commissars, Cheka, and so on—weighed heavily not only on genuine counterrevolutionaries (who were too weak, divided and demoralized to be a serious threat) but on active revolutionary forces—independent soviets, peasant communes and committees, democratic army committees, factory committees, and so on. It was in the name of their own vision, restricted to a tiny minority, that the Bolsheviks snuffed the life out of a wide variety of revolutionary forces. Stalinism spent most of its life doing exactly the same thing. The Bolsheviks set up a centralized party and state apparatus answerable to no one but themselves and legitimized by the superiority and correctness of their vision rather than that of the popular movement. One of the main purposes of that apparatus was not just to fight off the Whites but to build a new type of state and society best characterized in the Party Program of 1919 and in the *ABC of Communism*.

The second consequence is that Bolshevism faced its own dilemma, which persisted throughout its existence. It could only succeed by winning over the population to its values. The less the people shared those values, the more the Bolsheviks coerced them. The more dictatorial the authorities became, the less persuasive their arguments appeared. The less persuasive their arguments, the more they had to force them on the population. And so it continued. Periods of relative social peace, like the 1920s, were achieved only through the party slowing down on the long-term goals. Periods of upheaval, like 1928–32, were moments of reversion to attempted rapid advance.

Associated with this was the third consequence. Periods of relaxation brought with them the risk that the tiny band of proletarian Socialists might be swallowed up by the mass of the Russian people. Throughout its history Russian Communism was engaged in a battle between the transforming vision of the early revolutionaries and the enduring values of the population. Neither came out unscathed. Bolshevism was a form of Marxism filtered through the culture, institutions, and practices of Russian society with which it shared some key values. For instance, as we saw at the beginning, Bolshevism was much more aggressively atheistic and science-oriented than Marxist movements elsewhere. Bolshevism also built on central aspects of tsarist political culture, notably its contempt for Western-style democracy, as well as its constraints on the development of what is today thought of as civil society. Many of Bolshevism's key instruments were taken over from tsarism and expanded—notably censorship, political police, political imprisonment, and labor camps. Most fundamental of all the legacy of serfdom was incalculable both in an institutional sense—in that it had polarized the country and helped prevent the growth of a vigorous and independent middle class—but also culturally, in terms of creating polarized social attitudes and deeply antagonistic identities of *narod* and elite. Hayek identified Soviet-style state Socialism as the road to serfdom. The connection was right, the direction wrong. It was serfdom that helped pave the way to Stalinism. In the event, the long run of Soviet history shows that the values of each side influenced the other, eroding some aspects of traditional values but also blunting the edge of the early utopian, Socialist vision that faded into the background as the decades went by and the generations changed. It was replaced by modified forms of patriotism and nationalism, the focus of which was, for more than half of the Soviet period, the national achievement in World War II rather than the October victory. In the battle for cultural transformation the state backed away from Socialist values. Instead, imperialist impulses and the drive for great power status came flooding back. The conflicts this process entailed have not yet been resolved.

Notes

1. Moshe Lewin, *The Making of the Soviet System: Essays in the Social History of Interwar Russia* (London: Methuen, 1985), 6.

2. A. Gleason, P. Kenez, and R. Stites, eds., *Bolshevik Culture: Experiment and Order in the Russian Revolution* (Bloomington: Indiana University Press, 1985), 37.

3. Ibid., 39.

4. Ibid.

5. Chris Ward, *Stalin's Russia* (London: Edward Arnold, 1993), 70.

6. V. I. Lenin, "One of the Fundamental Questions of the Revolution," in *Between the Two Revolutions: Articles and Speeches of 1917* (Moscow: Progress Publishers, 1971), 379.

7. "The Tasks of the Revolution," in ibid., 388.

8. "Marxism and Insurrection," in ibid., 396.

9. Ibid.

10. "Letters on Tactics," in ibid., 73–74.

11. For instance, in his speech on the Land Decree at the Second All-Russian Congress of Soviets.

12. V. I. Lenin, "The Immediate Tasks of the Soviet Government," in *Selected Works* (Moscow: Progress Publishers, 1967), 2: 645.

13. Ibid., 646. Note, once again, the reversion to the "populist" category "working-people."

14. Ibid., 670.

15. Ibid., 672.

16. Ibid., 673.

17. Ibid.

18. Ibid., 675.

19. Ibid., 670.

20. Ibid.

21. Ibid., 669. A discussion of Lenin's complex attitude toward civil war would take us beyond the scope of this chapter. In this period he consistently believed that civil war was unavoidable, proclaiming in September 1914 that the world war should be transformed into a European civil war. At various points in 1917 he found it expedient to divert attention away from the prospect and expressed changing opinions about how deep and serious such a conflict might be.

22. R. McNeal, ed., *Resolutions and Decisions of the Communist Party of the Soviet Union* (Toronto: University of Toronto Press, 1974), 90–98.

23. Ibid., 94.

24. Ibid., 96, 97.

25. Ibid., 75, 76.

26. Ibid., 78.

27. Ibid., 100, 101.

28. Ibid., 63.

29. Ibid., 57, 62, 63.

30. N. Bukharin and E. Preobrazhensky, *ABC of Communism*, English ed. (Harmondsworth: Penguin, 1968), 116, 117.

31. Ibid., 119.

32. V. I. Lenin, "State and Revolution," in *Selected Works*, 2: 341.

33. L. Trotsky, *Literature and Revolution* (Ann Arbor: University of Michigan Press, 1971), 256.

Contributors

Vladimir N. Brovkin is an associate professor of history at Harvard University.

Jonathan W. Daly is an assistant professor of history at the University of Illinois, Chicago.

Delano DuGarm, educated at the University of Chicago and Stanford University, works at the World Bank.

Anna Geifman is an associate professor of history at Boston University.

Leonid Heretz is an assistant professor of history at Bridgewater State College.

Michael Melancon is an associate professor of history at Auburn University.

Taisia Osipova is a professor of Russian history at Moscow Pedagogical University.

Sergei Pavliuchenkov is an associate professor (dotsent) at the Social History of Russia department, Moscow State University for Social Studies.

N. G. O. Pereira is a professor of history at Dalhousie University.

Richard Pipes is professor emeritus, Harvard University.

Christopher Read is a professor of history at the University of Warwick, England.

Dmitry Shlapentokh is an assistant professor of history at Indiana University, South Bend.

Scott Smith is a lecturer in history at Harvard University.

O. V. Volobuev is a professor of Russian history at Moscow Pedagogical University.

Index